Federalism and the Law of Diversity

Studies in Territorial and Cultural Diversity Governance

VOLUME 23

The titles published in this series are listed at *brill.com/tcdg*

Federalism and the Law of Diversity

The Theoretical Contribution of Federalism to the Explanation of Emergent Models for the Accommodation of Diversity

Edited by

Nicolò P. Alessi and Martina Trettel

BRILL | NIJHOFF

LEIDEN | BOSTON

The open access publication of this book has been published with the support of the Swiss National Science Foundation.

Library of Congress Cataloging-in-Publication Data

Names: Alessi, Nicolò Paolo, editor. | Trettel, Martina, editor.
Title: Federalism and the law of diversity: the theoretical contribution of federalism to the explanation of emergent models for the accommodation of diversity / edited by Nicolò P. Alessi and Martina Trettel.
Description: Leiden; Boston: Brill/Nijhoff, 2025. |
Series: Studies in territorial & cultural diversity governance, 2213-2570; volume 23 | Includes index. | Summary: "The volume offers new and unexplored perspectives on federalism and its relationships with diversity accommodation. It represents the first structured attempt to use federal theory and practice to frame several phenomena of governance in the area of diversity management.
Identifiers: LCCN 2024052527 (print) | LCCN 2024052528 (ebook) |
ISBN 9789004707757 (hardback) | ISBN 9789004707764 (ebook)
Subjects: LCSH: Federal government. | Cultural pluralism. |
Minorities–Legal status, laws, etc.
Classification: LCC K3185.F437 2025 (print) | LCC K3185 (ebook) |
DDC 342.08–dc23/eng/20241105
LC record available at https://lccn.loc.gov/2024052527
LC ebook record available at https://lccn.loc.gov/2024052528

Typeface for the Latin, Greek, and Cyrillic scripts: "Brill". See and download: brill.com/brill-typeface.

ISSN 2213-2570
ISBN 978-90-04-70775-7 (hardback)
ISBN 978-90-04-70776-4 (e-book)
DOI 10.1163/9789004707764

This book is printed on acid-free paper and produced in a sustainable manner.

Contents

Foreword: The Inextricable Link between Federalism and the Law of Diversity

Francesco Palermo

1 The Federal Matrix for the Regulation of Pluralism (or: The Grandfather's Company)

When reading the title of this book, scholars from the field of minority rights and diversity management might wonder what federalism has to do not with the accommodation of diversity, but with its law: how can federalism produce rules to regulate diversity, if it is nothing else than a tool to split the cake among different groups and in this way to accommodate them (and their appetite)? Conversely, federal scholars are likely to have a similar reaction when looking at the table of contents: where is federalism left? What do non-territorial (i.e. essentially personal) forms of autonomy, legal pluralism and participatory democracy have to do with federalism? Something should be wrong here.

In fact, a recent field of studies (of which this book is one of the spearheads) investigates how federalism inspires several related instruments within the framework of constitutional pluralism. Many of such instruments are in some way derived from federalism, as they share the same goal: regulating pluralism.

Metaphorically, it can be argued that federalism is the grandfather of most other instruments for the constitutional management of pluralism. Federalism can be seen as the founder of a company that produces a whole set of tools that aim at managing ever more sophisticated pluralistic claims. Such tools being, inter alia (and particularly fit for the management of ethno-diversity pluralistic claims) non-territorial autonomy, legal pluralism and participatory democracy. Having become old, federalism increasingly operates through proxies, and spreads its genes through its grandsons and -daughters, who have been inheriting the company. The family remains the same, and so the company's products: constitutional tools to accommodate pluralism as the backbone of constitutionalism. But the actors evolve, change, bring with them some important elements or legacies of the progenitor while adding new features and elements and modernizing the company.

The metaphor describes what is happening to federalism in relation to the accommodation of ethno-national (linguistic, religious, etc.) diversity. For a long time, a sort of in-vitro combination of the goal (accommodating the claims of self-government by certain groups within unchanged national borders) and the tool (self-government for the territories where such groups reside) has produced a variety of territorial autonomy arrangements that have been more or less successful depending on how several factors have played out.[1] Actually, this function has been inherent to the idea of federalism, even long before the very concept emerged in modern (and then in contemporary) constitutionalism.[2] But contemporary societies are becoming too complex for such a simple approach based on a clear distinction between the goal (accommodation) and the tool (self-government): decision-making has become an extremely complicated task, and competence matters are too manifold and fragmented to be clear-cut and therefore attributed to the exclusive responsibility of one level of government only. Rather, societies are pluralizing also internally,[3] and functions become transversal. The exclusive power of a level of government and the exclusive ownership of a territory by a (assumingly homogenous) group are too fictious to be effective.[4] They were perfectly fitting the idea of the nation state and have tried to replicate it at subnational level, but are now inevitably aging like their prototypes.

The constitutional systems are pluralizing[5] and decisions are being made by a growing number of actors vested with different legitimacies beyond the mere political/electoral one. These actors are arrayed both vertically (levels of government) and horizontally (parliaments, governments, agencies, courts,

1 See inter alia Ruth Lapidoth, *Autonomy: Flexible Solutions to Ethnic Conflicts* (Washington: US Institute of Peace Press, 1996), Marc Weller and Stefan Wolff (eds.), *Autonomy, Self-Governance and Conflict Resolution* (London and New York: Routledge, 2005), Thomas Benedikter, *The World's Modern Autonomy Systems* (Bolzano: Eurac Research, 2009), and many more.

2 Studies confirm that already in ancient Greece this idea was widespread and largely used, despite the concept of federalism (and the very term) was still to be born and was distant from the contemporary understanding, which implies statehood and is thus a post-Westphalian product. See Hans Beck and Peter Funke, eds., *Federalism in Greek Antiquity* (Cambridge: Cambridge University Press 2015) and Elena Franchi, "Leghe e stati federali," in *Introduzione alla storia greca*, eds. Maurizio Giangiulio (Bologna: il Mulino, 2021), 185–196.

3 Petra Roter, "Commentary of article 5 of the Framework Convention for the Protection of National Minorities," in *The Framework Convention for the Protection of National Minorities: A Commentary*, eds. Rainer Hofmann, Tove H. Malloy and Detlev Rein (Leiden-Boston: Brill-Nijhoff, 2018), 126–147. See also Advisory Committee on the Framework Convention for the Protection of National Minorities, Third Thematic Commentary *The Language Rights of Persons Belonging to National Minorities under the Framework Convention* (ACFC/44DOC(2012)001), no. 17–18.

4 See Francesco Palermo, "Territory and the Law of Ownership: From Misunderstanding to Opportunity," in *Law, Territory and Conflict Resolution. Law as a Problem and Law as a Solution*, eds. Matteo Nicolini, Francesco Palermo and Enrico Milano (Leiden-Boston: Brill-Nijhoff, 2016), 16–38.

5 See among many others Nico Krisch, *Beyond Constitutionalism: The Pluralist Structure of Postnational Law* (Oxford: Oxford University Press, 2012).

administrations, interest groups, etc.). Numerous norm suppliers coexist and shape decision-making and implementation in each subject area, and, at each level, a plethora of actors access institutions in both formal and informal ways to make their claims heard and possibly influence legal norms. Subject matters become more articulated the more society and technology evolve. Thus, jurisdictions tend to overlap as no field can be clearly separated from others, and the legal and administrative regulation of each competence matter is subject to an entanglement of norms and procedures produced by several authorities at different levels, often in an uncoordinated manner.[6] At the same time, there seems to be no alternative to the evolution of governance towards greater complexity and pluralism, not only because societies are simply becoming more intricate, but also because democracy requires that many voices be heard and included in decision-making processes, especially in order to increase social acceptance of norms. Such a pluralizing context significantly involves groups and their rights and affects in particular groups that are likely to be in a structural minority position when decisions are made by majority rule.

This is why traditional self-government (federalism, autonomy and the like) is no longer enough to address the claims of an increasingly pluralizing society. At the same time, federalism is as critical as never before as it represents the prototype of institutional regulation of pluralism. As a matrix, it can hardly be used itself, at least not in the traditional way, but it remains the tool that inspires all the others as it has been the first one to deal with a pluralizing society. Initially in an institutional way only, now increasingly also within societies. The claim, however, remains the same: accommodating different needs within a unitary constitutional framework. Such claims are different from those of the past, but, at the same time, show that no other constitutional tool has more potential than federalism as a conceptual and practical matrix for providing the answers required by contemporary societies, since federalism is the most consolidated and sophisticated tool for regulating institutional and procedural complexity.

6 This might also involve the relationship between public and private spheres, thus going beyond the public law realm to imply the possibility and even the opportunity to create functional jurisdictions populated by private actors competing with or substituting for the public service providers. See Bruno S. Frey, "Functional, Overlapping, Competing Jurisdictions: Redrawing the Geographic Borders of Administration," *European Journal of Law Reform* v, no. 3/4 (2005): 543–555.

2 The Law of Diversity and Its Contribution to the Upgrade of Federalism

All the tools derived from the federal matrix can be subsumed under the heading of the "law of diversity".[7] The three instruments analyzed in this volume (non-territorial autonomy, participatory democracy, and legal pluralism) are particularly relevant in this context, as they are the most widespread, and probably the most advanced in constitutional terms.[8]

This book focuses on a number of paradigmatic examples of how the Law of diversity works and is evolving in different (groups of) countries and in diverse subject areas. All contributions describe how new institutions and procedures are being established and how they work in practice for the management of ethno-national complexity challenges. Most of them contribute to the development of an original methodological framework for the analysis of ever more intricate forms of diversity accommodation.

The analysis carried out in this volume shows that diversity governance cannot but be multi-level and multi-actor, with some important consequences following from this tendency. In the first place, what used to be the 'protection' of minorities ceases to be a 'competence matter' (if indeed it ever was such) vested with one subject or another. Rather, managing the diversity of and in societies (far more than 'protecting' certain groups) becomes a transversal and shared objective which is to be realized by different actors and instruments in a combined approach: while minimum denominators are determined at international and supranational level, the state acts as the motor for macro-policies in the field of equality, and subnational and local authorities and the minority groups themselves are in charge of micro-policies of diversity. What matters are in particular the procedures that make it possible for groups to engage, participate, self-govern and allow the system to be plural itself (legal pluralism).

Second – and as a consequence of the plurality of different actors actively engaged in reaching the common objective of celebrating diversity within a rule-of-law context – a permanent obligation of loyal cooperation should exist

---

7 See Francesco Palermo and Jens Woelk, "From Minority Protection to a Law of Diversity? Reflections on the Evolution of Minority Rights," *European Yearbook of Minority Issues* 3 (2003/2004): 5–13. The concept has been developed much further especially by Nicolò P. Alessi, *A Global Law of Diversity: Evolving Models and Concepts* (London-New York: Routledge, 2025), as well as in this very volume.

8 For further considerations on the variety of possible constitutional instruments dealing with pluralism (not limited to ethno-national claims) see inter alia Michael W. Dowdle, Michael A. Wilkinson, eds., *Constitutionalism Beyond Liberalism* (Cambridge: Cambridge University Press, 2017).

among all actors, which prevents against unilateral and imposed solutions while stressing the need for the continuous consideration of social, economic and normative complexity when adopting single solutions. This also implies a permanent openness towards adaptation of rules and instruments in a continuous process of negotiation in refining the instruments of the Law of diversity.

This is what allows for a gradual move from a majority-driven 'Law of minority protection' to a more complex 'Law of diversities', much more in line with today's culturally complex societies. A Law of diversity which is made of procedures that keep the system open and flexible and allows for the inclusion of further (potentially countless) factors of difference which compose a diverse society.[9] Such procedures work inasmuch as they avoid the structural domination of one position over the other and guarantee the necessary – permanent but never stable – balance between equality and difference, protection and living together, rights and obligations, autonomy and integration.[10]

The Law of diversity resulting from such procedures is necessarily characterized by three main elements: asymmetry regarding its application as well as the single instruments (differentiation in the legal position of the groups thus becomes the rule); pluralism of legal sources and of actors; permanent negotiation of its content in a quasi-contractual framework, i.e. going beyond pre-established majority and minority positions (and making the distinction between rule and exception as well as between majority and minorities increasingly difficult if not obsolete).

Why is all this tremendously relevant for federal studies? First, because asymmetry, pluralism of sources and actors as well as negotiation are precisely what federalism has always been about and what has determined its success or failure as an instrument of 'minority accommodation'. Now it's the time of the (federalism-inspired) Law of diversity to prove fit for the new challenge of the management of diverse societies.

Secondly, the link between the Law of diversity and federalism is not only 'generational', in the sense explained above (common genesis from the federal matrix). A strong link also exists with regard to the theory of federalism. In this regard, the editors also propose the term feder(ation)alism in order to emphasize the connection between the (theory of) federalism and its manifold constitutional manifestations like in particular the ones analyzed in this volume: an attempt that requires further investigation but already hints to the

9 See William Romans, Iryna Ulasiuk and Anton Petrenko Thomsen, eds., *Effective Participation of National Minorities and Conflict Prevention* (Leiden-Boston: Brill-Nijhoff, 2020).

10 See Joseph Marko and Sergiu Constantin, eds., *Human and Minority Rights Protection by Multiple Diversity Governance* (London-New York: Routledge, 2019).

need to combine the necessary resort to the concept of federalism and its contextual modernization.[11]

Third, pluralism is in fact the backbone of federalism since federalism is at odds with any constitutional framework aimed at protecting only one interest, such as the interest of the leader in autocratic states, that of the dominant denomination in religious states, that of the majority nation in nationalistic states, etc.

When the idea of federalism was first born, it was a philosophical approach to political organization, serving essentially economic and military purposes.[12] In legal terms, the early idea of federalism was closer to international rather than constitutional law, aimed at bringing together sovereign units that alone were no longer competitive in economic and military terms; this has been the case for historic federations, notably, the US, Switzerland, and Germany. The more federal systems established themselves (19th century) and significantly increased in number (20th century),[13] the more federalism became noteworthy not only to political philosophers and political scientists, but also to constitutional lawyers and economists. All of these methodological perspectives facilitated the study of how federations (and subsequently their derivative forms such as regional or devolved states)[14] work in practice, what are the comparative elements in common, how their functioning can be improved, and, above all, what institutions and procedures are needed in order to make federations work. And of course how they can be used to accommodate minority claims.

In the 21st century, the challenge is not so much the creation of new federations,[15] the federal idea has been sufficiently explored, and so are its

11 See inter alia Patricia Popelier, *Dynamic Federalism: A New Theory for Cohesion and Regional Autonomy* (London: Routledge, 2021), who introduces the concept of "multi-tiered systems" (MTS).

12 See in particular John Kincaid, *Federalism* (London: Sage, 2011); John Loughlin, John Kincaid and Wilfried Swenden, eds., *The Routledge Handbook of Regionalism and Federalism* (London-New York: Routledge, 2013); Daniel J. Elazar, *Exploring Federalism* (Tuscaloosa: University of Alabama Press, 1987).

13 The number of federal or quasi-federal countries has more than tripled in the course of the 20th century; at present, the majority of the world's population lives under federal or quasi-federal rule. See Thomas O. Hueglin and Alan Fenna, *Comparative Federalism: A Systematic Inquiry* (Peterborough, ON: Broadview Press, 2006), 3.

14 Ronald L. Watts, *Comparing Federal Systems* (3rd ed., Montreal-Kingston: McGill-Queens University Press, 2008).

15 For the distinction between federalism and federations, see in particular Michael Burgess, "The Penumbra of Federalism. A Conceptual Reappraisal of Federalism, Federation, Confederations and Federal Political System," in *The Routledge Handbook of Regionalism and Federalism*, eds. John Loughlin, John Kincaid and Wilfried Swenden (London-New York: Routledge, 2013), 45–60.

institutional mechanisms. Also the factors for success or failure of minority-based federal arrangements are sufficiently clear. Instead, the critical test that remains is the effective management of pluralism and its inherent complexity. The main complexity challenge to the accommodation of contemporary pluralism is the claim for the participation of a number of actors that are not institutional in nature. Consequently, federalism can no longer be seen as a pure institutional interplay, a system accommodating the coexistence of institutions belonging to different tiers of government, but becomes the engine that stimulates the establishment of new rules and procedures for the management of new diversity claims.

Federalism – with its institutions, procedures, structured relations, and mechanisms for the prevention and resolution of conflicts – is inspiring the development of procedural solutions for the growing demands for pluralist (participatory, inclusive, multilevel) democracy. As the older brother of complementary decision-making processes,[16] federalism, with its history and its machinery, is the unavoidable benchmark for the design and the development of new instruments and procedures for accommodating pluralism and participation. The family line continues, and the Law of diversity is the newborn.

Bibliography

Advisory Committee on the Framework Convention for the Protection of National Minorities. Third Thematic Commentary *The Language Rights of Persons Belonging to National Minorities under the Framework Convention* (ACFC/44DOC(2012)001).

Alessi, Nicolò P. *A Global Law of Diversity: Evolving Models and Concepts*. London-New York: Routledge, 2025.

Beck, Hans and Peter Funke, eds., *Federalism in Greek Antiquity*. Cambridge: Cambridge University Press 2015.

Benedikter, Thomas. *The World's Modern Autonomy Systems*. Bolzano: Eurac Research, 2009.

Burgess, Michael. "The Penumbra of Federalism. A Conceptual Reappraisal of Federalism, Federation, Confederations and Federal Political System." In *The Routledge Handbook of Regionalism and Federalism*, edited by John Loughlin, John Kincaid and Wilfried Swenden, 45–60. London-New York: Routledge, 2013.

16 The German scholar Peter Häberle once famously described regionalism as the younger brother of federalism (Peter Häberle, *Europäische Rechtskultur* (Berlin: Suhrkamp, 1997), 233). Federalism might thus have more little brothers than just regionalism.

Dowdle, Michael W. and Michael A. Wilkinson, eds. *Constitutionalism beyond Liberalism*. Cambridge: Cambridge University Press, 2017.

Elazar, Daniel J. *Exploring Federalism*. Tuscaloosa: University of Alabama Press, 1987.

Franchi, Elena. "Leghe e stati federali." In *Introduzione alla storia greca*, edited by Maurizio Giangiulio, 185–196. Bologna: il Mulino, 2021.

Frey, Bruno S. "Functional, Overlapping, Competing Jurisdictions: Redrawing the Geographic Borders of Administration." *European Journal of Law Reform* v, no. 3/4 (2005): 543–555.

Häberle, Peter. *Europäische Rechtskultur*. Berlin: Suhrkamp, 1997.

Hueglin Thomas O. and Alan Fenna. *Comparative Federalism: A Systematic Inquiry*. Peterborough, ON: Broadview Press, 2006.

Kincaid, John. *Federalism*. London: Sage, 2011.

Krisch, Nico. *Beyond Constitutionalism: The Pluralist Structure of Postnational Law*. Oxford: Oxford University Press, 2012.

Lapidoth, Ruth. *Autonomy: Flexible Solutions to Ethnic Conflicts*. Washington: US Institute of Peace Press, 1996.

Loughlin, John, John Kincaid and Wilfried Swenden, eds., *The Routledge Handbook of Regionalism and Federalism*. London-New York: Routledge, 2013.

Marko, Joseph and Sergiu Constantin, eds., *Human and Minority Rights Protection by Multiple Diversity Governance*. London- New York: Routledge, 2019.

Palermo, Francesco and Jens Woelk. "From Minority Protection to a Law of Diversity? Reflections on the Evolution of Minority Rights." *European Yearbook of Minority Issues* 3 (2003/2004): 5–13.

Palermo, Francesco. "Territory and the Law of Ownership: From Misunderstanding to Opportunity." In *Law, Territory and Conflict Resolution. Law as a Problem and Law as a Solution*, edited by Matteo Nicolini, Francesco Palermo and Enrico Milano, 16–38. Leiden-Boston: Brill-Nijhoff, 2016.

Popelier, Patricia. *Dynamic Federalism: A New Theory for Cohesion and Regional Autonomy*. London-New York: Routledge, 2021.

Romans, William, Iryna Ulasiuk and Anton Petrenko Thomsen, eds., *Effective Participation of National Minorities and Conflict Prevention*. Leiden-Boston: Brill-Nijhoff, 2020.

Roter, Petra. "Commentary of article 5 of the Framework Convention for the Protection of National Minorities." In *The Framework Convention for the Protection of National Minorities: a commentary*, edited by Rainer Hofmann, Tove H. Malloy, Detlev Rein, 126–147. Leiden-Boston: Brill-Nijhoff, 2018.

Watts, Ronald L. *Comparing Federal Systems*. 3rd ed., Montreal-Kingston: McGill-Queens University Press, 2008.

Weller, Marc and Stefan Wolff. *Autonomy, Self-Governance and Conflict Resolution: Innovative Approaches to Institutional Design in Divided Societies*. London-New York: Routledge, 2005.

Figures and Tables

Figures

Tables

Notes on Contributors

Nicolò P. Alessi
holds a MA degree in Law from the University of Torino and a PhD in Law and European and International Law at the universities of Verona and Fribourg/Freiburg (CH). His PhD thesis has been awarded the International Prize Giancarlo Doria for the best thesis in Italian and Comparative Constitutional Law. He currently is post-doctoral researcher in Comparative Public Law and European Law at UniDistance Suisse and the University of Bern. He was adjunct professor of Comparative Public Law at the University of Aosta Valley, junior researcher at the Institute for comparative federalism at Eurac research and guest researcher at the Institute of federalism of Fribourg/Freiburg. His main research interests are Italian and Comparative Constitutional Law, Diversity accommodation, Minority Rights, Autonomy Studies, Regionalism, and Federalism. He is also an expert on the Aosta Valley's legal system. He has authored numerous publications and an edited book on these topic areas.

Michael G. Breen
is a Lecturer in Public Policy (MECAF) in the School of Social and Political Sciences. After completing his PhD at Nanyang Technological University, Singapore, Michael was a McKenzie Postdoctoral Fellow at the University of Melbourne. His research focuses on federalism, political parties and electoral systems in Asia, and the management of ethnic diversity. He is the author of 'The Road to Federalism in Nepal, Myanmar and Sri Lanka: Finding the Middle Ground' (2018, Routledge) and was an advisor to Nepal's constitution-making process that established it as a federal democratic republic. Michael's research also explores the role of deliberative democracy and the use of deliberative polling in constitution-making and conflict management. Prior to academia, Michael was a policy maker, negotiator and project manager in various government departments in Australia and international organisations including the United Nations Development Programme. His professional background is in Indigenous rights and native title, political inclusion and environmental conservation.

Enriqueta Expósito
is full Professor of Constitutional Law at the University of Barcelona and member of the Study Group on Democracy and Constitutionalism (GEDECO). She has worked and published in various areas of constitutional law: institutions, rights and territorial organization of the State. Recently, she has focused on the

study of citizen participation. She has participated in numerous research projects funded under the R+D+i programme. She is currently co-principal investigator of the project "Counter-majoritarian Instruments in the Constitutional State" (PID2019- 104414GB-C32).

Karl Kössler

is Senior Researcher at the Institute for Comparative Federalism at Eurac Research Bolzano/Bozen (Italy). He obtained a PhD in comparative public law and political science from the University of Innsbruck (Austria) and his main fields of interest and expertise are comparative federalism and autonomy studies and, more broadly, constitutional design in diverse societies. He has provided consultancy to the Council of Europe as well as to various national and subnational governments. He has lectured on the above-mentioned subjects in Europe and beyond at universities, as well as in master programmes targeted at post-doc researchers, civil servants and political decision-makers. Kössler is the author of more than 30 peer-reviewed publications on the above-mentioned subjects, including five books. He is the co-author of the book *Comparative Federalism: Constitutional Arrangements and Case Law* (Oxford: Hart Publishing, 2017). Since 2018, he is representative for Austria in the Council of Europe's Group of Independent Experts on the European Charter of Local Self-Government. Moreover, he is the Coordinator of the five-year EU-funded project "LoGov – Local Government and the Changing Urban- Rural Interplay" which brings together 18 partner institutions from around the world.

Tove H. Malloy

teaches European Studies at the Europa-Universität Flensburg (EUF) and Global Studies at Roskilde University (RUC). She is a political theorist by background specialising in the political and legal aspects of national and ethnic minority rights in international relations and international law, especially in the European context. Her areas of expertise cover the major international organisations, the European Union as well as individual countries. Her current research interests include minority politics in the EU, the UN mandate system and Greenland, the emergence of minority rights in the Council of Europe system, non-territorial autonomy for ethno-cultural minorities, minority citizenship, agonistic democracy, ethno-ecologism, minority indicators, and inter-sectional discrimination. She is a co-founding member of the COST network ENTAN (European Non-Territorial Autonomy Network), where she is a member of the Action Core Group and also functions as the group leader of the working group on Regional and Socio-economic Development: Resources and Incentives. Prof. Malloy has been called upon for expert advisory opinions by local and national governments, the Council of Europe, the OSCE and the European Commission. Her research has been funded by the European Commission, governments and private foundations. She has previously taught at the University of Southern Denmark's European Studies Programme, the EU's Master Programme in Human Rights and Democratisation in Venice, Italy, the Master in European Integration and Regionalism in Bolzano and the University of Bologna's European Master in Peace-making and Peace-building. Previously, Prof. Malloy has served as Director of the European Centre for Minority Issues (ECMI) in Flensburg, Germany and as Senior Researcher and Consortium Director at the European Academy, Bolzano/Bozen, South Tyrol. In addition to her academic career, she has served in the Danish Foreign Service in numerous positions and represented the Danish Government in international fora on post-conflict resolution for Rwanda and Bosnia, transition and development for Albania as well as on indigenous affairs issues. She holds a doctorate in Government from the University of Essex (UK) and an MA in Humanities from the University of Southern Denmark. She was a member of the Advisory Committee to the European Framework Convention for the Protection of National Minorities (ACFC) at the Council of Europe from 2011 to 2018 and served as Gender Equality Rapporteur from 2016 to 2018.

Francesco Palermo
is Professor of comparative constitutional law at the University of Verona and Director of the Institute for Comparative Federalism at Eurac Research in Bolzano/Bozen. He worked for the OSCE High Commissioner on National Minorities and was member and president of the Council of Europe's Advisory Committee on the Framework Convention for the Protection of National Minorities. From 2013 to 2018 he served as a non-party member of the Italian Senate, Member of the Scientific Committee of the Fundamental Rights Agency of the EU for the term 2018–2023 and Constitutional Adviser to the Council of Europe's Congress of Local and Regional Autonomies since 2019. He has authored over 300 publications, including 11 monographs and 36 edited volumes.

Jared Sonnicksen
is Professor for Political Science and responsible for Political Systems at the RTWH Aachen University. He was Privatdozent and Researcher at the Institute for Political Science of the Technical University Darmstadt. In Winter Semester 2020/21 he was also Guest Professor. From Winter Semester 2012/12 to Summer Semester 2019 he was a Researcher and Instructor for working group "Political System of Germany and Comparative Government". He temporarily headed

this working area for Winter Semester 2019/20. In Summer Semester 2020 he was Guest Professor at the Otto-Suhr- Institute for Political Science at the Free University of Berlin. His interests in teaching and research are diverse, but refer especially to questions of democratic governing under conditions of complexity.

Roberto Toniatti

is Emeritus Professor of Comparative Constitutional Law at the University of Trento. After spending a year at the Institute for Government at the University of Virginia as a Fullbright Scholar, he was called as an associate professor at the Faculty of Law of the University of Trento in 1988. He became a full professor in 1994 and was Dean of the same Faculty from 1994 to 2000 and again from 2003 to 2009. Roberto Toniatti has been a visiting professor at University College Galway, University of Delaware, Universidad de Valencia, Universidad del Pais Vasco, Universitat Pompeu Fabra in Barcelona, University of Haifa (Israel), Kunmin University, Bahçesehir University in Istanbul, University of Singapore and University of Hong Kong.From 1995 to 1998 he was a member of the 'round table' of experts that designed the model of cross-border cooperation between Trentino, Adige/Südtirol and Tyrol and is an honorary member of the Euroregional Association of Comparative and European Public Law (www.jus-euroregionale.org), which he founded together with a group of lawyers from Innsbruck, Bolzano and Trento in 2004. In 2016–2017, he was a member of Convention 33 of the Autonomous Province of Bolzano for the reform of the autonomy statute. Since 2013, he has coordinated the activities of the 'Laboratory of Institutional Innovation for Integral Autonomy' at the University of Trento (www.liatn.eu).

Kyriaki Topidi

is head of the research cluster on "Culture & Diversity" and joined ECMI in 2019. She holds a degree in law from the Robert Schuman Faculty of Law in Strasbourg, an MA in International Studies from the University of Birmingham, a PhD in European Studies from Queen's University Belfast and a habilitation in Constitutional Law from the University of Fribourg. She has lectured extensively and researched in the areas of Public International Law, European Law, Human Rights and Comparative Law. In the past, she has occupied research positions in various institutions and was a senior lecturer at the Faculty of Law of the University of Luzern in Switzerland. She has also worked as managing director of the Centre for Comparative Constitutional Law and Religion at the same institution. She has been a guest scholar at Fordham University (US), the IDC (Israel) and the Max Planck Institute in Halle (Germany), the

Institute of Law and Religion of the University of Fribourg (Switzerland) as well as the National Law School Delhi (India) among others. Her research interests focus on diversity management, minority protection rights and mechanisms (with a special interest in religion) and human rights law. She is the author and editor of a number of volumes, including EU law, Minorities and Enlargement (Intersentia, 2010), Constitutional Evolution in Central and Eastern Europe: Expansion and Integration in the EU (Ashgate, 2011), Transnational Legal Process and Human Rights (Ashgate, 2013) and Religion as Empowerment: Global Legal Perspectives (Routledge, 2016). More recently, she has edited a collection on Normative Pluralism and Human Rights (Routledge, 2018). Her latest monograph focuses on The Right to Difference and Comparative Religious Diversity in Education (Routledge, 2020). At the ECMI, in addition to her expertise on minority rights in education, she is researching on minority identity and digital governance as well as on the intersection of minorities with social movements. She is also the editor of JEMIE.

Martina Trettel
is Senior Researcher at the Institute for Comparative Federalism of Eurac Research. She got her PhD in Constitutional and European Legal Studies at the Graduate School of Law of the University of Verona in 2017. Her main research interests are Participatory democracy and Institutional Innovation, Federal and Regional Studies and Comparative Constitutional Justice. Particularly, her doctoral research focused on participatory and deliberative democracy intended as complementary decisional mechanisms to the more traditional representative and direct democratic instruments. In the last five years she combined theoretical and empirical research on participatory mechanisms. To this extent, she took part in different European projects related to these topics. Among these, she co-managed the project GaYA (Governance and Youth in the Alps) and she is actively participating in the COST project "Constitution-making and deliberative democracy" that focuses on the deliberative/participatory turn that many countries in Europe and beyond are taking in order to reform their Constitutions. She authored several articles on these topics in academic journals as well as in edited books. She has provided consultancies on topics related to citizens participation to the Council of Europe and to regional and local governments in Italy, and beyond. She co-manages the Blog EUreka! (https://blogs.eurac.edu/eureka/) and co-created the simulation game Let's go federal!, a role play on decentralization and intergovernmental relations.

Introduction

*Nicolò P. Alessi and Martina Trettel**

1 The Variety of Diversity Accommodation in the Contemporary World

The accommodation of diversity in the – today rich and variegated – tradition of constitutionalism[1] is a multifaceted phenomenon, of which the mainstream practical and theoretical perspective is just one dimension.

It is indeed possible to observe the emergence of new and interesting legal responses beyond the most consolidated instruments for managing diversity within liberal-democratic constitutional systems – i.e. non-discrimination law and minority and indigenous peoples' rights law. Such innovative responses complement – and do not imply the demise of – the latter and enrich the understanding of diversity accommodation in the global constitutional tradition, within and outside liberal-democratic constitutionalism.

On the one side, novel regional macro-perspectives of diversity accommodation are emerging, which are integrating the very vocabulary of liberal-democratic constitutionalism, tied to national categories, with groundbreaking concepts and approaches. First, the South American and Southeast Asian regions host legal systems that have incorporated diversity at the very core of their constitutional structures. The case models of Bolivia and Ecuador represent the most innovative approaches of the South American continent. These add to the global discourse over diversity accommodation through the establishment of constitutional systems that affirm and variously implement the principles of plurinationality and interculturalism, thus acknowledging the

* This chapter was developed and written collaboratively. Nicolò P. Alessi is chiefly responsible for sections 2, 3 and 4 and Martina Trettel, for sections 1, 5 and 6.

1 On a plural conceptualization of constitutionalism, see: James Tully, *Strange Multiplicity: Constitutionalism in an Age of Diversity* (Cambridge: Cambridge University Press, 1995) and his proposed reconceptualization of constitutionalism as a plural concept embracing a vast array of constitutional experiences; Ran Hirschl, *Comparative Matters: The Renaissance of Comparative Constitutional Law* (Oxford: Oxford University Press, 2014), 205–223; on the need for an integration of the theory of constitutionalism with Global South perspectives, see Michael W. Dowdle and Michael A. Wilkinson, eds., *Constitutionalism Beyond Liberalism* (Cambridge: Cambridge University Press, 2017); Philipp Dann, Michael Riegner and Maxim Bönnemann, eds., *The Global South and Comparative Constitutional Law* (Oxford: Oxford University Press, 2020).

composite nature of their societies.[2] Singapore can be seen as a paradigmatic example to illustrate the innovations in Southeast Asia, where pluralism is not only a societal reality but also a basic constitutional principle in several countries. Pluralism, pragmatism, flexibility, persuasion and governance mechanisms over rights attribution are the pillars of Singapore's rather government-directed system, which constitutes an interesting alternative to liberal-democratic perspectives to constitutionalism and diversity accommodation.[3] Secondly, the Global North itself is experiencing notable developments in this area. European international law has tried to update its contents to respond to the challenges that contemporary times pose, especially in European societies. It has done so by proposing a renovated concept of integration and encouraging states to shift their focus from (selected ethno-cultural) minorities to the regulation of diversity as a global societal phenomenon.[4]

At the same time, one can observe the rise of several forms of emergent instruments for the accommodation of diversity in several countries of the Global North. They are particular types of legal – but variously institutionalized – devices that contribute to accommodating diversity in ways that are divergent from the classic minority rights law mechanisms and their structure.

The emergent models for the accommodation of diversity have been classified in three main (and internally differentiated) categories:[5] non-territorial autonomy, legal pluralism, and participatory democracy. They all can be framed as forms of "non-governmental autonomy": forms of decentralization of authority – or autonomous arrangements – that do not correspond to full-fledged subnational governments that increase the expression of pluralism and diversity. These are loose categories that contain a wealth of models, from the most consolidated to the most innovative ones.

In order to capture the described trends and reconnect traditional and contemporary perspectives in this area, the book employs the concept of the Law of diversity, which was developed in a recent publication.[6] The latter notion suggests that one refrains from framing diversity management only through the lens of minority rights, which may prove to be an epistemological

2 On this, see Nicolò P. Alessi, *A Global Law of Diversity: Evolving Models and Concepts* (London-New York: Routledge, 2025).

3 See Alessi, *A Global Law*.

4 See Alessi, *A Global Law*.

5 See Alessi, *A Global Law*.

6 The expression is borrowed from Francesco Palermo and Jens Woelk, "From Minority Protection to a Law of Diversity? Reflections on the Evolution of Minority Rights," *European Yearbook of Minority Issues* 3 (2003/2004): 5–13 and developed in the sense here endorsed in Alessi, *A Global Law*.

constraint.[7] This is so as it ties the study to some particular models that respect a specific essential structure (based on the national paradigm) and, accordingly, it restrains the scientific focus to them. The Law of diversity is a way to create an enabling theoretical framework, which, acting as a gate-opener, opens up the scientific observation and interest beyond the well-trodden path of minority rights-related practices and models.[8] In other words, the employment of the concept "Law of diversity" is meant to overcome the theoretical limitations one encounters when studying this area of law through the lens of minority (and indigenous peoples') rights categories.

Such a theoretical standpoint constitutes one of the premises of this edited book, as it allows to include the instruments that are dealt here within the legal analysis of diversity accommodation. The next sub-sections will provide a brief overview of the emergent models for the accommodation of diversity.

1.1 *Non-territorial Autonomy*

Different non-territorial autonomous arrangements fall within this category.

The most consolidated (and studied) models reproduce (at least on paper) the classic structure of minority rights law mechanisms: they are forms of public bodies that are attributed or delegated administrative and legislative functions (at least in theory, this is also the case for the so-called non-territorial cultural autonomy models) through constitutional provisions or statutes, and as such, form a part of the state system of government.[9]

The innovative forms of non-territorial autonomy are, conversely, various types of governance bodies with different degrees of institutionalization that complement state action in the interest of some non-majority communities. Their structure is typically private or hybrid public-private, and they provide services for the relevant communities along with the state. Notably, they all are potentially very inclusive instruments as none of them require state recognition of the non-majority group to be set up. In other words, state recognition is not a necessary condition for their emergence.

7 See Jean-F., Gaudreault-DesBiens, "Introduction to Part II," in *Cultural Diversity and the Law: State Responses Around the World*, eds. Marie-C. Foblets, Jean-F. Gaudreault-DesBiens and Alison Dundes Relteln (Bruxelles-Montréal: Bruylant and Yvon-Blais, 2010), 367–380.

8 See Alessi, *A Global Law*.

9 See Johanne Poirier, "Autonomie politique et minorités francophones du Canada: réflexions sur un angle mort de la typologie classique de Will Kymlicka," *Minorités linguistiques et société / Linguistic Minorities and Society* no. 1 (2012): 66–89.

Examples of this model are observable in Germany and Denmark,[10] as well as in Canada. The European version of innovative non-territorial autonomy has been framed as functional non-territorial autonomy. It is characterized by its limited institutionalization: the non-majority groups have created an array of minority associations that provide services and, more in general, act in the interest of the relevant groups in several areas, not limited to cultural issues. Similar to this experience, is the model of institutional completeness in Canada. This expression has been used to describe the emergence of forms of "private autonomy" – private associations or organizations, as well as private-public bodies – in the provision of services, especially in the areas of education and health – for the French minority communities in Canada.[11]

Other models that have been emerging in Canada and Australia have been defined as "nested federalisms" and represent innovative forms of indigenous autonomous arrangements.[12] They are complex governance devices that have been nested within unchanged federal structures, i.e. new layers of decentralization in federal states created without explicit changes in the constitutional legal framework. The most interesting experiences are the Inuit self-governance systems in the Arctic and the so-called model of "privatized autonomy" of the Noongar people in Australia. Both models rely on the existence of private companies that serve the interests of their communities, not only concerning cultural issues, but in a global manner, with a specific focus on practical solutions to ameliorate the socio-economic conditions of their members.

10 For a general overview, see Tove H. Malloy, Alexander Osipov and Balázs Vizi, eds., *Managing Diversity through Non-Territorial Autonomy. Assessing Advantages, Deficiencies, and Risks* (Oxford: Oxford University Press, 2015); Ephraim Nimni, Alexander Osipov and David J. Smith, eds., *The Challenge of Non-Territorial Autonomy: Theory and Practice* (Oxford: Peter Lang, 2013); on the German-Danish model, see Tove H. Malloy, "Functional Non-Territorial Autonomy in Denmark and Germany," in *Managing Diversity through Non-Territorial Autonomy: Assessing Advantages, Deficiencies, and Risks*, eds. Tove H. Malloy, Alexander Osipov and Balázs Vizi (Oxford: Oxford University Press, 2015), 183–204.

11 See Stéphanie Chouinard, "The Rise of Non-territorial Autonomy in Canada: Towards a Doctrine of Institutional Completeness in the Domain of Minority Language Rights," *Ethnopolitics* 13, no. 2 (2014): 141–158.

12 See Gary N. Wilson, Christopher Alcantara and Thierry Rodon, *Nested Federalism and Inuit Governance in the Canadian Arctic* (Vancouver: University of British Columbia Press, 2020); Bertus De Villiers, "Privatised Autonomy for the Noongar People of Australia: A New Model for Indigenous Self-Government," in *Indigenous, Aboriginal, Fugitive and Ethnic Groups Around the Globe*, ed. Liat Klain-Gabbay (London: Intech Open, 2019), 127–157.

1.2 *Participatory Democracy*

Participatory democracy and democratic innovations[13] are catch-all expressions that refer to institutions and mechanisms that foster the interaction between citizens and public bodies in decision-making processes aimed at enriching democratic procedures and complementing – not substituting – representative democracy.[14] In general, experiences of democratic innovations started to emerge during the 1970s and 1980s in various parts of the world. They have attracted the attention of scholars from a range of disciplines, most notably political science. However, it has been noticed that participatory democracy means are still largely overshadowed in theory and practice by interest in traditional channels of participation through representation in elected assemblies. Accordingly, while participatory instruments are implemented to different degrees or at least widely accepted, they seem to suffer from being overlooked theoretically and experience troublesome practical application. Participatory means beyond classic forms of representation – especially in the form of consultative bodies and co-management mechanisms – are presented here as at least partially innovative avenues of this area of law.

Among them, of particular interest are the advisory and co-decision structures, as they are "transversal bodies". The latter are not aimed at representing the voice of just one minority, but rather are designed to gather all the minority groups, thus creating a consultative body that does not serve the interest of a single group. They seem to imply a conception of diversity that does not exclusively identify a single minority that "owns" the body, but represents all groups bearing diversity. For instance, in Germany, the Minority Council, established in 2005, advises the federal government and federal parliament about matters that affect the Frisians, Sinti and Roma, Sorbian, and Danish minorities, particularly as concerns the protection and promotion of their language and culture. Even more in line with this perspective are what can be referred to as "transversal inclusivist bodies", which are characterized by having open membership criteria and do not – at least formally – exclude any form of (ethnocultural) group from being part of it. An example is the Croatian Council for National Minorities, established by the Constitutional Law on the Rights of

13 It must be said that most of the English-speaking literature on this theme employs the expression "democratic innovations" nowadays; on this, amongst others, see Graham Smith, *Democratic Innovations: Designing Institutions for Citizen Participation* (Cambridge: Cambridge University Press, 2009).

14 Martina Trettel, *La democrazia partecipativa negli ordinamenti composti: studio di diritto comparato sull'incidenza della tradizione giuridica nelle democratic innovations* (Naples: ESI, 2020), 23–52; Smith, *Democratic Innovations*, 8–29.

National Minorities of 2002, which follows the described structure. Besides the creation of non-territorial autonomous arrangements (national minority councils), the legal framework for minority protection in Croatia has established a government-funded structure that serves the interests of all minorities and manages the distribution of public funding to minority self-governments and associations.

A further noteworthy model of participation has been labeled as "co-management". This expression refers to the cooperative management between state/public institutions and non-majority (indigenous) groups in areas of interest to the latter. These bodies are interesting models for the accommodation of diversity as they focus on pragmatic governance issues and methods instead of traditional representation in elected bodies. Co-management bodies are present in Canada, in the framework of the Inuit and the French minority communities' self-governance systems.[15]

1.3 *Legal Pluralism*

The expression legal pluralism[16] refers to the coexistence of multiple legal orders in the same geographical and temporal space[17] and challenges the liberal assumption that law must equate to state law.

---

15 See Pierre Foucher, "Autonomie des communautés francophones minoritaires du Canada: le point de vue du droit," *Minorités linguistiques et société / Linguistic Minorities and Society* 1 (2012): 90–114; Daniel Bourgeois, "Administrative Nationalism," *Administration & Society* 39, no. 5 (2007): 631–655; *Id.*, "Territory, Institutions and National Identity: The Case of Acadians in Greater Moncton, Canada," *Urban Studies* 42, no. 7 (2005): 1123–1138; Gary N. Wilson and Christopher Alcantara, "Mixing Politics and Business in the Canadian Arctic: Inuit Corporate Governance in Nunavik and the Inuvialuit Settlement Region," *Canadian Journal of Political Science / Revue canadienne de science politique* 45, no. 4 (2012): 781–804.

16 The present section employs the expression legal pluralism, although, in legal studies, legal and normative pluralism are generally used interchangeably; a possible distinction between legal and normative pluralism is offered by Helen Quane, "Legal Pluralism, Autonomy and Ethno-Cultural Diversity Management," in *Non-Territorial Autonomy and Decentralization: Ethno-Cultural Diversity Governance*, eds. Tove H. Malloy and Levente Salat (London-New York: Routledge, 2021), 69: "Legal pluralism has generated considerable academic debate, but for present purposes it refers to the coexistence of more than one legal or "law like" normative system within the same geographical and temporal space. Of course, this presupposes that the relevant normative systems can be classified as "law" or "law like." If not, it may be more correct to refer to normative rather than legal pluralism".

17 William Twining, "Normative and Legal Pluralism: A Global Perspective," *Duke Journal of Comparative and International Law* 20 (2010): 473–518; Bryan S. Turner, "Legal Pluralism: Freedom of Religion, Exemptions and the Equality of Citizens," in *Religious*

Theories of legal pluralism arose in the 1970s and are now a central theme of legal research. Although several definitional conundrums characterize this area of legal study – especially when it comes to the definition of what is law – legal pluralism's core idea is that the legal phenomenon is not limited to official sources of law produced by the state, but comprises a variety of legal arrangements stemming from numerous state and non-state authorities and processes. Among the phenomena taken into account by legal pluralist theory, prominent are experiences of legal pluralism that derive from the coexistence of state law and non-state legal orders originating from ethnic (generally indigenous) or religious communities. This strand of literature has analyzed cases of legal pluralism in Global North and Global South countries and their varying relationship with state law, with specific regard to the issues of state recognition and the definition of rules to manage the coexistence between these legal orders.[18]

Other innovative phenomena of legal pluralism are currently emerging. Concretely, they take the shape of private courts or arbitration systems that apply religious (or customary) law to settle controversies of several types – including but not limited to family law – within a given community. And, notably, they are non-institutionalized forms, or types that are established following legal models that are provided for by non-minority-specific legislation. Two very interesting experiences are the religious alternative dispute resolution (ADR) systems in the UK and the US and the Gypsy tribunal – called *Kris* – in several European and North American countries.[19]

Not unlike the cases of non-governmental autonomy, such legal phenomena appear to illustrate the existence and potential of autonomous arrangements that, to different degrees, diverge from the traditional structure of minority rights and instruments, which are based on public law recognition, hard regulations and

---

Rules, State Law, and Normative Pluralism: A Comparative Overview, eds. Rossella Bottoni, Rinaldo Cristofori and Silvio Ferrari (Cham: Springer, 2016), 61–73.

18 Margaret Davies, "Legal Pluralism," in *The Oxford Handbook of Comparative Constitutional Law*, eds. Michel Rosenfeld and András Sajó (Oxford: Oxford University Press, 2012), 805–827, has identified three major strands of legal pluralist theory: the first is focused on the context of colonialism and post-colonialism; the second deals with normative pluralism that is present in any complex society; and a third has as its central focal point globalization and the consequent loss of power by states to supra- and international organizations and the consequent diminishment of its traditional legal functions.

19 On this, see Michael J. Broyde, *Sharia Tribunals, Rabbinical Courts, and Christian Panels: Religious Arbitration in America and the West* (Oxford: Oxford University Press, 2017); Levente Salat and Sergiu Miscoiu, "Roma Autonomous Lawmaking: The Romanian Case," in *Non-Territorial Autonomy and Decentralization: Ethno-Cultural Diversity Governance*, eds. Tove H. Malloy and Levente Salat (London-New York: Routledge, 2021), 167–194.

exclusive entitlements. Although these innovative models are not free from criticism[20] and significantly rely on constitutional and legal systems that are conducive to their emergence, they nonetheless contribute to expanding the legal and constitutional discourse over diversity accommodation.

2 The Aim of the Book: In Search of Theoretical Instruments to Understand the Law of Diversity

This book aims to propose the employment of federalism as a frame of understanding of the emergent instruments for the accommodation of diversity.[21] The latter indeed appear to be the most in need of a solid theoretical ground given their peculiar structure and dynamics. Similarly to any other emerging practice, the creation of a theoretical framework of understanding is key to providing a solid theoretical basis upon which their consolidation and development may be built. Resorting to federalism is considered worthwhile for it is thought to have a potential that goes far beyond its "form of government" dimension – i.e. its conceptualization as a form of (territorial) vertical division of powers between two institutional levels – which has been rather underexplored so far.

---

20 On this, see the considerations of Silvio Ferrari, "Religious Rules and Legal Pluralism: An Introduction," in *Religious Rules, State Law, and Normative Pluralism: A Comparative Overview*, eds. Rossella Bottoni, Rinaldo Cristofori and Silvio Ferrari (Cham: Springer, 2016), 21: "Is legal pluralism the best strategy to give citizens the opportunity to live according to their convictions without endangering social cohesion and fostering segregation? At first glance one could think that the more religious rules that are recognized and implemented in a State legal system, the more citizens have the possibility to run their lives according to the rules of their choice. […] Sometimes legal pluralism has encouraged religious conservatism […], in other cases the legal application of the principle of religious pluralism turned out to strengthen dominant cultural and religious identities […]. It is therefore wise to accept Michele Graziadei's remark that "legal pluralism as a theory, or as a set of theories, does not necessarily address how diversity can be turned into a resource for individuals and for society as a whole, rather than becoming a cause of fragmentation and anomie" or a ground for the oppression of the weakest components of society. At the same time the contributions in this book seem to suggest that there is a difference between a legal pluralism of choice and a legal pluralism of constraint […]. In both cases tensions and conflicts are to be expected in the long process of accommodating religious diversity in the State legal systems, but only the first has a good chance to help build an inclusive and, at the same time, even-handed society".

21 As hinted in Alessi, *A Global Law*; the latter publication has introduced this perspective, which the present volume aims to further elaborate on.

In other words, the main aim of the book is to offer the opportunity to reflect on this innovative perspective on federalism and diversity accommodation and test it.

3 Why Federalism to Frame the Law of Diversity?

While most philosophical and normative accounts have considered federalism as a (more or less successful) formula to manage (manifold forms of) societal diversity by building a state federal structure[22] (or a corporative society),[23] and most political scientists and lawyers have studied its features and evolution

22 For instance, among many, see Ronald L. Watts, *Comparing Federal Systems* (3rd ed., Montréal: McGill-Queen's University Press, 2008), 8: "the term "federalism" is used basically not as a descriptive but as a normative term and refers to the advocacy of multi-tiered government combining elements of shared-rule and regional self-rule. It is based on the presumed value and validity of combining unity and diversity, i.e of accommodating, preserving and promoting distinct identities within a larger political union. The essence of federalism as a normative principle is the value of perpetuating both union and non- centralization at the same time"; *Id.*, *Comparing*, 192; also, Michael Burgess, *Comparative Federalism: Theory and Practice* (London-New York: Routledge, 2006), 2: "In what follows, then, I shall take federalism to mean the recommendation and (sometimes) the active promotion of support for federation. A federation is a particular kind of state"; these and most American authors have conflated federalism with an ideal-typical model, federal democracy (based on the US example); see, for instance, Michael Burgess, *In Search of the Federal Spirit* (Oxford: Oxford University Press, 2012); Alfred Stepan, "Federalism and Democracy: Beyond the U.S. Model," in *Theories of Federalism: A Reader*, eds. Dimitrios Karmis and Wayne Norman (New-York-Basingstoke: Palgrave Macmillan, 2005), 255–268; this line of reasoning has characterized the origins of American thought on federalism: see, for instance, Alexander Hamilton, "Federalist No. 28," in *The Federalist Papers*, ed. Clinton Rossiter (New York: The New American Library, 1961), 178–182; see also the American Supreme Court ruling *Gregory v Ashcroft*, 501 U.S. 452, 458 (1991), per Justice O'Connor.

23 On the idea that federalism is the most suited form of government to manage human society, and on the model of a confederal corporative society, see Frederick S. Carney, *The Politics of Johannes Althusius* (Boston-Toronto: Beacon Press-S. J. Reginald Saunders and Co., 1964) (translation of Johannes Althusius, *Politica methodice digesta atque exemplis sacris et profanis illustrate*); some authors have tried to modernize Althusius's thought and apply it to post-modernity: Thomas O. Hueglin, *Early Modern Concepts for a Late Modern World: Althusius on Community and Federalism* (Waterloo: Wilfried Laurier University Press, 1999); *Id.*, "Johannes Althusius: Medieval Constitutionalist or Modern Federalist?," *Publius* 9, no. 4 (1979): 9–41; Nicolas Aroney, "The Federal Condition: Towards a Normative Theory," *The American Journal of Jurisprudence* 61, no. 1 (2016): 13–31.

as a constitutional state experience,[24] this book analyzes this concept from a different – and promising – angle.

In the chapters that endorsed the standpoint presented here, federalism is taken as a broad legal phenomenon that relates to the existence of governmental and governance structures and embeds any degree of diffusion of powers. Accordingly, a federal framing can be employed with regard to models that imply a total or partial diffusion of legal authority/power/autonomy in more than one center, having different degrees of public legal relevance (as a result of recognition or tolerance) in the same legal system.[25] In other words, federalism may be considered as a theoretical frame of reference for all those models that imply the expression of a certain degree of (more or less institutionalized) pluralism and autonomy and stay irreducible to its annihilation.

Such a wide framing of federalism is not for its own sake. To the contrary, it is, first, beneficial for the understanding of the emergent models for the accommodation of diversity. Indeed, based on this, federalism becomes an interesting standpoint from which one can look at complex governance structures, such as those that are emerging in the area of diversity accommodation. The theory and practice developed studying federal systems – which can be seen as vanilla models of pluralism management – has thus the potential to be used to analyze the functioning, possibly explain the dynamics and foresee the development of these (and possibly other) governance systems. Considering federalism as a wide phenomenon that embeds among its manifestations all the phenomena of diffusion of powers – from the most to the least institutionalized – allows the observer to reflect on these models as federal arrangements and to benefit from federal theory and practice to explain them. Notably, this perspective on federalism has been widely endorsed in modern and contemporary federal theory.[26] However, while accepted, the applications of this conceptualization have not been sufficiently studied so far.

Furthermore, this approach to federalism seems beneficial for federal theory itself. What actually distinguishes the theoretical approach of this book from others that have proposed a similar reading of federalism is indeed the fact that it proves the usefulness of this intuition. This perspective renovates and seems to give federal theory a new lease of life in times of increasing complexity.

---

24 For instance, see Francesco Palermo and Karl Kössler, *Comparative Federalism: Constitutional Arrangements and Case Law* (Oxford-Portland: Hart Publishing, 2019); Stephen Tierney, *The Federal Contract: A Constitutional Theory of Federalism* (Oxford: Oxford University Press, 2022).

25 See Alessi's chapter in this book.

26 See the next paragraphs.

In an era of interconnection and changing power structures,[27] a federal theory castled in its traditional (but not original) focus on state and governmental territorial structures can turn obsolete and risk heading to exhaustion.

For federal theory to keep and exploit its explanatory function, this change of perspective seems necessary.[28] In other words, to navigate contemporary complexity one should complexify and pluralize federalism itself.

4 Is (Diversity) Governance the New Dimension of Federalism? Unleashing Creative Thinking to Understand Contemporary Issues

Similarly to any other concept of constitutionalism, federalism has been so strongly tied to a specific human experience – the modern (nation and then multination) state – that it has been considered as coeval to it and almost meaningless without it. This has led to the prominence of what one may refer to as feder(ation)alism in federal studies.[29]

The term feder(ation)alism aims to highlight the elision between federalism and federation (as an overarching term for federal systems) as a form of government that most literature in this area appears to take as a given. The term emphasizes the implicit connection that political and constitutional theory establishes between the concept of federalism (in constitutional or philosophical terms) and its state-related manifestations.

More specifically, feder(ation)alism intrinsically ties federalism to two main issues. On the one hand, one may notice the widespread framing of federalism in terms of a form of government. This corresponds to a specific model of state organization – not necessarily the federal state in a strict sense – based on the institutionalization of two or more orders of full-fledged polities. The subnational levels of government reproduce or resemble the state and are entitled to varying degrees of legislative and administrative powers.[30] On the other,

27 On the evolution of human life towards an increasingly complex economic and social setting (at least in some parts of the world), mostly owing to the information revolution, see Sergio Ortino, *La struttura delle rivoluzioni economiche* (Bari: Cacucci, 2010).

28 As already suggested by Francesco Palermo, "Regulating Pluralism: Federalism as Decision-Making and New Challenges for Federal Studies," in *Federalism as Decision-Making: Changes in Structures, Procedures and Policies*, eds. Francesco Palermo and Elisabeth Alber (Leiden-Boston: Brill-Nijhoff, 2015), 499–513.

29 The term is borrowed from Nicolò P. Alessi, *A Global Law*.

30 This is particularly apparent in Patricia Popelier, *Dynamic Federalism: A New Theory for Cohesion and Regional Autonomy* (London-New York: Routledge, 2021), who built a theory of federalism as a value concept to be identified in a "proper balance" among layers of territorial government; however, the theoretical framework is somewhat conditioned by

federalism has constantly been described as a form of territorial government, having to do with the relations between territorial layers of authority. Indeed, a great number of contemporary studies take the territorial dimension of federalism as a postulate.[31]

This is not to say that federal research has not witnessed renovation. An increasing number of studies have revolved around the "post-modern epoch" and its consequences for the Westphalian model of state, mostly elaborating on the variety of new federal arrangements[32] and the process of European integration.[33] However, the centrality of the two abovementioned elements does not appear to have been called into question.

In addition, increasing attention to political behaviors and cultural components of federalism is observable. However, while today non-institutional factors affecting the dynamics of federal political systems are generally considered crucial to any analysis, this does not imply that the general focus has shifted to something different from the federal form of government. Rather, it is only that more attention has been devoted to the actors who live and perform within federal systems as well as to the social-cultural context.

Moreover, the analysis of the ongoing transition from the modern era to the so-called "post-modern epoch" has given rise to another parallel trend. Many authors have grasped the impact of post-modernity on the Westphalian model of the (federal) state. Generally, this has led to the acknowledgment of the increasing complexity characterizing the exercise of power, as a consequence of upward and downward drives stemming from global economic trends and

---

the basic initial tenet, stated at 50: "Federalism presupposes a subdivision of the political system in territorial entities with some political power".

31 For instance, Popelier, *Dynamic Federalism*, 50, justified her perspective with the following statement: "There is a common understanding that federalism is about the relationship between territorial levels of authority", similarly, Tierney, *The Federal Contract*, 161, defined "the constitutional focus of federalism as 'jurisdictional territorial pluralism': the creation of individual systems of government for the constituent territories as well as a state-wide system of government for the polity as a whole; and it is the ultimate purpose of federalism that these different governments be reconciled with each other through institutions of rule across the polity: an implicit logic of any constitutional system is efficacy".

32 Specific attention is drawn to federal arrangements for conflict resolution; on this, see Soeren Keil and Elisabeth Alber, eds., *Federalism as a Tool of Conflict Resolution* (London-New York: Routledge, 2021); Soeren Keil and Sabine Kropp, eds., *Emerging Federal Structures in the Post-Cold War Era* (Cham: Palgrave Macmillan, 2022).

33 In addition, one can also consider within this category those authors who have investigated the replication of federal patterns in state organization only with regard to some parts of the state territory, that is to say, those who have addressed autonomy as a form of federal arrangement; for instance, see Palermo and Kössler, *Comparative Federalism*, 58–61.

the emergence of compelling ethnocultural diversity issues in contemporary societies.[34] Nonetheless, this has not led to a considerable change in the heart of most inquiries, which have always directly or indirectly placed state-like full-fledged polities at the core of their analysis.

Conversely, numerous accounts have demonstrated that federalism can be seen as a phenomenon whose concrete manifestations have adapted to different human epochs and systems of thought, while at the same maintaining an unchanged and essential core content. Similarly to every social and legal phenomenon, it has followed the evolution of human organization and human thought, adapting to changing circumstances. Such a reading of federalism has been first evoked by some modern authors – Friedrich, Davis and Elazar[35] – and then specified by few contemporary accounts.[36]

Among them, of particular interest is Lépine's article "Federalism: Essence, Values and Ideologies",[37] which described the hermeneutical process of extracting a notion of federalism from the "federal phenomenon" and defined its stages of evolution as mirroring the increasing complexities of both societies and knowledge. Following his view, federalism corresponds to a synthetical idea capable of framing the federal phenomenon – which "encompasses federal institutional organizations in different times and places as well as federal thoughts about the diffusion of powers"[38] – and should thus mainly be addressed as an analytical rather than a purely normative or institutional concept.[39] As a result, on the one hand, an inner content of federalism is

---

34 See Daniel J. Elazar, *Exploring Federalism* (Tuscaloosa: The University of Alabama Press, 1987), 53; *Id.*, "From Statism to Federalism: A Paradigm Shift," *International Political Science Review / Revue internationale de science politique* 17, no. 4 (1996): 417–429; *Id.*, "The State System + Globalization (Economic plus Human Rights) = Federalism (State Federations plus Regional Confederations)," *South Texas Law Review* 40, no. 3 (1999): 555–566; Watts, *Comparing*, 6; Ortino, *La struttura*.

35 On this, see Alessi, *A Global Law*.

36 These are Frédéric Lépine, Roderick A. Macdonald, Francesco Palermo, Heather Gerken and James Tully: on this, see Alessi, *A Global Law*.

37 Frédéric Lépine, "Federalism: Essence, Values and Ideologies", in *Understanding Federalism and Federation*, eds. Alain-G. Gagnon, Soeren Keil and Sean Mueller (Farnham-Burlington: Ashgate, 2015), 31–48.

38 Lépine, "Federalism," 34.

39 *Contra*, starting from similar premises, Jean-F. Gaudreault-DesBiens, and Fabien Gélinas, "Opening New Perspectives on Federalism," in *Le fédéralisme dans tous ses états: gouvernance, identité et méthodologie – The States and Moods of Federalism: Governance, Identity and Methodology*, eds. Jean-F. Gaudreault-DesBiens and Fabien Gélinas (Cowansville-Bruxelles: Éditions Yvon Blais- Bruylant, 2005), 51–96, have alluded to the existence (or the need to study the existence) of a set of ethical values of federalism; a reasoning further expanded by Jean-F. Gaudreault-DesBiens, "Towards a Deontic Axiomatic Theory

acknowledged, but not identified as a prescriptive doctrine coinciding with a contingent ideology; on the other, the federal phenomenon was not reduced to a specific institutional manifestation, thus highlighting its trans-historical dimension and its continuous evolution.

Hence, federalism, rather than being identified in a particular prescriptive set of principles or institutional features, is mainly described as an analytical framework or an "interpretive paradigm"[40] that can explain much more than its closed state-related expression. Specifically, federalism is referred to as a notion, which "has to be considered as an elementary abstract mental representation of an object of studies, derived from empirical research and mental induction, allowing the capacity of bringing together a multiplicity of phenomena observed by the selection of some essential features, but not elaborated enough to be used in model or theory building".[41] According to this view, federalism underlies all those political systems that are characterized by the diffusion of autonomous powers in the same political space.

Based on this, federalism thus performs an analytical function leading to practical benefits, for it provides a common ground of understanding for countless practices, generalized enough to get rid of the contingencies that characterize the time and place in which these phenomena take place.[42]

Most importantly, this account illustrates that the notion of federalism has encountered several stages of evolution as regards its concrete manifestations, the last one being the "network of functional polities and institutions", a "new moment of complexity in federalism"[43] which reconnects it to the model of multi-level governance, considered as not only the latest expression of federalism,[44] but a "potential synthesis of most of the approaches of federalism [...],

of Federal Adjudication," in *The Federal Idea*, ed. Amnon Lev (Oxford-Portland: Hart Publishing, 2017), 90–91: according to this position, federalism embodies an ethics, a set of prescriptive constitutional-legal contents which make up its very core and are supposed to frame and direct the evolution of its concrete manifestations; it should be noted that these contents are referred to as legal, due to their nature as constitutional principles, and are derived from an inductive process stemming from the analysis of comparative practical experiences, together with a deductive method built upon the doctrinal discourse on federalism; this perspective is not fundamentally different from the political science approach which is intended to provide a normative account of federalism, stressing that it embeds a fundamental set of moral values and a strong linkage with the liberal ideology.

40 An expression employed by Gaudreault-DesBiens and Gélinas, "Opening New Perspectives," 71.

41 Lépine, "Federalism," 37.

42 Lépine, "Federalism," 36.

43 Lépine, "Federalism," 41.

44 Lépine, "Federalism," 41.

and mostly the different schools of studies of the analytical approach: it does consider federations and federal states (general jurisdictions) as well as federal institutions created for a specific purpose (task-oriented jurisdictions); it is able to reconcile domestic and international fields; and, eventually, it sets federalism free from the archetype American model and its inherited values".[45]

Endorsing this perspective frees federal thought from orthodoxy and from its supposed (but not proved) necessary premise, i.e. the focus on some specific forms of diffusion of powers – governmental and territorial. This allows to apply federal concepts and theories to the study of governance systems.[46]

Governance is the concept of the last decades, especially in the European continent, where multilevel governance is a consolidated frame of reference to explain the dynamics of the European Union system.[47]

At the same time, governance still is surrounded by a certain degree of obscurity. Governance and multi-level governance are generally studied by political scientists as natural phenomena of which one can describe the functioning but not infer generalized models, explanations or principles of functioning.[48] There seems to be a lack of a general reference system to frame this phenomenon, which also depends on the scarce involvement of legal and constitutional scholars in the analysis of this concept.

Such a general standpoint – that can be provided by public law perspectives – would help build a global and comprehensive view on governance systems by connecting their manifestations in a coherent way and providing the conceptual tools for their deeper understanding as well as possible solutions for their development.

---

45 Frédéric Lépine, "A Journey through the History of Federalism: Is Multilevel Governance a Form of Federalism?," *L'Europe en formation* 363, no. 1 (2012): 58.

46 This point of view takes inspiration from Lépine's article, which underscores the intimate connections between multilevel governance and federalism; however, it extends its analysis to governance systems in general and proposes that federalism is the most promising way to frame governance, and not the way round, which is the idea brought forward by this author.

47 On this, see for instance, Liesbet Hooghe and Gary Marks, "Unravelling the Central State, but How? Types of Multi-level Governance," *American Political Science Review* 97, no. 2 (2003): 233–243; Simona Piattoni, *The Theory of Multi-level Governance: Conceptual, Empirical and Normative Challenges* (Oxford: Oxford University Press, 2010); Maria Rosaria Ferrarese, *La governance tra politica e diritto* (Bologna: Il Mulino, 2010).

48 As Lépine, "A Journey," 57, suggested, "Multilevel governance appears more as a descriptive model than an explanatory theory"; also, see Michael Stein and Lisa Turkewitsch, "The Concept of Multi-level Governance in Studies of Federalism," in *2008 International Political Science Association (IPSA) International Conference; International Political Science: New Theoretical and Regional Perspectives* (Montréal: Concordia University, 2008), 10.

It seems critical that legal scholars consider those phenomena and add their specific perspective to those of other disciplines. The public law scholar's standpoint provides a crucial insight into the analysis of governance models, since it focuses on their relationships with the structures of representative government and decision-making as provided for by the constitutional framework.[49] Besides reconnecting the legal ideal reality to the concrete operation of legal systems, the systematization of governance within public law (and federal) theory – for instance, by studying its relationships with the content of constitutional principles, by complementing traditional approaches that heavily rely on the constitutional distribution of powers among state and substate institutions to explain the dynamics of public activity, and by providing solutions for the design of governance procedures to ensure their transparency and legitimacy – can arguably offer a fruitful explanatory standpoint as well as advance evolutionary proposals to address its possible further regulation.[50]

In particular, as seen, a federal perspective may fill the mentioned void in the study of governance systems.[51] It may indeed provide the tools for analyzing (diversity) governance systems adding to the focus on processes and factual competence ownership – typical of multilevel governance studies – a link to the implications of these systems to more general federal and constitutional issues. For instance, federal theory shifts the focus from concrete processes to how they affect (or are affected by) general (federal) principles, which consequences they bring to legitimate and democratic decision-making, and more generally, to the state and supranational structures as defined by their founding documents.

Diversity accommodation is a paradigmatic area in which governance increasingly complements government. Studying this phenomenon according to the proposed approach can give fruitful insights also to other fields

49 On this, see Ferrarese, *La governance*; *Id.*, "Governance: A Soft Revolution with Hard Political and Legal Effects," *Soft Power* 1, no. 1 (2014): 35–56.

50 On the reconciliation between the phenomenon of governance and legal theory, see Marco Dani and Francesco Palermo, "Della governance e di altri demoni (un dialogo)," *Quaderni costituzionali* 23, no. 4 (2003): 785–794; a study that follows the proposed perspective is Alessandro Arienzo and Francesca Scamardella, eds., *La governance tra legittimazione e vulnerabilità* (Naples: Guida editori, 2020).

51 On this, see Michael Keating, "Europe as a Multilevel Federation," *Journal of European Public Policy* 24, no. 4 (2017): 615–632: the author underlined that the evolution of the European Union, widely framed through the concept of multilevel governance, may be better understood if studied as a federal phenomenon.

where governance models are emerging and spreading, such as the climate or digital policy areas.

In the end, this federal theoretical perspective, freed of the nation-state epistemological constraints, can unleash creative and fruitful avenues of research far beyond the purposes of this book. This journey has just begun.

5 What to Expect from This Volume

These issues being so underexplored, and possibly full of unforeseeable perspectives of research, the editors purposely asked the authors to follow the standpoint they considered more promising. The goal was precisely to stimulate first impressions and insights, to pave the way for further and more structured research. Accordingly, the authors have been left a large margin of discretion and were simply suggested some loose guidelines for their contributions.

This has led to a variety of approaches to the relationships between federalism and the Law of diversity. Some chapters offer theoretical considerations on one or both concepts, others focus on case studies, others on both. The two concepts and their interactions are understood and interpreted in different ways, thus leading to a real kaleidoscope of theoretical and practical views.[52] The chapters here collected offer several significant insights and potential directions of research that are summarized here.

Firstly, the chapters remind the reader that the traditional understandings of both concepts and their interconnections are not being replaced by new perspectives but complemented by them. They remain a reality one should not overlook. The use of "orthodox" (even if evolving)[53] federal arrangements is still a powerful (and sometimes successful) tool to accommodate some forms of diversity,[54] as are consolidated diversity accommodation mechanisms (i.e. minority and indigenous peoples' rights mechanisms). As well, federal structures interact with the functioning of traditional instruments for the accommodation of

52 On the multifaceted nature of federalism and the use of the term kaleidoscope to describe it, see Roderick A. Macdonald, "Kaleidoscopic Federalism," in *Le fédéralisme dans tous ses états: governance, identité et méthodologie – The States and Moods of Federalism: Governance, Identity and Methodology*, eds. Jean-F. Gaudreault-DesBiens and Fabien Gélinas (Cowansville-Bruxelles: Éditions Yvon Blais- Bruylant, 2005), 261–283.

53 On the evolution of federal arrangements and their changing structures, see Keil and Kropp, eds., *Emerging Federal Structures*.

54 See Karl Kössler's chapter.

diversity, contributing to their further consolidation[55] or establishing complex relationships[56] that can also show some sorts of incompatibility.[57]

Looking at this issue from the opposite side, at the same time the book demonstrates that the traditional models and the relevant theoretical approaches should no longer be the exclusive interest of scholars in this area. On the one side, innovative models are enriching diversity accommodation and contributing to the emergence of complex systems of diversity governance. Such systems contemplate various forms of self-rule and shared rule that range from full-fledged federal arrangements to non-institutionalized forms of legal pluralism.[58]

On the other side, and most importantly, federal theory and practice have been suggested as frameworks of understanding for these innovative models with interesting results. It seems indeed possible to affirm that there is room for the theoretical proposals advanced in the introduction to be put in operation and bring useful perspectives that improve one's understanding of diversity accommodation and federalism in contemporary times. In several ways, federalism can be a useful framework to better understand the functioning of diversity accommodation and offer inspiration for its development. In particular, federal theory and practice are precious repositories of concepts, theories and experiences that can definitely give a contribution to explaining the emerging governance systems for the accommodation of diversity.[59]

Lastly, this publication underscores that putting in operation the proposed innovative use of federalism to frame emergent models for the accommodation of diversity is complex and needs refinement. Further research will hopefully unveil the promising results that are evoked here. However, suggesting them and test their theoretical legitimacy was the main goal of this book, which seems reached.

In other words, a first step and a long way ahead.

6 The Plan of the Book

As already indicated above, the editors identified three main areas where innovations in the realm of diversity accommodation are taking place, *i.e.*

55 See Michael Breen and Enriqueta Expósito's chapters.
56 See Martina Trettel and Jared Sonnicksen's chapters.
57 See Toniatti's chapter.
58 See Nicolò P. Alessi, Tove H. Malloy and Kyriaki Topidi's chapters.
59 See, in particular, Nicolò P. Alessi and Kyriaki Topidi's chapters.

non-territorial autonomy, legal pluralism and participatory democracy. To structure the book, it was decided to devote one section to each of these aspects. Each section comprises three chapters, each one providing a nuanced understanding of those legal phenomena and their relationships with federalism, spanning from foundational theories to contemporary applications of comparative federalism in today's ever-evolving global context.

Section one commences with the analysis of K. Kössler's "Federalism and Non-Territorial Autonomy: An Odd Couple?" where historical and conceptual dissimilarities between federalism and non-territorial autonomy are dissected. Their resurgence as potential solutions for ethno-cultural conflict management underscores fundamental differences in terms of history, theory, and core ideas.

Tove H. Malloy guides the reader then into the realm of legal frameworks with "The Law of Diversity and Non-Territorial Autonomy: Challenging Pre-established Positions in Domestic Law" which focuses on rights safeguarding non-territorial autonomy for ethno-cultural groups, revealing a growing desire for greater control among minority groups in matters of identity protection and showing that there is room for applying the Law of diversity as a research framework to NTA studies.

Nicolò P. Alessi closes this first section of the book on non-territorial autonomy by shifting the focus toward innovation with "Innovative Forms of Autonomy and the Role of Federalism: A Comparative and Theoretical perspective." His contribution proposes a classification of emerging models, emphasizing their divergence from traditional autonomous frameworks. Alessi argues for the utility of federal theory as a meta-theoretical tool to comprehend and address these new forms of autonomy.

The second section focuses on participatory democracy and its connections to federalism. It is opened by Jared Sonnicksen's contribution entitled "Federalism and Participatory Democracy: A Manifold Balancing Act", which explores the intricate relationship between federalism and participatory democracy. The focus here is on the complex interplay of the ideational and institutional dimensions of federalism and participatory democracy, considering the balancing act between self and shared rule within a framework of pluralism and diversity.

This chapter is followed by Martina Trettel's exploration on participatory democracy as a potential solution to the crisis of representative democracy with "Rethinking Participatory Democracy through Federalism: Citizen participation, Power-sharing and Decision-making Processes." Through the lens of federalism, she aims to redefine the scope of deliberative citizens' participation and enhance the effectiveness of participatory procedures.

The closing chapter of the second section is authored by E. Expósito Gomez. "Participatory Democracy in Spain's Autonomous Regions: some Tools to Strengthen Democratic Development" delves into the democratic principles underlying the Spanish autonomous state. The discussion highlights the natural alignment of participatory democracy in Spain with the logic of federalism and the management of pluralism.

Section three, dealing with legal pluralism, opens up with Kyriaki Topidi's "Federalism as Legal Pluralism?" that engages in an analysis of the affinities between legal pluralism and federalism within the context of the Law of diversity. The discussion revolves around notions such as negotiated federalism and hierarchical pluralism, proposing a preliminary framework embedding pluralist decision-making principles within federalism.

This chapter is followed by Michael G. Breen's "Measurement and Change in Federalism and Legal Pluralism" that explores the intersection of federalism and legal pluralism, particularly in ethnic federal systems. The paper demonstrates how the measurement of both concepts can shed light on the recognition and institutionalization of (or resistance to) legal pluralism.

Finally, in the last chapter, Roberto Toniatti offers broader considerations on diversities and federalism with "Some Ideas on Diversities, Federalisms, and Pluralisms," examining how federalism has addressed various forms of pluralism globally. The focus here is on the relationship between legal pluralism and the universalist approach of state law on fundamental human rights.

As readers traverse these thought-provoking contributions, a rich tapestry of ideas is woven, creating an intricate but meaningful embroidery. Beyond merely presenting individual viewpoints, the book encapsulates a collective journey that underscores federalism as a potent interpretive paradigm for emerging models in diversity accommodation. The insights shared by each author contribute to a deeper understanding of these issues, illuminating the potential of federalism as a guiding framework in navigating the challenges and opportunities presented by diverse cultural landscapes.

Bibliography

Alessi, Nicolò P. *A Global Law of Diversity: Evolving Models and Concepts*. London-New York: Routledge, 2025.

Arienzo, Alessandro and Francesca Scamardella, eds., *La governance tra legittimazione e vulnerabilità*. Naples: Guida editori, 2020.

Aroney, Nicolas. "The Federal Condition: Towards a Normative Theory." *The American Journal of Jurisprudence* 61, no. 1 (2016): 13–31.

Bourgeois, Daniel. "Administrative Nationalism." *Administration & Society* 39, no. 5 (2007): 631–655.
Bourgeois, Daniel. "Territory, Institutions and National Identity: The Case of Acadians in Greater Moncton, Canada." *Urban Studies* 42, no. 7 (2005): 1123–1138.
Broyde, Michael J. *Sharia Tribunals, Rabbinical Courts, and Christian Panels: Religious Arbitration in America and the West*. Oxford: Oxford University Press, 2017.
Burgess, Michael. *Comparative Federalism: Theory and Practice*. London-New York: Routledge, 2006.
Burgess, Michael. *In Search of the Federal Spirit*. Oxford: Oxford University Press, 2012.
Carney, Frederick S. *The Politics of Johannes Althusius*. Boston-Toronto: Beacon Press-S. J. Reginald Saunders and Co., 1964.
Chouinard, Stéphanie. "The Rise of Non-territorial Autonomy in Canada: Towards a Doctrine of Institutional Completeness in the Domain of Minority Language Rights." *Ethnopolitics* 13, no. 2 (2014): 141–158.
Dani, Marco and Francesco Palermo. "Della governance e di altri demoni (un dialogo)." *Quaderni costituzionali* 23, no.4 (2003): 785–794.
Dann, Philipp, Michael Riegner and Maxim Bönnemann, eds. *The Global South and Comparative Constitutional Law*. Oxford: Oxford University Press, 2020.
Davies, Margaret. "Legal Pluralism." In *The Oxford Handbook of Comparative Constitutional Law*, edited by Michel Rosenfeld and András Sajó, 805–827. Oxford: Oxford University Press, 2012.
De Villiers, Bertus. "Privatised Autonomy for the Noongar People of Australia: A New Model for Indigenous Self-Government." In *Indigenous, Aboriginal, Fugitive and Ethnic Groups Around the Globe*, edited by Liat Klain-Gabbay, 127–157. London: Intech Open, 2019.
Dowdle, Michael W. and Michael A. Wilkinson, eds. *Constitutionalism Beyond Liberalism*. Cambridge: Cambridge University Press, 2017.
Elazar, Daniel J. *Exploring Federalism*. Tuscaloosa: The University of Alabama Press, 1987.
Elazar, Daniel J. "From Statism to Federalism: A Paradigm Shift." *International Political Science Review / Revue internationale de science politique* 17, no. 4 (1996): 417–429.
Elazar, Daniel J. "The State System + Globalization (Economic plus Human Rights) = Federalism (State Federations plus Regional Confederations)." *South Texas Law Review* 40, no. 3 (1999): 555–566.
Ferrarese, Maria Rosaria. "Governance: A Soft Revolution with Hard Political and Legal Effects." *Soft Power* 1, no. 1 (2014): 35–56.
Ferrarese, Maria Rosaria. *La governance tra politica e diritto*. Bologna: Il Mulino, 2010.
Ferrari, Silvio. "Religious Rules and Legal Pluralism: An Introduction." In *Religious Rules, State Law, and Normative Pluralism: A Comparative Overview*, edited by Rossella Bottoni, Rinaldo Cristofori and Silvio Ferrari, 1–25. Cham: Springer, 2016.

Foucher, Pierre. "Autonomie des communautés francophones minoritaires du Canada: le point de vue du droit." *Minorités linguistiques et société / Linguistic Minorities and Society* 1 (2012): 90–114.

Gaudreault-DesBiens, Jean-F. and Fabien Gélinas. "Opening New Perspectives on Federalism." In *Le fédéralisme dans tous ses états: governance, identité et méthodologie – The States and Moods of Federalism: Governance, Identity and Methodology*, edited by Jean-F. Gaudreault-DesBiens and Fabien Gélinas, 51–96. Cowansville-Bruxelles: Éditions Yvon Blais-Bruylant, 2005.

Gaudreault-DesBiens, Jean-F. "Introduction to Part II." In *Cultural Diversity and the Law: State Responses Around the World*, edited by Marie-C. Foblets, Jean-F. Gaudreault-DesBiens and Alison Dundes Relteln, 367–380. Bruxelles-Montréal: Bruylant and Yvon-Blais, 2010.

Gaudreault-DesBiens, Jean-F. "Towards a Deontic Axiomatic Theory of Federal Adjudication." In *The Federal Idea*, edited by Amnon Lev, 75–103. Oxford-Portland: Hart Publishing, 2017.

Hamilton, Alexander. "Federalist No. 28." In *The Federalist Papers*, edited by Clinton Rossiter, 178–182. New York: The New American Library, 1961.

Hirschl, Ran. *Comparative Matters: The Renaissance of Comparative Constitutional Law*. Oxford: Oxford University Press, 2014.

Hooghe, Liesbet and Gary Marks. "Unravelling the Central State, but How? Types of Multi-level Governance." *American Political Science Review* 97, no. 2 (2003): 233–243.

Hueglin, Thomas O. *Early Modern Concepts for a Late Modern World: Althusius on Community and Federalism*. Waterloo: Wilfried Laurier University Press, 1999.

Hueglin, Thomas O. "Johannes Althusius: Medieval Constitutionalist or Modern Federalist?" *Publius* 9, no. 4 (1979): 9–41.

Keating, Michael. "Europe as a Multilevel Federation." *Journal of European Public Policy* 24, no. 4 (2017): 615–632.

Keil, Soeren and Elisabeth Alber, eds., *Federalism as a Tool of Conflict Resolution*. London-New York: Routledge, 2021.

Keil, Soeren and Sabine Kropp, eds., *Emerging Federal Structures in the Post-Cold War Era* (Cham: Palgrave Macmillan, 2022).

Lépine, Frédéric. "A Journey through the History of Federalism: Is Multilevel Governance a Form of Federalism?" *L'Europe en formation* 363, no. 1 (2012): 21–62.

Lépine, Frédéric. "Federalism: Essence, Values and Ideologies." In *Understanding Federalism and Federation*, edited by Alain-G. Gagnon, Soeren Keil and Sean Mueller, 31–48. Farnham-Burlington: Ashgate, 2015.

MacDonald, Roderick. "Kaleidoscopic Federalism." In *Le fédéralisme dans tous ses états: governance, identité et méthodologie – The States and Moods of Federalism: Governance, Identity and Methodology*, edited by Jean-F.

Gaudreault-DesBiens and Fabien Gélinas, 261–283. Cowansville-Bruxelles: Éditions Yvon Blais-Bruylant, 2005.

Malloy, Tove H., Alexander Osipov and Balázs Vizi, eds., *Managing Diversity through Non-Territorial Autonomy: Assessing Advantages, Deficiencies, and Risks*. Oxford: Oxford University Press, 2015.

Malloy, Tove H. "Functional Non-Territorial Autonomy in Denmark and Germany." In *Managing Diversity through Non-Territorial Autonomy: Assessing Advantages, Deficiencies, and Risks*, edited by Tove H. Malloy, Alexander Osipov and Balázs Vizi, 183–204. Oxford: Oxford University Press, 2015.

Nimni, Ephraim, Alexander Osipov and David J. Smith, eds., *The Challenge of Non-Territorial Autonomy: Theory and Practice*. Oxford: Peter Lang, 2013.

Ortino, Sergio. *La struttura delle rivoluzioni economiche*. Bari: Cacucci, 2010.

Palermo, Francesco and Karl Kössler. *Comparative Federalism: Constitutional Arrangements and Case Law*. Oxford-Portland: Hart Publishing, 2019.

Palermo, Francesco and Jens Woelk. "From Minority Protection to a Law of Diversity? Reflections on the Evolution of Minority Rights." *European Yearbook of Minority Issues* 3 (2003/2004): 5–13.

Palermo, Francesco. "Regulating Pluralism: Federalism as Decision-Making and New Challenges for Federal Studies." In *Federalism as Decision-Making: Changes in Structures, Procedures and Policies*, edited by Francesco Palermo and Elisabeth Alber, 499–513. Leiden-Boston: Brill-Nijhoff, 2015.

Piattoni, Simona. *The Theory of Multi-level Governance: Conceptual, Empirical and Normative Challenges*. Oxford: Oxford University Press, 2010.

Poirier, Johanne. "Autonomie politique et minorités francophones du Canada: réflexions sur un angle mort de la typologie classique de Will Kymlicka." *Minorités linguistiques et société / Linguistic Minorities and Society* no. 1 (2012): 66–89.

Popelier, Patricia. *Dynamic Federalism: A New Theory for Cohesion and Regional Autonomy*. London-New York: Routledge, 2021.

Quane, Helen. "Legal Pluralism, Autonomy and Ethno-Cultural Diversity Management." In *Non-Territorial Autonomy and Decentralization: Ethno-Cultural Diversity Governance*, edited by Tove H. Malloy and Levente Salat, 67–87. London-New York: Routledge, 2021.

Salat, Levente and Sergiu Miscoiu. "Roma Autonomous Lawmaking: The Romanian Case." In *Non-Territorial Autonomy and Decentralization: Ethno-Cultural Diversity Governance*, edited by Tove H. Malloy and Levente Salat, 167–194. London-New York: Routledge, 2021.

Smith, Graham. *Democratic Innovations: Designing Institutions for Citizen Participation*. Cambridge: Cambridge University Press, 2009.

Stein, Michael and Lisa Turkewitsch. "The Concept of Multi-level Governance in Studies of Federalism." In *2008 International Political Science Association* (IPSA)

International Conference; International Political Science: New Theoretical and Regional Perspectives, 1–35. Montréal: Concordia University, 2008.

Stepan, Alfred. "Federalism and Democracy: Beyond the U.S. Model." In *Theories of Federalism: A Reader*, edited by Dimitrios Karmis and Wayne Norman, 255–268. New-York-Basingstoke: Palgrave Macmillan, 2005.

Tierney, Stephen. *The Federal Contract: A Constitutional Theory of Federalism*. Oxford: Oxford University Press, 2022.

Trettel, Martina. *La democrazia partecipativa negli ordinamenti composti: studio di diritto comparato sull'incidenza della tradizione giuridica nelle democratic innovations*. Naples: ESI, 2020.

Tully, James. *Strange Multiplicity: Constitutionalism in an Age of Diversity*. Cambridge: Cambridge University Press, 1995.

Turner, Bryan S. "Legal Pluralism: Freedom of Religion, Exemptions and the Equality of Citizens." In *Religious Rules, State Law, and Normative Pluralism: A Comparative Overview*, edited by Rossella Bottoni, Rinaldo Cristofori and Silvio Ferrari, 61–73. Cham: Springer, 2016.

Twining, William. "Normative and Legal Pluralism: A Global Perspective." *Duke Journal of Comparative and International Law* 20 (2010): 473–518.

Watts, Ronald L. *Comparing Federal Systems*. 3rd ed., Montréal: McGill-Queen's University Press, 2008.

Wilson, Gary N. and Christopher Alcantara. "Mixing Politics and Business in the Canadian Arctic: Inuit Corporate Governance in Nunavik and the Inuvialuit Settlement Region." *Canadian Journal of Political Science / Revue canadienne de science politique* 45, no. 4 (2012): 781–804.

Wilson, Gary N., Christopher Alcantara and Thierry Rodon. *Nested Federalism and Inuit Governance in the Canadian Arctic*. Vancouver: University of British Columbia Press, 2020.

PART 1

Federalism and Non-territorial Autonomy

CHAPTER 1

Federalism and Non-territorial Autonomy: Revisiting Two Interrelated Concepts

Karl Kössler

1 Introduction

Federalism and non-territorial autonomy (hereinafter NTA) have both been proposed, especially in the post-Cold War era, as possible solutions for the successful management of ethno-cultural conflict, regarding both their prevention and solution. They are very different, however, in terms of their history in theory and practice, as well as their core idea. Federalism typically refers to a territorial arrangement, while NTA is, as the name suggests, a non-territorial one. Yet, things are not as unambiguous and clear-cut as they might seem at first glance.

Indeed, some theorists of federalism understood the concept in such a broad way that it would encompass also non-territorial arrangements as one of its many institutional manifestations. Daniel Elazar claimed, for instance, that federalism included "consociational unions on a nonterritorial basis".[1] Carl Friedrich elaborated even more on federalism's relationship with NTA. He defined federalism as geared towards the "value of the freedom and security of federally recognized communities" and acknowledged that "[h]istorically these have been territorially defined communities", but also made very clear that "this aspect is not necessarily implied in the concept". Interestingly, Friedrich also referred more explicitly to the "now forgotten yet highly imaginative idea of the Austrian socialists" like Karl Renner and others "for a solution of the nationality problems of the Austrian empire by organizing it in terms of corporative national bodies without defined boundaries" and considered these ideas reflective of "the broad possibilities of federalism".[2] He could not know in 1962, of course, that these ideas would experience a veritable

1 Daniel J. Elazar, *Exploring Federalism* (Tuscaloosa: University of Alabama Press, 1987), 44.

2 Carl J. Friedrich, "Federal Constitutional Theory and Emergent Proposals," in *Federalism: Mature and Emergent*, ed. Arthur W. MacMahon (New York: Russell&Russell, 1962), 517.

"resurrection" in the 1990s.[3] In a much more recent account, Frédéric Lépine pointed out that the political space that is characteristically shared by two or more self-governing communities "does not refer to a territorial dimension, which allows taking into account (non-territorial) personal and/or functional federal arrangements".[4] In spite of these voices, there is little doubt that most contemporary scholars of federalism still subscribe to a rather classical understanding of this concept which refers essentially to territorial arrangements. A recently published reconceptualization of federalism by Patricia Popelier, for example, emphasizes that there is "a common understanding that federalism is about the relationship between *territorial* [emphasis added] levels of authority".[5]

NTA,[6] on the other hand, is of course by nature non-territorial. This specific way in which it organizes the exercise of power contrasts with territorial forms of autonomy and is the least common denominator of the various arrangements subsumed under this umbrella term.[7] For Renner, NTA actually emerged from a critique of the logic of territorial autonomy, which aims to create homogeneous entities, a goal that cannot be achieved and instead always leaves new minority groups. In his thinking, an NTA arrangement offers the advantage that "the rule applies only to people who have accepted that they are members of the group in question".[8] The fact that autonomous competences are transferred not in relation to a specific territory but in relation to a certain community lowers the stakes concerning the issue of "possessing" territory as

3 Bill Bowring, "Burial and Resurrection: Karl Renner's Controversial Influence on the 'National Question' in Russia," in *National-Cultural Autonomy and its Contemporary Critics*, ed. Ephraim Nimni (London-New York: Routledge, 2005), 191–206. See on this "resurrection" also Section 2.1. below.

4 Frédéric Lépine, "Federalism: Essence, Values and Ideologies," in *Understanding Federalism and Federation*, eds. Alain-G. Gagnon, Soeren Keil and Sean Mueller (Farnham-Burlington: Ashgate, 2015), 37.

5 Patricia Popelier, *Dynamic Federalism: A New Theory for Cohesion and Regional Autonomy* (London-New York: Routledge, 2021), 37.

6 See section 2 of Alessi's chapter and section 2.2 of Malloy's chapter in this volume.

7 Suksi distinguishes three forms of NTA: institutional forms of civil law turning into functional autonomy, functional autonomy within line administration and national cultural autonomy. See Markku Suksi, "Non-Territorial Autonomy: The Meaning of (Non-)Territoriality," in *Minority Accommodation through Territorial and Non-territorial Autonomy*, eds. Tove H. Malloy and Francesco Palermo (Oxford: Oxford University Press, 2015), 87–93.

8 John McGarry and Margaret Moore, "Karl Renner, Power Sharing and Non-Territorial Autonomy," in *National Cultural Autonomy and its Contemporary Critics*, ed. Ephraim Nimni (London-New York: Routledge, 2005), 81.

a zero-sum game. Yet, NTA is in certain ways also territorial.[9] First, the very distinction between the majority and the minority groups benefitting from non-territorial powers has a territorial dimension, as this distinction regarding both the relative size and relative power of groups[10] needs a territorial frame of reference. In short, whether a group is a minority depends on where national borders were drawn. Secondly, even if territoriality is naturally much weaker in the case of NTA, it is inextricably linked with any form of autonomy. This is because even NTA requires a clearly delimited territorial scope of application of its legal framework and history demonstrates that this depends on a quite arbitrary decision. It can be determined to function within an entire country or only within a region, in a "pyramid-like" constellation within multiple levels of governments (e.g. Russia) or within what is sketched as historic homeland on a map (e.g. the Sami autonomy in Finland). Thirdly, the fact that NTA is offered to certain groups within a certain territory (often as surrogate for usually stronger territorial autonomy) implies the recognition of the legitimate claims to this territory based on historic settlement.[11]

While all this shows that a broader understanding of federalism may well include NTA and that the latter is not as non-territorial as it would seem at first glance, this chapter adopts a more classical view of federalism in the sense of territorial arrangements. The aim is to explore how federalism, understood in such a way, is related to NTA and compares to it. To this end, section 2 demonstrates how both have experienced a revival in the 1990s in political practice and in research. Section 3 then explores points of conceptual convergence or divergence and thereby analyses what federalism and NTA have in common (or not) with regard to four key issues: How do they come into being as institutional arrangements? How are they related to the idea of self-rule? How are they linked to the idea of shared rule? What role does democracy play as a presumably important context factor for both kinds of arrangements? Section 4 concludes.

---

9 Karl Kössler, "Conclusions: Beyond the Illusion of Ethno-culturally Homogenous Territory," in *Minority Accommodation through Territorial and Non-territorial Autonomy*, eds. Tove H. Malloy and Francesco Palermo (Oxford: Oxford University Press, 2015), 246–248.

10 Both these two elements are crucial for Capotorti's famous definition (see Francesco Capotorti, *Study on the Rights of Persons Belonging to Ethnic, Religious and Linguistic Minorities*, UN Doc E/CN.4/Sub.2/384/Add. 1–7).

11 Will Kymlicka, "National Cultural Autonomy and International Minority Rights Norms," *Ethnopolitics* 6, no. 3 (2007): 390.

2 Federalism and NTA in Political Practice and Research

2.1 *Political Practice in the 1990s: A Tale of Two Revivals*

There is a broad consensus that federalism experienced a renaissance in the 1990s. The context for this in international relations was the collapse of the Cold War constellation and ensuing claims to self-determination within (or sometimes outside of) many still relatively young and ethno-culturally diverse states around the globe. While in several parts of the world the initially strong belief in federalism as an almost magical solution subsided somewhat at the start of the new millennium,[12] it has been more recently at the centre of the political debate and (often) practice in a number of countries which have faced self-determination claims from ethno-cultural groups (e.g. Iraq and Nepal).

In these situations, federalism typically comes in the form of what is known, with some variation, as multinational, plurinational or ethnic federalism,[13] which suggests that the federal territorial structure should be based on ethno-cultural divisions. This implies that internal boundaries are drawn or redrawn so as to transform *nationwide minorities*, at least large ones with concentrated settlement areas, into *regional majorities* within "nationality-based units".[14] This logic is diametrically opposed to that of mononational federalism, which prevails in the United States, where territory is perceived as neutral, in fact as "a blank slate to be filled in by whoever lives on the territory".[15]

Whether multinational federalism has fulfilled its promise to successfully manage ethno-cultural conflicts has been a much-debated issue. Whereas its early critics pointed to the disintegration of the communist ethno-federations (the Soviet Union, Yugoslavia and Czechoslovakia) to speak – without recognizing their specific communist legacy – of "a terrible track record",[16] the

12 Francesco Palermo, "Concluding Remarks: New Regionalism in Central, Eastern and South-Eastern Europe: Traditional Models and Beyond," in *Regional Dynamics in Central and Eastern Europe*, eds. Francesco Palermo and Sara Parolari (Leiden-Boston: Martinus Nijhoff, 2013), 241–243.

13 For an introduction, see John McGarry and Brendan O'Leary, "Federation and Managing Nations," in *Multinational Federations*, eds. Michael Burgess and John Pinder (London-New York: Routledge, 2007), 180–211.

14 Will Kymlicka, "Is Federalism a Viable Alternative to Secession?," in *Theories of Secession*, ed. Percy B. Lehning, (London-New York: Routledge, 1998), 125; Kymlicka contrasts them with 'regional-based unities'.

15 John Kincaid, "Territorial Neutrality and Coercive Federalism in the United States," in *Federalism, Regionalism and Territory*, ed. Stelio Mangiameli (Milan: Giuffrè, 2013), 133–134.

16 Jack L. Snyder, *From Voting to Violence: Democratization and Nationalist Conflict* (New York: Norton, 2000), 327.

debate later became more nuanced. It started to focus on factors that may be secession-inducing and secession-preventing such as the federal design, separatist mobilization and socio-economic determinants,[17] as well as on the issue of internal minorities.[18]

Indeed, the latter issue is related to the inconsistency of multinational federalism's inherent ethnic-territorial link because it presumes that territories of subnational entities are homogenous, even though they are in reality almost always ethno-culturally diverse. The fact that dominant group(s) are thus seen as *owning* the autonomous territory and territorially based power instead of *sharing* it with other groups makes multinational federalism a double-edged sword. This has even been recognized by scholars like Yash Ghai who had tended to emphasize the merits of the concepts by defining autonomy "as device to allow minorities claiming a distinct identity to exercise control over affairs of special concern to them".[19] In a more recent publication, Ghai seems to acknowledge the potential negative consequences for internal minorities: "Autonomy is a response to marginalisation, or oppression, but can itself all too easily become an instrument for the marginalisation of others. ... Starting as a response to discrimination, it sets up its own orthodoxy. Justified in the name of diversity, it tends to entrench boundaries between cultures. Instead of defining identity as a composite of different values and multiple affiliations, identity is perceived as made up of a singular and exclusive affiliation."[20]

The fact that the practice of multinational federalism revealed two main problems, namely those regarding secession and internal minorities, is related to the revival of NTA because the latter purports to be unaffected by both these difficulties. Indeed, one of the main reasons for this revival was "autonomy-phobia",[21] that is, the widespread fear of governments that *territorial* autonomy

17 Jan Erk and Lawrence M. Anderson, *The Paradox of Federalism: Does Self-Rule Accommodate or Exacerbate Ethnic Divisions?* (London-New York: Routledge, 2012).

18 Francesco Palermo and Karl Kössler, *Comparative Federalism: Constitutional Arrangements and Case Law* (Oxford: Hart Publishing, 2017), 101–105.

19 Yash Ghai, "Autonomy as a Participatory Right in the Modern Democratic State: Public Participation, Autonomy and Minorities," in *Beyond a One-Dimensional State: An Emerging Right to Autonomy?*, ed. Zelim A. Skubarty (Leiden-Boston: Martinus Nijhoff, 2005), 38.

20 Sophia Woodman and Yash Ghai, "Comparative Perspectives on Institutional Frameworks for Autonomy," in *Practising Self-Government: A Comparative Study of Autonomous Regions*, eds. Yash Ghai and Sophia Woodman (Cambridge: Cambridge University Press, 2013), 485.

21 Francesco Palermo, "Central, Eastern and South-Eastern Europe and Territorial Autonomy: Are They Really Incompatible?," in *Political Autonomy and Divided Societies: Comparative Territorial Politics*, eds. Alain-G. Gagnon and Michael Keating (Basingstoke: Palgrave Macmillan, 2012), 82.

will be a stepping stone to secession. This change of emphasis towards a rediscovery of non-territorial autonomy is clearly visible if one analyses international documents between the Copenhagen Document of 1990 and the Lund Recommendations of 1999. It has been pointed out that the aim of the latter was exactly "to lead governments away from fearing territorial autonomy claims towards contemplating NTA as alternatives".[22] It has been observed that, more generally, international organizations "have appeared interested in supporting less threatening forms of NTA rather than TA".[23]

This trend must be called a *re*-discovery because NTA did not emerge out of nowhere. Instead, the European continent can look back to a long tradition of such arrangements ranging from the Jewish community within the Polish-Lithuanian Commonwealth until 1764 to the millets within the Ottoman empire.[24] A particularly well-known and often-mentioned example is Karl Renner's model of the *Nationalitätenbundesstaat* for the late Austro-Hungarian Empire which combined territorial and non-territorial elements.[25] While precisely this combination appears to be the main legacy of this model,[26] it has in common with other historical examples that non-territoriality was aimed at addressing, especially in Central and Eastern Europe, the issue of the intermingling of nationalities. Such cases risk the above-mentioned problem of internal minorities when addressed via territorial arrangements. This goal and geographical focus did not change when NTA was established in the 1990s in a number of countries such as Estonia (1993), Hungary (1993) and the Russian Federation (1996).[27] These laws have sometimes tied in with earlier experiences in these countries in terms of political theory (futile attempts in Russia to assert Karl Renner's above-mentioned ideas against the Bolshevik

22 Tove H. Malloy, "The Lund Recommendations and Non-Territorial Arrangements: Progressive De-territorialization of Minority Politics," *International Journal on Minority and Group Rights* 16, no. 4 (2009): 677.

23 John McGarry, Michael Keating and Margaret Moore, "Introduction: European Integration and the Nationalities Question," in *European Integration and the Nationalities Question*, eds. John McGarry and Michael Keating (London-New York: Routledge, 2006), 17.

24 For an overview, see John Coakley, "Approaches to the Resolution of Ethnic Conflict: The Strategy of Non-Territorial Autonomy," *International Political Science Review* 15, no. 3 (1994): 297–314.

25 Robert A. Kann, *The Multinational Empire: Nationalism and National Reform in the Habsburg Monarchy. 1848–1918. Vol. 2* (New York: Octagon Books, 1983), 159.

26 Kössler, "Conclusions," 267.

27 David J. Smith, "NTA as Political Strategy in Central and Eastern Europe," in *Minority Accommodation through Territorial and Non-territorial Autonomy*, eds. Tove H. Malloy and Francesco Palermo (Oxford: Oxford University Press, 2015), 161–178.

orthodoxy of territorial arrangements)[28] or even political practice (Estonia's NTA law of 1925).[29]

Irrespective of whether NTA was introduced in the 1990s or *re*-introduced, a still unsolved question concerns the actual significance of this trend. It is indeed puzzling that minority groups have made ample use of the opportunities offered by NTA arrangements, most notably in Hungary and the Russian Federation, even if these opportunities have been rather limited due to few competences, scarce funding, administrative obstacles, etc. This might have to do, for example, with communist (and pre-communist) institutional legacies[30] or with the fact that the groups concerned either do not want more or are not strong enough in the political arena to realistically demand more.[31]

One thing, however, can be definitively said about the revival of NTA in political practice: it demonstrated that there is another, second, dimension to autonomy. While many classical definitions had equated autonomy in general with its territorial variety,[32] a process of incremental dissociation of these two notions would now occur. Autonomy would thus become an umbrella term that comprises both territorial and non-territorial arrangements.

2.2 *Research on Federalism and NTA*

The preceding section explained the revivals of federalism and NTA in the 1990s and the ways in which they are linked, but there remains the question of links in research concerning these two topics. Ideally, with both gaining increasing prominence and being interconnected, their analysis by the scientific community should also grow.

What we can say for sure is that there is still a significant imbalance when it comes to the extent of studies on these issues. Comparative research on federalism already experienced an enormous boost from the 1970s[33] onwards through the work and international networks created by pioneering scholars

28 Bowring, "Burial and Resurrection," 191–206.

29 Kari Alenius, "The Birth of Cultural Autonomy in Estonia: How, Why and for Whom?," *Journal of Baltic Studies* 38, no. 4 (2007): 445–462.

30 Smith, "NTA as Political Strategy," 177–178.

31 Kössler, "Conclusions," 256.

32 See for an overview of these definitions, Geneviève Nootens, "Can Non-Territorial Autonomy Bring an Added Value to Theoretic and Policy-Oriented Analysis of Ethnic Politics?," in *Minority Accommodation through Territorial and Non-territorial Autonomy*, eds. Tove H. Malloy and Francesco Palermo (Oxford: Oxford University Press, 2015), 34–37.

33 See section 3.1 in Malloy's chapter in this volume.

such as Daniel Elazar[34] and Ronald Watts.[35] Similar efforts regarding NTA were only initiated in the 2010s, roughly four decades later,[36] which of course makes a difference. In fact, a few years ago a leading scholar on the topic still remarked that "the literature on non-territorial autonomy is sparse" and "completely overshadowed by a much larger literature that focuses on such well-known strategies as federation or consociation".[37] To correct this state of affairs, significant efforts towards more comprehensive research on NTA from both theoretical and empirical perspectives are already being undertaken.[38]

In light of federalism's much longer research tradition it is understandable that its scientific community seems to have looked more often into the topic of NTA than vice versa. Still, federalism scholars have not gone beyond occasional mentions of NTA and, at any rate, have failed to explore the issue more in depth. A case in point is Elazar's reference to "cultural home-rule, designed to preserve a minority language or religion".[39] Conversely, NTA scholars also sometimes mention federalism, but do not engage with it in a comprehensive and systematic manner. Yet, in spite of that, the two research communities have not remained entirely unconnected. An attempt to bring together the communities dealing with federalism and NTA was made at a workshop organized in 2011 in Bolzano/Bozen that eventually led to an edited book.[40] Another initiative has been the online resource "Autonomy Arrangements in the World", which is similarly inspired by the aim to bridge studies on territorial and non-territorial arrangements but also seeks to reach a non-academic audience with its case studies.[41] Finally, there have been links to the topic of NTA

34 On Elazar's legacy, see "Tributes to Daniel J. Elazar from Colleagues and Friends," on the Center for the Study of Federalism website, accessed on 8 June 2023, https://federalism.org/elazar-tribute/tributes/.

35 Nico Steytler and Balveer Arora, "Introduction," in *The Value of Comparative Federalism: The Legacy of Ronald L. Watts*, eds. Nico Steytler, Balveer Arora and Rekha Saxena (London-New York: Routledge, 2020), 2–12.

36 E.g. Tove H. Malloy, Alexander Osipov and Balázs Vizi, eds., *Managing Diversity through Non-Territorial Autonomy: Assessing Advantages, Deficiencies, and Risks* (Oxford: Oxford University Press, 2015).

37 John Coakley, "Introduction: Dispersed Minorities and Non-Territorial Autonomy," *Ethnopolitics* 15, no. 1 (January 2016): 1.

38 E.g. Marina Andeva et al., *Non-Territorial Autonomy: An Introduction* (Cham: Palgrave Macmillan, 2023).

39 Daniel J. Elazar, *Federal Systems of the World: A Handbook of Federal, Confederal and Autonomy Arrangements* (2nd ed., Harlow: Longman Group Limited, 1994), xvii.

40 Tove H. Malloy and Francesco Palermo, eds., *Minority Accommodation through Territorial and Non-territorial Autonomy* (Oxford: Oxford University Press, 2015).

41 "Autonomy Arrangements in the World," accessed 8 June 2023, http://www.world-autonomies.info.

even within the network created and shaped by the two federalism pioneers mentioned above, Elazar and Watts. Occasionally, attention has been drawn in conferences of the International Association of Centers for Federal Studies (IACFS) to the limits of federalism, seen as a purely territorial arrangement involving government levels, and to the possible role for NTA in this regard.[42] Overall, however, the traditional territorial approach to federalism has clearly remained predominant within this academic network.

3 Convergence and Divergence of Federalism and NTA

3.1 *Formation*

As for the formative processes that eventually led to arrangements of federalism or NTA, a point of departure may be the traditional view of federalism being based on an initial compact. According to this view, historically and legally sovereign entities form a federal government so that this very moment of a "federal big bang" turns their original sovereignty into autonomy as a result of the primacy of the national constitution.[43] This view purports further that this compact is one among equal partners and that this equality (albeit a fiction in view of typically unequal political power at the founding moment) is reflected in the idea of all subnational entities having the same competences and equal representation in a second chamber of the national parliament. Classical theorists of federalism argued that such a compact, with its Latin equivalent *foedus* being the etymological origin of federalism,[44] remains the core and basis of the "federal principle" and does not necessarily imply a compact between territorial entities. Interestingly, S. Rufus Davis asserts, for example, that if a *foedus* is there, this can be "connoting simply *any* cooperative association of groups, whether territorial or not".[45]

If we apply this to arrangements of NTA, it immediately becomes clear that their formative processes do not usually involve something that can be

42 E.g. Frédéric Lépine, "Non-territorial Federalism as an Answer to the Limits of the Territorial Approach," paper presented at the IACFS conference "*Federalism, Regionalism and Territory*" (Rome, 19–21 September 2012).

43 Palermo and Kössler, *Comparative Federalism*, 38–42. On the origins of the "federal big bang" notion in European integration studies, see Neil Walker, "The Shifting Foundations of the European Union Constitution," *University of Edinburgh School of Law, Research Paper Series*, no. 1 (2012), 1–27.

44 Palermo and Kössler, *Comparative Federalism*, 18–19.

45 Rufus S. Davis, *The Federal Principle: A Journey Through Time in Quest of a Meaning* (Berkeley-Los Angeles-London: University of California Press, 1978), 214.

called a compact and certainly not one among equals. NTA rather seems to be something that is granted in a top-down manner by the national government. Presumably, this also has to do with the contexts in which NTA is most often applied or at least in which it is applied with success. In fact, Will Kymlicka notes that such an arrangement "will work well in those countries which are essentially ethnically homogenous – where the dominant group forms 90–95 per cent of the population – and where the remaining ethnic groups are small, dispersed and already on the road to assimilation".[46] In such a constellation of inequality between the national government and the communities which shall benefit from NTA, granting such an arrangement often seems to be a minor concession and one that is sometimes as much made as a gesture to an international audience rather than these communities themselves. In fact, NTA legislation in Hungary and Estonia in the 1990s to some extent had the function to cultivate a positive image of these countries during their process of accession to the EU, especially to "compensate" for controversial policies such as Hungary's proactive approach to protecting its minorities in neighbouring countries[47] and Estonia's citizenship legislation adopted around the same time.[48] In some cases, however, national governments were even reluctant to make the relatively minor concession that an NTA implies. A case in point is the failure of such an arrangement in Romania in 2005, as any strengthening of the position of the Hungarian community was considered a potential threat to the integrity of the state.[49]

The key question is then whether NTA fundamentally differs from federalism in terms of the way in which it comes into being. This does not seem to be the case because federal arrangements are similar to those of NTA in that they often do not involve an initial compact among equals. Indeed, the above-mentioned traditional view about a "federal big bang" has been clearly refuted

46 Will Kymlicka, "The Evolving Basis of European Norms of Minority Rights: Rights to Culture, Participation and Autonomy," in *European Integration and the Nationalities Question*, eds. John McGarry and Michael Keating (London-New York: Routledge, 2006), 44.

47 See András L. Pap, "Minority Rights and Diaspora-Claims: Collision, Interdependence and Loss of Orientation," in *Beyond Sovereignty: From Status Law to Transnational Citizenship*, eds. Osamu Ieda and Balázs Majtényi (Sapporo: Hokkaido University, 2006), 243.

48 See David J. Smith and John Hiden, *Ethnic Diversity and the Nation State: National Cultural Autonomy Revisited* (London-New York: Routledge, 2012), 111.

49 D. Christopher Decker, "The Use of Cultural Autonomy to Prevent Conflict and Meet the Copenhagen Criteria: The case of Romania," in *Cultural Autonomy in Contemporary Europe*, eds. David J. Smith and Karl Cordell (London-New York: Routledge, 2008), 111–112.

by historical evidence. Both political scientists like Carl Friedrich[50] and lawyers like Koen Lenaerts[51] have pointed out that compact-based aggregative (or integrative) federalism is just one variety, another one being devolutionary (or differentiating) which involves a unitary state recognizing future autonomous entities through a process of decentralization.[52] A particularly clear example of such a formative process is Belgium. In its case federalism was not ushered in all at once but is the result of an incremental piecemeal process of six state reforms from 1970 until 2011 and each reform was meant to solve an immediate problem. It is certainly possible to see in these negotiated solutions (instead of a grand design) some kinds of repeated ex-post compacts. But Belgium and other devolutionary federal systems defy the traditional view of an *initial* "federal big bang" involving equal partners, which is therefore not something that fundamentally distinguishes federalism from NTA.

3.2 *Self-Rule*

It is widely recognized that the self-rule element, which is inherent to federalism (next to the shared rule element),[53] is much more far-reaching than merely the authority for subnational entities to enact their own laws and implement legislation, that is, legislative and administrative autonomy. In fact, self-rule also has a constitutional dimension (the power to adopt a subnational constitution), a financial dimension (the power to autonomously raise revenue and spend money) and sometimes even a judicial dimension (in case of subnational court systems).[54]

Yet, it is exactly legislative and administrative self-rule where NTA seems to be particularly and inherently limited in comparison to federalism. This is because there are certain powers that are by nature territorial and therefore cannot be transferred to authorities under NTA arrangements. Examples of such responsibilities which can only be exercised in the context of a territorial arrangement are policing (e.g. Catalonia's *Mossos d'Esquadra* and the Basque Country's *Ertzaintza*) and in some extraordinary cases even the military. In

50 Carl J. Friedrich, "New Tendencies in Federal Theory and Practice," *Jahrbuch des Öffentlichen Rechts* 14, no. 1 (1965): 1–14.

51 Koen Lenaerts, "Constitutionalism and the Many Faces of Federalism," *American Journal of Comparative Law* 38, no. 2 (1990): 205–264.

52 For a discussion of both varieties of federalism, see Karl Kössler, "Aggregative and Devolutionary Federalism Revisited: The Impact of the Founding on the Federal System," in *The Making and Ending of Federalism*, eds. Peter Bußjäger and Mathias Eller (Leiden-Boston: Brill-Martinus Nijhoff, forthcoming).

53 See section 3.3. below.

54 Palermo and Kössler, *Comparative Federalism*, 125–163 and 210–239.

fact, the federal country of Bosnia and Herzegovina maintained armed forces only in its two constituent entities for a decade, until 2005.[55] Other typical territory-bound competences are immigration, infrastructure and the regulation of the economy, areas in which the Canadian province of Quebec has, for example, significant responsibilities.

All such territorial powers are naturally out of reach for groups under any arrangement of NTA,[56] while many subnational entities in federal systems like Quebec or Catalonia have found precisely these competences important to underpin their nation-building projects. It hardly comes as a surprise, therefore, that large, territorially concentrated and politically powerful ethno-cultural groups usually prefer the typically much more far-reaching territorial solutions over mere cultural self-expression, as offered by non-territorial arrangements.[57] A question is then how big the gap actually is between what federalism and NTA have to offer. What can be said for sure is that the extent of territory-bound powers has massively increased over the 20th century with the expansion of governmental action more generally, and that this has entailed that NTA's inherent practical limitation is more deeply felt today than during Renner's times. This probably has to be borne in mind when observers state with a certain frustration that "[n]owhere in Eastern Europe do minorities possess the wide-ranging control over cultural matters that was envisaged by Renner".[58] Another thing to be aware of is that, as this quote says, Renner only "envisaged" a broader scope of powers, as his theoretical model remained just that and was never put into practice.[59]

This implies the question of whether the well-established fact that NTA arrangements do not confer much autonomy is because "little more than control over education, cultural affairs and relatively unimportant matters *can*

55 Only the founding of a Ministry of Defence of Bosnia and Herzegovina in 2004 and the creation of the unified Armed Forces of Bosnia and Herzegovin in 2005 ended the separate existence of the Bosniak-Croat Army of the Federation of Bosnia and Herzegovina (VFBiH) and the Bosnian Serbs' Army of Republika Srpska (VRS).

56 See already John Coakley, "National Territories and Cultural Frontiers: Conflicts of Principle in the Formation of States in Europe," *West European Politics* 5, no. 4 (1982): 36; McGarry and Moore, "Karl Renner", 82–83.

57 Michael Keating, "Europe, the State and the Nation," in *European Integration and the Nationalities Question*, eds. John McGarry and Michael Keating (London-New York: Routledge, 2006), 28.

58 McGarry and Moore, "Karl Renner," 84; similarly, on the limited extent of powers under NTA arrangements, see Suksi, "Non-Territorial Autonomy," 103.

59 Only some elements were adopted in the Moravian Compromise of 1905, as well as the arrangements for Bukovina 1910 and Galicia 1914.

[emphasis added] be devolved to a body lacking a defined territorial jurisdiction"[60] or because national governments have been reluctant to devolve all powers that they could have. In fact, Stefan Wolff and Marc Weller have argued that the post-Cold war era has seen a process of NTA being narrowed to a few policy areas, even if "there is no need to conceive of it as being in principle confined to cultural and educational matters only".[61] This echoes Ruth Lapidoth's view that some social affairs in a broader sense, such as some selected functions in healthcare and welfare matters, could well be managed autonomously under an NTA arrangement.[62] In a similar vein, Tove Malloy commented that NTA-related provisions of the OSCE Lund Recommendations are limited by "a narrow understanding of cultural autonomy" with the Explanatory Note to the recommendations lacking references, for example, "to the role of economic functions of culture". She concludes that "arguably culture in the 21st century is more than education, language, religion and recognition of names and symbols as suggested in the Lund Recommendations."[63] To be sure, with the OSCE being an international governmental organization, these recommendations reflect predominant views among governments which seem to be reluctant to fully exploit NTA's potential when it comes to legislative and administrative self-rule. However, a certain, quite significant gap will always remain in comparison with federalism, as only the latter may involve the transfer of a number of territory-bound powers.

3.3 *Shared Rule*

If federalism is understood, according to a widely accepted formula, as "self-rule plus shared rule",[64] it becomes clear that these two elements are complementary. In fact, while much emphasis is often placed on the self-rule element, instruments of shared rule are actually at least as important, especially in light of a general trend (for a number of reasons) from dual to cooperative federalism.[65] These instruments are key for the latter not to degenerate into coercive

60 John Coakley, "National Territories," 36.

61 Stefan Wolff and Marc Weller, "Self-Determination and Autonomy: A Conceptual Introduction," in *Autonomy, Self-Governance, and Conflict Resolution: Innovative Approaches to Institutional Design in Divided Societies*, eds. Marc Weller and Stefan Wolff (London-New York: Routledge, 2005), 15.

62 Ruth Lapidoth, *Autonomy: Flexible Solutions to Ethnic Conflicts* (Washington D.C.: United States Institute of Peace Press, 1996), 40.

63 Tove H. Malloy, "The Lund Recommendations," 675.

64 Elazar, *Exploring*, 12.

65 Palermo and Kössler, *Comparative Federalism*, 148–149 and 246–249.

federalism.[66] Given its actual importance, it is paradoxical that federal shared rule's traditional instrument, bicameralism, is widely seen as incapable of representing subnational interests at the national level. This incapability has been called "Madison's paradox"[67] because James Madison's claim that the Senate "will derive its powers from the states as political and coequal societies"[68] was not realized in practice, as the chamber has failed to become an institution of effective state representation. Bearing this failure of second chambers in mind, it is quite understandable that there is nowadays a trend towards intergovernmental institutions,[69] which most often bring together the executive branches of multiple government levels[70] and are frequently bilateral because powerful subnational entities prefer these over multilateral institutions.[71]

If we turn to the relationship between NTA and shared rule, Renner may again serve as a good starting point. For him it was clear that self-rule provided through the non-territorial exercise of certain autonomous competences is not sufficient and needs to be complemented by participation within institutions of the national government. Renner is therefore sometimes even seen as a precursor of the theory of consociationalism (or power-sharing),[72] which has been associated since the 1970s above all with the name of Arend Lijphart and has only recently seen an extension to power-sharing at the regional level.[73] Renner's writings are still relevant today because his concern for shared rule (or similar concepts such as participation or integration) was echoed in the 1990s both in international documents and in research. This concern is clearly visible in the OSCE Lund Recommendations[74] and in the work of academics who stress the importance of representation, understood as "having a say" in

66 John Kincaid, "From Cooperative Federalism to Coercive Federalism," *The Annals of the American Academy of Political and Social Science* 509 (1990): 139.

67 Renaud Dehousse, "Il paradosso di Madison: riflessioni sul ruolo delle camere alte nei sistemi federali," *Le Regioni* 17, no. 5 (1989): 1365–1400.

68 Alexander Hamilton et al., *Federalist Papers* (London: Penguin Books, 1987), 122.

69 On this, see Yonatan T. Fessha, Karl Kössler and Francesco Palermo, eds. *Intergovernmental Relations in Divided Societies* (London: Palgrave Macmillan, 2022).

70 Palermo and Kössler, *Comparative Federalism*, 253–256.

71 Francesco Palermo, "Beyond Second Chambers: Alternative Representation of Territorial Interests and Their Reasons," *Perspectives on Federalism* 10, no. 2 (2018): 61–64.

72 McGarry and Moore, "Karl Renner," 88.

73 Karl Kössler, "Beyond Majoritarian Autonomy? Legislative and Executive Power-sharing in European Regions," in *Law, Territory and Conflict Resolution*, eds. Matteo Nicolini, Francesco Palermo and Enrico Milano (Leiden-Boston: Brill-Martinus Nijhoff, 2016), 39–66.

74 *Lund Recommendations on the Effective Participation of National Minorities in Public Life* of 1999.

national institutions,[75] as a complement to autonomy or see autonomy, in a similar way, as being "congenial to integration which presupposes the recognition of distinctive identities and cultures and participation of the members of distinctive groups in political, economic and cultural structures of the state".[76] The last part of this quote ("participation of the members of distinctive groups") makes very clear, however, that there is a major difference between shared rule as a complement for minority communities exercising self-rule through NTA, on the one hand, and federalism, on the other hand. Shared rule is in these two cases only superficially similar because its beneficiary is a (minority) *group* in the first case and a *territory*, which is typically home to multiple groups, in the latter.[77] Yet, in spite of this important difference, there is a tendency under the paradigm of multinational federalism to (wrongly) see such a group as the owner of this territory.[78] Anyway, while shared rule is seen (together with self-rule) as inherent to federalism, it is not to NTA. It is rather a complement that can be (and according to Renner should be) provided in *addition* to the self-rule provided by NTA. As pointed out above,[79] the latter has a limited potential of self-rule compared to territorial forms of autonomy. Some observers argue that NTA is also weaker regarding the shared rule dimension because it would have less overall integrative effects than territorial arrangements.[80]

3.4 *Democracy*

Another issue that deserves closer analysis is how federalism and NTA are related to democracy. As for federalism's relation to democracy,[81] Carl Friedrich

---

75 Kristin Henrard, "'Participation', 'Representation' and 'Autonomy' in the Lund Recommendations and their Reflections in the Supervision of the FCNM and Several Human Rights Convention," *International Journal on Minority and Group Rights* 12, no. 2–3 (2005): 141.

76 Zelim A. Skubarty, "Introduction," in *Beyond a One-Dimensional State: An Emerging Right to Autonomy?*, ed. Zelim A. Skubarty (Leiden-Boston: Martinus Nijhoff Publishers, 2005), xxxi-lviii, at xxxiv.

77 Kössler, "Beyond Majoritarian Autonomy?," 44.

78 Francesco Palermo, "Owned or Shared? Territorial Autonomy in the Minority Discourse," in *Minority Accommodation through Territorial and Non-territorial Autonomy*, eds. Tove H. Malloy and Francesco Palermo (Oxford: Oxford University Press, 2015), 13–32; Karl Kössler, "Conclusions," 245–272; Karl Kössler, "Constitution-Making in Diverse Societies: The Rise of Multinational Federalism and its Pitfalls," *Ethiopian Journal of Federal Studies* 4, no. 1 (2018): 63–89.

79 See section 3.2. above.

80 Rainer Bauböck, "Territorial or Cultural Autonomy for National Minorities?," *IWE Working Paper Series* 22, (Vienna: Österreichische Akademie der Wissenschaften Forschungsstelle für institutionellen Wandel und Europäische Integration, 2001): 19.

81 See sections 2 and 3 in Sonnicksen's chapter.

was one of the most vocal theorists in this regard, as he not only drew attention to relevant discussions in the writings of Jean-Jacques Rousseau and Immanuel Kant[82] but also made his own intellectual contribution. While Friedrich emphasized federalism's linkage with constitutionalism, which he famously perceived as a form of democratic government, he also alluded to certain tensions between the two concepts. At least those who "identify democracy with the absolute and unrestrained will of the majority of a given community are confronted with an unresolvable dilemma by federalism since the 'sovereign will' of a constituent people might have to adjust to what other people want or reject".[83] Others highlighting the close relationship include Ivo Duchacek for whom federalism is "the territorial twin of democracy"[84] and Dimitris Chryssochoou for whom they are "predominantly an osmotic relationship since both concepts are insolubly linked and in constant interpenetration with each other".[85]

Yet, it needs to be pointed out that from an empirical perspective federalism has often operated in the past and still does operate nowadays in contexts with more or less severe democratic deficits. One must not only focus in this regard on a number of "fragile federations" on the African continent in which "the conditions for federalism, notably democracy and the rule of law, are either absent or brittle."[86] Even the United States, the home of modern federalism, has long been characterized by democratic deficits due to the limitation of voting rights to white male property owners. Actually, the Dorr rebellion (1841–1842) to extend suffrage in the state of Rhode Island to all white men was a first step against this state of affairs and led to a seminal US Supreme Court ruling at the intersection of federalism and democracy. The court failed to accept the rebels' view that the Rhode Island government was illegitimate because it violated Article 4, clause 4 of the US Constitution guaranteeing "a republican form of government" and left the assessment of such legitimacy to Congress.[87] It took until long into the 20th century for suffrage to be extended to all men and

82 Friedrich, "Federal Constitutional Theory," 513.

83 Ibid. 518.

84 Ivo Duchacek, "Perforated Sovereignties: Towards a Typology of New Actors in International Relations," in *Federalism and International Relations: The Role of Subnational Units*, eds. Hans J. Michelmann and Panayotis Soldatos (Oxford: Clarendon Press, 1990), 3.

85 Dimitris N. Chryssochoou, "Federalism and Democracy Reconsidered," *Regional & Federal Studies* 8, no. 2 (1998): 18.

86 Nico Steytler and Jaap de Visser, "'Fragile Federations' and the Dynamics of Devolution," in *Federalism as Decision-Making: Changes in Structures, Procedures and Policies*, eds. Francesco Palermo and Elisabeth Alber (Leiden-Boston: Brill-Martinus Nijhoff, 2015), 81.

87 *Luther v Borden*, 48 US 1 (1849).

women with clauses in mostly Southern states to suppress Black voting rights being systematically tackled only with the Voting Rights Act of 1965. Indeed, several observers emphasize that the United States have been characterized by democratic deficits, even to the point that one might speak of subnational authoritarianism.[88] The US case is not exceptional of course, as many of the "first generation" federations[89] formed before the 20th century have long operated in a context of democratic deficits.

A question for NTA is then whether such deficits are similarly part of the environment in which it functions or are to some extent inherent in such arrangements. The latter arguably holds true for the millets which existed for centuries in the Ottoman Empire, among others, for the benefit of adherents of various Christian and Jewish confessions.[90] While religious leaders had remarkable non-territorial autonomy regarding the own affairs of their millets, they had to be loyal to the Sultan, ensure tributes in the form of taxes or soldiers and it was not uncommon that they joined forces with the political authorities to extract as much as possible from their communities. It is therefore hardly surprising that democratic credentials were identified as a key difference between the millets and the NTA proposals of Austro-Marxists like Renner. The latter envisaged a system that is based on internal democracy within the autonomous communities and individual consent.[91] As with federalism above, we have to take into account of course the different historical contexts when considering democracy. In fact, the millets had been shaped for several centuries by the specific political circumstances of an empire, while Renner developed his model as a theory and during what would later be identified as the first wave of democratization.[92] There are, however, certain critical voices claiming that NTA arrangements suffer from inherent democracy-related deficiencies, either in specific countries or more generally. Alexander

88 Edward L. Gibson, "Boundary Control: Subnational Authoritarianism in Democratic Countries", *World Politics* 58 (2005): 107–08; Robert Mickey, *Paths out of Dixie: The Democratization of Authoritarian Enclaves in America's Deep South, 1944–1972* (Princeton: Princeton University Press, 2015).

89 Thomas Fleiner-Gerster, "Federalism in Australia and in Other Nations," in *Australian Federalism: Towards the Second Century*, ed. Greg Craven (Carlton, Vic.: Melbourne University Press, 1992), 14.

90 Jan Erk, "Non-Territorial Millets in Ottoman History," in *Minority Accommodation through Territorial and Non-territorial Autonomy*, eds. Tove H. Malloy and Francesco Palermo (Oxford: Oxford University Press, 2015), 119–131.

91 Ephraim Nimni, "Nationalist Multiculturalism in Late Imperial Austria as a Critique of Contemporary Liberalism: The Case of Bauer and Renner," *Journal of Political Ideologies* 4, no. 3 (1999): 296.

92 Samuel P. Huntington, "Democracy's Third Wave," *Journal of Democracy* 2, no. 2 (1991): 12.

Osipov, for instance, argues that NTA in Russia has had to some degree a detrimental effect on democracy because it served to direct attention away from equality and non-discrimination by enabling authorities to explain "exclusion and conflicts in terms of cultural differences rather than institutional deficiencies and social deprivation".[93] Rainer Bauböck even goes as far as to claim that incentives for illiberal government are inherent to NTA so that territorial arrangements should generally be preferred.[94]

4 Conclusions

It has been suggested that the added value of NTA in the context of ethno-culturally diverse societies depends, in essence, on three things, i.e. whether it lowers the stakes of conflicts regarding contested territory, whether it both empowers minority groups and strengthens their participation as equals (in other words, the safeguarding of both self-rule and shared rule) and whether it contributes in the long run to building a more inclusive democratic polity.[95] Much the same can be said about federalism in contexts of ethno-cultural diversity. While the effects of NTA and federalism in these three areas would deserve comprehensive empirical research, this chapter pursued the more modest aim of exploring how federalism, perceived in line with a classical view as referring to territorial arrangements, is related to NTA and compares to it with regard to four key issues.

As for the formation of arrangements of federalism and NTA, it is important to bear in mind that the "federal big bang" of an initial compact among equal partners is today a myth and certainly does not correspond (anymore) to empirical reality. In fact, it is a well-established fact that federal systems nowadays most often come into being through a gradual devolutionary process of a unitary state recognizing the claims of future autonomous entities. An original compact among equals is therefore practically as absent in the case of federalism as in that of NTA. What seems different, however, is that only in the case of some federal systems it is possible to speak of some kind of ex-post compact because the devolutionary process of transferring responsibilities occurred in a power constellation in which the national government could not and did not simply dictate the terms of negotiations (e.g. Belgium or Spain). As far as NTA

93 Alexander Osipov, "National Cultural Autonomy in Russia: A Case of Symbolic Law," *Review of Central and East European Law* 35, no. 1 (2010): 54.

94 Bauböck, "Territorial or Cultural Autonomy."

95 Nootens, "Can Non-Territorial Autonomy," 47.

arrangements are concerned, they are put in place in power constellations that are far more asymmetrical and lack large and powerful ethno-cultural groups able to challenge the national government. Granting such an arrangement is thus for the latter only a minor concession which does not cost much.

This is linked to the second issue explored in this chapter, namely how federalism and NTA are related to self-rule. The main reason why NTA does not cost much and is therefore "attractive (or at least acceptable)" from the national government's perspective is "the fact that there are real, practical limits to the amount of power that may be devolved in a community that does not have a territory of its own".[96] Even if this statement is from almost three decades ago, it still holds true today. There can be little doubt that federalism is more attractive for large, territorially concentrated and politically powerful ethno-cultural groups because it offers them a wider range of powers that are naturally inaccessible under an NTA arrangement. Besides this empirical fact, it is important to note that the expansion of governmental action over the 20th century has increased the scope of these territory-bound powers so that the gap between the potential maximum offers of federalism and NTA is today arguably wider than during the times of Karl Renner. Yet, there are clear indications that national governments are even reluctant to fully exploit this inherently limited potential of NTA regarding legislative and administrative self-rule. This reluctance is not least reflected in the rather traditional and narrow focus on issues of education, language and religion for which the OSCE Lund Recommendations have been criticized.

This chapter emphasized that shared rule is at least as important as self-rule, especially in light of an overall trend towards cooperative federalism. It also demonstrated that NTA theorists from Renner to the post-Cold War era have insisted that self-rule provided through the non-territorial exercise of certain autonomous powers needs to be complemented by shared rule within institutions of the national government. Importantly, however, the beneficiary of "having a say" in these institutions and target group of the integration into the state which presupposes such participation is a (minority) *group* in the case of NTA and a *territory* in that of federalism, even if the doctrine of multinational federalism all too often blurs this distinction. Another significant difference is that shared rule is seen (together with self-rule) as inherent to federalism, while it is, as said above, considered a complement in *addition* to non-territorial self-rule as the essence of NTA.

96 John Coakley, "Approaches," 311.

Finally, another key issue for both federalism and NTA is how they are related to democracy. Many theorists of federalism have emphasized the close link between federalism and democracy, characterizing them as twins or being in an osmotic relationship. This chapter has pointed out, however, that such a characterization is quite at odds with the reality of federalism often operating in contexts with significant democratic deficits, in some cases today but above all in federal systems established before the 20th century. It has also been pointed out that this is obviously linked in the latter cases, similar to older examples of NTA, to the historical circumstances at the time, i.e. the situation before repeated waves of democratization. As for NTA, however, there still is the question of whether it suffers from inherent democracy-related deficiencies, as some claim either regarding specific arrangements or the concept more generally. Overall, the relationship of democracy with NTA appears to be complex and still understudied, but the same probably holds true for its relationship with federalism, even in spite of a much longer research tradition. Both concepts and their interrelations therefore deserve and indeed require further research efforts.

Bibliography

Alenius, Kari. "The Birth of Cultural Autonomy in Estonia: How, Why and for Whom?" *Journal of Baltic Studies* 38, no. 4 (2007): 445–462.

Andeva, Marina et al. *Non-Territorial Autonomy: An Introduction*. Cham: Palgrave Macmillan, 2023.

Bauböck, Rainer. "Territorial or Cultural Autonomy for National Minorities?" In *IWE Working Paper Series* 22, 2–38. Vienna: Österreichische Akademie der Wissenschaften Forschungsstelle für institutionellen Wandel und Europäische Integration, 2001.

Bowring, Bill. "Burial and Resurrection: Karl Renner's Controversial Influence on the 'National Question' in Russia." In *National-Cultural Autonomy and its Contemporary Critics*, edited by Ephraim Nimni, 191–206. London-New York: Routledge, 2005.

Capotorti, Francesco. *Study on the Rights of Persons Belonging to Ethnic, Religious and Linguistic Minorities*, UN Doc E/CN.4/Sub.2/384/Add., 1–7.

Chryssochoou, Dimitris N. "Federalism and Democracy Reconsidered." *Regional & Federal Studies* 8, no. 2 (1998): 1–20.

Coakley, John. "Approaches to the Resolution of Ethnic Conflict: The Strategy of Non-Territorial Autonomy." *International Political Science Review* 15, no. 3 (1994): 297–314.

Coakley, John, "Introduction: Dispersed Minorities and Non-Territorial Autonomy." *Ethnopolitics* 15, no. 1 (January 2016): 1–23.

Coakley, John. "National Territories and Cultural Frontiers: Conflicts of Principle in the Formation of States in Europe." *West European Politics* 5, no. 4 (1982): 34–49.

Davis, Rufus S. *The Federal Principle: A Journey Through Time in Quest of a Meaning*. Berkeley-Los Angeles-London: University of California Press, 1978.

Decker, D. Christopher. "The Use of Cultural Autonomy to Prevent Conflict and Meet the Copenhagen Criteria: The case of Romania." In *Cultural Autonomy in Contemporary Europe*, edited by David J. Smith and Karl Cordell, 101–114. London-New York: Routledge, 2008.

Dehousse, Renaud. "Il paradosso di Madison: riflessioni sul ruolo delle camere alte nei sistemi federali." *Le Regioni* 17, no. 5 (1989): 1365–1400.

Duchacek, Ivo. "Perforated Sovereignties: Towards a Typology of New Actors in International Relations." In *Federalism and International Relations: The Role of Subnational Units*, edited by Hans J. Michelmann and Panayotis Soldatos, 1–33. Oxford: Clarendon Press, 1990.

Elazar, Daniel J. *Exploring Federalism*. Tuscaloosa: University of Alabama Press, 1987.

Elazar, Daniel J. *Federal Systems of the World: A Handbook of Federal, Confederal and Autonomy Arrangements*. 2nd ed., Harlow: Longman Group Limited, 1994.

Erk, Jan and Lawrence M. Anderson. *The Paradox of Federalism: Does Self-Rule Accommodate or Exacerbate Ethnic Divisions?*. London-New York: Routledge, 2012.

Erk, Jan. "Non-Territorial Millets in Ottoman History." In *Minority Accommodation through Territorial and Non-territorial Autonomy*, edited by Tove H. Malloy and Francesco Palermo, 119–131. Oxford: Oxford University Press, 2015.

Fessha, Yonatan T., Karl Kössler and Francesco Palermo, eds., *Intergovernmental Relations in Divided Societies*. London: Palgrave Macmillan, 2022.

Fleiner-Gerster, Thomas. "Federalism in Australia and in Other Nations." In *Australian Federalism: Towards the Second Century*, edited by Greg Craven, 14–32. Carlton, Vic.: Melbourne University Press, 1992.

Friedrich, Carl J. "Federal Constitutional Theory and Emergent Proposals." In *Federalism: Mature and Emergent*, edited by Arthur W. MacMahon, 510–533. New York: Russell&Russell, 1962.

Friedrich, Carl J. "New Tendencies in Federal Theory and Practice." *Jahrbuch des Öffentlichen Rechts* 14, no. 1 (1965): 1–14.

Ghai, Yash. "Autonomy as a Participatory Right in the Modern Democratic State: Public Participation, Autonomy and Minorities." In *Beyond a One-Dimensional State: An Emerging Right to Autonomy?*, edited by Zelim A. Skubarty, 38. Leiden-Boston: Martinus Nijhoff, 2005.

Gibson, Edward L. "Boundary Control: Subnational Authoritarianism in Democratic Countries", World Politics 58 (2005): 101–132.

Hamilton, Alexander et al. *Federalist Papers*. London: Penguin Books, 1987.

Henrard, Kristin. "'Participation', 'Representation' and 'Autonomy' in the Lund Recommendations and their Reflections in the Supervision of the FCNM and Several Human Rights Convention." *International Journal on Minority and Group Rights* 12, no. 2–3 (2005): 133–168.

Huntington, Samuel P. "Democracy's Third Wave." *Journal of Democracy* 2, no. 2 (1991): 12–34.

Kann, Robert A. *The Multinational Empire: Nationalism and National Reform in the Habsburg Monarchy. 1848–1918. Vol. 2*. New York: Octagon Books, 1983.

Keating, Michael. "Europe, the State and the Nation." In *European Integration and the Nationalities Question*, edited by John McGarry and Michael Keating, 23–34. London-New York: Routledge, 2006.

Kincaid, John. "From Cooperative Federalism to Coercive Federalism." *The Annals of the American Academy of Political and Social Science* 509 (1990): 139–152.

Kincaid, John. "Territorial Neutrality and Coercive Federalism in the United States." In *Federalism, Regionalism and Territory*, edited by Stelio Mangiameli, 133–147. Milan: Giuffrè, 2013.

Kössler, Karl. "Aggregative and Devolutionary Federalism Revisited: The Impact of the Founding on the Federal System." In *The Making and Ending of Federalism*, edited by Peter Bußjäger and Mathias Eller. Leiden-Boston: Brill-Martinus Nijhoff, forthcoming.

Kössler, Karl. "Beyond Majoritarian Autonomy? Legislative and Executive Power-sharing in European Regions." In *Law, Territory and Conflict Resolution*, edited by Matteo Nicolini, Francesco Palermo and Enrico Milano, 39–66. Leiden-Boston: Brill-Martinus Nijhoff, 2016.

Kössler, Karl. "Conclusions: Beyond the Illusion of Ethno-culturally Homogenous Territory." In *Minority Accommodation through Territorial and Non-territorial Autonomy*, edited by Tove H. Malloy and Francesco Palermo, 245–272. Oxford: Oxford University Press, 2015.

Kössler, Karl. "Constitution-Making in Diverse Societies: The Rise of Multinational Federalism and its Pitfalls." *Ethiopian Journal of Federal Studies* 4, no. 1 (2018): 63–89.

Kymlicka, Will. "Is Federalism a Viable Alternative to Secession?." In *Theories of Secession*, edited by Percy B. Lehning, 109–148. London-New York: Routledge, 1998.

Kymlicka, Will. "National Cultural Autonomy and International Minority Rights Norms." *Ethnopolitics* 6, no. 3 (2007): 379–393.

Kymlicka, Will. "The Evolving Basis of European Norms of Minority Rights: Rights to Culture, Participation and Autonomy." In *European Integration and the Nationalities Question*, edited by John McGarry and Michael Keating, 11–41. London-New York: Routledge, 2006.

Lapidoth, Ruth. *Autonomy: Flexible Solutions to Ethnic Conflicts*. Washington D.C.: United States Institute of Peace Press, 1996.

Lenaerts, Koen. "Constitutionalism and the Many Faces of Federalism." *American Journal of Comparative Law* 38, no. 2 (1990): 205–264.

Lépine, Frédéric. "Federalism: Essence, Values and Ideologies." In *Understanding Federalism and Federation,* edited by Alain-G. Gagnon, Soeren Keil and Sean Mueller, 31–48. Farnham-Burlington: Ashgate, 2015.

Lépine, Frédéric. "Non-territorial Federalism as an Answer to the Limits of the Territorial Approach." paper presented at the IACFS conference "*Federalism, Regionalism and Territory*". Rome, 19–21 September 2012.

Malloy, Tove H., Alexander Osipov and Balázs Vizi, eds., *Managing Diversity through Non-Territorial Autonomy: Assessing Advantages, Deficiencies, and Risks*. Oxford: Oxford University Press, 2015.

Malloy, Tove H. and Francesco Palermo, eds., *Minority Accommodation through Territorial and Non-territorial Autonomy*. Oxford: Oxford University Press, 2015.

Malloy, Tove H. "The Lund Recommendations and Non-Territorial Arrangements: Progressive De-territorialization of Minority Politics." *International Journal on Minority and Group Rights* 16, no. 4 (2009): 665–679.

McGarry, John and Brendan O'Leary. "Federation and Managing Nations." In *Multinational Federations,* edited by Michael Burgess and John Pinder, 180–211. London-New York: Routledge, 2007.

McGarry, John and Margaret Moore. "Karl Renner, Power Sharing and Non-Territorial Autonomy." in *National Cultural Autonomy and its Contemporary Critics,* edited by Ephraim Nimni, 74–94. London-New York: Routledge, 2005.

McGarry, John, Michael Keating and Margaret Moore. "Introduction: European Integration and the Nationalities Question." In *European Integration and the Nationalities Question,* edited by John McGarry and Michael Keating, 1–20. London-New York: Routledge, 2006.

Mickey, Robert. *Paths out of Dixie: The Democratization of Authoritarian Enclaves in America's Deep South, 1944–1972*. Princeton: Princeton University Press, 2015.

Nimni, Ephraim. "Nationalist Multiculturalism in Late Imperial Austria as a Critique of Contemporary Liberalism: The Case of Bauer and Renner." *Journal of Political Ideologies* 4, no. 3 (1999): 289–314.

Nootens, Geneviève. "Can Non-Territorial Autonomy Bring an Added Value to Theoretic and Policy-Oriented Analysis of Ethnic Politics?" in *Minority Accommodation through Territorial and Non-territorial Autonomy,* edited by Tove H. Malloy and Francesco Palermo, 33–56. Oxford: Oxford University Press, 2015.

Osipov, Alexander. "National Cultural Autonomy in Russia: A Case of Symbolic Law." *Review of Central and East European Law* 35, no. 1 (2010): 27–57.

Pap, András L. "Minority Rights and Diaspora-Claims: Collision, Interdependence and Loss of Orientation." In *Beyond Sovereignty: From Status Law to Transnational*

Citizenship, edited by Osamu Ieda and Balázs Majtényi, 243–252. Sapporo: Hokkaido University, 2006.

Palermo, Francesco and Karl Kössler. *Comparative Federalism: Constitutional Arrangements and Case Law*. Oxford: Hart Publishing, 2017.

Palermo, Francesco. "Beyond Second Chambers: Alternative Representation of Territorial Interests and Their Reasons." *Perspectives on Federalism* 10, no. 2 (2018): 50–70.

Palermo, Francesco. "Central, Eastern and South-Eastern Europe and Territorial Autonomy: Are They Really Incompatible?" In *Political Autonomy and Divided Societies: Comparative Territorial Politics*, edited by Alain-G. Gagnon and Michael Keating, 81–97. Basingstoke: Palgrave Macmillan, 2012.

Palermo, Francesco. "Concluding Remarks: New Regionalism in Central, Eastern and South-Eastern Europe: Traditional Models and Beyond." In *Regional Dynamics in Central and Eastern Europe*, edited by Francesco Palermo and Sara Parolari, 241–253. Leiden-Boston: Martinus Nijhoff, 2013.

Palermo, Francesco. "Owned or Shared? Territorial Autonomy in the Minority Discourse." In *Minority Accommodation through Territorial and Non-territorial Autonomy*, edited by Tove H. Malloy and Francesco Palermo, 13–22. Oxford: Oxford University Press, 2015.

Popelier, Patricia. *Dynamic Federalism: A New Theory for Cohesion and Regional Autonomy*. London-New York: Routledge, 2021.

Skubarty, Zelim A. "Introduction." In *Beyond a One-Dimensional State: An Emerging Right to Autonomy?*, edited by Zelim A. Skubarty, XXXI–LVIII. Leiden-Boston: Martinus Nijhoff Publishers, 2005.

Snyder, Jack L. *From Voting to Violence: Democratization and Nationalist Conflict*. New York: Norton, 2000.

Smith, David J. and John Hiden. *Ethnic Diversity and the Nation State: National Cultural Autonomy Revisited*. London-New York: Routledge, 2012.

Smith, David J. "NTA as Political Strategy in Central and Eastern Europe." In *Minority Accommodation through Territorial and Non-territorial Autonomy*, edited by Tove H. Malloy and Francesco Palermo, 161–178. Oxford: Oxford University Press, 2015.

Steytler, Nico and Balveer Arora. "Introduction." in *The Value of Comparative Federalism: The Legacy of Ronald L. Watts*, edited by Nico Steytler, Balveer Arora and Rekha Saxena, 2–12. London-New York: Routledge, 2020.

Steytler, Nico and Jaap de Visser. "'Fragile Federations' and the Dynamics of Devolution." In *Federalism as Decision-Making: Changes in Structures, Procedures and Policies*, edited by Francesco Palermo and Elisabeth Alber, 77–101. Leiden-Boston: Brill-Martinus Nijhoff, 2015.

Suksi, Markku. "Non-Territorial Autonomy: The Meaning of (Non-)Territoriality." In *Minority Accommodation through Territorial and Non-territorial Autonomy*, edited by Tove H. Malloy and Francesco Palermo, 87, 93. Oxford: Oxford University Press, 2015.

Walker, Neil. "The Shifting Foundations of the European Union Constitution." *University of Edinburgh School of Law, Research Paper Series*, no. 1 (2012), 1–27.

Wolff, Stefan and Marc Weller. "Self-Determination and Autonomy: A Conceptual Introduction." In *Autonomy, Self-Governance, and Conflict Resolution: Innovative Approaches to Institutional Design in Divided Societies*, edited by Marc Weller and Stefan Wolff, 1–25. London-New York: Routledge, 2005.

Woodman, Sophia and Yash Ghai. "Comparative Perspectives on Institutional Frameworks for Autonomy." In *Practising Self-Government: A Comparative Study of Autonomous Regions*, edited by Yash Ghai and Sophia Woodman, 449–486. Cambridge: Cambridge University Press, 2013.

CHAPTER 2

Non-territorial Autonomy and the Law of Diversity: Challenging Pre-established Positions in Domestic Law

Tove H. Malloy

1 Introduction

Accommodating non-territorial autonomy (NTA) arrangements for ethno-cultural groups has been approached differently by European countries. There is an increasing desire among ethno-cultural minority groups to have greater control in matters related to the protection of individual and group identities. Institutions, such as the family, educational structures, cultural and religious activities, and social care contribute to promoting the cultural capital of the members of such minority groups and thus to their cultural survival. Creating separate and distinct micro-societies through self-organization and self-rule of institutions that are essential to identity protection require the ability to be autonomous in the management of these while remaining integrated in the macro-society through mainstream institutions, activities and actions. However, while international standards allow for protecting and preserving cultural difference through human and minority rights, they do not prescribe activist promotion of distinct ethno-cultural identities through autonomy. This is still the prerogative of states. Ethno-cultural groups are thus dependent on domestic legal structures and the political will of the majority and the government when seeking to obtain NTA arrangements. They have to hope for a political climate that promotes deliberation and negotiation on their positions and requests for self-rule. Most importantly, they have to hope that the majority accepts cultural difference. Where this is not the case, achieving NTA arrangements may not be a given outcome, or it may be very difficult. The processes that lead to NTA arrangements can, therefore, be complicated and intricate.

There is no method of analysis that can facilitate a uniform scientific assessment of how countries and governments accommodate ethno-cultural demands for NTA arrangements. Aspects of historical legacy, state formation and political and legal traditions can influence how governments accommodate demands from ethno-cultural groups for self-rule in matters related to protection and promotion of their identity. How do NTA processes begin?

DOI:10.1163/9789004707764_004

What indicators to look for in terms of government actions and legal and political tools? What indicates that they have progressed, and are there any parameters for success? This paper seeks to answer some of these questions. First, it will discuss briefly the concept of ethno-cultural NTA arrangements in order to explain the context and the problematization. Next, it will examine a theory of law-making regarding diversity accommodation. The theory, called the "Law of Diversity", develops a number of indicators for law-making in diverse societies seeking to accommodate ethno-cultural difference and is thus useful as a research strategy for analysing NTA processes.[1] The Law of diversity seeks to question the pre-established positions of majorities and minorities in law-making through a perspective of societal action that questions the willingness of societies to allow for deliberation of cultural diversity and moral pluralism. Such is also the aim of social idealism, which promotes social exchange as the best tool to finding law. Drawing on the indicators of the Law of diversity and the perspective of social idealism, the main part of the paper will examine three cases of NTA processes in Europe. The cases of Hungary, Finland and Germany provide good materials and processes for applying the Law of diversity and testing the hypothesis that social idealism can challenge the pre-established positions of majorities and minorities in law and politics. In the Conclusion, a few thoughts on the success of the hypothesis will be offered.

2 Non-territorial Autonomy

NTA refers to the rights and capabilities of cohesive ethno-cultural groups, who live dispersed among the general population, to establish, manage, implement and regulate their own institutions or functions aimed at protecting, preserving and promoting a common cultural identity.[2] This is why NTA is often called *cultural* autonomy. In order to achieve NTA, members of ethno-cultural groups must also have special political rights to participation in decision-making about issues relevant to the identity of the groups, such as culture and

---

1 Francesco Palermo and Jens Woelk, "From Minority Protection to a Law of Diversity? Reflections on the Evolution of Minority Rights," *European Yearbook of Minority Issues* (*EYMI*) 3, no. 1 (2003–2004): 5–13; on the Law of Diversity as a theoretical framework to grasp the evolving instruments for the accommodation of diversity, see Nicolò P. Alessi, *A Global Law of Diversity: Evolving Models and Concepts* (Routledge: London-New York, 2025).

2 Tove H. Malloy, "Territorial and Non-Territorial Autonomy: The Tools for Governing Diversity," in *The Routledge Handbook of Comparative Territorial Autonomies*, eds. Brian C.H. Fong and Atsuko Ichijo (London-New York: Routledge, 2022), 48–66.

education. NTA is thus based on special personal autonomy rights provided to a number of individuals who belong to a specific national, ethnic, linguistic, religious, or indigenous group, and who have expressed an interest and desire to enjoy their special rights together by having independent authority over the areas of those special rights. Thus, NTA groups need not be in the majority nor in a dominant position. In fact, groups enjoying NTA are always numerically in the minority and thus non-dominant both at the national and the local level. Critical mass is not required in this scenario, and very small groups can be given authority over their own cultural affairs.

Policies for NTA are seldom directed by one piece of legislation or a single agreement.[3] Very few countries opt for including NTA status in the constitution. Instead, ethno-cultural groups may be mentioned in a preamble and/or in a general article setting out special rights for groups that have a historical and cultural significance for the country. Moreover, only a few countries have adopted specific and comprehensive NTA laws, but many countries have adopted laws that set out conditions for implementing ethno-cultural minority rights.[4] These laws are not usually considered NTA laws, and confusion between NTA rights and minority rights is thus quite common, and not without reason, because the two are dependent on each other. Minority rights established by law often help a minority group to claim NTA arrangements in areas covered by the minority rights legislation. The difference between the two is that minority rights entitle a member of a minority to certain individual rights, whereas NTA legislation and policies entitle a group of minority members to decide for each other within the group.

In the absence of a comprehensive NTA law, a government can agree to delegate some authority to minority groups via statutes or other means of implementing minority rights.[5] It may consequently be necessary to amend existing laws and statutes with specific clauses or sub-sections on minority rights. This is a piecemeal approach that is likely to be slow and lengthy without any binding timetable. In addition to codifying via public statutes, a government and the legislators can also decide to amend private law. Many minority activities will likely be regulated as civil society activities under private law. And it is often in private law organizations that there is room for developing

3 Tove H. Malloy, "Concepts of Non-Territorial Autonomy: Agreements, or Arrangements?," *German Yearbook of International Law* 63, no. 1 (2020): 255–276.

4 See, for instance, Ljubica Djordjević, Tove H. Malloy, and Stanislav Cernega, "Drafting Domestic Legislation Provisioning National Minority Rights: The Dos and Don'ts According to the Council of Europe," ECMI *Working Paper 104* (December 2017): 3–53.

5 Malloy, "Territorial and Non-Territorial Autonomy," 48–66.

NTA authority by establishing internal governance regulations, for instance through bylaws, statutes, strategies, guidelines, etc. as is usually required by private law. NTA arrangements are, therefore, often characterized by a mix of public and private law amendments combined together in a cluster of regulations that function as NTA.

Theoretically, NTA for ethno-cultural groups may be conceptualized as 'institutions-within-institutions,' or ethno-cultural institutions functioning on separate mandates within mainstream governing institutions.[6] For this reason, it would not seem logical to define NTA arrangements as another full-fledged level of multilevel governance, including federalism, because they do not constitute a horizontal level like the central, regional and local, and they seldom exist at all levels of the state. Moreover, they should be distinguished from civil society and social movements, which are based on universal access. They could perhaps be described as a 'subsidiary' to the political organisation of society since they co-exist within state institutions of similar functions. The key is that they represent added value as opposed to merely juxtaposed value. On this view, NTA arrangements could be seen as a very specific layer of decentralization.[7]

The study of NTA has provided some tools that can be useful in assessing the institutional framework of such models. Scholarly debates over the years have resulted in a combined knowledge production of typologies of NTA that provide labels indicating legal entrenchment and political empowerment. The type that is based on a comprehensive legal framework and involves constitutional recognition and legislative powers is sometimes referred to as legislative autonomy,[8] whereas a comprehensive legal framework with constitutional recognition but no legislative powers has been referred to as traditional autonomy.[9] NTA arrangements based on a cluster of provisions found in public and private law without having the strong legal guarantees of the two first models have been called functional or administrative NTA.[10] Finally, NTA

6 Tove H. Malloy and Levente Salat, "Towards New Paradigms?," in *Non-Territorial Autonomy and Decentralization: Ethno-Cultural Diversity Governance*, eds. Tove H. Malloy and Levente Salat (London-New York: Routledge, 2020), 244.

7 This chapter is mainly focused on investigating the emergence and functioning of NTA arrangements and their inclusion in the framework of the Law of Diversity; thorough considerations on the connections between federalism and NTA are provided by Alessi and Kössler's chapters in this volume.

8 Michael Tkacik, "Characteristics of Forms of Autonomy," *International Journal on Minority and Group Rights* 15, no. 2–3 (2008): 369.

9 Malloy, "Concepts of Non-Territorial Autonomy," 255–276.

10 See Markku Suksi, "Functional Autonomy: The Case of Finland with some Notes on the Basis of International Human Rights Law and Comparisons with Other Cases,"

is increasingly discussed as a phenomenon of legal pluralism, mainly in post-colonial countries. Often legal pluralism arrangements are a carry-over from pre-colonial arrangements that survived informally during colonial rule, and still today many survive without any strong legal guarantees.[11] This typology is not the main concern in this discussion, which focuses primarily on the processes that form NTA. It is nevertheless useful as it provides indicators for the end-result of these processes.

NTA arrangements are formed on the basis of formal or informal processes of power delegation. Formal processes are usually initiated top-down at the seat of power and follow rather fixed paths to settlement, for instance through commissions or temporary functions of dispute settlement. With regard to the institutionalization of informal processes, these are often bottom-up, like social movements, but they do not have the purpose of radical change. Mostly, bottom-up development of NTA arrangements emerge in response to a need to fill gaps in service delivery by the state. In other words, they seek to, or offer to, create institutions or organisations that provide thematic support with regard to the specific ethno-cultural group. Whether formal or informal, NTA arrangements are usually the result of years of negotiations and legal adjustments of domestic law to ensure that the rights of the NTA beneficiaries, i.e., the minorities, are protected.

There is no simple or fixed road to defining and codifying such rights, and adjustments to incorporate rights that promote and protect NTA arrangements will often require unique approaches. For this reason, comparison of NTA models in terms of approaches to legal codification is virtually impossible. Countries have very diverse systems of constitutional and primary law frameworks usually defined by historical events, societal and cultural developments, and external relations. In other words, the study of NTA arrangements and their processes is complex and requires sophisticated scientific tools of research and understanding.

Since the focus of this discussion is on the processes of NTA in terms of politics and policy-making with subsequent codification in law or other means of empowerment, an interpretive approach to understanding NTA processes is applied through a qualitative analysis of examples of NTA arrangements in

---

International Journal on Minority and Group Rights 15, no. 2–3 (2008): 195 and Malloy "Concepts of Non-Territorial Autonomy," 255–276.

11 See for instance, Levente Salat and Sergiu Miscoiu, "Roma Autonomous lawmaking: The Romanian Case," in *Non-Territorial Autonomy and Decentralization: Ethno-Cultural Diversity Governance*, eds. Tove H. Malloy and Levente Salat (London-New York: Routledge, 2020), 167–194.

Hungary, Finland and Germany. This will involve interpreting historical contexts as well as political systems of democracy and public management. It will also ask whether policy-makers insist on formal equality and egalitarian societies, or whether they accept deviances from such approaches by acknowledging substantive equality and asymmetry in rights. While legal entrenchment is important in terms of the degree of autonomy and empowerment of ethno-cultural groups, the scope of application is more relevant when trying to interpret whether pre-established norms influence the NTA processes. Moreover, do they accept a variety of legal sources that are conducive to accepting NTA institutions within state institutions? Finally, it is also important to interpret the implementation of the processes. What characterizes the processes that lead to codification of NTA arrangements? Is there a political climate of deliberation and negotiation? Are the processes tolerant and respectful? Have the processes come about voluntarily or through international pressure? In short, what solutions have been applied in the efforts to agree on NTA arrangements and to adjust domestic legal systems in Hungary, Finland and Germany?

3 The Law of Diversity

Notwithstanding the many obstacles of analysing NTA policy-making processes, there have been attempts to develop guidelines for the overarching rules that governments could follow. One such effort was presented by Francesco Palermo and Jens Woelk in 2003.[12] Their proposal for a Law of diversity allows for differentiation in the legal position of ethno-cultural groups, for pluralism in terms of legal and non-legal sources as well as for renegotiation of the status of actors in the specific situation of a societal relationship. They argued that minority law-making in multi-ethnic and multi-cultural societies should be characterized by three main elements:

> *asymmetry* regarding its application as well as the single instruments (differentiation in the legal position of the groups thus becomes the rule); *pluralism* of legal sources and of subjects (creating the obligation of mutual recognition, consideration of the position and interests of others and, in the end, mutual acceptance; mutual trust and cooperation are the most important non-legal preconditions for the acceptance of the single solutions) as well as the *negotiation* of its content in a quasi-contractual

12 Palermo and Woelk, "From Minority Protection to a Law of Diversity," 5–13.

> framework, i.e. going beyond pre-established majority and minority positions (and making the distinction between rule and exception increasingly difficult if not obsolete).[13]

According to Palermo and Woelk, the Law of diversity should not be seen as a system of justice as this usually entails ideological bias; rather, it should be a prescription for procedures aiming at determining the common ground. It should not determine the details but become detached as a regulator whose services are only needed as a "referee."[14] On this view, the Law of diversity would be substantively determined by the minority groups themselves and the local governments under whose jurisdiction they belong. Like the owners of shops around the city square, they decide on the substantive issues of co-operation. Palermo and Woelk make it clear that co-operation is paramount for the Law of diversity to function well. This includes the willingness on behalf of minorities to co-operate and become integrated. At the same time, this will force the majority to understand that their society is complex and thus needs complex solutions. In other words, simple rules are not efficient when dealing with minority law-making. Although the Law of diversity is defined mainly as a tool for describing territorial autonomy processes, it has many elements that are relevant for NTA processes. The rest of this section provides a brief examination of the three main elements proposed by Palermo and Woelk.

3.1 *Asymmetry Regarding Application*

Collective autonomy, such as NTA arrangements, is one example of asymmetric rights that ethno-cultural minorities and indigenous groups enjoy at the domestic level. They are asymmetric rights and duties because they are rights that only pertain to a minority living within a territory that fulfils certain criteria set out in the negotiated agreements. Palermo and Woelk's argument that asymmetry defines the instruments and the application of the Law of diversity is interesting for a number of reasons. First, with regard to applicability, it challenges the formal equality approach that has characterized the liberal paradigm of international law for decades. Secondly, it implies that applying corporate rights to groups could be necessary. Thirdly, it entails a conceptual challenge to the universal buttresses of international human rights law by which human rights are seen as belonging to all humankind. The conceptual aspect of asymmetry poses a number of problems in law-making inasmuch as

13 Palermo and Woelk, "From Minority Protection to a Law of Diversity," 12.
14 Palermo and Woelk, "From Minority Protection to a Law of Diversity," 13.

asymmetric rights in legal theory are special institutional rights that give members of society particular entitlements to a range of benefits subject to meeting certain well-defined criteria.

Onora O'Neill has explained that asymmetric relationships are perilous, not only because they must rely on a moral justification of the asymmetric rights granted, but also because the value of the political institutions supporting the asymmetric rights-holders must be ethical.[15] This is because special obligations always presuppose special relationships according to which duty-bearers are allocated to recipients. Moreover, they are always subject to two levels of ethical vindication or query so that both the ethical claims that arise within special relationships and those of the background practices, institutions and relationships that establish or enable special relationships can be questioned.[16] Essentially, this means that to justify the granting of asymmetric rights there must be evidence of both moral justification for imposing asymmetric duties on others and ethical reasons and behaviour among the rights-holders to claim such rights. Thus, the ethical reason for a recipient of special benefits must be that she can prove that she cannot exist without this special entitlement. In terms of minority rights, it means that minorities must prove both that they are better off if they receive special group protection and that they are worthy of such special protection. Otherwise, the political will to institutionalize asymmetric rights is not likely to materialize.

The issue of institutional rights is at the core of the problem of minority rights and is one of the reasons why minorities are not granted corporate rights in public international human rights law. This is partially due to the fact that claims to have rights amount only to rhetoric if obligation-bearers are not identifiable by rights-holders, and in public international human rights law it is very difficult to identify who the bearers of obligations are.[17] Special asymmetric rights impose two categories of obligations. In one category, the *imperfect* category of special obligations, obligations may not correspond to a right. For instance, the obligations that good parents will feel they should extend to their children in terms of love, attention and support are particular to the relationship between parents and child, but it is questionable whether parents owe these obligations to their children. Thus, they are not institutional rights. Whereas it is debatable whether children have a right to emotional or moral support, arguably they have the right to substantive support. In fact,

15 Onora O'Neill, *Towards Justice and Virtue: A Constructive Account of Practical Reasoning* (Cambridge University Press: Cambridge, 1998).

16 O'Neill, *Towards Justice*, 148.

17 O'Neill, *Towards Justice*, 129.

most Western democratic states consider this a legal right. The other category, the *perfect* category of special obligations, "require[s] social structure or practices that connect specific agents to specified recipients of action, to whom they owe and for whom they are bound to perform, who are the holders of the equivalent special rights."[18] The rights that correspond to these duties are far from rhetoric. They are very definite entitlements that are distributed according to a scheme and whose enforcement would have to justify institutional structures as well as more abstract principles. Thus, the definition of a *special* and *perfect obligation* is a right "held by some; owed to specified others; counterpart special rights; fixed by structure of specific transactions and relationships; [which] can be distributively universal given appropriate institutions".[19] Examples of rights in this category are the special relationships that states, markets, firms and families define and create, as well as specified welfare rights and time-restricted rights. Inasmuch as the special obligations that are imposed following this definition may be rather burdensome at times to some members of society but not to others, these obligations and their corollary rights are *asymmetric*. This is in contradistinction to universal rights, which are mainly liberty rights. While not dismissing universal rights as applicable to special protection, universal rights may be illusionary if they do not specifically identify the bearers of the duty. This may result in inflated expectations while masking a lack of claimable entitlements.[20] Therefore, while asymmetric duties and rights may be distributed universally given appropriate institutions, they are usually distributed within a confined system, such as domestic legal systems, to a particular group of people.

3.2 *Pluralism of Legal Sources*

Pluralism in law-making is not a question of reconciling divergent values but of reconciling divergent factual existences in an ethical manner. This is also what Palermo and Woelk would like to achieve with the Law of diversity when they argue for a set of non-legal preconditions for the acceptance of the single solutions. These preconditions must include mutual recognition, consideration of the position and interests of others, mutual trust and co-operation, as well as acceptance.[21] Thus, the notion of a fixed, perfect model of justice representing common values is simply not feasible. Moreover, justice should not be seen as static and inflexible. Rather, justice is non-static and unsettled

18 O'Neill, *Towards Justice*, 147.
19 O'Neill, *Towards Justice*, 142.
20 O'Neill, *Towards Justice*, 133.
21 Palermo and Woelk, "From Minority Protection to a Law of Diversity," 12.

in that it is constantly renegotiated through a dialectical process among the people to whom it pertains.[22] Dialectic here means rather than deriving *ought* from *is*, the process requires us to see justice not as something we *should* have but something we *could* have. In a sense, the dialectic process derives *could* from *is*. In other words, when we negotiate about conceptions of justice we seek to establish, not what we *ought* to support as an ethical model, but what we *could* support. It goes without saying that in such a process it is vital that no absolutes are exhibited and that the individual is capable of critical practical reasoning. Therefore, by substituting *could* for *ought*, we take the ideological debate out of the social interaction and, thus, set the stage for negotiation that is based on facts rather than values.

3.3 *Negotiation of Content*

The Law of diversity approach is akin to the model of democracy based on the procedural republic, constitutionalism, communicative action and representative government. In procedural democracy, law is the structure that defines proceduralism. Procedural democracy is also referred to as deliberative democracy.[23] Deliberative democracy refers to the ideal of reaching agreement through communicative action. The rules that guide deliberative democracy are procedural inasmuch as they set a standard for how the deliberation process should be ordered. Hence, ethics are regulated by the procedures of law where law is discursively agreed upon through communicative action. On this view, the rules that people follow when they negotiate substantive matters are based neither on the universal liberal ideology of individualism nor on the particularistic communitarian tradition of civic humanism; rather, the rules follow a discourse principle that is explained from the point of view of which norms of action can be impartially justified. It wishes to give power to the state on the basis of a discursive character of public reason.

Law then is seen as the medium by which public reason is transformed into administrative power, and the proceduralist model insists on the empirical relevance of democratic ideals accepted by citizens. On this view, proceduralism is a combination of the juridical and the political, or a combined model of

---

22 Jacques Derrida, "Force of Law: The 'Mystical Foundation of Authority'," in *Deconstruction and the Possibility of Justice*, eds. Drucilla Cornell, Michel Rosenfeld and David Gray Carlson (London-New York: Routledge, 1992), 3–67.

23 Jürgen Habermas, *The Theory of Communicative Action, I*, trans. Thomas McCarthy (Heinemann: London, 1984) and Id., *The Theory of Communicative Action, II*, trans. Thomas McCarthy (Polity Press: Cambridge, 1987).

the constitutional and the political state.[24] Whereas the constitutional state adjudicates rights by means of institutions and procedures, the political state operates in a public arena where collectivities contend with and interpret collective goals and collective goods. This model of proceduralism suggests mediation by just individuals who are able to disengage any self-interest in that process. This way, the parties to the deliberation will evidence trust in each other as well as in the final result. In this process, citizens debate and deliberate in public on the kind of rights they regard as fair and necessary for the protection of both private liberties and public participation.

4 Social Exchange and Pragmatism

Minority law-making has a variety of options to choose from to achieve the goals set out in the Law of diversity. While the view based on pragmatism sees the law-making process as a contingent act of creative problem-solving,[25] the deconstructivist view holds that law-making is an ongoing inter-cultural multilogue about constitutional arrangements[26] defined by a dialectic process of constant redefinition and contestation.[27] Moreover, the goal of law-making has been fiercely debated by critical theorists who criticize the injustice of the liberal dogma of neutrality in favour of contextual justice.[28] Finally, there is the social idealism view, which sees law as a result of the systematic way in which social exchange is organized.[29] This is the view that oils the machinery of the Law of diversity.

Social idealism speaks to the view that minority law-making is a systematic process of social exchange. This exchange takes place between actors who are willing to serve society's purposes. According to Philip Allott, law-making is

---

24 Jürgen Habermas, "Struggles for Recognition in the Democratic Constitutional State," in *Multiculturalism*, ed. Amy Gutmann (Princeton: Princeton University Press, 1994), 107–149; see also, Melissa S. Williams, "Justice toward Groups. Political Not Juridical," *Political Theory* 23, no. 1 (1995): 67–91.

25 Siegfried Schieder, "Pragmatism as a Path towards a Discursive and Open Theory of International Law," *European Journal of International Law* (EJIL) 11, no. 3 (2000): 663–698.

26 James Tully, *Strange Multiplicity: Constitutionalism in an Age of Diversity* (Cambridge University Press: Cambridge, 1995).

27 Derrida, "Force of Law," 3–67.

28 Martti Koskenniemi, "The Politics of International Law," *European Journal of International Law* (EJIL) 1, no. 4 (1990): 4–32.

29 Philip Allott, "Reconstituting Humanity: New International Law," *European Journal of International Law* (EJIL) 3, no. 2 (1992): 219–252.

an element of societies that are self-organizing, and it functions as the means to actualize social objectives.[30] This confronts law-making with a number of dilemmas. First, the subjects of the law are not only individuals but also groups. Second, law must pertain to the actual society as well as to all members of society. Third, law must represent both social unity and human diversity in the struggles for recognition, and it must consider the positives and negatives of such struggles. Fourth, law must settle tensions that arise in the processes that seek to define justice and thus be able to accept that value is modifiable. Fifth, law must, therefore, continuously renew itself.

The social idealism view of law draws on pragmatism, which requires the procedural process to look for 'real possibilities' within our thoughts and actions. In doing so, pragmatism employs the relational logic of finding the law. By being relational, pragmatism employs an approach that seeks to remove the opposition between reality and appearance. Instead of asking why things are as they are, pragmatism asks whether we have the best possible system for bringing things into relation to other things in such a way as to better meet our needs by more appropriately fulfilling them. This ties the pragmatism view to the argument noted earlier that, rather than deriving *ought* from *is*, we should endeavour to derive *could* from *is*. Moreover, as pragmatism finds law through a relational method based on empirical facts and history, it is discursive. Law is discursive when it is understood as a creative and situational act of creative problem-solving which is flexible and open in its adaptation to the conditions of life. In other words, it is not substance but discursive relations seeking to arrive at the norms that are relevant for the actual situation. Pragmatism, therefore, helps social idealism find law through particular social action and particular social contexts.

A key aim of the Law of diversity is to challenge pre-established positions of majority and minority groups in domestic law, making the distinction between rule and exception increasingly difficult to define, if not obsolete. This is what social idealism proposes with the idea of finding law through social exchange. Allowing inclusive and deliberative NTA processes will by nature challenge fixed views and inflexible approaches. If NTA processes are pluralistic in approach and outcome, boundaries for norms will become adaptable and accommodating. Thus, the state-of-the-art of law-making regarding NTA arrangements for ethno-cultural groups concerns both processes and end-results.

---

30 Tove H. Malloy, "Towards a New Paradigm of Minority Law-Making: A Rejoinder to Palermo and Woelk's Law of Diversity," *European Yearbook of Minority Issues* (EYMI) 4, no. 5 (2004–2005): 5–29.

5 Three Processes

The cases of Hungary, Finland and Germany provide useful examples of how different political processes have led to different policy-making and codification outcomes, i.e., how these countries have found law through NTA processes. The caveat is that there is no generic norm for the processes that lead to NTA arrangements. Each country is influenced by its historical and cultural context and its moral outlook. First, Hungary and Finland are unitary states, while Germany is a federal state. This influences their approaches at the constitutional level. Second, Hungary and Finland differ further in that Hungary has been through a transition from authoritarian to democratic rule and thus a total refurbishing of the legal framework, while Finland has adopted a two-nation system as its overarching constitutional framework, albeit not a federal one like the German system. Notwithstanding these immediate differences, all three countries have accepted NTA self-rule at various degrees for ethno-cultural groups.

Drawing on the indicators of the Law of diversity, this section will present and examine NTA processes in the three country cases in terms of

- Historical context
- Political system of democracy
- Egalitarianism vs. moral pluralism
- Public management systems
- Scope of application of minority rights
- Asymmetry in terms of formal equality vs. substantive equality
- Variety of legal sources
- Process implementation and initiative
- Political climate of cooperation and negotiation
- Political climate of tolerance and respect
- External pressure and kin-state relations

Clearly, not all these can be discussed in detail in the space of a single, short paper. Only a superficial assessment can be attempted.

5.1 *Hungary*

The Hungarian NTA process started immediately after the breakup of the Soviet Union when the country sought membership in the European peace institutions, such as the Council of Europe. Membership required adherence to the European human rights standards and the minority rights regime. Hungary had prepared for this by adopting a constitution that respected national minorities[31] and granted recognized minorities certain self-government rights.[32]

In fact, Hungary opted for a comprehensive legal agreement for ethno-cultural NTA through a combination of constitutional recognition and an NTA single act that is applied equally to all recognised minorities, called nationalities. The Law on Nationalities, which substituted an earlier Law on the Rights of National and Ethnic Minorities from 1993,[33] was adopted by the Hungarian Parliament in 2011.[34] It followed a revision of the Hungarian Constitution, which redefined national and ethnic minorities as nationalities.[35] Like the 1993 Law, the 2011 Law on Nationalities recognises certain nationalities as legal entities, and provides them with an art of self-governance, called 'self-government.' The 2011 Law identifies cultural autonomy as its main aim and guarantees a great variety of collective rights, of which the establishment of 'self-government' is one. Thus, 'self-government' is the institutionalisation of cultural autonomy by being both a representative forum and an administrative tool for realising cultural autonomy. NTA self-governments do not, however, have legislative powers. The Hungarian NTA arrangement is, therefore, not a legislative but a traditional model that can be subsumed in the category of classic non-territorial autonomy arrangements.[36]

The Law on Nationalities gives detailed provisions on the internal structure of the 'self-governments', and elections to the self-governments follow the territorial division of Hungary and are held together with general and local elections. The Law also stipulates their functions and competences, including specifying these as mandatory public duties – that is, an obligation to share competences and co-governance with the central administration. These duties include the maintenance of schools and cultural institutions, fulfilment

31 Art. 29, Fundamental Law of Hungary (*Magyarország Alaptörvénye*), available at https://www.refworld.org/pdfid/53df98964.pdf (accessed 30 June 2022).

32 There are currently 14 recognised nationalities in Hungary.

33 Act LXXVII of 1993 on the Rights of National and Ethnic Minorities (*Magyar törvény a nemzeti és etnikai kisebbségek jogairól*), arts. 21–54, available at https://www.refworld.org/docid/4c3476272.html (accessed 30 June 2022).

34 Act CLXXIX of 2011 on the Rights of Nationalities in Hungary (*A nemzetiségi jogok Magyarországon*), available at https://njt.hu/translated/doc/J2011T0179P_20171221_FINrev.pdf (accessed 30 June 2022).

35 This discussion benefits greatly from the analysis offered by Balazs Vizi, "Minority Self-Government in Hungary – a Special Model of NTA?," in *Managing Diversity through Non-Territorial Autonomy: Assessing Advantages, Deficiencies, and Risks*, eds. Tove H. Malloy, Alexander Osipov, and Balazs Vizi (Oxford: Oxford University Press, 2015), 31–52.

36 On the differences between classic and governance forms of NTA, see Alessi's chapter in this volume.

of responsibilities and competences delegated by local governments, duties related to the maintenance of organisations taken over from state or local institutions, duties related to the interests of the community, and creating equal opportunities in relation to the enforcement of nationality rights. The duties also involve decision-making and co-operation, serving to reinforce the cultural autonomy of nationality communities in connection with the operation and responsibilities of institutions operated by other agencies in the self-government's jurisdiction. Further duties may include supporting community initiatives with organisational and operational services, liaising with local nationality civil organisations and initiatives of the community and local church organisations, initiating measures necessary for the preservation of cultural heritage, participating in the preparation of development plans, and assessing demand for education and training in nationality languages. In short, they are shared competences with duties attached to ensure the administration of public services delivery in a great variety of public and communal life.

With regard to general politics and policy-making, the Hungarian government is obliged to consult with nationality 'self-governments' at the state level about issues concerning education of members of nationalities. Thus, the Law on Nationalities provides the 'self-governments' with the right to consultation in matters of both public education and cultural self-administration.[37] Again, duties are formulated concretely. Nationality 'self-governments' at the state level are expected to act as interest representation for all NTA organisations in the country, and to this effect, to maintain a national network. Each nationality elects a representative to the Hungarian Parliament, called an advocate. They do not have voting rights, but act on behalf of all the 'self-governments' within their own community. The Hungarian government must furthermore consult 'self-governments' on bilateral and multilateral international agreements related to the protection of nationalities. To maintain oversight, the 'self-governments' may request information relevant to the nationality from public authorities and agencies, and they may exercise their right of consent on issues directly affecting the nationalities in connection with development plans. This is not an absolute veto right, but within a time limit, 'self-governments' can voice their position on the matter. If no comments are received, a court may take a decision on the matter. In other words, the NTA arrangement in Hungary ensures co-governance at the national level on matters vital to the survival of the cultures of the nationality. The NTA arrangement in Hungary is, therefore,

37 Act CLXXIX of 2011, arts. 27 and 33–49.

both a top-down and bottom-up approach placing obligations on both the national government and the minority 'self-governments.'

When Hungary established itself as a unitary state after the demise of the Soviet bloc, it adopted a parliamentary system based on liberal democracy principles. The country is divided into territorial units, or regions, but matters regarding managing diversity and minority rights, including the system of NTA 'self-governments', are decided at the central level. From the first liberal constitution in 1991 and the first law on minorities of 1993, there was a clear acceptance of asymmetry in terms of substantive equality and pluralism of nationalities. Given the detail of the current Law on Nationalities, deliberation and negotiation are required when preparing policies pertaining to the areas of cultural autonomy. The external pressure exerted by the Council of Europe early on has continued during the country's accession process to the European Union (EU), and the 1993 law was in fact heavily criticised by the EU resulting in major changes to the law. The kin-states that are members of the EU have been able to exert pressure this way, whereas other countries with kin-minorities in Hungary have had to use bilateral means. Notwithstanding recent changes in Hungary's political climate towards foreigners, the approach towards nationalities remains open. There have been complaints from the international community about Hungary's treatment of the Roma community, which is one of the fourteen recognized nationalities.[38] This has not influenced the framework for the NTA arrangement, and the comprehensive system of constitutional guarantees combined with a very detailed primary law of protection remains in place.

5.2 *Finland*

Due to the Swedish colonialization of Finland since the Middle Ages, Finland has been a *de facto* dual nation for centuries. With the decision of the Åland Islands' Commission of the League of Nations, which granted the right to territorial autonomy to the archipelago in 1921,[39] the country began its journey towards legal codification as a dual nation with two official languages. The occupation by the Russian Empire from 1809 to 1917 did not influence the dual nation sentiment. Rather, in the years that followed independence from Russia

38 Se for instance, Advisory Committee on the Framework Convention for the Protection of National Minorities, "Fourth Opinion on Hungary," adopted on 25 February 2016, no. ACFC/OP/IV(2016)003.

39 Act 1991/1144 on the Autonomy of Åland (*Självstyrelselag för Åland/Ahvenanmaan itsehallintolaki*), available at https://www.finlex.fi/sv/laki/ajantasa/1991/19911144 (accessed 4 July 2022), regulates the TA agreement for the Islands and will not be discussed here.

and the League of Nations decision, Finland continued to develop the dual nation also on the mainland. This created the administrative NTA arrangements for the Swedish speakers living mixed with the rest of the population in the coastal areas and big cities. Today, Finland protects the Swedish communities and their language rights through a sophisticated matrix of legislation that covers the entire territory of Finland and application of a plurality of legal instruments.

The NTA arrangement in Finland is constitutionally recognised as part of Finland's bilingual setup. The 1919 Constitution determines in Section 17(1) that there are two official languages in Finland: Finnish and Swedish.[40] This provides a strong guarantee to the Swedish-speakers of Finland. Essentially, NTA in Finland is a language agreement setting up an arrangement for bilingualism, meaning that all matters pertaining to the NTA guarantees are language matters. Thus, it functions primarily through a universal act of parliament, the Language Act of 2003.[41] This Act regulates the entire public administration of Finland, and subsidiary legislation has been adopted in specific areas, such as local government, civil servant personnel, and administrative regulations.[42] This is particularly evident in the field of education, where forms of administrative or sectorial non-territorial autonomy are in place.[43] Sub-sections of several pieces of education legislation specifically regulate languages.[44] For instance, the Basic Education Act and the Act on General Upper Secondary Education provide for teaching in Swedish, while the Decree on Qualification Requirements for Teaching Staff requires language proficiency in Swedish.[45] The Universities Act provides for unilingual and bilingual universities in

---

40 This section relies on the analysis provided by Suksi, "Functional Autonomy," 195–225.

41 Act 423 of 2003 on Language rights (*Språklag/Kielilaki*), available at https://finlex.fi/en/laki/kaannokset/2003/en20030423.pdf. (accessed 4 July 2022).

42 Section 18 of the Act 410 of 2015 on Local Government (*Kommunallag/Kuntalaki*), available at https://finlex.fi/en/laki/kaannokset/2015/en20150410 (accessed 4 July 2022).; Act 424 of 2003 on Knowledge of Languages Required of Personnel in Public Bodies (*Lag om de språkkunskaper som krävs av offentligt anställda/Laki julkisyhteisöjen henkilöstöltä vaadittavasta kielitaidosta*), available at https://finlex.fi/en/laki/kaannokset/2003/en20030424 (accessed 4 July 2022).

43 On this concept, see Alessi's chapter in this volume.

44 Local Government Act, *supra* note 40, for school boards.

45 Section 10, Act 628 of 1998 on Basic Education (*Lag om grundläggande utbildning/Perusopetuslaki*), available at https://finlex.fi/en/laki/kaannokset/1998/en19980628 (accessed 4 July 2022); Section 6, Act 629 of 1998 on General Upper Secondary Education (*Gymnasielag/Lukiolaki*), available at https://finlex.fi/en/laki/kaannokset/1998/en19980629 (accessed 4 July 2022); Section 9, Decree 986 of 1998 on Qualification Requirements for Teaching Staff (*Förordning om behörighetsvillkoren för personal inom*

Finland.[46] Indirect NTA administration seems less evident in the area of religion, where the Church Act ensures bilingualism in the administration within the Evangelic-Lutheran Church, but is not guaranteed in other religious denominations.[47] Language rights in the military have also been guaranteed through the Act on Military Duty, which provides for Swedish-speakers to serve in a Swedish army section within the military.[48] The judiciary has ensured shared competences through an amendment to the Act on Courts of First Instance that provides for special internal divisions within the court system to operate entirely in Swedish.[49] Finally, the Act on the Finnish Broadcasting Company Ltd. (Act on *Yleisradio Oy*) provides for representation of Swedish-speakers on the board of governors,[50] and the Local Government Act provides for the option to receive healthcare and social care services in Swedish.[51] This means that the scope of application of minority rights is broader than most other NTA arrangements in Europe.

Like Hungary, Finland is a unitary state with minimal decentralization, and all decisions on language issues are taken at the central level. Notwithstanding this, the Local Government Act provides for participation by Swedish speakers in local government and local administration and for the option to establish Swedish municipal councils within Finnish majority municipalities.[52] The powers of these are nevertheless purely administrative. Lack of powers is also evident in the participation in politics and policy-making. The Law on the Swedish Assembly of Finland (*Folketing*) guarantees Swedish-speakers administrative self-decision powers, but neither legislative powers nor self-government.[53] The Assembly is a consultative body to the Finnish Parliament

---

undervisningsväsendet/ Asetus opetustoimen henkilöstön kelpoisuusvaatimuksista), available at https://finlex.fi/en/laki/kaannokset/1998/en19980986 (accessed 4 July 2022).

46 Section 4, Act 645 of 1997 on Universities (*Universitetslag/Yliopistolaki*), available at https://finlex.fi/en/laki/kaannokset/1997/en19970645 (accessed 4 July 2022).

47 Sections 2 and 3, Act 1054 of 1993 on Churches (*Kyrkolag/Kirkkolaki*), available at https://finlex.fi/sv/laki/ajantasa/1993/19931054 (accessed 4 July 2022).

48 Section 51, Act 452 of 1950 on Military Duty (*Värnpliktslag/Asevelvollisuuslaki*), available at https://www.finlex.fi/sv/laki/ajantasa/kumotut/1950/19500452 (accessed 4 July 2022).

49 Section 18 of the Act 581 of 1993 on Courts of First Instance (*Tingsrättslag/Käräjäoikeuslaki*), available at https://www.finlex.fi/sv/laki/smur/1993/19930581 (accessed 4 July 2022).

50 Act 1380 of 1993 on *Yleisradio Oy* (*Lag om Rundradion Ab/Laki Yleisradio Oy:stä*), available at https://www.finlex.fi/sv/laki/smur/1993/19931380 (accessed 4 July 2022).

51 Section 18(2)(4), Act 410 of 2015 on Local Government.

52 Section 18(2)(4), Act 410 of 2015 on Local Government.

53 Act 1331 of 2003 on the Swedish Assembly (*Lag om Svenska Finlands folkting/ Laki Svenska Finlands folktingnimisestä järjestöstä*), available at https://www.finlex.fi/sv/laki/ajantasa/2003/20031331 (accessed 4 July 2022).

and municipal bodies but does not provide any administrative functions in relation to the Swedish-speakers. In other words, this arrangement limitedly reproduces the original model of NTA; it instead represents an example of participatory democracy instrument for the accommodation of diversity.[54] Elections are held every four years, and candidates are nominated by the political parties, which are either bilingual or Swedish-speaking. The Assembly has 75 seats, where 70 are filled on the basis of municipal election results, and five are appointed by the Parliament of Åland (*Lagtinget*).[55] In addition, the Swedish People's Party of Finland has been in the national parliament since 1870, and between 1979 and 2015 it was a member of the Finnish cabinet.

The Finnish system of protection for the NTA arrangement is based on a political view of moral dualism in terms of diversity of languages and cultures. Moreover, recent years have also shown that moral pluralism has developed with other national and ethno-cultural groups being granted rights beyond formal equality.[56] The scope of application of the rights of the Swedish speakers is very broad, and while the process of arriving at the current NTA arrangement has taken most of the 20th century, it continues to develop and expand using all political and legal tools available, including the court system. The approach is entirely top-down with decision powers held at the top level of the state but with room for deliberation and negotiation at the local level as well as juridical evaluations. Unlike Hungary, external pressure has not been a major element with the exception of the mediation by the League of Nations at the beginning of the 20th century, nor has the relations to the kin-state Sweden been decisive.

5.3 *Germany*

Unlike Hungary and Finland, Germany is not a unitary state but a union of federal sub-states with equal powers devolved from the central level. The political and legal systems of Germany were established by the Allied Powers after World War II, who laid the grounds for a liberal and parliamentarian democracy. The constitution or the Basic Law does not address ethno-cultural diversity but follows a formal equality doctrine. In that sense Germany is a very egalitarian society; moral pluralism has come later through the country's memberships of international organisations and extensive immigration. Matters of culture and education are devolved to the federal sub-states. However, recognition

---

54 On this, see the Introduction and Section 2 of this volume.

55 The Parliament of Åland also appoints one representative to the Finnish Parliament.

56 See for instance, Advisory Committee on the Framework Convention for the Protection of National Minorities, "Reports on Finland," available at https://www.coe.int/en/web/minorities/finland (accessed 4 July 2022).

of ethno-cultural groups requires approval at both the central and regional levels given the country's international responsibilities regarding minority protection. There are four recognized minorities in Germany, but not all of them have achieved NTA arrangements. As NTA is not part of the constitutional structure of Germany, there have not been any universal primary law adopted like in Hungary and Finland. A system that resembles NTA has been achieved in Germany by only one ethno-cultural group, the Danish minority in Schleswig-Holstein.

Historically, the Danish minority emerged after the division of the Duchy of Schleswig in 1920. A plebiscite stipulated by the Paris Peace Agreement of 1919 moved the border between Denmark and Germany south providing self-determination for parts of the Duchy but not all. In the part remaining under German rule, a Danish community was left without protection, as the League of Nations had not stipulated any such protection in the peace agreement. It was not until after World War II that Germany and Schleswig-Holstein recognised the cultural rights of the Danish minority with the Kiel Declaration in 1949.[57] The Declaration reiterated the universal rights of the federal German Basic Law but also included the right to freedom of affiliation with the minority and to send children to Danish minority schools.[58] The Schleswig-Holstein (constitutional) Statute of 1949 incorporated the rights of the Danish minority.[59] When the Statute was transformed into a constitution in 1990, the rights of minorities were expanded to include protection of political participation.[60] This was also codified in Schleswig-Holstein through the 1956 federal law exempting minorities from the five percent threshold for political parties.[61] Schleswig-Holstein further established protection in its election legislation in 1991.[62] With the help of the exemption from the five percent threshold, the Danish minority is represented in the Schleswig-Holstein *Landtag* and has participated directly in government from 2012–2017.

The first regulation on minority schools was issued in 1950, but the schools were not legalised until 1978. Currently, the schools are regulated by the

---

57 Kiel Declaration (*Kieler Erklärung*) of 26 September 1949.

58 This section is based on Tove H. Malloy, "Functional Non-Territorial Autonomy in Denmark and Germany," in *Managing Diversity through Non-Territorial Autonomy: Assessing Advantages, Deficiencies, and Risks*, eds. Tove H. Malloy, Alexander Osipov, and Balazs Vizi (Oxford: Oxford University Press, 2015), 183–202.

59 Arts. 5 and 6, Schleswig-Holstein Constitution (*Verfassung des Landes Schleswig-Holstein*).

60 Art. 5, Schleswig-Holstein Constitution.

61 Arts. 6, 20, and 27, Act of 7 May 1956 on Federal Elections (*Bundeswahlgesetz*).

62 Art. 3(1), Act of 7 October 1991 on Elections in Schleswig-Holstein (*Wahlgesetz für den Landtag Schleswig-Holstein*).

Education Act of 1990, which provides that minority schools in Schleswig-Holstein are categorised as private schools or substitute schools (*Ersatzschulen*) but hold recognition as public schools so long as they fulfil public school requirements.[63] Thus, there are no obligations on the minority to perform duties of the state in education; they decide to do it voluntarily. The fusion between public and private law is unique here and ensures that diplomas from Danish minority schools are recognised officially in all of Germany. Minority cultural education in kindergartens is guaranteed through the general requirement to accommodate the wishes of parents in provisions of the legislation on day care.[64] Other minority institutions include culture and sports associations, as well as institutions of cultural heritage maintenance and social care for the elderly. Since all minority organisations are private entities, their ability to be self-managed requires that those organisations that act as public service providers must abide by the general principles of the German Basic Law. The fact that all minority organisations are private entities means that the NTA arrangement is primarily bottom-up. If the minority does not establish organisations under private law, there will be no basis for indirect administration in service delivery.

In addition, Schleswig-Holstein has accommodated the Danish minority through special provisions in other legislative instruments. For instance, mainstreaming of language rights in public administration statutes at the local level has begun at limited speed, but this does not lead to any indirect administrative competences.[65] Moreover, participation in decision-making is secured in legislation on the media.[66] A representative of the minority's cultural organisation is a member of the Schleswig-Holstein supervisory authority for private broadcasters (*Unabhängige Landesanstalt für den Rundfunk – ULR*) as well as the Television Board of Second German (public) Television (*Zweites Deutsches Fernsehen – ZDF*). Several consultative bodies also exist at the political level; they provide for consultation in political matters related to NTA.[67] These are

---

63 Arts. 4, 58, 60, and 63, Act of 2 August 1990 on Education (*Schleswig-Holsteinisches Schulgesetz*).

64 Arts. 5, 7, and 12, Act of 12 December 2019 on Day Care (*Kindertagesförderungsgesetz*).

65 See Tove H. Malloy and Sonja Wolf, "Linguistic Minority Rights in the Danish-German Border Region: Reciprocity and Public Administration Policies," *International Journal on Minority and Group Rights* 23, no. 4 (2016): 485.

66 Act of 25 July 1996 on Telecommunications (*Telekommunikationsgesetz*); and Interstate Broadcasting Agreement (*Rundfunkstaatsvertrag*) of 31 August 1991.

67 See Schleswig-Holsteinischer Landtag, "Minderheiten- und Volksgruppenpolitik in der 18. Legislaturperiode (2012–2017): Minderheitenbericht 2017," https://www.landtag.ltsh.de/infothek/wahl18/drucks/5200/drucksache-18-5279.pdf (accessed 6 July 2022).

usually mixed bodies with representation of both public and private actors. The legal sources that underpin the NTA arrangement in Schleswig-Holstein are clearly a mix of legal instruments and non-legal tools.

Like the case of Finland, the NTA arrangement in Schleswig-Holstein – an example of functional autonomy[68] – has taken years to develop and continues to expand into new domains. The scope of application is not as broad as in Finland. On the other hand, the degree of self-administration is higher as long as public policies are followed. A number of organisations for deliberation and negotiation exist and function on a permanent basis.[69] Moreover, the threshold exemption of five percent for political parties of national minorities ensures access to the political processes in both the national parliament and local parliaments. Unlike Hungary and Finland's focus on consultative bodies, the direct participation with voting rights provides guarantees of participation in the debates and deliberations on issue relevant to NTA arrangements. Finally, the kin-state relations with Denmark have functioned as a strict oversight with multiple opportunities to exert pressure when necessary.

6 Challenging the Status Quo

One of the key aims of the Law of diversity is to challenge pre-established positions of majority and minority groups in domestic law, making the distinction between rule and exception increasingly difficult if not obsolete. An example of pre-established positions is the egalitarian notion of formal equality, or the idea that non-discrimination standards are applied uniformly and universally across all levels and for all groups of society.

This is in contradistinction to substantive equality, which recognizes that some segments of society need special rights in order to arrive at a level playing field in outcome. Such segments are not only ethno-cultural groups but also groups characterized by special needs, such as the disabled or women in very disadvantaged positions, to mention just a few. Another example is the notion that a society is mono-cultural, and thus the state represents one culture and other cultures are less important and subjected to the private sphere of life. Even societies that recognize established, historical and numerically non-dominant groups, such as ethno-cultural groups with indigenous roots in the homeland, do not always acknowledge this in the common narrative. The

68 On this, see Alessi's chapter in this volume.

69 See for instance overview of these in Tove H. Malloy, "Functional Non-Territorial Autonomy," 183–204.

common narrative maintains that the culture of the dominant group rules and any other groups abide by those rules. Such rules cement the positions of dominant groups, and any rules that are applied to non-dominant groups are considered exceptions rather than new general rules of a complex multidimensional and multicultural system. The question in this section is, therefore, have the legal and political systems in Hungary, Finland and Germany accommodated ethno-cultural groups as exceptions or as part of a multi-faceted society?

First, the three indicators of the Law of diversity – asymmetry in application, pluralism of legal sources and negotiation of content – have been useful in assessing the sub-themes of NTA approaches. Comparison is not the aim, nor is it possible, but in all three cases studied, these indicators have been examined and have indicated the presence of strong elements of NTA processes. Asymmetry in application is evident in that all three countries have adopted special rights for minorities. They have opted to go beyond formal equality and accepted that substantive equality is necessary in order to establish levelled playing fields between the majority and the minorities. Pluralism of legal sources is also clearly evident. Two of the countries, Hungary and Finland, have combined constitutional recognition and protection through primary laws, while Germany has combined political rights at the federal constitutional level with recognition at the regional constitutional level and statutes protecting cultural rights. Negotiation of content has been stable throughout the 20th century with Finland starting after World War I and Germany after World War II. Both countries have added domains to the arrangements. While Finland has added Swedish language units in the military, Germany has expanded media rights and language rights. Hungary's negotiation process started when the country adopted a democratic constitution, and following external pressure, the scope of application has expanded to the political domain with the option to elect representatives to the parliament. Thus, all three countries continue to amend and expand the rights of minorities through negotiation of content.

Second, with regard to the other relevant indicators discussed earlier, it is clear that induced by historical events and external pressure, all three countries have not only initiated NTA processes but also continue them. So far, there has been no withdrawal of rights, and goals achieved have been preserved. This would indicate that minority rights are no longer seen as an exception. Thus, maintaining the status quo in terms of legal and political approaches has not been an option in the three country cases examined. However, there is not enough evidence in this short examination to discuss political climates of co-operation, tolerance and respect, but the fact that goals have been achieved and preserved would indicate that there is a political willingness to accept moral pluralism and cultural diversity, respect difference and embrace democratic deliberation.

7 Conclusions

The Law of diversity is primarily a legal framework for assessing political, legal and social developments in societies with regard to minority rights claims, developments and settlements. It is not specifically designed for analysis of NTA arrangements, but its focus on the asymmetric rights of ethno-cultural groups in minority and non-dominant positions allows for a good match with the study of NTA arrangements precisely because NTA arrangements are asymmetric constellations and solutions for multicultural and multi-nation societies. The fact that the three country cases fairly easily verified the indicators of the Law of diversity, and the key objective of challenging pre-established positions shows that there is basis for applying the Law of diversity as a research framework to NTA studies. Moreover, it proved that the perspective of social idealism is a good lens for explaining and prescribing how law should be found and developed in democratic societies. If NTA processes are inclusive and deliberative, they will challenge the fixed views and inflexible approaches prevalent in many societies, and boundaries for norms will become adaptable and accommodating.

Bibliography

Alessi, Nicolò P. *A Global Law of Diversity: Evolving Models and Concepts*. Routledge: London-New York, 2025.

Allott, Philip. "Reconstituting Humanity: New International Law." *European Journal of International Law* (*EJIL*) 3, no. 2 (1992): 219–252.

Derrida, Jacques. "Force of Law: The 'Mystical Foundation of Authority.'" In *Deconstruction and the Possibility of Justice*, edited by Drucilla Cornell, Michel Rosenfeld and David Gray Carlson, 3–67. London-New York: Routledge, 1992.

Djordjević, Ljubica, Tove H. Malloy, and Stanislav Cernega. "Drafting Domestic Legislation Provisioning National Minority Rights: The Dos and Don'ts According to the Council of Europe." *ECMI Working Paper 104* (December 2017): 3–53.

Habermas, Jürgen. "Struggles for Recognition in the Democratic Constitutional State." In *Multiculturalism*, edited by Amy Gutmann, 107–149. Princeton: Princeton University Press, 1994.

Habermas, Jürgen. *The Theory of Communicative Action, I*, trans. Thomas McCarthy. Heinemann: London, 1984.

Habermas, Jürgen. *The Theory of Communicative Action, II*, trans. Thomas McCarthy. Polity Press: Cambridge, 1987.

Koskenniemi, Martti. "The Politics of International Law." *European Journal of International Law* (EJIL) 1, no. 4 (1990): 4–32.

Malloy, Tove H. and Levente Salat. "Towards New Paradigms?" in *Non-Territorial Autonomy and Decentralization: Ethno-Cultural Diversity Governance*, edited by Tove H. Malloy and Levente Salat, 243–266. London-New York: Routledge, 2020.

Malloy, Tove H. and Sonja Wolf. "Linguistic Minority Rights in the Danish-German Border Region: Reciprocity and Public Administration Policies." *International Journal on Minority and Group Rights* 23, no. 4 (2016): 485–504.

Malloy, Tove H. "Concepts of Non-Territorial Autonomy: Agreements, or Arrangements?" *German Yearbook of International Law* 63, no. 1 (2020): 255–276.

Malloy, Tove H. "Functional Non-Territorial Autonomy in Denmark and Germany." In *Managing Diversity through Non-Territorial Autonomy: Assessing Advantages, Deficiencies, and Risks*, edited by Tove H. Malloy, Alexander Osipov, and Balazs Vizi, 183–202. Oxford: Oxford University Press, 2015.

Malloy, Tove H. "Territorial and Non-Territorial Autonomy: The Tools for Governing Diversity." In *The Routledge Handbook of Comparative Territorial Autonomies*, edtied by Brian C.H. Fong and Atsuko Ichijo, 48–66. London-New York: Routledge, 2022.

Malloy, Tove H. "Towards a New Paradigm of Minority Law-Making: A Rejoinder to Palermo and Woelk's Law of Diversity." *European Yearbook of Minority Issues* (EYMI) 4, no. 5 (2004–2005): 5–29.

O'Neill, Onora. *Towards Justice and Virtue: A Constructive Account of Practical Reasoning*. Cambridge University Press: Cambridge, 1998.

Palermo, Francesco and Jens Woelk. "From Minority Protection to a Law of Diversity? Reflections on the Evolution of Minority Rights." *European Yearbook of Minority Issues* (EYMI) 3, no. 1 (2003–2004): 5–13.

Salat, Levente and Sergiu Miscoiu. "Roma Autonomous lawmaking: The Romanian Case." In *Non-Territorial Autonomy and Decentralization: Ethno-Cultural Diversity Governance*, edited by Tove H. Malloy and Levente Salat, 167–194. London-New York: Routledge, 2020.

Schieder, Siegfried. "Pragmatism as a Path towards a Discursive and Open Theory of International Law." *European Journal of International Law* (EJIL) 11, no. 3 (2000): 663–698.

Suksi, Markku. "Functional Autonomy: The Case of Finland with some Notes on the Basis of International Human Rights Law and Comparisons with Other Cases." *International Journal on Minority and Group Rights* 15, no. 2–3 (2008): 195–225.

Tkacik, Michael. "Characteristics of Forms of Autonomy." *International Journal on Minority and Group Rights* 15, no. 2–3 (2008): 369–401.

Tully, James. *Strange Multiplicity: Constitutionalism in an Age of Diversity*. Cambridge University Press: Cambridge, 1995.

Vizi, Balazs. "Minority Self-Government in Hungary – a Special Model of NTA?" In *Managing Diversity through Non-Territorial Autonomy: Assessing Advantages, Deficiencies, and Risks*, edited by Tove H. Malloy, Alexander Osipov, and Balazs Vizi, 31–52. Oxford: Oxford University Press, 2015.

Williams, Melissa S. "Justice Toward Groups. Political Not Juridical." *Political Theory* 23, no. 1 (1995): 67–91.

CHAPTER 3

Innovative Forms of Autonomy and the Role of Federalism: A Comparative and Theoretical Perspective

Nicolò P. Alessi

1 Emergent Instruments for the Accommodation of Diversity in the Global North

The present chapter aims to show how variegate and evolving the Law of diversity is in contemporary times. In particular, the focus will be on emerging and innovative forms of autonomy, whose distinctive feature is the divergence from the consolidated autonomous models that stem from the liberal-democratic tradition.

These innovations – mainly taking place in the Global North[1] – appear to lack comprehensive recognition or conceptual framing. This chapter intends to address this deficiency. It will do this firstly by recognizing these instruments as some of the most innovative tendencies of the Law of diversity. Secondly, it will propose to frame these developments as part of a broad federal phenomenon, which provides solid theoretical tools to better understand them and explain their functioning.

1 This does not mean that the Global South is not showing very promising models in this area; especially the South American and Southeast Asian regions of the world display very interesting instruments for the accommodation of diversity that add to the traditional ones generally stemming from liberal-democratic constitutionalism; a renovated interest in this areas of the world is observable, together with a new decolonial approach; on this, see, for instance, Lena Salaymeh and Ralf Michaels, "Decolonial Comparative Law: A Conceptual Beginning," *Max Planck Institute for Comparative and International Private Law Research Paper Series* 22, no. 1 (2022): 166–188 and Werner Menski, "Beyond Europe," in *Comparative Law: A Handbook*, eds. Örücü, Esin and Nelken, David (Oxford-Portland: Hart, 2007), 189–216; the present chapter draws the attention on the innovative trends in the Global North, which appear to represent another strand of recent innovation in the area of diversity accommodation with its own features. Such innovations seem to be very unrecognized and undertheorized from a legal standpoint, given their peculiar forms and limited institutionalization; however, when useful, examples from Global South legal systems will be presented.

Accordingly, the next section aims to propose a brief classification of these emergent models of what will be referred to as "governance autonomy" – mainly non-territorial – providing several examples that are solely touched upon but not delved into as comprehensive case studies. Thereafter, an attempt at theoretically framing them based on a federal perspective will be advanced.[2]

2 Emerging Governance Forms of Autonomy

2.1 *A Shift towards Governance*

The expression "governance forms of autonomy" is meant to encapsulate various types of self-governance, which are differentiated from the classic structure of territorial and non-territorial autonomy. The latter, as instruments for the accommodation of diversity, are marked by the following characteristics: a. they are based on the top-down institution of public bodies to which are attributed or delegated wide or general competences; b. those bodies are vested with administrative and legislative functions; c. they are entrenched in the legal system of a country through constitutional provisions or statutes; d. they are designed to protect the interests of a specific minority: in territorial arrangements, the minority is turned into a majority in a given territory, while in non-territorial ones the minority "owns" the institution; consequently, e. they have been created for security and/or protection reasons;[3] f. ultimately, their functioning resonates with nation-state logic as they represent the state in small-scale.[4]

All the types of autonomy addressed here deviate from this structure to different extents and complement the traditional approaches regarding the issue of autonomy in diversity accommodation. For this reason, the expressions "non-orthodox", "non-governmental" or "governance" forms of autonomy may be employed to describe them.

---

2 This chapter takes inspiration from a wider study on these models presented in Nicolò P. Alessi, *A Global Law of Diversity: Evolving Models and Concepts* (London-New York: Routledge, 2025).

3 Tove H. Malloy, "Functional Non-Territorial Autonomy in Denmark and Germany," in *Managing Diversity through Non-Territorial Autonomy: Assessing Advantages, Deficiencies and Risks*, eds. Tove H. Malloy, Alexander Osipov and Balázs Vizi (Oxford: Oxford University Press, 2015), 184; on this, see also Marc Weller and Stefan Wolff, *Autonomy, Self-Governance and Conflict Resolution: Innovative Approaches to Institutional Design in Divided Societies* (London-New York: Routledge, 2005).

4 See Johanne Poirier, "Autonomie politique et minorités francophones du Canada: réflexions sur un angle mort de la typologie classique de Will Kymlicka," *Minorités linguistiques et société / Linguistic Minorities and Society*, no. 1 (2012): 66–89.

2.2 *Functional Non-territorial Autonomy*

It has been observed that, in this epoch, several kinds of governance bodies along the public-private divide complement the state in the provision of services and functions that were once exclusively managed by public structures.[5] Notably, some authors have pointed out that the same phenomenon is taking place in the area of diversity accommodation, as flexible and less institutionalized forms of autonomy are emerging. One of them has been referred to as functional non-territorial autonomy.[6] Focusing on this form of non-territorial autonomy and theoretically framing it as such enables a better understanding of how broad the universe of tools for the accommodation of diversity is, beyond the most consolidated and top-down, hard, defensive and paternalistic models.[7]

Functional autonomy is the outcome of bottom-up processes whereby private organizations are created to cooperate with the state in the provision of services in favor of a non-dominant group.

In practice, functional non-territorial autonomy may assume several forms and take place through "informal mechanisms, such as dialogue mechanisms, specific management agreements, *ad hoc* and footnote budgeting, specific programming, or public-private partnerships".[8] The areas in which functional autonomy operates are varied and include education and culture, politics, media, medical care, and economic and social support.

Interesting cases of functional non-territorial autonomy can be found in South Africa – related to Afrikaners' self-governance[9] – and, to a certain extent,

---

5 On this, see Eva Sørensen and Jacob Torfing, eds., *Theories of Democratic Network Governance* (Basingstoke-New York: Palgrave Macmillan, 2007).

6 The most comprehensive study of these phenomena, which explicitly connected emerging forms of functional autonomy to the concepts of network governance and legal pluralism, is Tove H. Malloy and Levente Salat, eds., *Non-Territorial Autonomy and Decentralization: Ethno-Cultural Diversity Governance* (London-New York: Routledge, 2021), and esp. the introductory and final chapters. These, however, do not specifically use the expression "functional non-territorial autonomy"; this section follows the conceptualization offered by Tove H. Malloy, "Non-Territorial Autonomy: Traditional and Alternative Practices," in *Effective Participation of National Minorities and Conflict Prevention*, eds. William Romans, Iryna Ulasiuk and Anton Petrenko Thomsen (Leiden-Boston: Brill-Nijhoff, 2020), 105–122, who significantly contributed to theoretically consolidating and giving conceptual clarity to the concept.

7 Malloy, "Functional Non-Territorial Autonomy," 187.

8 Malloy, "Functional Non-territorial Autonomy," 188.

9 On this, see Deon Geldenhuys, "Autonomy Initiatives of the Afrikaner Community in South Africa," in *Non-Territorial Autonomy and Decentralization: Ethno-Cultural Diversity Governance*, eds. Tove H. Malloy and Levente Salat (London-New York: Routledge, 2021), 91–114; Bertus De Villiers, "Community Government for Cultural Minorities: Thinking beyond "Territory" as a Prerequisite for Self-government," *International Journal on Minority and Group Rights* 25, no. 4 (2018): 576, where he described the case of the

the UK,[10] Ireland and Northern Ireland, with the latter concerning patterns of functional self-rule of the Irish-speaking population.[11]

However, one of the most interesting – and by far the most structured – examples is located at the border between the German Land of Schleswig-Holstein and the regions of Southern Denmark, which serves the interests of, respectively, the Danish and German minorities.[12]

Functional non-territorial autonomy seems to emerge as a very flexible tool for the accommodation of diversity. Less institutionalization does not imply legal irrelevance. In this case, law is much less direct and "hard", but not less significant to the functioning of the model. Similarly, autonomy is much less institutionalized but not less functional. Moreover, and most importantly, such autonomous arrangements appear to be potentially very inclusive, in the sense that state legal recognition does not seem to be a precondition for the exercise of self-governance instruments. Hence, the groups potentially using them are not limited to traditional minorities.[13] In addition, the peculiar private form of the functional non-territorial autonomous arrangements allows them to operate regardless of existing political boundaries, including international ones.

The rights of the minorities enjoying this form of autonomy are much more proactively practiced than legally recognized and their exercise flows from active involvement in legal systems where horizontal subsidiarity is encouraged or at least admitted. Interestingly, state support for minority activities and institutions is not lacking. This creates a form of horizontal cooperation – resonating with the concept of subsidiarity – which is in the interest of both parties. In any case, the public legal frameworks serve a significant function as

---

Helpmekaar Kollege MSV (RF) operating in Johannesburg and providing education in Afrikaans: this private institution has been set up by the Afrikaans community and is entirely self-funded as it does not receive any government grant.

10 As for the UK, Kyriaki Topidi, "Faith Education in Britain," in *Non-Territorial Autonomy and Decentralization: Ethno-Cultural Diversity Governance*, eds. Tove H. Malloy and Levente Salat (London-New York: Routledge, 2021), 215–239.

11 On this, see Steve Coleman and Éamon Ó Ciosáin, "The Irish Gaeltacht as a Trans-Local Phenomenon," in *Non-Territorial Autonomy and Decentralization: Ethno-Cultural Diversity Governance*, eds. Tove H. Malloy and Levente Salat (London-New York: Routledge, 2021), 153–164.

12 On the features of functional autonomy in this border region, see Malloy, "Functional Non-Territorial Autonomy," 183–204.

13 This expression refers to cultural, linguistic, religious or ethnic minorities, which have traditionally been the beneficiaries of minority rights ad instruments. As the instruments analysed here are all supposed to have a (at least potential) wider reach in terms of beneficiaries than traditional minority rights models, the terms "minority groups" or "non-majority groups" are used.

they allow various forms of non-territorial autonomous arrangements to blossom rather than directly regulating them. Such legal systems enable autonomous action and institutions for diversity accommodation by attributing a "power to" take autonomous action, unlike the traditional minority rights law approach to autonomy that gives minorities "freedom from" state institutions and control.[14] In other words, functional non-territorial autonomy may be understood as something that persons belonging to minorities or other groups make use of because they are entitled to it as civic freedom and not as anything granted by the state under the public law of a country.[15]

2.3 *Institutional Completeness and Administrative Autonomy in Canada and Beyond*

Institutional completeness is an expression that has been recently used to describe forms of self-governance in Canada. The concept emphasizes the relationship between the endurance of a community and the existence of a manifold set of non-governmental institutions that operate in its interest in various sectors.

The expression was coined by the sociologist Raymond Breton in a study that delved into the forms of integration of ethnic communities.[16] The analysis revealed that the integration of immigrant communities is directly influenced and shaped by their institutional completeness, i.e. the extent to which those communities have created their own formal and informal organizations operating in numerous areas, such as religion, welfare, information, and culture. More importantly, Breton demonstrated how the degree of institutional completeness – i.e. the extent to which ethnic institutions exist and are stable – has a direct impact on a given community's survival and endurance.[17] The notion was subsequently used by the sociologist in regard to the francophone minority communities (FMCs) in Canada (outside Québec) and the dynamics of their integration.[18]

---

14 Malloy, "Functional Non-Territorial Autonomy," 199.

15 Markku Suksi, "Personal Autonomy as Institutional Form: Focus on Europe against the Background of Article 27 of the ICCPR," *International Journal on Minority and Group Rights* 15, no. 2–3 (2008): 163.

16 Raymond Breton, "Institutional Completeness of Ethnic Communities and the Personal Relations of Immigrants," *American Journal of Sociology* 70, no. 2 (1964): 193–205; see also *Id.*, "The Structure of Relationships between Ethnic Collectivities," in *The Canadian Ethnic Mosaic*, ed. Leo Driedger (Toronto: McClelland and Stewart, 1978), 55–73.

17 Breton, "Institutional Completeness," 196–200.

18 Raymond Breton, "L'intégration des francophones hors Québec dans des communautés de langue française," *Revue de l'Université d'Ottawa* 55, no. 2 (1985): 77–90.

From a legal perspective, research has been conducted on the phenomenon of institutional completeness with regard to the FMCs in Canada, and, to a lesser extent, the English community in Québec.

Chouinard has demonstrated that this concept has been increasingly employed by courts in Canada to recognize forms of autonomy in the provision of services that favor FMCs in several areas, and in particular in the realm of education and health services.[19] Her studies have illustrated that the courts – and, gradually, the Legislatures – have increasingly recognized the importance of self-managed organizations delivering services in French to ensure the preservation of this minority group. In addition, Foucher and Bourgeois have provided an overview of the vast array of autonomous arrangements for the FMCs that have emerged in Canada, referred to as forms of sectorial (or administrative) autonomy by the authors.[20]

Regardless of the different categorizations employed, all the accounts have essentially drawn attention to the same phenomenon, namely, the creation of public or private-public autonomous arrangements that do not correspond to traditional – and more frequently discussed – state-like autonomies (be they territorial or non-territorial). These instruments for the accommodation of diversity provide the targeted minority group with different degrees of self-governance over the institutions which deliver specific services – including but not limited to schools – in its favor.

Institutional completeness and sectorial autonomy take two general forms: the first consists of self-managed private institutions that cooperate with public structures, while the second – much more developed – involves the creation of public independent organisms governed by the non-majority group in certain administrative sectors. The main areas where institutional

19 See Stéphanie Chouinard, "The Rise of Non-territorial Autonomy in Canada: Towards a Doctrine of Institutional Completeness in the Domain of Minority Language Rights," *Ethnopolitics* 13, no. 2 (2014): 141–158; *Id.*, "Quand le droit linguistique parle de sciences sociales: l'intégration de la notion de completude institutionnelle dans la jurisprudence canadienne," *Revue de Droit Linguistique* 3 (2016): 60–93; such a perspective was criticized by Rémi Léger, "Non-territorial Autonomy in Canada: Reply to Chouinard," *Ethnopolitics* 13, no. 4 (2014): 418–427.

20 See Pierre Foucher, "Autonomie des communautés francophones minoritaires du Canada: le point de vue du droit," *Minorités linguistiques et société / Linguistic Minorities and Society*, no. 1 (2012): 90–114; Daniel Bourgeois, "Administrative Nationalism," *Administration & Society* 39, no. 5 (2007): 631–655; *Id.*, "Territory, Institutions and National Identity: The Case of Acadians in Greater Moncton, Canada," *Urban Studies* 42, no. 7 (2005): 1123–1138.

completeness and sectorial autonomy have been envisaged are education and healthcare.

It must also be noted that forms of private-public partnerships have emerged in several parts of Canada through agreements for the provision of some services between various levels of government and minority associations. Research in this area is very limited and focuses more on the evolution of the role of representative associations than on their actual powers and duties.[21]

The models of institutional completeness and sectorial autonomy are of clear interest and seem to add to the general theory on diversity accommodation. In this case, it must be noted that the legal framework has played a significant and active role in fostering the emergence of these autonomous arrangements, especially when it comes to the two major French-speaking communities outside Québec.[22] Moreover, a notable element favoring the establishment of sectorial autonomies is the fact that French is an official language of the country (and of New Brunswick). Therefore, the French-speaking communities (partially) enjoy a legally recognized differential position in the constitutional system. In other words, "hard" legal frameworks concerning these communities are present, even if they are not considered national or traditional minorities.[23]

The tools analyzed here are forms of autonomy that shy away from the idea of a fully-fledged system of government and instead imply self-governance in a limited area that contributes to the minority's survival. In turn, this contributes to relativizing the centrality of a rather univocal discourse over this topic in literature dealing with diversity accommodation.

2.4 *Nested Federalism(s)*

Nested federalism(s) is an expression that refers to complex governance structures where public and private bodies exert several duties for the sake of (generally indigenous) communities within the existent (generally) federal constitutional structure, without modifying its fundamental features.[24] Put differently, there is evidence of the emergence of further layers

21 Foucher, "Autonomie des communautés," 108.

22 On this, see Alessi, *A Global Law*, 153–155.

23 On the rather difficult systematization of the FMCs within the consolidated theoretical categories of minority rights law, see Poirier, "Autonomie politique," 73–84.

24 The concept of nested federalism has been derived from Gary N. Wilson, Christopher Alcantara and Thierry Rodon, *Nested Federalism and Inuit Governance in the Canadian Arctic* (Vancouver: University of British Columbia Press, 2020), who, in turn, were inspired by Liesbet Hooghe and Gary Marks, *Community, Scale, and Regional Governance: A Post-Functionalist Theory of Governance* (Oxford: Oxford University Press, 2016).

of decentralization in federal states. These differentiate from the traditional model of self-government, as they are forms of self-management that do not fully fit into the classical model of political subnational autonomy.

At the same time, such autonomous systems, which are to different degrees related to the notion of functional non-territorial autonomy, rely upon the basic logic of federalism. This is visible in the fact that they are based on agreements and compromise and take the form of modern treaties or agreements between state and (indigenous) groups.

Cases of nested federalism(s) have been found in Canada and Australia and all concern innovative forms of indigenous self-governance.

As regards the Canadian experience, the Inuit self-governance models of Inuvialuit, Nunavik and Nunatsiavut, all located in the Canadian Arctic, present the features of nested federalisms.[25] While all have peculiar characteristics – not least as they are all are nested in and parallel to an unchallenged constitutional federal structure – the Inuvialuit is arguably the most fascinating case.[26]

The latter model is of specific interest in that it is not structured following a public autonomy model, but rather it is completely centered on private corporations that serve the needs of the relevant community. Indeed, the Inuvialuit Final Agreement (IFA) provides for a unique private governance structure nested within the Northwest Territories.

The case of the Noongar indigenous people in Australia has several similarities with the Canadian experience of nested federalism.[27]

In both cases, the peculiar nature of the bodies entitled to serve the community's interests challenges the monolithic theoretical concept of autonomy

25 On this, Wilson, Alcantara and Rodon, *Nested Federalism*, esp. 43–158; other forms of nested federalism, similarly stemming from modern treaties, have been established for the Nisga'a indigenous peoples in British Columbia and eleven First Nations in Yukon (Wilson, Alcantara and Rodon, *Nested Federalism*, 9).

26 The Inuit self-governance system is not the only emerging model of self-management occurring in Canada, as several other forms of complex governance have also arisen over the last decades; among them, Métis and francophone Franzaskois self-governance have also been described as innovative; on this, see Janique Dubois and Kelly Saunders, " "Just Do It!": Carving Out a Space for the Métis in Canadian Federalism," *Canadian Journal of Political Science / Revue canadienne de science politique* 46, no. 1 (2013): 187–214; Janique Dubois, "The Fransaskois' Journey from Survival to Empowerment through Governance," *Canadian Political Science Review* 11, no. 1 (2017): 37–60.

27 On this, see Bertus De Villiers, "Privatised Autonomy for the Noongar People of Australia: A New Model for Indigenous Self-Government," in *Indigenous, Aboriginal, Fugitive and Ethnic Groups around the Globe*, ed. Liat Klain-Gabbay (London: Intech Open, 2019), 127–157.

that revolves around public forms, and urges the observer to appreciate the variety of shapes an autonomous arrangement can take and their effective functioning.

In fact, the authority exercised by these bodies is different from traditional state-like jurisdiction, typical of traditional versions of territorial and non-territorial autonomy. The focus here is on delivering services and redistributing wealth, with this implying a fundamentally practical approach to the issue of diversity accommodation that shies away from reproducing traditional liberal public forms of government and instead aims to employ flexible private instruments to achieve community survival and empowerment in every aspect of life.

The private or quasi-private status of the autonomous models seems to allow a high degree of flexibility and appears to be a pragmatic tool to manage the communities' interests. At the same time, though the legal framework is not absent, it mainly offers a platform for negotiation and sealing agreements to create such forms of governance autonomy. In fact, besides the private-law nature of the corporations charged with the management of community interests, another notable element of this model is, in both cases, the centrality of negotiation. This implies an active role of the relevant communities as subjects in the definition of the rules governing diversity.

In addition, this model has been defined as holistic,[28] in the sense that it implies a (peculiar) form of non-territorial self-governance which is designed to accommodate diversity by serving all the needs of the community and not only cultural ones. In other words, the private-body system seems to provide a model underpinned by a comprehensive view of the relevant community's interests and suggests a strict interlinkage between cultural and socio-economic needs.

Furthermore, it must be noted that both forms of autonomy imply a different relationship between territory and the communities exercising powers over it, as well as a different conception of autonomous jurisdiction. Both are peculiar forms of non-territorial autonomy where a softer connection with territory is observable, as both provide services and activities that add to and do not exclude the action of governmental bodies. Therefore, it seems that rather than being a precondition for the achievement of autonomy, territory (and land rights) act as an avenue[29] or extension for the exercise of autonomous powers.

28 De Villiers, "Privatised Autonomy," 145.

29 De Villiers, "Privatised Autonomy," 132, indeed stated that land rights constitute an avenue to privatized autonomy for the Noongar people.

The particular role of territory is a central element of the last case analyzed in this section, namely, the so-called urban reserves for indigenous peoples in Canada.

The establishment of urban reserves is an emerging phenomenon occurring in Canada, whereby First Nations acquire ownership of lands outside their traditional reserves through special treaties called Treaty Land Entitlement Framework Agreements (TLEFA). The most implemented examples of urban reserves are located in the Province of Saskatchewan, where a TLEFA was adopted in 1992.[30] The establishment of an urban reserve means attributing reserve status to portions of urban areas, with this implying the application of the same special regime in force in the indigenous homelands. This means, for instance, that those areas can be governed by bands under the Indian Act and subject to the same tax exemptions.[31] At the same time, the management of an urban reserve is nested within the complex institutional framework of the cities and Provinces where it has been established and coexists with them.

The most interesting feature of this case concerns the relationship between territory and self-governance. Indeed, urban reserves constitute an interesting example of self- and shared governance, whereby the indigenous communities residing in cities are allowed to create and develop their own institutions, businesses, and services for their socio-economic and cultural survival and empowerment. The acquisition of land ownership (which in any case grants some additional advantages for the indigenous communities) allows them to exercise a rather flexible form of self-governance that consists of managing their institutions – from businesses to service-delivering bodies – in an urban setting and not on isolated reserves.

What is fascinating is that, as in the previous cases, self-governance is exercised through complex structures aimed at creating a non-isolationist ecosystem conducive to economic and cultural survival and self-sufficiency. Consequently, territory is not a fundamental precondition but an enabling

30 Already in 1988, the city of Saskatoon created the urban reserve of Muskeg Lake Cree Nation, which was the first case in Canada; on this, see Joseph Garcea, "First Nations Satellite Reserves: Capacity-Building and Self-Government in Saskatchewan," in *Aboriginal Self-Government in Canada: Current Trends and Issues*, ed. Yale D. Belanger (Saskatoon: Purich Publishing, 2008), 240-259.

31 On this, see Evelyn Peters, "Urban Reserves," Research paper for the National Centre for first Nations Governance, August 2007, available at the following link: https://fngovernance.org/wp-content/uploads/2020/09/e_peters.pdf, 3.

element.[32] Additionally, as in the previous cases, the control over territory does not entail exclusive sovereign jurisdiction, but a more pragmatic and relational form of autonomy.[33]

2.5 *Revitalized Inclusive Forms of Territorial and Non-territorial Subnational Autonomy for Diversity Accommodation*

A final category of autonomous arrangement that appears to diverge from the traditional employment of autonomy for diversity accommodation purposes – based on the idea that a national minority becomes a regional majority – is what can be referred to as "revitalized forms of subnational autonomy". These arrangements exhibit an inclusive structure in that they are not premised on the reproduction of nation-state logic on a smaller scale. On the contrary, they are designed to embed and foster the expression of the many diversities that characterize their societies.

Such a model, which implies an inclusive revision of autonomy for diversity accommodation, has been encouraged by European international soft law and has increasingly drawn scholarly interest. In this sense, it has been pointed out that the model of subnational ethnic government based on "minority ownership" is limited in its ability to manage the growing complexity that characterizes several contemporary societies.[34] This is also the case with complex regional multinational power-sharing systems, which go beyond models designed exclusively for the benefit of a single regional majority: they are confronted with the challenge of increasing diversity that originates from migration flows, and, in general, the rise of "others" that challenge the rigid structure of arrangements based on an ethnic distribution of power and ethnic representation in administration.[35]

---

32 Janique Dubois, "Beyond Territory: Revisiting the Normative Justification of Self-Government in Theory and Practice," *The International Indigenous Policy Journal* 2, no. 2 (2011): 5–10.

33 On the concept of relational autonomy, which entails the need for complex, shared, or co-operative forms of governance to manage diverse societies, especially in urban areas, see Michael Murphy, "Relational Self-Determination and Federal Reform," in *Canada: The State of the Federation 2003: Reconfiguring Aboriginal-State Relations*, ed. Micheal Murphy (Montréal: McGill-Queen's University Press, 2005), 3-35.

34 Francesco Palermo, "Owned or Shared? Territorial Autonomy in the Minority Discourse," in *Minority Accommodation through Territorial and Non-Territorial Autonomy*, eds. Tove H. Malloy and Francesco Palermo (Oxford: Oxford University Press, 2015), 19–21.

35 On this, see Arianna Piacentini, " 'Others' and Consociational Democracy: Citizens, Civil Society, and Politics in South Tyrol and Bosnia Herzegovina," Project Report (Eurac Research-Provincia Autonoma di Bolzano, Bolzano/*Bozen*, 2021); on the condition of "others" in the context of autonomous arrangements, see also Timofey Agarin

It seems that this model is attracting growing attention in the Global North, and in some cases, the need to update self-government systems in this direction has been on the agenda for several years or practiced to a limited extent. For instance, the Province of South Tyrol in Italy has slowly been moving towards more flexibility in its organization and activity.[36]

A fascinating – though still evolving – case is represented by the experiment of democratic confederalism in the Autonomous Administration of North and East Syria (Rojava), which has elements of both territorial and non-territorial autonomy.[37] However, this is still more of theoretical ideal-typical model than a fully implemented arrangement.

3 Can Federalism Contribute to Framing the Emergent Models for the Accommodation of Diversity?

3.1 *Theoretical References: The Meta-Theoretical Approach to Federalism*

This section argues that a federal standpoint could provide a promising standpoint to better understand and theoretically frame the governance forms of autonomy described above.

This perspective relies on the studies that have delved into the "meta-theoretical" dimension of federalism, in turn inspired, to a greater or lesser extent, by the critical contributions of some modern federal scholars.[38]

---

and Allison McCulloch, "How Power-Sharing Includes and Excludes Non-Dominant Communities: Introduction to the Special Issue," *International Political Science Review* 41, no. 1 (2020): 3–14, and the other articles in this issue.

36 Francesco Palermo, "Implementation and Amendment of the Autonomy Statute," in *Tolerance through Law: Self Governance and Group Rights in South Tyrol*, eds. Jens Woelk, Joseph Marko and Francesco Palermo (Leiden-Boston: Martinus Nijhoff, 2008), 158; the possible revision of the power-sharing system has been on the agenda in South Tyrol for several years and is still a politically contentious matter.

37 The Syrian case appears to rely on a democratic form of subnational government that is in line with the theoretical underpinnings of the liberal-democratic constitutional tradition; on this experience, see, among others, Rosa Burç, "Non-Territorial Autonomy and Gender Equality: The Case of the Autonomous Administration of North and East Syria – Rojava," *Philosophy and Society* 31, no. 3 (2020): 321–340; Cengiz Gunes, "Accommodating Kurdish National Demands in Turkey," in *The Challenge of Non-Territorial Autonomy: Theory and Practice*, eds. Ephraim Nimni, Alexander Osipov and David J. Smith (Bern: Peter Lang, 2013), 71–84.

38 Namely, Daniel J. Elazar, *Exploring Federalism* (Tuscaloosa: The University of Alabama Press, 1987); Carl J. Friedrich, *Trends of Federalism in Theory and Practice* (London: Pall Mall Press, 1968); Rufus S. Davis, *The Federal Principle: A Journey Through Time in Quest of a Meaning* (Berkeley-Los Angeles-London: University of California Press, 1978).

Following these accounts, federalism is theorized as an autonomous legal (and/or political) concept[39] that is derived from the observation of its various manifestations. Accordingly, federalism is meant to be a general, synthetical and analytical legal notion, not unlike a constitution, for instance. And, like "constitution", federalism may thus be seen as an interpretive legal model embodying some essential features replicated in innumerably varied ways.[40] It is, in the end, the meta-theoretical common core, super-code or framework able to bring all of these concrete manifestations together.

Federalism is intertwined and inseparable from its materializations, which form what one may call the "federal phenomenon".[41] The latter is multifaceted, with its concrete shape being affected by the cultural, political, economic, and philosophical contexts underlying the different epochs of human history and acting as contingencies of the federal theme.[42] Accordingly, the state-related dimension of federalism as a form of government is considered to be one of the possible replications of the legal concept – or, one of the manifestations of the federal phenomenon – having a legal-constitutional significance.

The employment of the adjective "meta-theoretical" to describe the perspective adopted here is meant to suggest that federalism is taken at a more abstract level than a (conceptual or) theoretical one. It is used as a lens or a framework of understanding through which one may grasp the structure and functioning of several phenomena – especially those analyzed above – and consequently apply to them the federal wisdom that derives from federal theory and practice. A theoretical perspective, which would arguably imply analyzing federalism as a constitutional concept, i.e. as a specific form of government provided by a constitution,[43] would limit the scope of the observation

39 A legal concept is here regarded as the outcome of a process of abstraction of general legal categories typical of the comparative inquiry; on this, see Jean-F. Gaudreault-DesBiens and Fabien Gélinas, "Opening New Perspectives on Federalism," in *Le fédéralisme dans tous ses états: governance, identité et méthodologie – The States and Moods of Federalism: Governance, Identity and Methodology*, eds. Jean-F. Gaudreault-DesBiens and Fabien Gélinas (Cowansville-Bruxelles: Éditions Yvon Blais-Bruylant, 2005), 70.

40 Gaudreault-DesBiens and Gélinas, "Opening New Perspectives," 70–71.

41 On this, see Frédéric Lépine, "Federalism: Essence, Values and Ideologies," in *Understanding Federalism and Federation*, eds. Alain-G. Gagnon, Soeren Keil and Sean Mueller (Farnham-Burlington: Ashgate, 2015), 31–48.

42 In this sense, Lépine, "Federalism," 36–37.

43 On this, see Stephen Tierney, *The Federal Contract: A Constitutional Theory of Federalism* (Oxford: Oxford University Press, 2022), esp. 151–182; another author that framed federalism as a "constitutionally defined concept" implying a form government characterized by the existence of a multi-tiered structure is Patricia Popelier, *Dynamic Federalism: A New Theory for Cohesion and Regional Autonomy* (London-New York: Routledge, 2021), esp. 46–74.

to institutional or governmental features.[44] The approach taken here is aimed at demonstrating that federalism can be used as a frame to recognize a vast range of more or less institutionalized instruments for the accommodation of diversity that have public legal relevance. Accordingly, it is not the aim of this chapter to dive into the very essence of federalism, but to provide arguments that sustain the idea of employing it as a general inter-temporal matrix for understanding complex systems of governance (as those stemming from the evolution of the Law of diversity), which implies going beyond its traditional description.

As a result, not only does the meta-theoretical angle extend the scope of federalism as an analytical tool, it also broadens its potential as an inspiring method for the regulation of pluralism which embeds a large and varied "baggage" (or "wisdom") made up of institutions and practices. Consequently, once an observed phenomenon is framed as part of federalism, it will be possible to apply "federal wisdom" to understand it and eventually draw practical lessons (stemming from federal theory and trends) related to its possible developments.

The latter perspective rests upon the idea that federalism has a far-reaching analytical scope. As a consequence, it claims that the traditional focus of legal and political federal thought could hinder the theoretical and analytical potential of federalism and thus act as an epistemological obstacle.

This theoretical proposal is capable of challenging the discussed basic epistemological assumptions underpinning the traditional focus of federal studies and seems particularly worthwhile for the present study. Several recent accounts seem to have endorsed this perspective and sought to overcome the state-centered vision expressed by the bulk of the scholarship on federalism,[45] not to reveal its true nature, but to heighten its analytical potential and its ability to perform explanatory functions as regards a vast array of phenomena.

44 See Frédéric Lépine, "A Journey through the History of Federalism: Is Multilevel Governance a Form of Federalism?," *L'Europe en formation* 363, no. 1 (2012): 60.

45 According to Antoine Messarra, "Principe de territorialité et principe de personnalité en fédéralisme comparé: le cas du Liban et perspectives actuelles pour la gestion du pluralisme," in *Le fédéralisme dans tous ses états: governance, identité et méthodologie – The States and Moods of Federalism: Governance, Identity and Methodology*, eds. Jean-F. Gaudreault-DesBiens and Fabien Gélinas (Cowansville-Bruxelles: Éditions Yvon Blais-Bruylant, 2005), 227–260, this position is principally due to the fact that most Western scholars are somewhat affected by a nation-state frame of mind or cryptotype, which has led to consideration of territorial polities as the fundamental elements of the general definition of "true" federalism.

In line with the latter accounts, federalism is here proposed as a theoretical tool that can help frame, understand and explain the functioning of the emerging instruments for the accommodation of diversity, such as governance forms of autonomy. In turn, this is thought to contribute to the advancement of federal and public law research in a time of increasing complexity, by freeing them from the straitjacket of the nation-state.[46]

The meta-theoretical dimension of federalism is far from absent in recent research, but it has barely been structured or even recognized as a completely developed theoretical mode of inquiry. As there is no room for a thorough review of the relevant literature that has opened up the perspective advanced here and of its (alleged) authors,[47] the analysis will go on to explain in which sense applying a federal framing to the emergent models for the accommodation of diversity could be theoretically beneficial.

3.2 *Federalism and the Federal Phenomenon: Why Another Definition Is Not Needed and How the Concept Can Be Theoretically Employed*

If the proposed reading of federalism is accepted, then it seems that a federal framing can be employed with regard to phenomena that imply a total or partial diffusion of legal authority/power/autonomy in more than one center, having different degrees of public legal relevance (as a result of recognition or tolerance) in the same legal system. Therefore, if all the emergent instruments of the Law of diversity analyzed here can be read as peculiar forms of autonomous arrangements having a major governance dimension, there seems to be room for them to be framed through a federal lens.

To this end, one may perhaps use the concept of federal arrangement to describe the particular features that characterize the analyzed tools. This concept has already been used to describe forms of emerging federal structures that do not correspond to classic ones.[48]

Notably, a federal framing is not intended to describe the truly federal nature of these instruments, which seems inconclusive (and useless), but is the conceptual key to productively applying federal wisdom to them. In other words, considering a phenomenon as federal is a way to provide a structured set of tools to better understand it. Such a perspective has a significant

46 Borrowing an expression formulated by Lépine, "A Journey," 47; *contra*, suggesting that the state remains the natural dimension of federalism, see Tierney, *The Federal Contract*, 287–297, esp. 292.

47 On this, see Alessi, *A Global Law*.

48 For instance, recently, see Soeren Keil and Sabine Kropp, eds., *Emerging Federal Structures in the Post-Cold War Era* (Cham: Palgrave Macmillan, 2022).

practical advantage,[49] which also represents a further theoretical justification for its use. Indeed, the main reason why this idea of federalism as a common explanatory ground for various phenomena is supported is its overall usefulness. The rules, the processes and the dynamics of the most structured federal manifestations – the federal states and federal political systems – can help lay the groundwork for the theoretical and practical development of phenomena that share the same core logic. In this sense, once a phenomenon is framed as (to a certain degree) federal, then it becomes possible to apply the "federal (theoretical and practical) toolbox" to understand and explain it, thus creating room for its further refinement and advancement.

Accordingly, federal systems thus act as a "vanilla example" of pluralism and governance at work,[50] i.e. a "simple" model of how a plurality of legal authorities and actors can be organized, how they interact and how their possible conflicts are regulated.

3.3 *Federalism and the Law of Diversity: The Theoretical Potential of Federalism*

This last section aims to propose some preliminary thoughts on the possible use of federalism to frame and explain emergent models for the accommodation of diversity. To this end, some themes related to federal theory and practice will be presented that may contribute to a better understanding of emergent models for the accommodation of diversity, and, among them, governance forms of autonomy.[51]

3.3.1 Negotiation and Asymmetry: A Federal Model for the Law of Diversity

It has been illustrated that the Law of diversity increasingly relies upon instruments based on promoting an active role for diverse groups in the regulation of

49 Francesco Palermo, "Regulating Pluralism: Federalism as Decision-Making and New Challenges for Federal Studies," in *Federalism as Decision-Making: Changes in Structures, Procedures and Policies*, eds. Francesco Palermo and Elisabeth Alber (Leiden-Boston: Brill-Nijhoff, 2015), 499–513.

50 On federalism as a "vanilla example" of managed pluralism, see Erin Ryan, "Federalism as Legal Pluralism," in *The Oxford Handbook of Global Legal Pluralism*, ed. Paul S. Berman (Oxford: Oxford University Press, 2020), e-book version, 491–527.

51 Several indications are drawn from the considerations put forward by Palermo, "Regulating Pluralism," 508–513 and extended in their theoretical scope; on this, see also Topidi's chapter in this volume, which suggested that federalism, as a "strategy for good governance", provides solutions to better accommodate legal pluralism.

diversity, i.e. on their self-management through governance in the framework of a state legal system.

Concerning the organization of complex legal systems, federal theory and practice have illustrated the centrality of negotiation and compromise as founding elements as well as working instruments for the successful operation and evolution of composite state structures like federal systems.

Consequently, drawing from federal studies, one may presume the concept of negotiation and its operation will take an ever more central role in the evolution of the Law of diversity.

Furthermore, the Law of diversity is marked by a great deal of differentiation of legal solutions. Similarly, federal theory has progressively taken into account the evolution of federal structures and acknowledged a trend towards increasing asymmetry. This has, for several authors, always been, albeit to different extents, a feature of federal systems – especially in what are referred to as "holding-together" federal systems.[52]

In this sense, federal studies may be of help in that they provide structured models to regulate the increasing differentiation of legal arrangements while maintaining the unity of the state, and help understand all the concrete issues (like, for instance, the financial aspects related to the management of asymmetric systems) that are at stake when dealing with the creation of differentiated solutions for differentiated claims.

3.3.2 Complex Decision-Making Processes

All the cases studied above determine the addition of new layers of governance that continuously and variously interact with different public entities in very complex settings. Federal theory and the actual functioning of federal systems may contribute to promoting solutions for the improvement of the complex decision-making processes that take place in these settings and analyzing their functionality.

In this sense, the variety of the actors and the manifold dynamics that arise from these developments create a complex and intricate system of multilevel decision-making that may benefit if lessons are drawn from federal studies. The latter may provide inspiration for possible further regulation, or at least

52 Several reasons account for the increasing differentiation in federal organization; on this, see Francesco Palermo and Karl Kössler, *Comparative Federalism: Constitutional Arrangements and Case Law* (Oxford-Portland: Hart Publishing, 2019), 34–66; on asymmetry as a feature of multi-tiered systems, and especially the European Union and multinational systems, see also Michael Keating, "Asymmetrical Government: Multinational States in an Integrating Europe," *Publius* 29, no. 1 (1999): 71–86.

facilitate the understanding of trends. Indeed, as is evident in federal systems, traditional decision-making processes based on democratic institutions are increasingly complemented by the contribution of various types of governmental, administrative, or hybrid bodies. This is also the case with the Law of diversity.

Hence, given that federal theory has traditionally revolved around institutional analysis and intergovernmental cooperation, the rules and mechanisms that have been developed in and for federal systems, aimed at fostering coordination among various authorities, may contribute to identifying dynamics and designing solutions to problematic issues that can arise in the area of diversity accommodation. In this sense, complex "federal-like" settings such as the European Union may provide several models for the regulation of public and private actors' involvement in policymaking, especially from a procedural point of view.[53]

3.3.3 Definition of Areas of Jurisdiction in Complex Policy Areas: Coordination over Division

Some recent publications on the functioning of federal systems have moved their focus to the issue of policy analysis from a legal perspective, studying the numerous actors involved in critical areas of regulation – such as environment, security, immigration and fiscal federalism – and their relationships.[54] Accordingly, they have underscored how the reality of policy-making is far more multifaceted and composite than that provided for by rigid constitutional texts that allocate powers to different levels of government.

In a way, the Law of diversity may be seen as another complex policy area,[55] where, especially as regards the most recent developments and instruments, a vast array of actors is involved in manifold ways. Thus, analysis of the operation of federal systems and their trends, such as the move towards coordination rather than separation of powers – which reached its peak during the recent coronavirus crisis – offers useful insights for the evolution of the Law of diversity and its governance means. Accordingly, it seems that the more

---

53 The area of climate policy may be of particular interest; on this, see Mariachiara Alberton, "Climate Governance and Federalism in the European Union," in *Climate Governance and Federalism: A Forum of Federations Comparative Policy Analysis*, eds. Alan Fenna, Sébastien Jodoin and Joana Setzer (Cambridge: Cambridge University Press, 2023), 128–149.

54 For instance, see Palermo and Kössler, *Comparative Federalism* and Francesco Palermo and Elisabeth Alber, eds., *Federalism as Decision- Making: Changes in Structures, Procedures and Policies* (Leiden- Boston: Brill-Nijhoff, 2015).

55 Francesco Palermo and Jens Woelk, "From Minority Protection to a Law of Diversity? Reflections on the Evolution of Minority Rights," *European Yearbook of Minority Issues* 3 (2003–2004): 7.

complex and broader (also from a strictly territorial standpoint) the area of management, the greater the need for coordination among the numerous actors involved.[56] Consequently, theoretical concepts such as "shared rule" and "subsidiarity", as well their manifold implementations in federal systems, may constitute important points of reference for understanding and developing the Law of diversity.

3.3.4 Conflicts of Jurisdictions: Trends and Tools for Their Resolution

The approaches of federal systems towards possible conflicts of jurisdiction among different authorities and the tools developed for their resolution are another source of interesting insights to explain and possibly further regulate the emergent instruments for the accommodation of diversity.

In this sense, two main issues arise. The first is a trend in federal systems towards the creation of increasing *loci* and mechanisms of dialogue and coordination among different authorities, especially after the coronavirus crisis.[57] The second is the critical role played by the judiciary when the mechanisms of coordination do not work. Both issues may help analyze the recent developments of the Law of diversity: one would expect that the complex systems of governance stemming from its recent evolution would need to foster the creation of stable dialogic and cooperative mechanisms to help the collaborative management of diversity accommodation. And, if they are not implemented, one would expect an increase in jurisdictional conflict.[58]

Bibliography

Agarin, Timofey and Allison McCulloch. "How Power-Sharing Includes and Excludes Non-Dominant Communities: Introduction to the Special Issue." *International Political Science Review* 41, no. 1 (2020): 3–14.

56 In this sense, coordination may not be limited to the boundaries of the state but also imply a strong role for trans-border cooperation (as well as, as seen, international bodies), especially when it comes to the accommodation of diversity.

57 On this, see Nico Steytler, ed., *Comparative Federalism and Covid-19: Combating the Pandemic* (London-New York: Routledge, 2021); Rupak Chattopadhyay et al., eds., *Federalism and the Response to COVID-19* (London-New York: Routledge, 2022).

58 On the possible further increase in jurisdiction conflict, and, more in general, the possible greater role of the judiciary in this area, and the parallel trends in federal systems, see Nicholas Aroney and John Kincaid, eds., *Courts in Federal Countries: Federalists or Unitarists?* (Toronto: University of Toronto Press, 2017); Delaney, Erin F., "The Federal Case for Judicial Review," *Oxford Journal of Legal Studies* 42, no. 3: 733–757.

Alberton, Mariachiara. "Climate Governance and Federalism in the European Union." In *Climate Governance and Federalism: A Forum of Federations Comparative Policy Analysis*, edited by Alan Fenna, Sébastien Jodoin and Joana Setzer, 128–149. Cambridge: Cambridge University Press, 2023.

Alessi, Nicolò P. *A Global Law of Diversity: Evolving Models and Concepts*. London-New York: Routledge, 2025.

Aroney, Nicholas and John Kincaid, eds., *Courts in Federal Countries: Federalists or Unitarists?* Toronto: University of Toronto Press, 2017.

Breton, Raymond. "L'intégration des francophones hors Québec dans des communautés de langue française." *Revue de l'Université d'Ottawa* 55, no. 2 (1985): 77–90.

Breton, Raymond. "Institutional Completeness of Ethnic Communities and the Personal Relations of Immigrants." *American Journal of Sociology* 70, no. 2 (1964): 193–205.

Breton, Raymond. "The Structure of Relationships Between Ethnic Collectivities." In *The Canadian Ethnic Mosaic*, edited by Leo Driedger, 55–73. Toronto: McClelland and Stewart, 1978.

Bourgeois, Daniel. "Administrative Nationalism." *Administration & Society* 39, no. 5 (2007): 631–655.

Bourgeois, Daniel. "Territory, Institutions and National Identity: The Case of Acadians in Greater Moncton, Canada." *Urban Studies* 42, no. 7 (2005): 1123–1138.

Burç, Rosa. "Non-Territorial Autonomy and Gender Equality: The Case of the Autonomous Administration of North and East Syria – Rojava." *Philosophy and Society* 31, no. 3 (2020): 321–340.

Chattopadhyay, Rupak, et al., eds., *Federalism and the Response to COVID-19*. London-New York: Routledge, 2022.

Chouinard, Stéphanie. "Quand le droit linguistique parle de sciences sociales: l'intégration de la notion de completude institutionnelle dans la jurisprudence Canadienne." *Revue de Droit Linguistique* 3 (2016): 60–93.

Chouinard, Stéphanie. "The Rise of Non-territorial Autonomy in Canada: Towards a Doctrine of Institutional Completeness in the Domain of Minority Language Rights." *Ethnopolitics* 13, no. 2 (2014): 141–158.

Coleman, Steve and Éamon Ó Ciosáin. "The Irish Gaeltacht as a Trans-Local Phenomenon." In *Non-Territorial Autonomy and Decentralization: Ethno-Cultural Diversity Governance*, edited by Tove H. Malloy and Levente Salat, 153–164. London-New York: Routledge, 2021.

Davis, Rufus S. *The Federal Principle: A Journey Through Time in Quest of a Meaning*. Berkeley-Los Angeles-London: University of California Press, 1978.

Delaney, Erin F., "The Federal Case for Judicial Review." *Oxford Journal of Legal Studies* 42, no. 3: 733–757.

De Villiers, Bertus. "Community Government for Cultural Minorities: Thinking beyond "Territory" as a Prerequisite for Self-government." *International Journal on Minority and Group Rights* 25, no. 4 (2018): 561–590.

De Villiers, Bertus. "Privatised Autonomy for the Noongar People of Australia: A New Model for Indigenous Self-Government." In *Indigenous, Aboriginal, Fugitive and Ethnic Groups Around the Globe*, edited by Liat Klain-Gabbay, 127–157. London: Intech Open, 2019.

Dubois, Janique and Kelly Saunders. ""Just Do It!": Carving Out a Space for the Métis in Canadian Federalism." *Canadian Journal of Political Science / Revue canadienne de science politique* 46, no. 1 (2013): 187–214.

Dubois, Janique. "Beyond Territory: Revisiting the Normative Justification of Self-Government in Theory and Practice." *The International Indigenous Policy Journal* 2, no. 2 (2011): 5–10.

Dubois, Janique. "The Fransaskois' Journey from Survival to Empowerment through Governance." *Canadian Political Science Review* 11, no. 1 (2017): 37–60.

Elazar, Daniel J. *Exploring Federalism*. Tuscaloosa: The University of Alabama Press, 1987.

Foucher, Pierre. "Autonomie des communautés francophones minoritaires du Canada: le point de vue du droit." *Minorités linguistiques et société / Linguistic Minorities and Society*, no. 1 (2012): 90–114.

Friedrich, Carl J. *Trends of Federalism in Theory and Practice*. London: Pall Mall Press, 1968.

Garcea, Joseph. "First Nations Satellite Reserves: Capacity-Building and Self-Government in Saskatchewan." In *Aboriginal Self-Government in Canada: Current Trends and Issues*, edited by Yale D. Belanger, 240–259. Saskatoon: Purich Publishing, 2008.

Gaudreault-DesBiens, Jean-F. and Fabien Gélinas. "Opening New Perspectives on Federalism." In *Le fédéralisme dans tous ses états: governance, identité et méthodologie – The States and Moods of Federalism: Governance, Identity and Methodology*, edited by Jean-F. Gaudreault-DesBiens and Fabien Gélinas, 51–96. Cowansville-Bruxelles: Éditions Yvon Blais-Bruylant, 2005.

Geldenhuys, Deon. "Autonomy Initiatives of the Afrikaner Community in South Africa." In *Non-Territorial Autonomy and Decentralization: Ethno-Cultural Diversity Governance*, edited by Tove H. Malloy and Levente Salat, 91–114. London-New York: Routledge, 2021.

Gunes, Cengiz. "Accommodating Kurdish National Demands in Turkey." In *The Challenge of Non-Territorial Autonomy: Theory and Practice*, edited by Ephraim Nimni, Alexander Osipov and David J. Smith, 71–84. Bern: Peter Lang, 2013.

Hooghe, Liesbet and Gary Marks. *Community, Scale, and Regional Governance: A Post-Functionalist Theory of Governance*. Oxford: Oxford University Press, 2016.

Keating, Michael. "Asymmetrical Government: Multinational States in an Integrating Europe." *Publius* 29, no. 1 (1999): 71–86.

Keil, Soeren and Sabine Kropp, eds., *Emerging Federal Structures in the Post-Cold War Era*. Cham: Palgrave Macmillan, 2022.

Léger, Rémi. "Non-territorial Autonomy in Canada: Reply to Chouinard." *Ethnopolitics* 13, no. 4 (2014): 418–427.

Lépine, Frédéric. "A Journey through the History of Federalism: Is Multilevel Governance a Form of Federalism?" *L'Europe en formation* 363, no. 1 (2012): 21–62.

Lépine, Frédéric. "Federalism: Essence, Values and Ideologies." In *Understanding Federalism and Federation*, edited by Alain-G. Gagnon, Soeren Keil and Sean Mueller, 31–48. Farnham-Burlington: Ashgate, 2015.

Malloy, Tove H. and Levente Salat, eds., *Non-Territorial Autonomy and Decentralization: Ethno-Cultural Diversity Governance*. London-New York: Routledge, 2021.

Malloy, Tove H. "Functional Non-Territorial Autonomy in Denmark and Germany." In *Managing Diversity through Non-Territorial Autonomy: Assessing Advantages, Deficiencies and Risks*, edited by Tove H. Malloy, Alexander Osipov and Balázs Vizi, 182–204. Oxford: Oxford University Press, 2015.

Malloy, Tove H. "Non-Territorial Autonomy: Traditional and Alternative Practices." In *Effective Participation of National Minorities and Conflict Prevention*, edited by William Romans, Iryna Ulasiuk and Anton Petrenko Thomsen, 105–122. Leiden-Boston: Brill-Nijhoff, 2020.

Menski, Werner. "Beyond Europe." In *Comparative Law: A Handbook*, edited by Örücü, Esin and Nelken, David, 189–216. Oxford-Portland: Hart, 2007.

Messarra, Antoine. "Principe de territorialité et principe de personnalité en fédéralisme comparé: le cas du Liban et perspectives actuelles pour la gestion du pluralism." In *Le fédéralisme dans tous ses états: governance, identité et méthodologie – The States and Moods of Federalism: Governance, Identity and Methodology*, edited by Jean-F. Gaudreault-DesBiens and Fabien Gélinas, 227–260. Cowansville-Bruxelles: Éditions Yvon Blais-Bruylant, 2005.

Murphy, Michael. "Relational Self-Determination and Federal Reform." In *Canada: The State of the Federation 2003: Reconfiguring Aboriginal-State Relations*, edited by Micheal Murphy, 3–35. Montréal: McGill-Queen's University Press, 2005.

Palermo, Francesco and Jens Woelk. "From Minority Protection to a Law of Diversity? Reflections on the Evolution of Minority Rights." *European Yearbook of Minority Issues* 3 (2003–2004): 5–13.

Palermo, Francesco and Karl Kössler. *Comparative Federalism: Constitutional Arrangements and Case Law*. Oxford-Portland: Hart Publishing, 2019.

Palermo, Francesco. "Implementation and Amendment of the Autonomy Statute." In *Tolerance through Law: Self Governance and Group Rights in South Tyrol*, eds. Jens

Woelk, Joseph Marko and Francesco Palermo, 143–159. Leiden-Boston: Martinus Nijhoff, 2008.

Palermo, Francesco. "Owned or Shared? Territorial Autonomy in the Minority Discourse." In *Minority Accommodation through Territorial and Non-Territorial Autonomy*, edited by Tove H. Malloy and Francesco Palermo, 13–32. Oxford: Oxford University Press, 2015.

Palermo, Francesco. "Regulating Pluralism: Federalism as Decision-Making and New Challenges for Federal Studies." In *Federalism as Decision-Making: Changes in Structures, Procedures and Policies*, edited by Francesco Palermo and Elisabeth Alber, 499–513. Leiden-Boston: Brill-Nijhoff, 2015.

Peters, Evelyn. "Urban Reserves." Research paper for the National Centre for first Nations Governance, August 2007, available at the following link: https://fngovernance.org/wp-content/uploads/2020/09/e_peters.pdf, 3.

Piacentini, Arianna. "'Others' and Consociational Democracy: Citizens, Civil Society, and Politics in South Tyrol and Bosnia Herzegovina." Project Report. Eurac Research-Provincia Autonoma di Bolzano, Bolzano/*Bozen*, 2021.

Poirier, Johanne. "Autonomie politique et minorités francophones du Canada: réflexions sur un angle mort de la typologie classique de Will Kymlicka." *Minorités linguistiques et société / Linguistic Minorities and Society*, no. 1 (2012): 66–89.

Popelier, Patricia. *Dynamic Federalism: A New Theory for Cohesion and Regional Autonomy*. London-New York: Routledge, 2021.

Ryan, Erin. "Federalism as Legal Pluralism." In *The Oxford Handbook of Global Legal Pluralism*, edited by Paul S. Berman, 491–527. E-book version, Oxford: Oxford University Press, 2020.

Salaymeh, Lena and Ralf Michaels. "Decolonial Comparative Law: A Conceptual Beginning." *Max Planck Institute for Comparative and International Private Law Research Paper Series* 22, no. 1 (2022): 166–188.

Steytler, Nico, ed., *Comparative Federalism and Covid-19: Combating the Pandemic*. London-New York: Routledge, 2021.

Suksi, Markku. "Personal Autonomy as Institutional Form: Focus on Europe Against the Background of Article 27 of the ICCPR." *International Journal on Minority and Group Rights* 15, no. 2–3 (2008): 157–178.

Sørensen, Eva and Jacob Torfing, eds., *Theories of Democratic Network Governance*. Basingstoke-New York: Palgrave Macmillan, 2007.

Tierney, Stephen. *The Federal Contract: A Constitutional Theory of Federalism*. Oxford: Oxford University Press, 2022.

Topidi, Kyriaki. "Faith Education in Britain." In *Non-Territorial Autonomy and Decentralization: Ethno-Cultural Diversity Governance*, edited by Tove H. Malloy and Levente Salat, 215–239. London-New York: Routledge, 2021.

Weller, Marc and Stefan Wolff. *Autonomy, Self-Governance and Conflict Resolution: Innovative Approaches to Institutional Design in Divided Societies.* London-New York: Routledge, 2005.

Wilson, Gary N., Christopher Alcantara and Thierry Rodon. *Nested Federalism and Inuit Governance in the Canadian Arctic.* Vancouver: University of British Columbia Press, 2020.

PART 2

Federalism and Participatory Democracy

CHAPTER 4

Federalism and Participatory Democracy: A Manifold Balancing Act

Jared Sonnicksen

1 Introduction

Federalism and territorial (re-)scaling, alongside democracy and democratization with participatory democracy, are critical current issues in light of changing societies and patterns of governance. Such changes give renewed impetus to scholarly and practical considerations for adapting federal and democratic institutions and practices. It is a tall order to undertake an exploration of federalism and participatory democracy – this no less so when considering them in connection with diversity and pluralism, and their potential accommodation in complex societies or polities. Taken together, the respective features and principles, and their potential linkages, may comprise a seemingly overwhelming territory of complexity. However, this chapter does not embark on that endeavor without navigational assistance. It aims instead to provide for a possible orientation and prompt further reflection. Territory is here a particularly fitting term for multiple reasons as well. Its organization lies at the heart of principles and many institutions and practices of federalism, democracy and constitutions, as well as the rule of law in and the organization of modern states and polities[1] – yet these principles are not intractably bound to particular territories or regional jurisdictions, but may also cut across them in variable ways, including federalism and federative forms of (self-)governance.[2] Indeed, federalism, democracy, law and diversity (its accommodation in particular) may each be conceived on their own and in distinction. Yet there may also

1 Cf. recent on theory of territory, relationship between people and polity, borders among others, e.g. Jenna Bednar, "Federalism Theory: The Boundary Problem, Robustness and Dynamics," in *A Research Agenda for Federalism Studies*, ed. John Kincaid (Cheltenham: Edward Elgar, 2019), 27–38; John Gerring and Wouter Veenendaal, *Population and Politics: The Impact of Scale* (Cambridge: Cambridge University Press, 2020); Margaret Moore, *A Political Theory of Territory* (Oxford: Oxford University Press, 2015).

2 See especially the introduction by Alessi and Trettel as well as the chapters by Alessi, Kössler and Malloy in this volume.

be deep foundational linkages connecting them below the surface. Moreover, they surely become interlinked in political practice.

Federalism and democracy represent particular principles of political organization, for one, and distinct dimensions of government each based on division of powers, for another. Federalism and democracy encompass multiple meanings and link with various ideas and institutional arrangements. Each is thus complex on its own, and their complexity grows when combined into one polity. Against this backdrop, this contribution explores the relationships and linkages between federalism and democracy. It draws on recent comparative federalism research that has taken a more differentiated view of the relationship between federalism and democracy as one of complexity, i.e. not just mutual compatibility, but rather also tensions, and this not least in diverse societies.[3] Furthermore, the chapter sets a particular focus on participatory democracy. To this end, it first revisits in compact fashion federalism and democracy as organizational principles and arrangements of division of powers. Secondly, it provides an overview of the linkages between federalism and democracy and their various potentials for tensions. They arise on account of different ideational, structural and functional logics, though also because of commonalities in shared principles, but that are grounded in different points of reference. Thirdly, an outline is proposed regarding the complex relationship between federalism and participatory democracy. This requires examining the ideational dimension and several facets of the institutional dimension regarding structural, functional and procedural arrangements. Accordingly, a variety of participatory democratic channels and the potential for their implementation in federal or multilevel systems is surveyed, which may prove particularly conducive to the establishment and expansion of participatory democracy. Finally, the chapter reflects on this relationship anew in line with the main themes of the edited volume. It considers how to conceptualize the relationship between federalism and participatory democracy not only as one

3 Arthur Benz, *Föderale Demokratie: Regieren im Spannungsfeld zwischen Interdependenz und Autonomie* (Baden-Baden: Nomos, 2020); Arthur Benz and Jared Sonnicksen, eds., *Federal Democracies at Work. Varieties of Complex Government* (Toronto: University of Toronto Press, 2021); Arthur Benz and Jared Sonnicksen, "Patterns of Federal Democracy: Tensions, Friction, or Balance between two Government Dimensions," *European Political Science Review* 9, no. 1 (2017): 3–25; Cristina Fraenkel-Haeberle et al., eds., *Citizen Participation in Multi-Level Democracies*, eds. (Leiden-Boston: Brill-Nijhoff, 2015); Alain-G. Gagnon, *The Legitimacy Clash: Challenges to Democracy in Multinational States* (Toronto: University of Toronto Press, 2023); Alain-G. Gagnon, "Multinational Federalism: Challenges, Shortcomings and Promises," *Regional & Federal Studies* 31, no. 1 (2021): 99–114.

of complexity, but also as balancing acts of accommodating pluralism and diversity along with self and shared rule in complex polities.

2 Delineating Federalism and Democracy

Federalism and other forms of non-unitary division of powers have long been viewed as fundamentally conducive to democracy. Many features of federalism support the premise of an inherently democratic quality to federalism, rendering it quite plausible to presuppose a mutual compatibility between federalism and democracy. For one, they are both grounded in norms and principles of not only liberty and equality, but also self-government. For another, federalism thus seemingly benefits democracy, and vice-versa democracy would be beneficial to federalism. They multiply the spaces and places for institutionalizing and continuously actualizing those underlying norms and principles, i.e. liberty, equality, and self-government, among others. The potential advantages of federalism and democracy span across a wide range: from providing room for maneuver for democratic policy experimentalism, to engendering competition for good policies or citizens who are endowed with rights to participate in (self-)government or defect (e.g. 'voting by feet') to other jurisdictions; from imbuing the polity on the whole with multiple layers of checks, balances and safeguards against government encroachment on liberties and rights, to guaranteeing protections for and even empowering minorities.[4] Regarding the latter, federalism is also commonly purported to exhibit the comparative advantage of an integral capacity to foster and adapt to diversity and assorted minority groups.[5] Moreover, federalism has been often deemed the most democratic way of facilitating a fair accommodation of multiple identities.[6] This potential property attributed to federal arrangements bears, of course, fundamental relevance in the context of diversity and pluralism. Federalism has

4 See e.g. comprehensive Michael Burgess and Alain-G. Gagnon, eds., *Federal Democracies* (London-New York: Routledge, 2010). On the wider democratic-theoretical implications of 'exit', see e.g. Mark E. Warren, "Voting with Your Feet: Exit-based Empowerment in Democratic Theory," *American Political Science Review* 105, no. 4 (2011): 683–701.

5 Cf. e.g. Will Kymlicka, *Politics in the Vernacular: Nationalism, Multiculturalism, and Citizenship* (Oxford: Oxford University Press, 2001); Luis Moreno, César Colino and John Kincaid, eds., *Diversity and Unity in Federal Countries* (Montreal: McGill-Queen's University Press, 2010); see also the chapters by Kössler and by Malloy in this volume.

6 Helder De Schutter, "Federalism as Fairness," *Journal of Political Philosophy* 19, no. 2 (2011): 167–189.

even been treated in the classic typology of patterns of democracy by Lijphart[7] as a constitutive feature of the consensus-democratic type – i.e. as opposed to majoritarian, power-concentrating type – given its in-built propensity to power-sharing. This feature may in turn underscore the appropriateness of adopting federalism in diverse or divided societies.

Federalism and democracy have a great deal in common. Beyond a grounding in principles of freedom, equality and self-determination, they both have deep developmental links with constitutions, and with that, separation of powers, but also constituency and representation.[8] However, the features of *constitutionalism* and *division of powers*, as well as *constituencies* and the presupposition of their *equality* with need for effective *representation*, have different points of reference (see also Figure 4.1 below).[9] This warrants a brief, albeit schematic, re-summary of federalism and democracy. In democracy and democratic government, the constitutional compact emanates from a people, conceived as a *demos* presupposed to enjoy popular sovereignty, and thus a collective right to self-determination. In modern constitutions moreover (i.e. as opposed to antiquity, or the Western 'Medieval' times etc.), the division of powers in popular government, which is predominantly representative-democratic government, runs chiefly between branches of government. Here, the popularly elected legislative and executive ones have pivotal democratic significance. Accordingly, the constituents, who in constitutional terms also comprise a collective *pouvoir constituant*, are citizens or the citizenry. Democratic equality refers foremost to their equal rights and value, which is not only, but prominently embodied in the electoral rules of 'one person, one vote' (of equal value; i.e. counting the same). The institutions and procedures of political representation are, moreover, principally based on population as well as people as individuals or diverse groups. The social contract of federalism, on the other hand, comprises a *foedus*, a compact or "covenant"[10] among communities. In modern federal systems, they have (ideal-)typically either aggregated or 'come together' as sovereign units, or have disaggregated from a

7 Arend Lijphart, *Patterns of Democracy: Government Forms and Performance in Thirty-Six Countries* (New Haven: Yale University Press, 1999).

8 Jared Sonnicksen, "Federalism and Democracy," in *Encyclopedia of Contemporary Constitutionalism*, eds. Javier Cremades and Cristina Hermida (Cham: Springer, 2022a), 1–17, https://doi.org/10.1007/978-3-319-31739-7_207-1.

9 See e.g. overviews in Sonnicksen "Federalism and Democracy," and Jared Sonnicksen, *Tensions of American Federal Democracy: Fragmentation of the State* (London-New York: Routledge, 2022), 48–50.

10 Daniel J. Elazar, "The Political Theory of Covenant: Biblical Origins and Modern Developments," *Publius* 10, no. 4 (1980): 3–30.

FIGURE 4.1 Democratic and federal principal features and points of reference

Features	Democracy	Federalism
Constitution	Demos	Foedus
Division of powers	Branches of government	Levels of government
Constituency	Citizens	Constituent units (e.g. states, regions, or other communities)
Equality		
Representation	Population-, group-based	Territory/region/community-based

SOURCE: OWN DEPICTION

preceding unitary polity into a federal union so as to 'hold together'[11] – though there are also many other forms, shades and constellations of federal unions, not to mention non- or cross-territorial based ones. Depicted in similar vein for federalism, the division of powers runs chiefly between governmental levels: a federal, national or otherwise superordinate one, and the constituent unit ones. The latter, irrespective of denomination (e.g. autonomous regions, cantons, Länder, provinces, or states), represent the *pouvoirs constituants*, i.e. in chiefly territorial based federal systems at least. They hold (ideal-)typically equal partial sovereignty or constituent power – though asymmetric allocations of authority are both theoretically conceivable and existent in practice –, which is also institutionalized in their respective governmental level, while political representation is accordingly foremost territorially, regionally or community based.

In line with the different points of reference, federal and democratic governments involve different institutions, institutional arrangements and procedures.

Democratic governments, again in modern polities, are by and large constituted as representative democracies. Yet, the principle of popular government based on citizen equality, voting rights, and other forms of co-determination, do not implicate one specific institutional set-up. Democratic theory and practice reveal a wide variety of democratic government arrangements. They

11 Alfred C. Stepan, "Federalism and Democracy: Beyond the U.S. Model," *Journal of Democracy* 10, no. 4 (1999): 19–34.

include (see also Figure 4.2 below) the constitutional *form of government* and its division of powers among government branches, which may be rather prone toward separation of powers or a more fluid, fused relationship. In the former, executive and legislative branches are elected separately and enjoy fixed terms of office as typified by presidential systems – e.g. USA, but also many Central and South American countries –; while in the latter case, the executive emanates from the legislative (i.e. parliament) and remains dependent on its confidence. In the parliamentary case, the executive can be removed prematurely through votes of no confidence, though it often also has power to dissolve parliament early.[12] Moreover, a further series of *structural* features determines the rules and organization of democratic government, most notably (though not exhaustively) the electoral system, other electoral or popular voting procedures (e.g. referenda, initiatives), the party system, and the system of interest mediation. Each of them may correspond with various forms or sub-types. While by no means solely deterministic, these structural-institutional features have fundamental impact on the functional logic and operation of democratic governance: for instance, whether democratic governance conforms to (simple) majoritarian or consensus patterns,[13] whether the dynamics of decision making conform to government-versus-opposition dualism or more variable coalitions, among others.

This outline is limited in referring to democracy as form of government in contemporary political systems and not the spectrum of democracy in theory. Capturing the latter would require a much more multifaceted review of democracy from, for example, further normative perspectives and even as a way of life. Instead, this depiction focused first on representative institutions. However, while participation inheres to any democratic government – elections being part and parcel of representative democracy, and thus a pivotal avenue of citizen participation –, participatory democracy extends and multiplies the channels and mechanisms of participation (which is explored further below and in relation to federalism). To be sure, democratic government is organized not only in a polity. It is also, fundamentally, constituted with a

12 Most European countries and majority of other modern democracies including federal ones like Australia, Austria, Belgium, Canada, Germany, India and Spain; see e.g. typology by Matthew Søberg Shugart and John M. Carey, *Presidents and Assemblies: Constitutional Design and Electoral Dynamics* (New York: Cambridge University Press, 1992); cf. also for comprehensive review by Mahir Tokatlı, *Auf dem Weg zum ‚Präsidialsystem alla Turca'? Eine Analyse unterschiedlicher Regierungsformen in der Türkei seit 1921* (Baden-Baden: Nomos, 2020), 61–118.

13 Lijphart, *Patterns of Democracy*.

FIGURE 4.2 Democratic-government arrangements

Form of government	Executive-legislative relationship	*Separation of powers (separate elections)* e.g. presidential system *Fusion of powers (confidence relationship)* e.g. parliamentary system
Structures of politics	Electoral system	e.g. plurality / majority v. proportional
	Further voting	e.g. direct democracy and plebiscites;
	Party system	e.g. two v. multiparty; moderate v. polarized
	Interest mediation	e.g. pluarlist v. corporatist, lobbying
Logics of operation	Majoritarianism	e.g. competition, "winner takes all", "minimum-winning" coalitions
	Consensus	e.g. concordance / 'Proporz'; consociational; negotiation; concertation

SOURCE: OWN DEPICTION

respective jurisdiction linking people or *demos* to governmental institutions elected by and (supposed to be) responsible and accountable to the people. This polity with constitutive democratic jurisdiction linking government and citizenry becomes even more multidimensional in a federal system.

Federalism likewise encompasses various forms, types and ideas[14] (see also Figure 4.3 below), and entail an own kind of division of powers. A federal system is most typically conceived as an organization of the state or polity with a territorial-based allocation of powers that is primarily *vertical*, i.e. between levels of government. However, even when the constituent units are on equal footing, the federal *division of power* does not prescribe one particular arrangement. From the outset, the constitution may set forth a stricter separation of powers and/or functions between levels as typified in dual federal systems, or variable arrangements spanning from flexible to compulsory cooperation, sharing of responsibilities or joint-decision making (i.e. common tasks that require cross-level decision making and/or implementation). The diversity of

14 See e.g. comprehensive review by Ronald L. Watts, "Federalism, Federal Political Systems, and Federations," *Annual Review of Political Science* 1, no. 1 (1998): 117–137.

formal federal arrangements expands in light of models such as asymmetric federalism. For instance, not all regions or constituent units may enjoy the same scope of powers, authority, autonomy, etc. The division of powers can apply to specific functions (e.g. a division of labor in legislating vs. implementation, revenue raising vs. expenditure) or rather groups (e.g. linguistic, religious, ethnic, various minorities or indigenous population), which may or may not be territorially concentrated, while federal governance may also be configured in non-territorial terms.[15]

The relationship between government levels may change over time. This also points toward the relevance of an elemental feature of federalism, namely *intergovernmental relations*. Their institutions and practices may correspond to the formal structural and constitutional division of powers. Again, they may be more prone to separation and therefore possibly competition or, instead, favor unilateralism between levels of government and among constituent units, or rather lean more toward cooperation. Shifts in practice occur such as when stricter dualistic systems develop arenas and fora for voluntary cooperation and coordination of cross-jurisdictional political tasks and problems. Yet, intergovernmental relations serve not only effectiveness of policy making, but also democratic ends.[16] They can contribute to managing the 'balancing act' between upholding self-rule and autonomy and to coping with interdependencies that arise from innumerable challenges of modern government and societies.[17] In addition, federal systems exhibit different *logics of operation*. They may coincide, in variable fashions and extents, with the institutional arrangements of separation or sharing between government levels as well as among constituent units and communities.

Democratic and federal arrangements reveal a spectrum of variety in their respective institutional designs as well as structural and functional propensities. This applies already with a selective view to conventional representative democratic government and to federalism as a system. Each may tend toward separation of powers with more or less 'checks and balances'; toward variable forms of power sharing; or different patterns and intensities of cooperation, interlinkage and interaction. They share common features embedded in

---

15 See e.g. César Colino, "Varieties of Federalism and Propensities for Change," in *Federal Dynamics: Continuity, Change, and the Varieties of Federalism*, eds. Arthur Benz and Jorg Broschek (Oxford: Oxford University Press, 2013), 48–69; see also again chapters by Alessi, Malloy, and Kössler in this volume.

16 Samuel Beer, "Federalism, Nationalism, and Democracy in America," *American Political Science Review* 72, no. 1 (1978): 9–21.

17 Arthur Benz, *Föderale Demokratie*.

FIGURE 4.3 Federal-system arrangements

Division of powers	between levels of government	strict separation of powers (e.g. dualistic) sharing of powers (e.g. cooperative) symmetric or asymmetric based on e.g. territory, function, group, sector
Intergovernmental relations	vertical relations	e.g. separated jurisdictions and/or tasks vs. cross-level cooperation and coordination; informal or institutionalized relations
	horizontal relations	e.g. separated jurisdictions and/or autonomy vs. Interstate/-regional cooperation and/ or joint tasks; informal or institutionalized relations
Logics of operation	self-rule	e.g. distinction-emphasis, competition, unilateralism
	shared rule	e.g. coordination/cooperation-emphasis, multilateralism

SOURCE: OWN DEPICTION

constitutionalism, the modern state, notions of equality, constituency, and collective self-government, among others. Yet, their points of reference differ: the constituent people, *demos* or citizenry, on the one hand, and the constituent *places*, territorial units or otherwise demarcated communities, for another. What is more, federalism comprises manifold jurisdictions of autonomy or self-rule. It can thus multiply democratic *governments* and hence linkages with *demoi* endowed with rights and eligibility of participation. However, this does not implicate a necessary compatibility or necessarily produce compounded democratization. In short, more federalism does not equate to more democracy per se. However, it *can* enable and even foster democratic government, not least in diverse societies. Federalism may invite a particularly suitable framework for the institutionalization of participatory democracy beyond regular elections.[18] Democratic government and federalism create a complex and multidimensional relationship when combined. This warrants on the other hand examining the linkages and potential tensions underlying this relationship.

18 See also the chapter by Trettel in this volume.

3 The Linkages, Tensions and Complexity between Federalism and Democracy

Federalism and democracy each have a long history reaching back millennia into the past. They have changed tremendously, moreover, with the evolution of modern states, constitutionalism and governance. Further transformations in the complexity of society as well as the extent and diversity of belongingness have prompted federal and democratic changes that help integrate pluralism. Institutions and practices include meanwhile core features such as mass political parties and interest group mediation in democracy, or bicameralism and cross-level intergovernmental relations in federalism. Hence, federalism and democracy are much more diverse in their respective variants than their historical predecessors. Earlier modern thinkers such as Montesquieu or the U.S. *Federalists* supposed an inherent or 'natural' congruence between federalism and democracy. Their ideas are influential to this day. However, such premises were derived from different conditions and a much more limited scale and range of government, state capacity, and even the demos itself.

Federalism and democracy can and have been able to exist with and without the other. Whether democracy is better in a federal system is an unresolved question in philosophy, social science and political science.[19] Moreover, having a federal system does not automatically qualify a democracy as a specific variant, like a 'consensus democracy', as the majoritarian democracies of Canada, the U.S. or India demonstrate. Empirically there are more non-federal than federal democracies to be found – though in a globalized world, and within the EU of a 'Europeanized' union, they often find themselves embedded in integrated and intersected multilevel systems. Conversely, from a normative standpoint, federalism, and arguably any political system for that matter, is preferable when it is democratic. Historical experience and current practices attest to a desirability of democratic federalism too. If anything, this holds true since non-democratic federations, while constituting an arrangement of divided authority, strictly limit the scope of eligible participation in self- or co-government and fail to protect citizens' rights and liberties. All the same, with a focus on federalism *and* democracy, it remains necessary to capture the complex relationship, with manifold interconnections but also potential tensions and challenges.

19 Cf. e.g. John Gerring, Strom C. Thacker and Carola Moreno, "Centripetal Democratic Governance: A Theory and Global Inquiry," *American Political Science Review* 99, no. 4 (2005): 567–581.

A federal democracy with its multiple levels of government and democratic jurisdictions and/or other demarcated communities offers additional constitutional provisions of rights and protections against their violation, and thus inversely safeguards liberty vis-à-vis the state, or the states. Theoretically, this arrangement offers checks and balances for limited government, as well as constructive opportunities for 'voice' and 'vote' in, but also 'exit' from and 'switch' to, multiple jurisdictions.[20] The actual exercise of these powers by the citizenry or *demoi* – as well as their anticipation (e.g. the threat of exit, the anticipation of elections, the threat of vetoes) – engender and incentivize processes and dynamics of representation and responsiveness. The constitution of a federal democracy firmly, though not unalterably, allocates rights, responsibilities and restrictions across multiple government branches and levels. It empowers, endows and enables both constituent units (or communities) and citizen constituents to collective self-government(s). The potential mutual advantages may be enjoyed irrespective of the composition of the society. They would be beneficial for a rather homogenous demos. However, they take on particular relevance, and even necessity, for multinational, heterogeneous and diverse plural societies as well as affected minorities. Otherwise, regular majoritarian democratic rules and institutions without federalism could lead or contribute to recurring overruling, marginalization, and other detrimental effects.

At the same time, as the previous section elaborated, federalism and democracy differ with regard to their respective institutions and structures, while many of their fairly common or analogous principles differ in their points of reference. This may lead to tensions, contradictions, and even dilemmas. As such, they cannot be solved per se, but they can be coped with.[21] From a theoretical standpoint, the additional levels and communities of government in federalism could be construed as multiplying spaces and channels for participation and protection of liberty. Yet this also suggests multiplication of governmental institutions and powers, and thus potentials for rule, coercion, taxation and so forth that citizens are subject to. Historical cases and current federal autocracies show that federal systems cannot only be undemocratic, but may also provide institutional structures and constitutional rules that wind up serving the continuation of sub-national authoritarianism.[22] This warrants

---

20 See e.g. Jacob T. Levy, "Federalism, Liberalism, and the Separation of Loyalties," *American Political Science Review* 101, no. 3 (2007): 459–477; Wallace E. Oates, "An Essay on Fiscal Federalism," *Journal of Economic Literature* 37, no. 3 (1999): 1120–1149.

21 Arthur Benz and Jared Sonnicksen, "Patterns of Federal Democracy," 3–25.

22 Edward L. Gibson, *Boundary Control: Subnational Authoritarianism in Federal Democracies* (Cambridge: Cambridge University Press, 2013); see also the chapter by Kössler in this volume.

caution against attributing to federalism a built-in democratic-promoting nature or character, at least wholesale. However this does not permit the inverse conclusion that federalism hinders democracy either. Nor is the potential for normative transfer of federalism theories and ideas to democratic government diminished. Nevertheless, potentials for institutional, structural and functional inconsistencies and mismatches remain.

The linkage of territory with the political in general is multifaceted. Federalism has conventionally been an organization of the state or polity into levels of government and constituent units. Though again, territory is constitutive for any modern state and democratic government, while – as several chapters in this volume address – federalism is by no means limited to a territorial-unit basis. Federal territorial and jurisdictional architecture – or otherwise configured federative communities – bring along multiple spaces and places of self-government. Yet, this also implicates necessities of coordination and challenges to politics, e.g. in processes like elections, interest mediation, and representation in line with the multiple levels of the polity.[23] Moreover, in the context of adapting to pluralism, the allotment of autonomous territory may be a suitable measure to serve minority protection and accommodate diversity, but this is an ambivalent issue for multiple reasons.[24] There may be non-territorially concentrated minorities or plural groups, while notions of pluralism as well as affected or defined groups may change incongruently with constitutionally delineated units. The diversity warranting accommodation may not necessarily match with certain territorial boundaries: e.g. a specific significant minority that is dispersed across the polity, or new autonomy-aspiring groups may have emerged elsewhere or increased in another jurisdiction. Subsequent re-apportionments, re-scaling or redistributions may pose a challenge to a federal democracy since the rules for amending the constitution typically involve high super-majoritarian thresholds of consent.[25]

23 For overview, see e.g. Klaus Detterbeck and Eve Hepburn, eds., *Handbook of Territorial Politics* (Cheltenham: Edward Elgar, 2018).

24 Francesco Palermo, "Owned or Shared? Territorial Autonomy in theMinority Discourse," in *Minority Accommodation throughTerritorial and Non-territorial Autonomy*, eds. Tove H. Malloy and Francesco Palermo (Oxford: Oxford University Press, 2015), 13–32.

25 Arthur Benz, *Constitutional Policy in Multilevel Government: The Art of Keeping the Balance* (Oxford: Oxford University Press, 2016); Richard Simeon, "Constitutional Design and Change in Federal Systems: Issues and Questions," *Publius* 39, no. 2 (2009): 241–261.

Separation of powers and the division of authority is characteristic of both democracy and federalism. However, neither subsumes the other. They are distinct and have different points of reference (like with the principle of equality) for different kinds of structural and functional arrangements. In addition to presupposing popular sovereignty in the demos, democratic government divides power between branches of government on one level. Conversely, federalism entails the division of powers between governments at different levels, though also among the constituent-unit ones and, as case may be, other communities. While simplified, this outline provides for orientation. However, these division-of-power models actually interact and can even blur upon closer inspection, thus becoming difficult to distinguish. As one example, the second chamber of a legislature at the federal level of government is often understood as a typically federal feature. It allows for representation and participation of lower-level governments, whether the representatives are popularly elected, appointed or otherwise delegated. However, bicameralism is immediately relevant to the division of powers at one level of government, namely the federal level, and thus impacts *its own* democratic government.

In terms of representation, the combination of federalism and democracy generates "compounded" principles and modes of democratic and federal representation[26] of constituent people and communities. Federal representation and democratic representation become entangled or interspersed. A democratic federal system encompasses numbers and types of veto 'players'.[27] This has extensive ramifications for political decision making and propensities for policy change – from competitive to cooperative, from negotiating, collaborating and bargaining to defections and blockades. Furthermore, federalism and democracy combine institutions that follow different and often "rival institutional logics"[28] in government. Gerhard Lehmbruch conceptualized one type of incongruity of institutional rules and arrangements conducive to frictions as a "rupture" or collision between the "tectonic plates" of competitive government-versus-opposition party politics of parliamentary government, on one hand, and the intergovernmental coordination and negotiation logics of

26 Thomas D. Lancaster, "Complex Self-identification and Compounded Representation in Federal Systems," *West European Politics* 22, no. 2 (1999): 59–89.

27 George Tsebelis, "Decision Making in Political Systems: Veto Players in Presidentialism, Parliamentarism, Multicameralism and Multipartyism," *British Journal of Political Science* 25, no. 3 (1995): 289–325.

28 Campbell Sharman, "Parliamentary Federations and Limited Government: Constitutional Design and Redesign in Australia and Canada," *Journal of Theoretical Politics* 2, no. 2 (1990): 205–230.

cooperative federalism, on the other.[29] The rules of democratic government induce a particular logic of politics linked with "responsible government" between executive and party- or coalition majority in parliament. Yet, they can contravene the federal logic of politics when partisan dualism permeates into decisions on policies requiring formal consent or effective coordination by governments representing constituent units. Nevertheless, this friction of democratic-party politics in federal governance is not merely an interference or disturbance. It is likewise expression of the compounded principles and modes of representation in federal democracy. Put simply, federalism affects and changes how democratic government works and vice-versa.[30] The cross-level organization of parties – or other political and civil societal actors – may prove in many cases just as conducive to absorbing tensions, aggregating, channeling and negotiating differences and thus accommodating or ameliorating divides that would otherwise prove too difficult to bridge.[31]

Interest group and association representation as part of democratic governance is also affected by federalism. The federal system opens up and fosters multiple channels of inclusion and diversified participation for interest group mediation. There are comparatively more opportunities for gaining access to or being consulted by democratic actors and institutions. This bears relevance for intergovernmental relations in general. Intergovernmental relations may complicate the attribution of responsibility, e.g. when actors from different levels negotiate and reach compromises in multi-level settings. However, they may also be conceived as furthering democratic governance overall.[32] While there is a preponderance of executive actors in these arenas – as implied by *intergovernmental* –, they remain accountable to legislatures and citizens. Intergovernmental relations also may create additional arenas and processes for further types of civil society actors and interest groups to enter into consultation and even cooperation. On the whole, the development and dynamics of

---

29 Gerhard Lehmbruch, *Parteienwettbewerb im Bundesstaat. Regelsysteme und Spannungslagen im politischen System der Bundesrepublik Deutschland*, (3rd ed., Wiesbaden: Westdeutscher Verlag, 2000).

30 These tensions are not limited to federal systems with parliamentary government, as the politically polarized U.S. case – a separation-of-powers presidential government with dual federalism – shows; see e.g. Sonnicksen, *Tensions of American Federal Democracy*.

31 See e.g. Jared Sonnicksen, "Konträr oder konstruktiv? Zur produktiven Widersprüchlichkeit zwischen Föderalismus und parlamentarischer Demokratie," *Zeitschrift für Parlamentsfragen* 55, no. 1 (2024): 93–108.

32 Thomas O. Hueglin, "Federalism and Democracy: A Critical Reassessment," in *The Global Promise of Federalism*, eds. Grace Skogstad, David Cameron, Martin Papillon, and Keith Banting (Toronto: University of Toronto Press, 2013), 17–42.

a democratic federal system can affect both democratic governance and federalism in practice. These manifold dynamics stem from the combination of differently configured government dimensions but also their logics of politics, which may evolve through mutual influence.

Veritable frictions can emerge between the two institutional arrangements due to 'rival' logics and contradictions and on account of overlaps and ambiguities. Cross-cutting both the federal and democratic dimensions are, again, the analogous principles of individual and collective self-determination, between self and shared rule, and between different constituencies. Democracies as government by popular rule, are always bound to a territory and in many respects organized territorially (e.g. electoral districts, the *demos* at large, etc.), while federal governance cuts across boundaries of territories and jurisdictions. Popularly elected parliaments and accountability of executives for one, and cross-level coordination, intergovernmental relations and constitutional amendments for another, link institutions and actors. They also generate multiple, yet often incongruous accountability and representation relations. Political actors of multiple branches and at different levels of government must grapple, wittingly or not, with the tensions arising out of different and at times conflicting political logics – of representation, accountability, constituency and appropriateness. The government dimensions interlink, and their respective institutions interact, not least because numerous public policy problems transcend the institutional structures of levels of government in federal systems. The different governments and even individual institutions remain bounded to the respective democratic representation, accountability and legitimacy structures of their constituencies. Nevertheless, inter-branch, -level and -governmental relations across jurisdictions develop in democratic multilevel systems.

The operation and dynamics of federal democratic government result from the way democratic and federal politics are linked, the *coupling* between federalism and democracy.[33] Again, federalism and democracy are distinct institutional dimensions of government operating by their own logic and mechanisms of collective action. They become linked not merely through their formal conjunction or co-existence, but also and above all through practices. The institutions of the federal system and democratic government allocate powers and mechanisms in ways that affect the dynamics of governing. Coupling then refers to how these powers and mechanisms are linked. The type and intensity

33 Arthur Benz, "Ein gordischer Knoten der Politikwissenschaft? Zur Vereinbarkeit von Föderalismus und Demokratie," *Politische Vierteljahresschrift* 50, no. 1 (2009): 3–22; Benz and Sonnicksen, "Patterns of Federal Democracy," 3–25.

of structural and functional linkage between levels, branches and arenas of democratic and federal government and politics of course differ, ranging from tightly to loosely coupled to decoupled altogether.

These different constellations may foster negotiation or underline autonomy, reinforce competition or encourage cooperation. Coupling of federalism and democracy entails both complexity and the potential for tensions. However, it also implies patterns and processes for coping with tensions and differences. This bears particular relevance for accommodating diversity and pluralism in particular as well as managing complexity in general. Federalism and democracy have a complex relationship given their joint multidimensionality. Their mutual interaction, influence and co-evolution create compounded forms of constituency and institutions as well as processes of representation and participation.

4 Exploring Federalism and Participatory Democracy

Federalism and participatory democracy comprise a special relationship, especially given the potential suitability of federalism for participatory democracy. This applies all the more so when also considering federalism from an ideational perspective, theoretical lens, or as a way of power sharing and shared rule.[34] Moreover, federalism may be compatible with participatory democracy in fashions that differ from the relationship to conventional representative democracy.

Representative democracy offers one possible way of organizing popular rule by the many. It is a predominant model in modern democratic governments with different possible arrangements. Without expounding on varieties of democracy in depth, numerous grounds invite reflection on democratizing reforms within established democracies as well as federal or otherwise multilevel and non-centralistic ones. The conditions underpinning and surrounding the exercise of popular rule have been in transition on multiple accounts. From changing patterns of governance to value reorientations, demographic shifts and growing diversity of societies, issues of democratic participation "beyond the vote" appear increasingly relevant and in demand.[35] Of course,

34 Sean Mueller, "Federalism and the Politics of Shared Rule," in *A Research Agenda for Federalism Studies*, ed. John Kincaid (Cheltenham: Edward Elgar, 2019) 162–174.

35 Henrik S. Christensen, *Political Participation Beyond the Vote: How the Institutional Context Shapes Patterns of Political Participation in 18 Western European Democracies* (Åbo: Åbo Akademi University Press, 2011).

there is a large variety of democratic-reform perspectives. However, taken together, they point to limits in conventional representative democracy as overly reliant on elections with an aggregative model. The latter may comply with rather economic-rational or market (e.g. Downsian, Schumpeterian) democratic theories, but are unsuitable or have become insufficient for contemporary pluralism.[36]

Democratic challenges do not just arrive on account of practical problems. They are also posed by democracy itself and several of its corresponding normative requisites. They include congruence – i.e. the 'match' between being affected by something and capacity to co-decide on it; effective articulation – i.e. expression of interests, ideas and identities; responsivity – ensuring consideration and attentiveness on the part of political actors and institutions; and representation – i.e. the effective reflection of citizens and groups in their diversity. These requisites comprise cardinal questions of democracy to establish and enable participation and inclusion of all members of the demos as equals. Limits and perceived deficits to fulfilling democratic goods and promises have elicited reform discourse on democratizing democracy by introducing and expanding elements of "strong"[37] and "vital"[38] democracy and thus respective participatory reforms. The introduction and expansion of direct democratic instruments provide one immediately relevant tool for potential democratization. Plebiscitary democratic procedures enable citizens to take part directly – i.e. not mediated via (elected) representatives – in popular co-determination, whether through popular initiatives or citizen-legislation like referenda and other plebiscites such as popular ratification of constitutional amendments. They pose but one set or type of participatory democracy that is still fundamentally voting-based.

The fulfilment of democratic requisites becomes more complex – and from normative perspective increasingly necessary – on account of heightened sensitivity to inclusion, and against marginalization of minority and underprivileged persons and groups and toward the inclusive representation, ideally, of all societal groups.[39] For the most part, and even including certain

36 See e.g. Alberto Melucci and Leonardo Avritzer, "Complexity, Cultural Pluralism and Democracy: Collective Action in the Public Space," *Social Science Information* 39, no. 4 (2000): 507–527.

37 Benjamin R. Barber, *Strong Democracy: Participatory Politics for a New Age* (20th Anniversary ed., Berkeley: University of California Press, 2009).

38 Frank Hendriks, *Vital Democracy: A Theory of Democracy in Action* (Oxford: Oxford University Press, 2010).

39 Iris M. Young, *Inclusion and Democracy* (Oxford: Oxford University Press, 2000).

adjustments and protections (like various thresholds, reserved seats, eligibility rules), voting-based procedures – whether regular elections or plebiscitary-direct democratic votes – correspond to an aggregative model that ultimately tends to result in winning majorities and losing minorities. Participatory approaches like deliberative democracy[40] emphasize inclusion of affected groups in decision-making processes to participate in discourse, exchange and argumentation. Deliberative and participatory forms and processes, moreover, allow citizens opportunities of direct exchange of opinions and position transformation, as well as experiences of empowerment and political efficacy in general, and autonomy and self-determination in particular.[41] These demands take on particular weight and necessity in heterogeneous and divided societies.[42] Under such conditions, democratic majoritarianism may prove untenable. It could even reinforce divisions, for instance when democratic procedures enable or perpetuate the 'majoritarization' or overruling and exclusion of minorities.

Other forms of participatory processes and institutions, as conceptualized in associative democracy, prescribe a manifold corporative, co-op type organization of political decision-making processes and co-determination by associative groups.[43] With affinities to neo-corporatist interest mediation, the associative-democratic participation of associations, civil society actors, and other groups extends further. They can be linked with one another and with governmental institutions to provide for further democratic anchorage – i.e. in addition to representative-democratic based ones – of decentralized and network-type arrangements of governance.[44] The participatory-democratic

---

40 James S. Fishkin, *Democracy and Deliberation* (New Haven: Yale University Press, 1995); Jürgen Habermas, *Between Facts and Norms* (Cambridge: Polity Press, 1996); see also comprehensive e.g. Stephen Elstub and Peter McLaverty, eds., *Deliberative Democracy: Issues and Cases* (Edinburgh: Edinburgh University Press, 2014); see also the chapter by Trettel in this volume.

41 See e.g. Archon Fung, *Empowered Participation: Reinventing Urban Democracy* (Princeton: Princeton University Press, 2004).

42 See e.g. Ian O'Flynn, "Pulling Together: Shared Intentions, Deliberative Democracy and Deeply Divided Societies," *British Journal of Political Science* 47, no. 1 (2017): 187–202.

43 Paul Hirst and Veit Bader, eds., *Associative Democracy: The Real Third Way* (London: Frank Cass, 2001).

44 *Ibid.*; Veit Bader, "Associative Democracy: From 'the Real Third Way' back to Utopianism or Towards a Colourful Socialism for the 21st Century?'," *Thesis Eleven* 167, no. 1 (2021): 12–41; Sabine Kropp, "Federalism, People's Legislation and Associative Democracy," in *Citizen Participation in Multi-Level Democracies*, eds. Cristina Fraenkel-Haeberle et al. (Leiden-Boston: Brill-Nijhoff, 2015), 48–66; Eva Sørensen, "Democratic Theory and Network Governance," *Administrative Theory and Praxis* 24, no. 4 (2002): 693–720; Eva Sørensen

spectrum extends to a large variety of potential internet, digital or e-democratic procedures and practices (e.g. polling, e-voting, forums, and liquid democracy).[45] Another arrangement that has found increasing attention in both scholarship and practice in multiple countries concerns citizen assemblies. Typically they are composed of randomly selected citizens, convened on ad-hoc or recurring basis, for regular policy- or constitutional political issues, at various levels of government, and operate as consultative deliberative 'mini-publics' and even co-determining governance bodies.[46] The preceding reveals a selection of assorted democratic possibilities. While different, they share basic commonalities of fundamental interest in political equality, inclusion and their improved realization in political practice.

Transformations of governance, societies and democracy elicit several overarching problems and challenges. The latter relate to congruence, representation, inclusion and participation in principle and their realization under conditions of complex governance, societal pluralism and manifold diversity. Democracy commits governments and communities to ensuring possibilities for citizens to have an effective say in how they live together. In turn, it is necessary to ask how living together can be shaped so that there are adequate spaces within which democratic promises can be fulfilled for diverse social groups. In the history, theory and practice of democracy, numerous models are available that provide potential answers to these questions, including for heterogeneously composed polities with multiple demoi. At the same time, federalism provides a particularly suitable framework to these ends. From the structural and constitutional perspective, the federal division of powers with multiple levels of government is inherently open to multiple channels of access and thus input. Moreover, federalism bears an affinity to pluralism, with self-rule underlining self-governance in a pluralism of communities, while shared rule implicates a general thrust toward cooperation and coping necessary in light of the virtual inevitability of diversity of citizens and groups with multiple to overlapping identities and memberships.

---

and Jacob Torfing, "The Democratic Anchorage of Governance Networks," *Scandinavian Political Studies* 28, no.3 (2005): 198–200.

45 See e.g. Stephen Coleman and Jay G. Blumler, *The Internet and Democratic Citizenship: Theory, Practice and Policy* (Cambridge: Cambridge University Press, 2009).

46 See e.g. Hubertus Buchstein, "Democracy and Lottery: Revisited," *Constellations* 26, no. 3 (2019): 361–377; Nicole Curato and Marit Böker, "Linking Mini-Publics to the Deliberative System: A Research Agenda," *Policy Science* 49, no. 2 (2016): 173–190; Kimmo Grönland, André Bächtiger and Maija Setälä, eds., *Deliberative Mini-Publics: Involving Citizens in the Democratic Process* (Colchester: ECPR Press, 2014).

Various institutions of federalism already reveal possibilities of participatory democratic anchorage. As with intergovernmental relations, an elaborate spectrum of arenas, fora and channels emerge in federal systems in order to manage the complexity and cross-cutting interdependencies in a system with multiple levels and jurisdictions.[47] They also, however, engender participatory democracy, at least in broad sense, because governmental actors in multiple branches and from multiple levels must interact, coordinate and negotiate. This may not conform to majoritarian democracy, but it certainly complies with consensus-democratic notions. Such complementary participatory and inclusionary democratic forms, in turn, may be preferable for distinct minorities and political-social identity oriented or based groups,[48] rather than reliance on only representative-democratic, and especially (simple) majoritarian ones. Federalism does not prescribe one particular form of democratic participation (nor even one particular form of federalism). However, its fundamentally multi-level and multi-jurisdictional character opens up the spaces and arenas that are particularly conducive to such complementary participatory democracy.

Again, not all federal systems are democratic. Nor does federalism imply one particular kind of democracy. Moreover, even with majoritarian constituted democratic regimes, federalism changes democratic governance on account of the compounded majoritarianism resulting from the multiple levels and tiers of governance. Federalism shows an affinity for, and is likely on the whole more supportive of, consociational or consensus-democratic regimes.[49] What is more, the relationship between federalism and participatory democracy implies not only multiple levels and arena for participation, but also an array of different procedures and mechanisms.[50] As federal systems already demonstrate, participatory democracy is possible even as part of constitutional reform processes[51] – e.g. Australia, Belgium, Canada, Switzerland and to an extent even the European Union – in various procedures, from deliberative citizen assemblies and 'mini publics' to obligatory referenda. Moreover, drawing on the prior review of participatory democracy, it is possible to outline a

47 See e.g. Johanna Schnabel, *Managing Interdependencies in Federal Systems: Intergovernmental Councils and the Making of Public Policy* (Cham: Palgrave Macmillan, 2020).

48 Thomas D. Lancaster, "Complex Self-identification," 59–89.

49 Daniel J. Elazar, "Federalism and Consociational Regimes," *Publius* 15, no. 2 (1985): 17–34.

50 See e.g. Fraenkel-Haeberle et al., eds., *Citizen Participation*.

51 Benz, *Constitutional Policy*; Francesco Palermo, "Towards Participatory Constitutionalism? Comparative European Lessons," in *Constitutional Acceleration within the European Union and Beyond*, ed. Paul Blokker (London-New York: Routledge, 2018), 25–47.

further series of types of democratic modes and mechanisms that each connect with multiple levels and among assorted communities.

In addition to *direct democracy*, participatory democratic types may include, in summary (see also Figure 4.4 below): *citizen assemblies* such as randomly-selected citizen councils or deliberative 'mini-publics'; more policy-sectional, function-oriented group-based (*neo-*)*corporatist mediation* akin to associative democracy or civil-society and interest-group councils; open plenary forums like *town hall meetings* for public debates, hearings and exchanges; and many *other forms* that may comprise distinct procedures such as participatory budgeting and deliberative polling or venues like round tables and variegated digital or online platforms. Each of these types allows for an 'internal' diversity of possible forms, arrangements and procedures as well as compositions or memberships. Moreover, their respective networks of linkages in federal or multilevel systems can run more *vertically*, such as from a lower level or tier like local and regional levels, to the national, federal or (supra-)national level as well as to different institutions such as representative-democratic legislative or executive bodies. At the same time, they could equally take on more *horizontal* relationships. Accordingly, the participatory models link communities to representative-democratic institutions or link the communities to each other, akin to intergovernmental and interparliamentary relations common to federal systems. Furthermore, the different participatory-democratic types may be linked to *constitutional revisions* as a distinct policy category, whether regarding amendments of polity-wide or sub-national constitutions. They may also connect to the *federal government* and to its particular institutions, similarly to *state or other regional governments* as well as to *local-level governments*, or rather to variable *inter-level and intergovernmental arenas*, be they already established inter-ministerial, -parliamentary, -administrative or further sectoral and group-based conferences.

Finally, these different types of participatory democracy present manifold possibilities for federal and multilevel systems, whether they are introduced and expanded at one or several levels. Beyond this quantitative propensity, federalism in qualitative principle can also foster realizations of participatory democracy for and even democratization of plural and diverse societies, precisely on account of its constitutive features of power-sharing and polycentricity. It is also capable of engendering and accommodating multiple coinciding as well as overlapping identities and memberships of *demoi*. The latter in turn need not only be territorially defined within distinct and among cross-jurisdictional constituencies, but also along variable identity-, minority, cross-sectoral and functional lines and terms. At the same time, of paramount concern is the type of inclusion of participatory forms, arrangements and

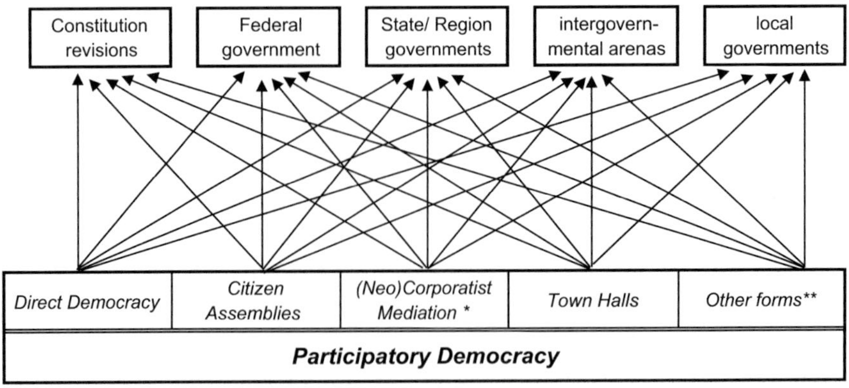

FIGURE 4.4 Linking federal/multilevel systems and participatory democracy
* e.g. civil society inclusion, consultation, and/or co-production
** e.g. deliberative fora & polling; e-government; e-/liquid democracy; participatory budgeting; round-tables
SOURCE: OWN DEPICTION

procedures. Indeed, allocations of powers and roles may vary substantially. They span from inclusion and inputs at different stages such as agenda setting to the final decision or its ratification, and range from consultative and monitory to co-determinant and co-productive competences over policies and other collectively binding decisions. These issues related to participatory design and positioning in political processes also apply to democratic-theoretical perspectives in general. They pose challenges of both organization and legitimacy. However, the challenges and necessities gain special relevance and urgency when linked with the autonomy and shared-rule requisites of federalism. While not participatory democracy per se, federalism entails commitment to equality and collective self- and co-determination of places and communities. Federalism entails thus a promise to their – however calibrated, designed and positioned – participation in shaping collective life. Realizing these promises is never easy, but federalism can contribute effectively to their realization in diverse and complex polities.

5 Conclusion

There may be a common foundation from which federalism and democracy emerged, this basis being present most notably in the development of modern states, constitutions, rule of law, and division-of-power arrangements, among others. On the other hand, state modernization has never been monolithic or unidirectional toward centralization and monocratic rule. It proceeded in a number of contexts in conjunction with decentralized and even polycentric arrangements.[52] Thus, the relationship between federalism and democracy comprises, in developmental and structural-functional terms and principles, more an entangled knot than separated strands. Certainly the division of powers among branches and among levels of government renders the polity both structurally and functionally multidimensional. The preceding sections aimed to delimit the contours of different governmental dimensions, organizational principles and structures, and to capture their interconnecting processes and linkages that compound to a multidimensional net- or latticework. In other words, federal governmental structures and constituted jurisdictions and communities are distinct from democratic governmental ones. At the same time, the participatory processes – from forms of coordination and exchange, to processes of participatory democracy in stricter sense – provide for linkages, interactions and the connective bridges between the 'nodes' of autonomy. This complexity, of course, is by no means an uncharted territory. This chapter nevertheless has sought at least to provide an own productive scheme of orientation.

The institutions and processes of politics are always linked to people and places. In federalism and democracy in particular, they connect to multiple principles and multidimensional division of powers as well as diverse groups, societal pluralism and the demos and demoi. Federalism and democracy hold promises, but their concurrence holds tensions, potential frictions and discontinuities. At the same time, the interlinkages between the democratic and the federal institutions and procedures can offer precisely the means and ways for coping with them in order to balance self- and shared rule with diversity and pluralism. Finally, the lens of federalism offers perhaps the most powerful theoretical perspective for reflecting on how to accommodate and interlink diverse people and plural communities without domination. Federalism can offer a framework for democratically maintaining and fostering equality, and squaring autonomy with shared ruled for the management of complexity in an increasingly diverse and interdependent world.

52 Arthur Benz, *Der moderne Staat: Grundlagen der politologischen Analyse* (2nd ed., Munich: Oldenbourg, 2008); see also e.g. Daniel Ziblatt, "Rethinking the Origins of Federalism: Puzzle, Theory, and Evidence from Nineteenth-Century Europe," *World Politics* 57, no. 1 (2004): 70–98.

Bibliography

Bader, Veit. "Associative Democracy: From 'the Real Third Way' back to Utopianism or Towards a Colourful Socialism for the 21st Century?'." *Thesis Eleven* 167, no. 1 (2021): 12–41.

Barber, Benjamin R. *Strong Democracy: Participatory Politics for a New Age*. 20th Anniversary ed., Berkeley: University of California Press, 2009.

Bednar, Jenna. "Federalism Theory: The Boundary Problem, Robustness and Dynamics." In *A Research Agenda for Federalism Studies*, edited by John Kincaid, 27–38. Cheltenham: Edward Elgar, 2019.

Beer, Samuel. "Federalism, Nationalism, and Democracy in America." *American Political Science Review* 72, no. 1 (1978): 9–21.

Benz, Arthur and Jared Sonnicksen, eds., *Federal Democracies at Work. Varieties of Complex Government*. Toronto: University of Toronto Press, 2021.

Benz, Arthur and Jared Sonnicksen. "Patterns of Federal Democracy: Tensions, Friction, or Balance between two Government Dimensions." *European Political Science Review* 9, no. 1 (2017): 3–25.

Benz, Arthur. *Constitutional Policy in Multilevel Government: The Art of Keeping the Balance*. Oxford: Oxford University Press, 2016.

Benz, Arthur. *Der moderne Staat: Grundlagen der politologischen Analyse*. 2nd ed., Munich: Oldenbourg, 2008.

Benz, Arthur. "Ein gordischer Knoten der Politikwissenschaft? Zur Vereinbarkeit von Föderalismus und Demokratie." *Politische Vierteljahresschrift* 50, no. 1 (2009): 3–22.

Benz, Arthur. *Föderale Demokratie: Regieren im Spannungsfeld zwischen Interdependenz und Autonomie*. Baden-Baden: Nomos, 2020.

Buchstein, Hubertus. "Democracy and Lottery: Revisited." *Constellations* 26, no. 3 (2019): 361–377.

Burgess, Michael and Alain-G. Gagnon, eds., *Federal Democracies*. London-New York: Routledge, 2010.

Christensen, Henrik S. *Political Participation Beyond the Vote: How the Institutional Context Shapes Patterns of Political Participation in 18 Western European Democracies*. Åbo: Åbo Akademi University Press, 2011.

Coleman, Stephen and Jay G. Blumler. *The Internet and Democratic Citizenship: Theory, Practice and Policy*. Cambridge: Cambridge University Press, 2009.

Colino, César. "Varieties of Federalism and Propensities for Change." In *Federal Dynamics: Continuity, Change, and the Varieties of Federalism*, edited by Arthur Benz and Jorg Broschek, 48–69. Oxford: Oxford University Press, 2013.

Curato, Nicole and Marit Böker. "Linking Mini-Publics to the Deliberative System: A Research Agenda." *Policy Science* 49, no. 2 (2016): 173–190.

De Schutter, Helder. "Federalism as Fairness." *Journal of Political Philosophy* 19, no. 2 (2011): 167–189.

Detterbeck, Klaus and Eve Hepburn, eds., *Handbook of Territorial Politics*. Cheltenham: Edward Elgar, 2018.

Elazar, Daniel J. "Federalism and Consociational Regimes." *Publius* 15, no. 2 (1985): 17–34.

Elazar, Daniel J. "The Political Theory of Covenant: Biblical Origins and Modern Developments." *Publius* 10, no. 4 (1980): 3–30.

Elstub, Stephen and Peter McLaverty, eds., *Deliberative Democracy: Issues and Cases*. Edinburgh: Edinburgh University Press, 2014.

Fishkin, James S. *Democracy and Deliberation*. New Haven: Yale University Press, 1995.

Fraenkel-Haeberle, Cristina et al., eds., *Citizen Participation in Multi-Level Democracies*. Leiden-Boston: Brill-Nijhoff, 2015.

Fung, Archon. *Empowered Participation: Reinventing Urban Democracy*. Princeton: Princeton University Press, 2004.

Gagnon, Alain-G. "Multinational Federalism: Challenges, Shortcomings and Promises." *Regional & Federal Studies* 31, no. 1 (2021): 99–114.

Gagnon, Alain-G. *The Legitimacy Clash: Challenges to Democracy in Multinational States*. Toronto: University of Toronto Press, 2023.

Gerring, John, Strom C. Thacker and Carola Moreno. "Centripetal Democratic Governance: A Theory and Global Inquiry." *American Political Science Review* 99, no. 4 (2005): 567–581.

Gerring, John and Wouter Veenendaal. *Population and Politics: The Impact of Scale*. Cambridge: Cambridge University Press, 2020.

Gibson, Edward L. *Boundary Control: Subnational Authoritarianism in Federal Democracies*. Cambridge: Cambridge University Press, 2013.

Grönland, Kimmo, André Bächtiger and Maija Setälä, eds., *Deliberative Mini-Publics: Involving Citizens in the Democratic Process*. Colchester: ECPR Press, 2014.

Habermas, Jürgen. *Between Facts and Norms*. Cambridge: Polity Press, 1996.

Hendriks, Frank. *Vital Democracy: A Theory of Democracy in Action*. Oxford: Oxford University Press, 2010.

Hirst Paul and Veit Bader, eds., *Associative Democracy: The Real Third Way*. London: Frank Cass, 2001.

Hueglin, Thomas O. "Federalism and Democracy: A Critical Reassessment." In *The Global Promise of Federalism*, edited by Grace Skogstad, David Cameron, Martin Papillon, and Keith Banting 17–42. Toronto: University of Toronto Press, 2013.

Kropp, Sabine. "Federalism, People's Legislation and Associative Democracy." In *Citizen Participation in Multi-Level Democracies*, edited by Cristina Fraenkel-Haeberle et al., 48–66. Leiden-Boston: Brill-Nijhoff, 2015.

Kymlicka, Will. *Politics in the Vernacular: Nationalism, Multiculturalism, and Citizenship*. Oxford: Oxford University Press, 2001.

Lancaster, Thomas D. "Complex Self-identification and Compounded Representation in Federal Systems." *West European Politics* 22, no. 2 (1999): 59–89.

Lehmbruch, Gerhard. *Parteienwettbewerb im Bundesstaat. Regelsysteme und Spannungslagen im politischen System der Bundesrepublik Deutschland.* 3rd ed., Wiesbaden: Westdeutscher Verlag, 2000.

Levy, Jacob T. "Federalism, Liberalism, and the Separation of Loyalties." *American Political Science Review* 101, no. 3 (2007): 459–477.

Lijphart, Arend. *Patterns of Democracy: Government Forms and Performance in Thirty-Six Countries.* New Haven: Yale University Press, 1999.

Melucci, Alberto and Leonardo Avritzer. "Complexity, Cultural Pluralism and Democracy: Collective Action in the Public Space." *Social Science Information* 39, no. 4 (2000): 507–527.

Moore, Margaret. *A Political Theory of Territory.* Oxford: Oxford University Press, 2015.

Moreno, Luis, César Colino and John Kincaid, eds., *Diversity and Unity in Federal Countries.* Montreal: McGill-Queen's University Press, 2010.

Mueller, Sean. "Federalism and the Politics of Shared Rule." In *A Research Agenda for Federalism Studies*, edited by John Kincaid 162–174. Cheltenham: Edward Elgar, 2019.

Oates, Wallace E. "An Essay on Fiscal Federalism." *Journal of Economic Literature* 37, no. 3 (1999): 1120–1149.

O'Flynn, Ian. "Pulling Together: Shared Intentions, Deliberative Democracy and Deeply Divided Societies." *British Journal of Political Science* 47, no. 1 (2017): 187–202.

Palermo, Francesco. "Owned or Shared? Territorial Autonomy in the Minority Discourse." In *Minority Accommodation through Territorial and Non-territorial Autonomy*, edited by Tove H. Malloy and Francesco Palermo, 13–32. Oxford: Oxford University Press, 2015.

Palermo, Francesco. "Towards Participatory Constitutionalism? Comparative European Lessons." In *Constitutional Acceleration within the European Union and Beyond*, edited by Paul Blokker, 25–47. London-New York: Routledge, 2018.

Schnabel, Johanna. *Managing Interdependencies in Federal Systems: Intergovernmental Councils and the Making of Public Policy.* Cham: Palgrave Macmillan, 2020.

Sharman, Campbell. "Parliamentary Federations and Limited Government: Constitutional Design and Redesign in Australia and Canada." *Journal of Theoretical Politics* 2, no. 2 (1990): 205–230.

Simeon, Richard. "Constitutional Design and Change in Federal Systems: Issues and Questions." *Publius* 39, no. 2 (2009): 241–261.

Sonnicksen, Jared. "Federalism and Democracy." In *Encyclopedia of Contemporary Constitutionalism*, edited by Javier Cremades and Cristina Hermida, 1–17. Cham: Springer, 2022.

Sonnicksen, Jared. *Tensions of American Federal Democracy: Fragmentation of the State.* London-New York: Routledge, 2022.

Sonnicksen, Jared. "Konträr oder konstruktiv? Zur produktiven Widersprüchlichkeit zwischen Föderalismus und parlamentarischer Demokratie," *Zeitschrift für Parlamentsfragen* 55, no. 1 (2024): 93–108.

Stepan, Alfred C. "Federalism and Democracy: Beyond the U.S. Model." *Journal of Democracy* 10, no. 4 (1999): 19–34.

Søberg Shugart, Matthew and John M. Carey. *Presidents and Assemblies: Constitutional Design and Electoral Dynamics*. New York: Cambridge University Press, 1992.

Sørensen, Eva and Jacob Torfing. "The Democratic Anchorage of Governance Networks." *Scandinavian Political Studies* 28, no.3 (2005): 198–200.

Sørensen, Eva. "Democratic Theory and Network Governance." *Administrative Theory and Praxis* 24, no. 4 (2002): 693–720.

Tokatlı, Mahir. *Auf dem Weg zum Präsidialsystem alla Turca? Eine Analyse unterschiedlicher Regierungsformen in der Türkei seit 1921*. Baden-Baden: Nomos, 2020.

Tsebelis, George. "Decision Making in Political Systems: Veto Players in Presidentialism, Parliamentarism, Multicameralism and Multipartyism." *British Journal of Political Science* 25, no. 3 (1995): 289–325.

Warren, Mark E. "Voting with Your Feet: Exit-based Empowerment in Democratic Theory." *American Political Science Review* 105, no. 4 (2011): 683–701.

Watts, Ronald L. "Federalism, Federal Political Systems, and Federations." *Annual Review of Political Science* 1, no. 1 (1998): 117–137.

Young, Iris M. *Inclusion and Democracy*. Oxford: Oxford University Press, 2000.

Ziblatt, Daniel. "Rethinking the Origins of Federalism: Puzzle, Theory, and Evidence from Nineteenth-Century Europe." *World Politics* 57, no. 1 (2004): 70–98.

CHAPTER 5

Rethinking Participatory Democracy through Federalism: Citizen Participation, Power-Sharing and Decision-Making Processes

Martina Trettel

1 The Extent to Which Democracy Is in a Crisis and Participatory Democracy Is a Possible Way Out. Where Does Federalism Come In?

At the risk of stating the obvious, democracy is undergoing a deep crisis.[1] This holds true especially when looking at the so-called "mature democracies".[2] A clear majority of scholars working in the field of democracy highlight that democratic institutions do not work as they are supposed to anymore and refer to this situation using a wide range of terminology: disease, malaise, discomfort, illness and so on.[3] The negativity permeating democratic systems could suggest that democracy is declining and slowly approaching its final stage. The question would then be if there are alternative decision-making structures and if these would be able to effectively replace democratic instruments. The answer seems to be a negative one. The literature indicates that democracy is the only way through which to govern complex and diverse societies.[4] Using one of Churchill's most popular quotes: "Many forms of Government have been tried and will be tried in this world of sin and woe. No one pretends that democracy is perfect or all-wise. Indeed, it has been said that democracy is the worst form of Government except all those other forms that have been tried

1 See among others Mark A. Graber, Sanford Levinson and Mark V. Tushnet, eds, *Constitutional Democracy in Crisis?* (Oxford: Oxford University Press, 2018) and Carl Schmitt and Ellen Kennedy, *The Crisis of Parliamentary Democracy* (Cambridge MA: MIT Press, 2000).

2 Robert A. Dahl and Ian Shapiro, *On Democracy* (New Have: Yale University Press, 2015); nonetheless some authors ask themselves if this holds true also with regard to emerging democracies, see Paul Blokker, *New Democracies in Crisis?* (London-New York: Routledge, 2015).

3 See for example, Brigitte Geissel and Kenneth Newton, *Evaluating Democratic Innovations: Curing the Democratic Malaise?* (London-New York: Routledge, 2012).

4 See Gianfranco Pasquino, *Strumenti della democrazia* (Bologna: Il Mulino, 2007), 7.

DOI:10.1163/9789004707764_007

from time to time".[5] More than seventy years later, this quote still mirrors the *status quo*.

To this extent, it is natural to ask ourselves if, and eventually how, this contradiction can be solved. Put differently, on one side it seems that democracy is not working anymore as it should, and on the other side democracy appears to be the only means to govern contemporary and plural societies, assuring at the same time protection of fundamental rights and the constitutional principle of popular sovereignty.

A closer look at the terminology can help find a way to interpret this contrast. "Democracy" is a term that dates back to the ancient Greeks and has endured through countless stages of philosophy and politics. As Dahl observed: "today the term democracy is like an ancient kitchen midden packed with assorted leftovers from twenty-five hundred years of nearly continuous usage".[6] The meaning assigned to this expression changed profoundly throughout historical eras. It is not surprising to observe that what we define as democracy nowadays is very different from what the ancient Greeks had in mind when referring to democratic instruments. This might suggest that what is undergoing a deep crisis is not democracy in its long-standing theoretical conception, but the instruments through which in recent times the principle has been put into practice, especially through representative democracy.[7] Low turnout at the polls, disaffection from political parties and a widespread disinterest in issues linked to society and citizenship are the most evident symptoms of the crisis representative democracy is going through.[8]

Against this background, it remains hard to imagine an effective approach through which dysfunctionalities of representative democracy could be treated. Many academics suggest that a possible solution is to be found in one of the fundamental cornerstones of democratic systems: the participation of citizens. Even if it can sound redundant – since democracy overlaps with the concept of participation –, this approach values a specific (and somehow

5 Winston Churchill and Robert R. James, *Complete Speeches, 1897–1963* (Langhorne: Chelsea House Publishers, 1974) vol. 7, 7566.

6 Robert A. Dahl, *Dilemmas of Pluralist Democracy: Autonomy vs. Control* (New Haven: Yale University Press, 1982), 5.

7 Selen A. Ercan and Jean-P. Gagnon, "The Crisis of Democracy Which Crisis? Which Democracy?," *Democratic Theory* 1, no. 2 (2014): 1.

8 Sara Parolari and Martina Trettel, "Democratic Quality and Territorial Distribution of Power in Italy," in *Calidad democrática y organización territorial*, eds. Jose Tudela et al. (Madrid: Marcial Pons, 2018), 281.

innovative) type of citizens' involvement in decision-making, described as "deliberative democracy" or "participatory democracy".[9]

To sum up, deliberative and participatory theories of democracy rely on a critique of the aggregative view of democracy and propose tools which tend to enhance public reasoning and argumentation with the ultimate aim of improving the quality of democracy and overcoming the majoritarian rationale.[10] A lot has been written on the topic, and deliberative democracy has become one of the most popular issues in democracy studies.[11] Most academics see in procedures that enhance deliberation and participation the starting point for a renewal of decision-making processes. They agree that these renovations should not overturn classical representative decisional mechanisms. In fact, it only would complement the latter by means of a deliberative involvement of citizens in specific decisional processes.[12]

With regard to definitions, it has to be noted that there is still a lot of uncertainty as far as the boundaries between participatory democracy, deliberative democracy and democratic innovations are concerned. For the purposes of this paper all three terms will be used interchangeably referring to those tools that aim at introducing ordinary citizens into representative decision-making procedures through deliberative methodologies.[13]

---

9 Stephen Elstub, "Deliberative and Participatory Democracy," in *The Oxford Handbook of Deliberative Democracy*, eds. André Bächtiger et al. (Oxford: Oxford University Press, 2018), 186.

10 See Simone Chambers, "Deliberative Democratic Theory," *Annual Review of Political Science* 6 (2003): 307.

11 See Stephen Elstub, "The Third Generation of Deliberative Democracy," Political Studies Review 8 (2010): 291; Amy Gutmann and Dennis F. Thompson, *Why Deliberative Democracy?* (Princeton: Princeton University Press, 2004); Jürg Steiner, *The Foundations of Deliberative Democracy: Empirical Eesearch and Normative Implications* (Cambridge: Cambridge University Press, 2012); James Bohman and William Rehg, *Deliberative Democracy: Essays on Reason and Politics* (Cambridge MA: MIT, 1997).

12 David J. Kahane, *Deliberative Democracy in Practice* (Vancouver: UBC Press 2010).

13 Different disciplines from different parts of the globe have dissimilar views and give, consequently, diverse definitions of these concepts. Among many others, André Bächtiger et al., eds., *The Oxford Handbook of Deliberative Democracy* (Oxford: Oxford University Press, 2018); John Gastil and Peter Levine, *The Deliberative Democracy Handbook: Strategies for Effective Civic Engagement in the Twenty-first Century* (San Francisco: Jossey-Bass, 2005); Raphaël Kies, *Promises and Limits of Web-deliberation* (Basingstoke: Palgrave Macmillan, 2010), 7; Graham Smith, *Democratic Innovations: Designing Institutions for Citizen Participation* (Cambridge: Cambridge University Press, 2009); Joan Font, Donatella Della Porta and Yves Sintomer, *Participatory Democracy in Southern Europe: Causes, Characteristics and Consequences* (Lanham: Rowman & Littlefield International, 2014).

The majority of studies on deliberative democracy present some analogies and common patterns in their approach to the topic. They mainly focus on subjects and methodologies in deliberative experiments, their conceptual qualification and their possible use.[14] However, some features regarding the way in which these processes work and how they could be defined and classified are mostly neglected. Better said, the proliferation of so-called participatory processes throughout the world offers several interesting and unedited readings that still remain unexplored.[15]

For instance, a comparative observation of how democratic innovations are theorized and work in practice suggest that institutional decentralization is one of the influential elements on the development of these concepts and their practices.[16] Thus, we could identify at least three potential ways through which deliberative democracy interacts with federalism, here to be understood as an organizational principle "that applies to systems consisting of at least two constituent parts that are not wholly independent but together form the system as a whole".[17]

First, it is generally recognized that the involvement of citizens in deliberative processes happens mostly at the local or subnational level, even though examples of participatory instances at national and supranational levels are also found.[18] In this regard, it is interesting to investigate if the level of

14 See Birte Gundelach, Patricia Buser and Daniel Kübler, "Deliberative Democracy in Local Governance: The Impact of Institutional Design on Legitimacy," 43(2) *Local Government Studies* 43, no. 2 (2017): 219; Luigi Bobbio, "Types of Deliberation," (2010) 6(2) *Journal of Public Deliberation* 6, no. 2 (2010): 1; James S. Fishkin, *Democracy when the People are Thinking: Revitalizing our Politics through Public Deliberation* (Oxford: Oxford University Press, 2018).

15 For example, other readings of the topic are suggested by the observations of the dynamics on legal traditions and forms of government. Both issues represent possible innovative approaches to deliberative democracy and their interactions could be the ground for future in depth analysis.

16 Ex *plurimis*, see Arend Lijphart, "Non-Majoritarian Democracy: A Comparison of Federal and Consociational Theories," (1985) *Publius* 15, no. 3 (1985): 3; Alfred Stepan, "Democrazia e federalismo: un'analisi comparata," *Rivista Italiana di Scienze Politiche* 28, no. 1, (1998): 5.

17 Anna Gamper, "A "Global Theory of Federalism": The Nature and Challenges of a Federal State," *German Law Journal* 6, no. 10 (2005): 1299. For a comprehensive overview on the concept of federalism see, among others, George Anderson, "An Overview on Federalism," in *Federalism: An Introduction*, ed. George Anderson (Oxford: Oxford University Press, 2008); Michael Burgess, *Comparative Federalism: Theory and Practice* (London-New York: Routledge, 2006); Francesco Palermo and Karl Kössler, *Comparative Federalism: Constitutional Arrangements and Case Law* (Oxford-Portland: Hart Publishing, 2017).

18 For a comprehensive perspective on deliberative democracy on different levels of government see Cristina Fraenkel-Haeberle et al., eds., *Citizen participation in multi-level*

government in which participatory processes take place has an impact on the functioning of participatory democracy and, further, if the decentralized institutional structure evidently affects the development of participatory processes.

Second, a trend is emerging towards the institutionalization of participatory democracy in legal norms. Therefore, the distribution of decision-making powers on the different levels of government could influence the existence and the structure of these pieces of legislation and how they accommodate deliberative elements and to what extent they interact with other levels of government.

Third, even if the concept of participatory democracy is relatively recent, some connect it to conceptualizations of democracy that date back to experiences of direct democracy in ancient Greece.[19] Nevertheless, looking at how deliberative democracy works in practice, it seems more likely to find some similarities with the theories on federalism than with direct democratic schemes. To this respect, both federal theory and deliberative democracy perceive the "sharing of power among multiple centers (non-centralization) as the keystone of popular government".[20]

For all the above reasons, this paper will try to delve into the relation between participatory democracy and federalism,[21] through comparative examples and explaining where, how and to what extent they interact.

The research goal is to display the points of contact between the two concepts aiming at offering a new perspective on deliberative democracy and federalism. This could help both to improve the effectiveness of participatory processes and develop a definition that considers the actual potential of deliberative citizens' participation for bettering the conditions of representative democracy.[22]

---

democracies (Leiden: Brill-Nijhoff, 2015) and Caroline Patsias, Anne Latendresse and Laurence Bherer, "Participatory Democracy, Decentralization and Local Governance: The Montreal Participatory Budget in the light of 'Empowered Participatory Governance'," *International Journal of Urban & Regional Research* 37, no. 6 (2013): 2214.

19 See Daniela Cammack, "Deliberation and Discussion in Classical Athens," *Journal of Political Philosophy* 29, no. 2 (2021): 135–166.

20 Daniel J. Elazar, *Exploring Federalism* (Tuscaloosa: The University of Alabama Press, 1987), 146.

21 For a deeper examination of the relationship between federalism and democracy, see Sonnicksen's chapter in this volume.

22 On effectiveness and democratic quality see André Bächtiger and John Parkinson, *Mapping and Measuring Deliberation: Towards a New Deliberative Quality* (Oxford: Oxford University Press, 2019); Joan Font, Sara Pasadas del Amo and Graham Smith, "Tracing the Impact of Proposals from Participatory Processes: Methodological Challenges and Substantive Lessons," *Journal of Public Deliberation* 12, no. 1 (2016): 1.

2 The Multi-level Approach to Participatory Democracy

One of the main reasons for adopting a decentralized structure of government is that it enhances democratic participation, representation, and accountability. In fact, the decentralization of central decision-making to democratically elected local and regional bodies functions as a multiplier, giving citizens numerous points of access, enhancing opportunities for political participation, increasing the accountability and responsiveness of elected officials to the citizens, and hence providing incentives for more responsive democratic government.[23]

In this regard, it could be argued that deliberative democracy takes root and proliferates more easily in multi-level structures of government, given the greater range of democratic tiers, and therefore it can be beneficial to approach the analysis of democratic innovations by searching for experiences on lower levels of government.[24]

Following this approach, and looking comparatively at the development of deliberative democracy, it is evident that most experiences took place at municipal level or even on a smaller scale.[25] For example, what is generally understood as the ancestor of all deliberative democratic experiences – participatory budgeting – was born precisely at the local level. This very well-known participatory process was invented in the Brazilian city of Porto Alegre in 1989 and aimed at including all citizens of a municipality in the discussion about the allocation of a specific portion of the local budget.[26] The beneficial effects of this experience on the local community led to a very broad and fast dissemination of local participatory budgeting throughout the world, and more generally to a quick spreading of deliberative experiments at local level.[27]

---

23 Karl-Peter Sommermann, "Citizen Participation in Multi-Level Democracies – An introduction," in *Citizen Participation in Multi-level Democracies*, eds. Cristina Fraenkel-Haeberle et al. (Leiden: Brill-Nijhoff, 2015), 7–8.

24 See Marcus A. Melo and Gianpaolo Baiocchi, "Deliberative Democracy and Local Governance: Towards a New Agenda," *International Journal of Urban & Regional Research* 30, no. 3 (2006): 587.

25 Umberto Allegretti, "Participatory Democracy in Multi-Level States," in *Citizen participation in multi-level democracies*, eds. Cristina Fraenkel-Haeberle et al. (Leiden: Brill-Nijhoff, 2015), 211.

26 Boaventura De Sousa Santos, "Participatory Budgeting in Porto Alegre: Toward a Redistributive Democracy," *Politics & Society* 26, no. 4 (1998): 469.

27 Yves Sintomer, Carsten Herzberg and Anja Röcke, "Participatory Budgeting in Europe: Potentials and Challenges," *International Journal of Urban & Regional Research* 32, no. 1 (2008): 164.

Why is that so? Like participatory budgeting, all kinds of deliberative democratic tools revolve around the opening of the political arena in order to multiply decision making centers through the participation of civil society. This is pursued through the development of a set of different decision-making procedures – participatory budgeting being just one of these – that apply deliberation theories and make use of citizenship expertise for containing potential conflicts in particularly sensitive decision-making fields. Moreover, in contrast to direct democracy, these tools do not lead to 'yes-or-no' decisions but to a compromised (consultative) outcome that represents a synthesis of the diversified interests of pluralist societies and that aim at complementing the traditional decision-making procedure.[28]

Hence, the small scale (both territorial and demographic) of local entities favored the conception of such decision-making structures because of two main elements: the closeness between citizens and policy-makers and the issues at stake, that at local level are more familiar to the citizens and directly affect their day to day life. Despite that, studies that described deliberative practices have proven that even if the dimensions of a region (province or state) within a federal (or regional) country are generally larger than those of a municipality, it does not mean that the intermediate level of government is incompatible with participatory democracy. Logically, such models cannot be copied from the local level and must be redesigned to fit the larger dimension.[29]

In this regard, three well-known examples illustrate how deliberative democracy has been adapted to the needs of the subnational level of government: the 2004 British Columbia Citizens' Assembly on electoral reform,[30] the Vorarlberg Citizens Juries (*Bürgerrat*)[31] and the Citizens Initiative Review established in Oregon.[32]

Besides using deliberative methodologies for coming to consensual solutions, these experiences had to face the issue of the much higher number of

28 Antonio Floridia, "Beyond Participatory Democracy, Towards Deliberative Democracy: Elements of a Possible Theoretical Genealogy," *Rivista italiana di scienza politica*, no. 3 (2014): 299; Palermo and Kössler, *Comparative Federalism*, 115.

29 Allegretti, "Participatory Democracy," 211; Sommermann, "Citizen Participation," 22.

30 See Mark E. Warren and Hilary Pearse, *Designing Deliberative Democracy: The British Columbia Citizens' Assembly* (Cambridge: Cambridge University Press, 2008).

31 See Peter Bußjäger, "Entwicklungen in der direkten Demokratie und Bürgerbeteiligung in Vorarlberg," in *Parlamentarische Rechtsetzung in der Krise*, ed. Georg Lienbacher (Wie: Sramek, 2014), 151.

32 On the topic Katherine R. Knobloch et al., "Did They Deliberate?: Applying an Evaluative Model of Democratic Deliberation to the Oregon Citizens' Initiative Review," *Journal of Applied Communication Research* 41, no. 2 (2013): 105.

possible participants. Thus, all three adapted deliberative *fora* by employing stratified random selection of participants to form what in deliberative studies are known as "mini-publics".[33] As to differences, the Canadian Citizens Assembly was instituted *ad hoc* for a specific policy objective, e.g. reforming the electoral law, while the *Bürgerrat* is intended as a general framework for transforming deliberative democracy into a permanent decision-making pattern to be used in different policy fields, at both the local and the subnational level. On the other hand, the Oregon Citizen Initiative Review had the specific intention to bring citizens together to deliberate on all ballot measures.[34] The goal of this participatory design is again different from the two above since it aims at smoothing out the polarizing effects of direct democracy through the consensual logic of participatory democracy.[35] This shows that deliberative democracy not only complements representative democracy, but it can also influence direct democratic procedures.

Having observed that deliberative democracy can be employed both at local and subnational level, it is now time to investigate if deliberative practices have been tested also at a higher level. The answer is positive as anticipated in the introductory paragraph: democratic innovations have been tried out also at central and supranational level. The reference goes not only to the countless online consultations spread all over the world,[36] but also to the 2009 Australia Citizens' Parliament – a nation-scale three-day deliberation process established in Canberra between randomly selected citizens to address pivotal questions on the institutional architecture of the country[37] – or to the Public debate in France[38] – recently adopted also in Italy.[39] The constitution-making

33 For an overview on this concept we make reference to Graham Smith and Maija Setälä, "Mini-Publics and Deliberative Democracy," in *The Oxford Handbook of Deliberative Democracy*, eds. André Bächtiger et al. (Oxford: Oxford University Press, 2018); Archon Fung, "Minipublics: Deliberative Designs and Their Consequences," in *Deliberation, Participation and Democracy: Can the People Govern?*, ed. Shawn W. Rosenberg (Basingstoke: Palgrave Macmillan, 2014).

34 A proposed law or constitutional amendment that is drafted by, and can be enacted by a direct vote of, citizens – that will be voted on in an upcoming election.

35 See John Gastil and Robert Richards, "Making Direct Democracy Deliberative through Random Assemblies," *Politics & Society* 41, no. 2 (2013): 253.

36 James Fishkin, "Making Deliberative Democracy Practical: Public Consultation and Dispute Resolution," *Ohio State Journal on Dispute Resolution* 24, no. 4 (2011): 611.

37 For an overview on this experience see Lyn Carson, ed., *The Australian Citizens' Parliament and the Future of Deliberative Democracy* (Philadelphia: Pennsylvania State University Press, 2013).

38 See par. 3.

39 See Martine Revel, *Le débat public: une expérience française de démocratie participative* (Paris: Découverte, 2007); Umberto Allegretti, "Un caso di attuazione del principio

experiences that took place in Ireland and in Iceland through deliberative assemblies consisting of ordinary citizens are also paradigmatic.[40] The high popularity reached by these two particular experiments introduced a new terminology for this typology of instruments. We can in fact use the formula "deliberative constitutionalism" for referring to the involvement of citizens through deliberative *fora* in constitution-making process.[41] These procedures show not only that the higher source of state law can be amended through such procedures, but also that deliberative democracy can without a doubt be employed at the central level of government.

Nonetheless, it must be emphasized that the two countries mentioned above – Iceland and Ireland – are geographically and demographically particularly small. It has to be considered that certain subnational entities or even some cities are larger than these nation-states. In this regard, it could be argued that the functioning of deliberative democratic instruments probably does not directly depend on the level of government, but rather on the size of a territorial entity.[42]

The descriptive perspective adopted by this paragraph shows that decentralized countries can be considered as valid containers for the development of deliberative instruments offering multiple levels on which these tools can be deployed. Moreover, considering that democratic innovations can take place at all levels of government, the analysis raises awareness on the importance of the dimensional scale of a constituency to the development and the outcomes of the procedure.[43]

---

costituzionale di partecipazione: il regolamento del dibattito pubblico sulle grandi opere," *Rivista Associazione Italiana Costituzionalisti*, no. 3 (2018): 1.

40 Silvia Suteu, "Constitutional Conventions in the Digital Era: Lessons from Iceland and Ireland," *Boston College International and Comparative Law Review* 3, no. 2 (2015): 251.

41 Ron Levy, ed., *The Cambridge Handbook of Deliberative Constitutionalism* (Cambridge: Cambridge University Press, 2018); Gabriel L. Negretto, "Democratic Constitution-Making Bodies: The Perils of a Partisan Convention," *International Journal of Constitutional Law* 16, no. 1 (2018): 254; Suteu, "Constitutional Conventions," 251. Such procedures were employed also at subnational level, especially in the making of four out of five subnational constitutions of the Italian special regions, as stated in Martina Trettel, "La democrazia partecipativa nelle Regioni a Statuto Speciale: tendenze e prospettive di sviluppo," in *Le variabili della specialità: evidenze e riscontri tra soluzioni istituzionali e politiche settoriali*, eds. Francesco Palermo and Sara Parolari (Napoli: Edizioni Scientifiche Italiane, 2018), 199.

42 See Umberto Allegretti, "Recenti costituzioni "partecipate": Islanda, Ecuador, Bolivia," Quaderni costituzionali, no. 3 (2013): 689.

43 On this see Adrian Bua, "Scale and Policy Impact In Participatory-Deliberative Democracy: Lessons From A Multi-Level Process," *Public Administration* 95, no. 1 (2017): 160.

Clearly, decentralization at the local level has been pivotal for the conception and experimentation of deliberative democratic instruments which are then exported to higher levels of government, but there still isn't any strong evidence proving the actual influence of institutional decentralization on the development and effectiveness of democratic innovations, besides the fact that on lower levels of government these are quantitatively more consistent.[44] Thus, in the following paragraph the focus will move to the second point of intersection, looking at the institutional aspects of deliberative democracy and its connection with the distribution of decision-making powers in decentralized constitutional settings.

3 Power-Sharing and the Institutionalization of Participatory Democracy

The issue of the institutionalization of deliberative practices is highly debated in the literature.[45] Institutionalizing deliberative democracy through laws for transforming it into a routine-practice is rather uncommon and one-shot experiences are much more widespread. However, not only can institutionalization "enhance qualitative standards of participatory processes as well as upgrade opportunities to exert some actual influence on choices and policies", but it also makes them easier to recall and to frame.[46]

This issue is evidently connected with the division of legislative powers on different levels of government. In Allegretti's words: "who has the power to set the rules for the implementation of participatory democracy"[47]? There is no certain answer to this question, given the fact that constitutions generally do not foresee a specific competence field related to participatory and deliberative democracy. Hence, the lack of a specific division of powers might create new (somehow unexpected) problems in need of a prompt and clear solution.

44 As stated in Bächtiger and Parkinson, *Mapping and Measuring Deliberation*.

45 See Mark E. Warren, "Institutionalizing Deliberative Democracy," in *Deliberation, Participation and Democracy: Can the People Govern?*, ed. Shawn W. Rosenberg (Basingstoke: Palgrave Macmillan, 2014) and Robert Hoppe, "Institutional Constraints and Practical Problems in Deliberative and Participatory Policy Making," *Policy & Politics* 39 (2011): 163 and Claus Offe, "Crisis and Innovation of Liberal Democracy: Can Deliberation Be Institutionalized?," *Czech Sociological Review* 47, no. 3 (2011): 447.

46 Rodolfo Lewanski, "The Challenges of Institutionalizing Deliberative Democracy: The 'Tuscany Laboratory'," *Journal of Public Deliberation* 9, no. 1 (2013): 12.

47 Allegretti, "Participatory Democracy," 212.

If we look at the different countries that institutionalized deliberative democracy we realize that most regulations are adopted at subnational level.[48] There are two kinds of possible regulations for participatory processes: sectorial ones – meaning those that foresee participatory procedure for making decisions in a specific policy sector – and organic ones – those that create a general framework for deliberative practices. About the first ones, it is of course a very difficult task to track them, given the high number of sectorial laws that foresee some kind of citizen participation in administrative procedures. However, in this case it is easier to identify the legitimate holder of the competence to adopt such instruments, looking at the government level constitutionally entitled with the related competence field.[49]

Coming to the second category of sources, it is interesting to analyze three examples in particular, Austria, Spain and Italy, where respectively *Länder*, Autonomous Communities and Regions adopted in recent years pieces of legislation that created general frameworks for deliberative democracy.

First, the Austrian Land of Vorarlberg enacted in 2013 a soft-law regulation on the functioning of the above described *Burgerräte* and in the same year the formula "participatory democracy" was introduced in the subnational Constitution, proving how highly Vorarlberg institutions regard these instruments, as they have become a stable part of the constitutional framework.[50]

The Autonomous Community of Aragon is another interesting example, having experimented with participatory procedures in different policy fields and involving citizens both at local and regional level.[51] After a long phase testing deliberative policymaking, in 2015 Aragon adopted a law (n. 8/2015) on participatory democracy and instituted a corresponding office at the regional level responsible for deliberative procedures. The law foresees that all the citizens of Aragon and the "organized civil society" can take part in deliberative

48 For a case study analysis on how participatory democracy has been institutionalized in a decentralized state, see Exposito Gomez's chapter on Spain in this volume.

49 With regard to the sharing of competences and the Italian case see Cecilia Corsi, "La democrazia partecipativa tra fonti statali fonti degli enti territoriali," *Osservatorio sulle fonti*, no. 1 (2009), available at: https://www.osservatoriosullefonti.it/mobile-saggi/fascicoli/fascicolo-n-1-2009/241-1-cecilia-corsi.

50 See Peter Bußjäger, "Participatory Initiatives and New Instruments of Direct Democracy in Austrian Federalism," in *Federalism as Decision-making: Changes in Structures, Procedures and Policies*, eds. Francesco Palermo and Elisabeth Alber (Leiden: Brill-Nijhoff, 2015), 417.

51 In the activity of the Spanish Autonomous Communities we can recognize two paths of development of participatory democracy: one of juridification (e.g. Valencia and Canaria) and one of experimentation, as the one of Aragon. On this see Sergio Castel Gayan, "Descentralizacion politica, participacion ciudadana y renovacion juridica: hacia una democracia participativa?," *Revista catalana de dret public* 43 (2011): 284.

procedures. The law lists some instruments of participatory democracy such as citizens' juries or citizens' panels, but also leaves space for the creation of other kinds of deliberative frameworks that can be activated both by the local entities or by the subnational administration.[52]

Even more fascinating is the case of the Italian Region of Tuscany that adopted a (first of its kind) law (n. 69/2007) specifically devoted to the organic regulation of deliberative democracy.[53] The law, renovated in 2013 (n. 46/2013), sets a general framework for participatory procedures, identifying the subjects who can activate participatory procedures, the functioning of the related financial support, and suggesting possible methodologies. Local entities are the main target of the law as they are the subject entitled with the power to activate participatory processes. Moreover, a regional participatory procedure, the public debate, is mandatory: it must be activated to involve all potentially interested parties in the planning procedure of environmentally relevant infrastructures. Furthermore, the law set up a new independent administrative body made of three members in charge of activating, monitoring, financing and concluding all participatory processes: the independent authority on participation.[54]

Undoubtedly, the regional legislature drew inspiration from the French experience of public debate for introducing the two latter elements in its legislation.

In fact, the first sectorial law ever adopted for permanently establishing the frame for a participatory process is the "*Loi Barnier*" on environmental protection adopted in France in 1995. The law provided for the establishment of the *Commission Nationale du Débat Public*, an independent administrative authority responsible for starting the public debate, managing the entire process and ensuring the planning of infrastructural projects in the national interest through deliberative discussion between all interested parties.[55] The main aim of the so called *debat public* is in fact to create a discussion arena where all

52 Sergio Castel Gayan, "Civil Participation Policy and Democratic Innovation in the Autonomous Community of Aragon," *Perspectives on Federalism* 4, no. 1 (2012): 235.

53 Lewanski, "The Challenges," 12.

54 Elisabeth Alber and Alice Valdesalici, "Framing Subnational 'Institutional Innovation' and 'Participatory Democracy' in Italy: Some Findings on Current Structures, Procedures and Dynamics," and Matteo Nicolini, "Theoretical Framework and Constitutional Implications: Participatory Democracy as Decision-Making in Multilayered Italy," both in *Federalism as Decision-Making: Changes in Structures, Procedures and Policies*, eds. Francesco Palermo and Elisabeth Alber (Leiden: Brill-Nijhoff, 2015).

55 Yves Mansillon, "L'esperienza del débat public in Francia," *Democrazia e diritto*, no. 3 (2006): 101.

opinions are collected, and potential conflicts are watered down, while looking for an acceptable compromise between all different positions at stake.[56]

As to the effects of this deliberative procedure, again, this is a merely consultative procedure. Despite that, the *debat public* can have very influential effects to the point that in the past some projects were recalled by the proponent, or in many others major changes were made to the initial projects.[57]

Not only the Region of Tuscany followed the French example, but also the Italian central government (Dpcm 76/2018) and the Apulia Region (l.r. n. 28/ 2017), adopted laws that enacted the "public debate" procedure. However, while in Tuscany the legislative measure on the public debate has remained in force undisturbed until now, the regional provision of Apulia was promptly challenged by the government which raised a question on the constitutional legitimacy of the law for violating the constitutional allocation of powers.[58] The issue was decided by Constitutional Court ruling No. 235/2018, in which some articles of the Apulian law were declared unconstitutional. Without going into the details of the decision, this ruling opens further doubts not only on the future of the regional public debates in Italy, but more generally with regard to the modulation of participatory democracy on multiple levels of government, to the possible interactions among different procedures and to the possibility of introducing mechanisms for coordination between processes taking place at the national level and those with regional relevance.[59]

This ruling shows that participatory democracy and its instruments end up thickening the network of relations between levels of government, from the local to the national, creating paths that can simultaneously affect different institutional spheres, each committed to implementing the deliberative frameworks made available by the competent level of government. Depending on the scope of their autonomy, not only local and subnational authorities are

56 See Alban Bouvier, "Démocratie délibérative, démocratie débattante, démocratie participative," *Revue européenne des sciences sociales* 45, no. 136 (2007): 5.

57 All information on the "public debate" procedure is available at: https://www.debatpublic.fr .

58 The growing role of judges in issues related to deliberative instruments has been anticipated by Francesco Palermo, "Regulating Pluralism: Federalism as Decision-Making and New Challenges for Federal Studies," *Federalism as Decision-Making: Changes in Structures, Procedures and Policies*, eds. in Francesco Palermo and Elisabeth Alber (Leiden: Brill-Nijhoff, 2015): 508. See also Kenneth P. Miller, *Direct Democracy and the Courts* (Cambridge: Cambridge University Press, 2009).

59 See Martina Trettel, "Discutere per deliberare: prime impressioni sulla recente introduzione del "Dibattito pubblico" in Italia," *Rivista il Mulino* (2018), available at: https://www.rivistailmulino.it/news/newsitem/index/Item/News:NEWS_ITEM:4488.

relevant in this interaction, but the central level of government can also play a role, adopting sources of law that impact local and regional governments by calling for the introduction of participatory decision-making processes. Moreover, the central government can develop valid and effective deliberative processes to take place at national level, as demonstrated by the case of the public debate in France, a traditionally unitary system.

Therefore, it could be stated that the allocation of powers on several levels of government and the decentralized structure of a country can undoubtedly help participatory democracy take root in the legal structures, although this is not a necessary precondition for its successful realization. On the contrary, among the elements that most strongly influence the positive outcome of democratic innovations, the "participatory" culture of a certain territory has to be considered, along with the will of political actors to engage effectively in their implementation.

It is undoubtedly true that a strong and clear decentralization strategy encourages pluralism and diversification, and thus it facilitates engagement in the implementation of participatory democracy, giving territories the possibility to structure their decision-making procedures in an innovative and more inclusive way. However, the involvement of citizens in the development of public decisions can only function when the cultural substratum is inherently acquainted with the participatory dimension of politics.[60]

4 The Paradigm of Federalism for a New Way of Looking at Deliberative Democracy

Having seen that institutional decentralization of powers only partially influences the development and employment of deliberative democratic instruments, we come now to the third, and last, tier of potential interaction between federalism and deliberative democracy. The starting point for this reflection resides in the simple observation that deliberative democracy and federalism partly pursue the same goals. We refer to the sharing of decision-making powers among multiple centers (both people and territories) for the improvement of democratic procedures and popular government.

In fact, bearing in mind the previous paragraphs, we are now aware that it is not only the decentralized structure of the State that induces a higher or lower degree of deliberative experimentation. On the contrary the link between

60 See Parolari and Trettel, "Democratic Quality," 301.

participatory democracy and federalism could be identified on a more theoretical and conceptual level.

Both federalism and deliberative democracy seek procedures, methods and institutional arrangements for distributing decision-making powers among multiple subjects, each holding a specific portion of sovereignty, in order to increase the degree of diversification and pluralism in the rule-making processes.

This way of approaching the issue can be tied to a "long tradition in political thought of linking federalism and other forms of non-centralism with separation of powers that reinforces rule of the people. Such notions have fostered the premise of an inherently democratic quality of federalism".[61]

At a first glance the federal (or regional) organization of a State constitutes a way for establishing democratic innovations on multiple levels of government. As Palermo points out, "federalism […] is a mode of organizing state structures in a way that preserves the plurality of levels of government and their decisional autonomy. As such, it does not per se include citizens in decision-making more than other systems, even though in federations citizens are involved more often, if nothing else then at least through various levels of election. Moreover, the wider the sub-national and local autonomy, the more these levels of government can experiment with forms of participatory democracy".[62] Here, however, we want to suggest a different perspective in which federalism offers institutional means for vertically multiplying representative decision-making centers and participatory democracy, and as its natural continuation, horizontally opening up these centers to create an even stronger connection with the civil society and citizens.[63]

Participation is pivotal both for federalism – where all territorial entities participate in governing the federal/regional state through shared-rule and self-rule[64] – and deliberative democracy – to the extent to which the related procedures require citizen participation for their positive outcome. Thus, participation represents the glue that ties federalism and deliberation on the common ground of democracy.

61 Jared Sonnicksen, "Federalism and Democracy: A Tense Relationship," in *Calidad democrática y organización territorial*, eds. Jose Tudela et al. (Madrid: Marcial Pons, 2018), 30.

62 Palermo, "Regulating Pluralism," 506.

63 The concept of representation in federalism is deeply analyzed in *Comparative Federalism*, 192.

64 Elazar, *Exploring Federalism*, 5.

The idea of distributing powers over several decision-making centers, all endowed with a portion – more or less extensive – of sovereignty, is inherent both to federalism and deliberative democracy. Whereas in the former case the reference is made to institutions, territories, and citizens in a collective perspective, in the latter, the term of reference is the citizens in their individual sphere, to be considered as centers of interests, potentially relevant to law. While federalism, on one side, is based on institutional instruments through which democratic capacity is shared vertically among different levels of government, deliberative democracy, on the other, manifests itself as a form of subjective exercise of popular sovereignty, distributed among all the individuals of a constituency.[65]

In the theoretical conception, the distribution of decision-making powers among several levels of government aims at improving the functionalities of democracy; with an analogous approach, the creation of deliberative phases aims at involving different instances in decision-making processes with a similar goal, albeit with partially different procedural outcomes.

How is this approach useful to the further development of both studies on federalism and on participatory democracy? In replying to this question, participatory democracy should be intended – similarly to federalism – as a tool of government that aspires at renewing traditional representative schemes and integrating additional levels and phases of decision-making. In this conception federalism and its way of dealing with complex issues through institutional means and flexible solutions could be seen as a paradigm, or a matrix, to be employed for devising valid answers to the "growing demands for pluralist (participatory, inclusive, multilevel) democracy".[66] While federalism has traditionally been a tool of regulating government, today it seems fruitful to consider its role to regulate or at least explain and frame phenomena of governance, like participatory democracy, which imply the same logic of multiplying the decision-making centers.

Such an approach might perhaps underpin the definitory work-in-progress that characterizes this field of research. To this extent, considering federalism as a tool for interpretation may allow, on one side, a new labeling of participatory processes and, on the other, their placement in a category that will more accurately describe the phenomenon. In fact, what is commonly found in studies that deal with participatory democracy is the opposition between

---

65 See Maria Margherita Procaccini, "Partecipazione e federalismo: lessico e strumenti di un metodo di governo," in *Le regole della democrazia partecipativa: itinerari per la costruzione di un metodo di governo*, ed. Alessandra Valastro (Napoli: Jovene, 2010).

66 Palermo, "Regulating Pluralism," 507.

three categories – representative, direct and deliberative democracy – as if these were strictly alternative one to the other. Not only is this not true, but it offers a confusing perspective on democratic innovations.

Relevantly, some accuse participatory democratic practices of being naïve, arguing that these cannot represent a valid alternative to representative structures of government, especially in complex societies.[67] Here we can only agree with these claims since participatory democracy does not suffice by itself.[68] By looking at the practical uses made of participatory democracy though, it is evident that democratic innovations are designed to integrate decision-making procedures already in place, whether they are representative or direct democracy.[69] Therefore, placing these instruments in their own category juxtaposed against the latter two does not accurately depict the reality of the facts. On the contrary, conceiving participatory practices as an organizational principle for integrating – when needed – policy-making procedures and horizontally expanding the plethora of subjects involved better conveys the true essence of such instruments. From this perspective participatory democracy practices imply a shift from government to governance in public decision-making processes in which federalism may provide theoretical framing, explanation and solutions, being the most consolidated set of tools and principles for the regulation of institutional and procedural complexity.

This perspective could also support public decision-makers in understanding that the powers they are vested with are not indivisible and monolithic; on the contrary, power-sharing – as federalism has taught over the centuries – induces greater democratic legitimacy and leads to decisions that are more appropriate to the context of reference. Like federalism, this type of civic participation is a method of government that encourages a reconsideration of decision-making processes for transforming these into something more complex, pluralistic, reticular, diversified; in brief, more similar to contemporary society.

67 Nicole Curato, Marit Hammond and John B. Min, *Power in Deliberative Democracy: Norms, Forums, Systems* (Basingstoke: Palgrave Macmillan, 2018), 1; Ron Levy and Graeme Orr, *The Law of Deliberative Democracy* (London-New York: Routledge, 2017), 46–47.

68 See Frank I. Michelman, "How Can the People Ever Make the Law?," *The Modern Schoolman* 74, no. 4 (1997): 311.

69 For example see Marlène Gerber and Sean Mueller, "When the People Speak – and Decide: Deliberation and Direct Democracy in the Citizen Assembly of Glarus, Switzerland," *Policy & Politics* 46, no. 3 (2018): 371.

5 Concluding Remarks

After having analyzed the three intersections between federalism and participatory democracy, as proposed in the introduction it is now possible to draw some conclusions.

The first level of connection could be defined as a practical and descriptive one. To this extent the level of government in which the participatory democratic process takes place is used as a lens through which it is possible to observe democratic innovations, for evaluation and descriptive purposes. Certainly, without some kind of decentralization participatory democracy would not have been born at all. In fact, the small scale of a territory and its closeness to citizens helped the conceptualization and the development of such instruments,[70] and its consequent transfer to other levels of government. However, it does not really matter from this way of looking at the issue what kind of decentralization is adopted in a specific country. Decentralization is only instrumental to the possibility for a participatory process to be established and properly function. In other words, in unitary countries – such as France – there are only two levels of government on which this kind of democratic experience can be started – the local and the national – while in regional or federal countries there are more possibilities. This does not change the way in which participatory processes are, on one hand, structured and implemented and, on the other hand, analyzed and presented. So, this multi-level approach represents mainly a "profiling model" of participatory democracy and is not properly able to prove any actual correlation between institutional decentralization and the successful development of its instruments.

The second level of interaction looked more at the ties between power sharing and the development of democratic innovations. This connection could be defined as the institutional one. It can be observed that more relevant experiences of institutionalizing participatory democracy have taken place at the subnational level of government. Therefore, this kind of decentralization has concretely influenced the further development of participatory practices in many decentralized countries, as seen in paragraph 3.

The institutionalization of participatory practices is important for ensuring the constant functioning of these practices and guaranteeing their

70 Also in light of the long-standing experiences of the New England Town-meetings and the Swiss Landsgemeinden. See for an overview Joseph F. Zimmerman, *The New England Town Meeting: Democracy in Action* (Westport: Praeger, 1999) and Hans-Peter Schaub, "Maximising Direct Democracy – by Popular Assemblies or by Ballot Votes?," *Swiss Political Science Review* 18, no. 3 (2012): 305.

independence from political interference. Writing down ground rules to be respected by all actors involved can avoid the manipulations of the outcomes of such processes. However, as seen, translating participatory democracy into legal norms is not very common, even if it is becoming more and more common practice. In this way, decentralization of powers certainly has to be considered as a support for developing legal frameworks that could accommodate participatory instances in different means. Subnational entities can function as living laboratories for the experimentation of deliberative institutional settings to be than copied and rearranged from other regions or even other levels of government.[71] This goes hand in hand with the very well-known statement according to which in federal systems a "single courageous state may, if its citizens choose, serve as laboratory, and try novel social and economic experiments without risk to the rest of the Country".[72] However, all this does not exclude the rise of participatory institutional settings in centralized countries, as successfully happened in France.[73]

To this extent, decentralization is a plus for establishment of participatory institutional structures, even if the positive outcome of a participatory experience depends upon many more factors: among these is also political culture, civic education and the strong will of all actors involved to effectively take part in the deliberative process.

The most innovative way of looking at participatory democracy, the third one, makes a different use of federalism for analyzing the issue. We could refer to it by the word "theoretical". In this respect, having excluded the possibility of proving any strong correlation between levels of government, their powers and the successful implementation of participatory processes, it has been argued that federalism and participatory democracy share some features mostly on a conceptual level. In fact, both pursue the sharing of powers between multiple decision-making centers to guarantee more pluralism and diversity and at the same time enhance the functionality of representative democracy, adapting it to current necessities.[74] To this extent, the parallelism between federalism and

---

71 See Nicolas Schmitt, "Subnational Institutional Innovation and Participatory Democracy: The Case of Switzerland," in *Federalism as Decision-Making: Changes in Structures, Procedures and Policies*, eds. Francesco Palermo and Elisabeth Alber (Leiden: Brill-Nijhoff 2015), 479 and Karl Kössler, "Laboratories of Democratic Innovation? Direct, Participatory, and Deliberative Democracy in Canadian Provinces and Municipalities," in *Citizen Participation in Multi-level Democracies*, eds. Cristina Fraenkel-Haeberle et al. (Leiden: Brill-Nijhoff, 2015) 290.

72 New State Ice Co. v. Liebmann, 285 U.S. 262, 311 (192).

73 Palermo and Kössler, *Comparative Federalism*, 122.

74 Palermo and Kössler, *Comparative Federalism*, 114–122.

participatory democracy lies at the structural-institutional level, in fact institutions are designed against an assumption of democracy, whether federalist or participatory.

Overall, what is clear is that participation through deliberation of citizens and civil society will become more and more a key element of the traditional decision-making process. To this extent, a change of perspective that transforms participatory democracy into a methodology would undeniably represent a big step forward in this sector. This is highly desirable for building new learning paths and expertise on participatory democracy and looking at new possible usages for federalism in the future.

Bibliography

Alber, Elisabeth and Alice Valdesalici. "Framing Subnational 'Institutional Innovation' and 'Participatory Democracy' in Italy: Some Findings on Current Structures, Procedures and Dynamics." In *Federalism as decision-making: Changes in structures, procedures and policies*, edited by Francesco Palermo and Elisabeth Alber, 448–478. Leiden: Brill-Nijhoff, 2015.

Allegretti, Umberto. "Un caso di attuazione del principio costituzionale di partecipazione: il regolamento del dibattito pubblico sulle grandi opere." *Rivista Associazione Italiana Costituzionalisti*, no. 3 (2018): 1–13.

Allegretti, Umberto. "Participatory Democracy in Multi-Level States." In *Citizen Participation in Multi-level Democracies*, edited by. Cristina Fraenkel-Haeberle et al., 205–215. Leiden: Brill-Nijhoff, 2015.

Allegretti, Umberto. "Recenti costituzioni "partecipate": Islanda, Ecuador, Bolivia." *Quaderni costituzionali*, no. 3 (2013): 689–708.

Anderson, George. "An Overview on Federalism." In *Federalism: An Introduction*, edited by George Anderson, 1–6. Oxford: Oxford University Press, 2008.

Bächtiger, André and John Parkinson. *Mapping and Measuring Deliberation: Towards a New Deliberative Quality*. Oxford: Oxford University Press, 2019.

Bächtiger, André et al., eds., *The Oxford Handbook of Deliberative Democracy*. Oxford: Oxford University Press, 2018.

Blokker, Paul, *New Democracies in Crisis?*. London-New York: Routledge, 2015.

Boaventura, De Sousa Santos. "Participatory Budgeting in Porto Alegre: Toward a Redistributive Democracy." *Politics & Society* 26, no. 4 (1998): 461–510.

Bobbio, Luigi, "Types of Deliberation." *Journal of Public Deliberation* 6, no. 2 (2010): 359–384.

Bohman, James and William Rehg. *Deliberative Democracy: Essays on Reason and Politics*. Cambridge MA: MIT, 1997.

Bouvier, Alban. "Démocratie délibérative, démocratie débattante, démocratie participative." *Revue européenne des sciences sociales* 45, no. 136 (2007): 5–34.

Bua, Adrian. "Scale and Policy Impact in Participatory-Deliberative Democracy: Lessons from a Multi-level Process." *Public Administration* 95, no. 1 (2017): 160–177.

Burgess, Michael. *Comparative Federalism: Theory and Practice.* London-New York: Routledge, 2006.

Bußjäger, Peter. "Participatory Initiatives and New Instruments of Direct Democracy in Austrian Federalism." In *Federalism as Decision-making: Changes in Structures, Procedures and Policies,* edited by Francesco Palermo and Elisabeth Alber, 415–427. Leiden: Brill-Nijhoff, 2015.

Bußjäger, Peter. "Entwicklungen in der direkten Demokratie und Bürgerbeteiligung in Vorarlberg." In *Parlamentarische Rechtsetzung in der Krise,* edited by Georg Lienbacher, 151–162. Wien: Sramek, 2014.

Cammack, Daniela. "Deliberation and Discussion in Classical Athens." *Journal of Political Philosophy* 29, no. 2 (2021): 135–166.

Carson, Lyn. *The Australian Citizens' Parliament and the Future of Deliberative Democracy.* Philadelphia: Pennsylvania State University Press, 2013.

Castel Gayan, Sergio. "Civil Participation Policy and Democratic Innovation in the Autonomous Community of Aragon." *Perspectives on Federalism* 4, no. 1 (2012): 230–251.

Castel Gayan, Sergio. "Descentralizacion politica, participacion ciudadana y renovacion juridica: hacia una democracia participativa?" *Revista catalana de dret public* 43 (2011): 279–316.

Chambers, Simone. "Deliberative Democratic Theory." *Annual Review of Political Science* 6 (2003): 307–326.

Churchill, Winston and Robert R. James. *Complete Speeches* 1897–1963. Langhorne: Chelsea House Publishers, 1974.

Corsi, Cecilia. "La democrazia partecipativa tra fonti statali fonti degli enti territoriali." *Osservatorio sulle fonti,* no. 1 (2009): 1–16.

Curato, Nicole, Marit Hammond and John B. Min. *Power in Deliberative Democracy: Norms, Forums, Systems.* Basingstoke: Palgrave Macmillan, 2018.

Dahl, Robert A. and Ian Shapiro. *On Democracy.* New Have: Yale University Press, 2015.

Dahl, Robert A. *Dilemmas of Pluralist Democracy: Autonomy vs. Control.* New Haven: Yale University Press, 1982.

Elazar Daniel J. *Exploring Federalism.* Tuscaloosa: The University of Alabama Press, 1987.

Elstub, Stephen. "Deliberative and Participatory Democracy." In *The Oxford Handbook of Deliberative Democracy,* edited by André Bächtiger et al., 187–202. Oxford: Oxford University Press, 2018.

Elstub, Stephen. "The Third Generation of Deliberative Democracy." *Political Studies Review* 8, no. 3 (2010): 291–307.

Ercan, Selen A. and Jean-P. Gagnon. "The Crisis of Democracy Which Crisis? Which Democracy?" *Democratic Theory* 1, no. 2 (2014): 1–10.

Fishkin, James S. *Democracy when the People are Thinking: Revitalizing our Politics through Public Deliberation*. Oxford: Oxford University Press, 2018.

Fishkin, James. "Making Deliberative Democracy Practical: Public Consultation and Dispute Resolution." *Ohio State Journal on Dispute Resolution* 24, no. 4 (2011): 611–626.

Floridia, Antonio. "Beyond Participatory Democracy, Towards Deliberative Democracy: Elements of a Possible Theoretical Genealogy." *Rivista italiana di scienza politica*, no. 3 (2014): 299–326.

Font, Joan, Donatella Della Porta and Yves Sintomer. *Participatory Democracy in Southern Europe: Causes, Characteristics and Consequences*. Lanham: Rowman & Littlefield International, 2014.

Font, Joan, Sara Pasadas del Amo and Graham Smith. "Tracing the Impact of Proposals from Participatory Processes: Methodological Challenges and Substantive Lessons." *Journal of Public Deliberation* 12, no. 1 (2016): 1–25.

Fung, Archon. "Minipublics: Deliberative Designs and Their Consequences." In *Deliberation, Participation and Democracy: Can the People Govern?*, edited by Shawn W. Rosenberg, 159–183. Basingstoke: Palgrave Macmillan, 2014.

Gamper, Anna. "A "Global Theory of Federalism": The Nature and Challenges of a Federal State." *German Law Journal* 6, no. 10 (2005): 1297–1318.

Gastil, John and Peter Levine. *The Deliberative Democracy Handbook: Strategies for Effective Civic Engagement in the Twenty-first Century*. San Francisco: Jossey-Bass, 2005.

Gastil, John and Robert Richards. "Making Direct Democracy Deliberative through Random Assemblies." *Politics & Society* 41, no. 2 (2013): 253–281.

Geissel, Brigitte and Kenneth Newton. *Evaluating Democratic Innovations: Curing the Democratic Malaise?*. London-New York: Routledge, 2012.

Gerber, Marlène and Sean Mueller. "When the People Speak – and Decide: Deliberation and Direct Democracy in the Citizen Assembly of Glarus, Switzerland." *Policy & Politics* 46, no. 3 (2018): 371–390.

Graber, Mark A. Sanford Levinson and Mark V. Tushnet, eds., *Constitutional Democracy in Crisis?*. Oxford: Oxford University Press, 2018.

Gundelach, Birte, Patricia Buser and Daniel Kübler. "Deliberative Democracy in Local Governance: The Impact of Institutional Design on Legitimacy." *Local Government Studies* 43, no. 2 (2017): 218–244.

Gutmann, Amy and Dennis F. Thompson. *Why Deliberative Democracy?*. Princeton: Princeton University Press, 2004.

Hoppe, Robert. "Institutional Constraints and Practical Problems in Deliberative and Participatory Policy Making." *Policy & Politics* 39 (2011): 163–186.

Kahane, David J. *Deliberative Democracy in Practice*. Vancouver: UBC Press, 2010.

Kies, Raphaël. *Promises and Limits of Web-deliberation*. Basingstoke: Palgrave Macmillan, 2010.

Knobloch, Katherine R. et al. "Did They Deliberate?: Applying an Evaluative Model of Democratic Deliberation to the Oregon Citizens' Initiative Review." *Journal of Applied Communication Research* 41, no. 2 (2013): 105–125.

Kössler, Karl. "Laboratories of Democratic Innovation? Direct, Participatory, and Deliberative Democracy in Canadian Provinces and Municipalities." In *Citizen Participation in Multi-level Democracies*, edited by Cristina Fraenkel-Haeberle et al., 286–308. Leiden: Brill-Nijhoff, 2015.

Levy, Ron and Graeme Orr. *The Law of Deliberative Democracy*. London-New York: Routledge, 2017.

Levy, Ron, ed. *The Cambridge Handbook of Deliberative Constitutionalism*. Cambridge: Cambridge University Press, 2018.

Lewanski, Rodolfo. "The Challenges of Institutionalizing Deliberative Democracy: The 'Tuscany Laboratory'." *Journal of Public Deliberation* 9, no. 1 (2013): 1–16.

Lijphart, Arend. "Non-Majoritarian Democracy: A Comparison of Federal and Consociational Theories." *Publius* 15, no. 3 (1985): 3–15.

Mansillon, Yves. "L'esperienza del débat public in Francia." *Democrazia e diritto*, no. 3 (2006): 1–14.

Melo, Marcus A. and Gianpaolo Baiocchi. "Deliberative Democracy and Local Governance: Towards a New Agenda." *International Journal of Urban & Regional Research* 30, no. 3 (2006): 587–600.

Michelman, Frank I. "How Can the People Ever Make the Law?" *The Modern Schoolman* 74, no. 4 (1997): 311–330.

Miller, Kenneth P. *Direct Democracy and the Courts*. Cambridge: Cambridge University Press, 2009.

Negretto, Gabriel L. "Democratic Constitution-Making Bodies: The Perils of a Partisan Convention." *International Journal of Constitutional Law* 16, no. 1 (2018): 254–279.

Nicolini, Matteo. "Theoretical Framework and Constitutional Implications. Participatory Democracy as Decision-Making in Multilayered Italy." In *Federalism as Decision-making: Changes in Structures, Procedures and Policies*, edited by Francesco Palermo and Elisabeth Alber, 428–447, Leiden: Brill-Nijhoff, 2015.

Offe, Claus. "Crisis and Innovation of Liberal Democracy: Can Deliberation Be Institutionalized?" *Czech Sociological Review* 47, no. 3 (2011): 447–472.

Palermo, Francesco and Karl Kössler. *Comparative Federalism: Constitutional Arrangements and Case Law*. Oxford-Portland: Hart Publishing, 2017.

Palermo, Francesco. "Regulating Pluralism: Federalism as Decision-Making and New Challenges for Federal Studies." In *Federalism as Decision-making: Changes in Structures, Procedures and Policies*, edited by Francesco Palermo and Elisabeth Alber, 497–513, Leiden: Brill-Nijhoff, 2015.

Parolari, Sara and Martina Trettel. "Democratic Quality and Territorial Distribution of Power in Italy." In *Calidad democrática y organización territorial*, edited by Jose Tudela et al., 281–302. Madrid: Marcial Pons, 2018.

Pasquino, Gianfranco. *Strumenti della democrazia*. Bologna: Il Mulino, 2007.

Patsias, Caroline, Anne Latendresse and Laurence Bherer. "Participatory Democracy, Decentralization and Local Governance: The Montreal Participatory Budget in the light of 'Empowered Participatory Governance'." *International Journal of Urban & Regional Research* 37, no. 6 (2013): 2214–2230.

Procaccini, Maria Margherita. "Partecipazione e federalismo: lessico e strumenti di un metodo di governo." in *Le regole della democrazia partecipativa: itinerari per la costruzione di un metodo di governo*, edited by Alessandra Valastro, 57–80. Napoli: Jovene, 2010.

Revel, Martine. *Le débat public: une expérience française de démocratie participative*. Paris: Découverte, 2007.

Schaub, Hans-Peter. "Maximising Direct Democracy – by Popular Assemblies or by Ballot Votes?" *Swiss Political Science Review* 18, no. 3 (2012): 305–331.

Schmitt, Carl and Ellen Kennedy. *The Crisis of Parliamentary Democracy*. Cambridge MA: MIT Press, 2000.

Schmitt, Nicolas. "Subnational Institutional Innovation and Participatory Democracy: The Case of Switzerland." In *Federalism as Decision-making: Changes in Structures, Procedures and Policies*, edited by Francesco Palermo and Elisabeth Alber, 479–495, Leiden: Brill-Nijhoff, 2015.

Sintomer, Yves, Carsten Herzberg and Anja Röcke. "Participatory Budgeting in Europe: Potentials and Challenges." *International Journal of Urban & Regional Research* 32, no. 1 (2008): 164–178.

Smith, Graham and Maija Setälä. "Mini-Publics and Deliberative Democracy." In *The Oxford Handbook of Deliberative Democracy*, edited by André Bächtiger et al., 300–314. Oxford: Oxford University Press, 2018.

Smith, Graham. *Democratic Innovations: Designing Institutions for Citizen Participation*. Cambridge: Cambridge University Press, 2009.

Sommermann, Karl-Peter. "Citizen Participation in Multi-Level Democracies – An introduction." In *Citizen Participation in Multi-level Democracies*, edited by Cristina Fraenkel-Haeberle et al., 1–12. Leiden: Brill-Nijhoff, 2015.

Sonnicksen, Jared. "Federalism and Democracy: A Tense Relationship." In *Calidad democrática y organización territorial*, edited by Jose Tudela et al., 29–50. Madrid: Marcial Pons, 2018.

Steiner, Jürg. *The Foundations of Deliberative Democracy: Empirical Research and Normative Implications*. Cambridge: Cambridge University Press, 2012.

Stepan, Alfred. "Democrazia e federalismo: un'analisi comparata." *Rivista Italiana di Scienze Politiche* 28, no. 1 (1998): 5–54.

Suteu. Silvia. "Constitutional Conventions in the Digital Era: Lessons from Iceland and Ireland." *Boston College International and Comparative Law Review* 3, no. 2 (2015): 251–276.

Trettel, Martina. "Discutere per deliberare: prime impressioni sulla recente introduzione del "Dibattito pubblico" in Italia." *Rivista il Mulino* (2018).

Trettel, Martina. "La democrazia partecipativa nelle Regioni a Statuto Speciale: tendenze e prospettive di sviluppo." In *Le variabili della specialità: evidenze e riscontri tra soluzioni istituzionali e politiche settoriali*, edited by Francesco Palermo and Sara Parolari, 199–224. Napoli: Edizioni Scientifiche Italiane, 2018.

Warren, Mark E. "Institutionalizing Deliberative Democracy." In *Deliberation, Participation and Democracy: Can the People Govern?*, edited by Shawn W. Rosenberg, 272–288. Basingstoke: Palgrave Macmillan, 2014.

Warren, Mark E. and Hilary Pearse. *Designing Deliberative Democracy: The British Columbia Citizens' Assembly*. Cambridge: Cambridge University Press, 2008.

Zimmerman, Joseph F. *The New England Town Meeting: Democracy in Action*. Westport: Praeger, 1999.

CHAPTER 6

Participatory Democracy in Spain's Autonomous Regions: Some Tools to Strengthen Democratic Development

Enriqueta Expósito

1 Introduction

Democracy and decentralisation came hand in hand in Spain. After a 40-year-long dictatorship, the transition to democracy pivoted on two axes. The first axis defined how Spain would move from an authoritarian regime to a democratic system. The second axis was territorial. It dictated the transformation of a unitary, strongly centralistic state into a decentralised state. The Spanish Constitution approved in 1978 (hereinafter "SC") combined these two elements to varying degrees.

Politically, the SC aimed to enable democracy. The Preamble to the SC specifically proclaims the political will to "establish an advanced democratic society". Article 1 of the SC also explicitly defines the state as a social and democratic State of Law.

From a territorial point of view, the SC mandated decentralization of political power. This process included forming the self-governing autonomous regions (*Comunidades Autónomas*) that currently make up the Spanish state, to which the democratic principle contained in Article 1.1 SC was extended. At this level of government, democracy was established in a form that mirrored the State's model. Until the end of the 20th century, the autonomous regions almost perfectly replicated the State's rules for the operation of representative democracy, including the shortcomings of direct democracy. This model did not provide any forms of citizen participation other than elections. Awareness that proximity to citizens was an added value only arose in the 2000s. This reinforced the "democratic quality" of sub-state entities. This proximity was helpful in articulating mechanisms to facilitate the interaction between public authorities and citizens. They seemed to be the most appropriate testing ground testing all these approaches.

The purpose of this chapter is to analyse how the territorial decentralisation of political power[1] contributes to increasing the democratic quality of the government of the autonomous regions. The analysis is strictly limited to the case of the Spanish state and its unique territorial structure. The hybrid nature of Spain as a state made up of autonomous regions determines the development of democracy in these sub-state entities, while promoting a shift towards a different model from the one advocated at state level, namely, participatory democracy.[2] The form and scope of its regulation in the autonomous regions is based on the same logic that is behind the exercise of power in federal systems: bringing decision making closer to the citizen.

First, the chapter will briefly analyse the constitutional framework on which citizen participation stands and the link between the democratic principle and territorial decentralisation. The central part of the chapter focuses on two main issues. The first considers the main factors that have contributed to the improvement of democratic quality in the autonomous regions. The second focuses on and outlines the main instruments of participation that sub-state lawmakers developed to promote citizens' participation.

2 The Constitutional Framework of Citizen Participation and the Decentralised Structure of the Spanish State

2.1 *Constitutional Perspectives on Citizen Participation*

Citizen participation, as an inherent element of the democratic exercise of power, was proclaimed as a fundamental right in the SC. Article 23 SC states: "Citizens have the right to participate in public affairs, directly or through representatives freely elected in periodic elections by universal

1 The use of the concept of 'decentralization' and not of federalism is due to the hybrid nature of the Spanish Autonomous State. In its constitutional configuration, the decentralization designed by the Constitution is not comparable to federalism. It is closer to a 'reinforced' regional model. And this is evidenced by the regulation contained in article 2 of the Constitution and in articles 137 to 159 of the Constitution. Only the evolution of the constitutional model, especially from the Statutes of Autonomy – without any reform of the constitutional text in this matter – the federal logic was introduced.

2 The autonomous State is a territorial form that is built on the unity of the State. It is based on the existence of a single and indivisible sovereign subject: the Spanish people. Everything related to the exercise of this sovereignty is a state matter. For this reason, the development of the exercise of the right to political participation – directly or through representatives – is regulated by the State. The Autonomous Communities have, however, a wide margin of autonomy in the organization of participation in those areas in which the sovereign subject is not involved: the sphere of participatory democracy.

suffrage". Article 23 is included in Title I of the SC, specifically, in section 1 of Chapter 2 ("Fundamental Rights and Public Liberties"). It relates to fundamental rights and duties, which provide mandatory safeguards of citizen participation. This special protection encompasses regulation under an organic law (Article 81 SC), direct access to the Constitutional Court through an individual appeal for protection (*recurso de amparo*, Article 161.1.b SC), and a requirement for a special or exceptional procedure (*procedimiento agravado*) for constitutional reform (Article 168 SC).

However, the wording of Article 23 SC implies that not all participation is protected as a fundamental right of citizens; protection only extends to participation that is related to public affairs. The expression *public affairs* has been deemed to mean *political affairs* in constitutional jurisprudence. Therefore, only political participation is considered a fundamental right. It is only political participation that constitutes:

> "a manifestation of people's sovereignty, which is normally exercised through representatives and which, exceptionally, can be directly exercised by the people; this leads to the conclusion that these rights are limited to the scope of the direct democratic legitimation of the State and of the different territorial entities within it".[3]

In other words, only where the call to participation ultimately involves the exercise of political power, directly or through representatives, that is, only where that power is conferred on the people, is it considered to be in the scope of Article 23.1 SC and, therefore, can it be invoked as a fundamental right.[4] In this way, the right to political participation under the SC is linked to forms of representative democracy and direct democracy. Its proclamation as a fundamental right is an expression of the "subjective aspect of the entire structure of the democratic State".[5]

Despite the apparent "neutrality" of Article 23 SC regarding both types of participation, a systematic interpretation of the SC has made it possible to identify representative democracy as the pillar of Spanish constitutional democracy. But it is not only representation that constitutes the central axis of the democratic system. This model is also characterised by limitations on the mechanisms of direct democracy – restricted to those cases in which the

3 Constitutional Court Judgment number 119, of 17 July 1995.

4 Constitutional Court Judgment number 119/1995.

5 Juan Alfonso Santamaría Pastor, "Comentario al artículo 23.1 CE," in *Comentarios a la Constitución Española de 1978*, ed. Fernando Garrido Falla (Madrid: Civitas, 1985), 443.

Constitution explicitly imposes them or those which are explicitly allowed and are subject to the authorisation of the representative of the sovereign people – basically, a referendum or a *citizens' legislative initiative*.[6] This has been confirmed by the extensive Constitutional Court case law on the matter, which has extolled representation as a source of democratic legitimation of political power and the instrument of participation *par excellence*. To the extent that the exercise of representation links the active and passive aspects of the right to vote, it is conceived as the "nerve and support of democracy".[7]

Beyond the strictly political vision of citizen participation, the SC incorporates multiple perspectives and refers to different subjects (citizens, nationals, consumers, workers, users, etc.). It is also applicable to other areas (social, economic and cultural) and the exercise of the state's legislative, executive and judicial powers is informed by different (organic and functional) perspectives. But in all these different appearances it does not refer to a fundamental right, but rather they are usually allusions to duties for all public powers – from the local to the state. Only when direct citizen participation is regulated is a fundamental right. This serves "to facilitate the participation of all citizens in political, economic, cultural and social life" under Article 9.2 SC. This constitutional mandate makes it possible to establish other forms of participation in public spheres, including those referring to political institutions, although they are not deemed to be constitutional rights for the purposes of Article 23 SC. All of these forms of participation constitute what has come to be identified as participatory democracy.

2.2 *The Democratic Principle and the Decentralised Structure of the State*

Over time, the democratic principle explicitly provided for in Article 1.1 of the SC inevitably extended to all levels of government. As noted by the Constitutional Court,[8] this principle requires that the citizens of an autonomous region also participate in shaping the powers of their region through the means set out in the regional Statutes and in the SC "precisely because they are recipients of the mandates of that public power".

This ensured that the representative model of democracy would be applied in these sub-state entities. But not only was the representative model of democracy applied, but a limited form of direct democracy was also "imposed".

6 The use of these mechanisms in Franco's dictatorship led to great caution around their inclusion in the SC.

7 Constitutional Court Judgment number 24, of 15 February 1990.

8 Specifically in Judgment number 31, of 28 June 2010.

As each of these models was linked to the fundamental right of participation in Article 23 SC, the autonomous regions enjoyed a very limited margin of manoeuvre to act within the model of political democracy, be it representative or direct. Rather, they were "condemned" to reproduce the state model with few innovations. There were several reasons for this.

In the system of distribution of powers designed by the SC, exclusive jurisdiction is attributed to the state for the "regulation of the basic conditions guaranteeing the equality of all Spaniards in the exercise of their rights and in the fulfilment of their constitutional duties" (Article 149.1.1 SC). As mentioned earlier, this right must be regulated by an organic law (pursuant to Article 81 SC), which can only be approved by the Spanish Parliament. Organic laws are not within the legal remit of the autonomous regions. The general electoral system is also regulated by an organic law and is therefore solely subject to the action of the state.[9] The power that the SC grants to the autonomous regions so that they can adopt their own electoral laws was also subject to the requirement of a system of proportional representation in their legislative Assemblies (pursuant to Article 152.1 SC).[10] All these conditions basically require legislators in the autonomous regions to choose an electoral scheme that specified the proportionality outlined by the SC.[11] In addition, it restricted their power to decide on the issue of constituency[12] and on the determination of the electoral threshold.[13]

9 This expression encompasses all those rules "that must govern the generality of elections to constitute the representative institutions of the state as a whole and in those of the territorial entities into which it is organised, in accordance with Article 137 of the SC" (Constitutional Court Judgment number 38, of 16 May 1983). That is, the establishment of the rules "relating to who can elect, who can be elected and under what conditions, for what period of time and under what organisational criteria from a procedural and territorial point of view" (Constitutional Court Judgment number 72, of 14 July 1984).

10 All the autonomous regions have approved their own electoral laws, with the sole exception of Catalonia. The elections to the Catalan Parliament continue to be governed by the Fourth Transitory Provision of the 1979 Statute of Autonomy of Catalonia, currently repealed.

11 At present, all regional electoral laws apply the d'Hont formula, which is the one used in the Spanish Congress.

12 As a general rule, the electoral constituency is the province (or the island in the Balearic and Canary Islands). Only in the case of Asturias is an infra-provincial territorial demarcation – the council – identified as a constituency. The case of the Canary Islands is unique in that it combines a single autonomous region and seven constituencies, each corresponding to one island.

13 In Spanish general elections, the electoral threshold is set at 3%. Therefore, any candidates that fail to obtain at least this percentage of valid votes cast in their constituency are not considered for the allocation and distribution of seats in those constituencies. This percentage has also been included in the majority of regional electoral laws. In some

The autonomous regions have practically no room to manoeuvre when it comes to direct democracy, especially with regard to holding a referendum. The omission of the autonomous region referendum from Organic Law 2/1980, of 18 January 1980, on the regulation of the different forms of referendum, and the extensive interpretation made by the Constitutional Court of the State's powers set forth in Article 149.1.32 SC regarding the "authorisation for citizens' consultations through the holding of referendums" deprived the autonomous regions of the ability to act in the regulatory organisation of this form of participation *par excellence*.[14]

Nevertheless, the logic is reversed when citizen participation is outside the protection of the right proclaimed in Article 23 of the SC. It is in this area that the autonomous regions play a crucial role. In compliance with the mandate of Article 9.2 SC, the public powers in the autonomous regions have ample authority to regulate other forms of participation, which enables them to foster a more participatory model of democracy. Self-governance involves determining the way in which the institutions of an autonomous region relate to their own citizens. The scope and extent of citizen participation is one of the essential elements that define these relationships and must be decided upon by the autonomous regions' institutions.

In this area, there are no limitations arising from the link between political democracy and the concept of sovereignty. Article 1.2 SC proclaims that "national sovereignty resides in the Spanish people, from whom the powers of the State emanate", thereby identifying the Spanish people as the undivided holder of sovereignty.[15] This unitary vision makes it difficult for autonomous regions to exercise direct democracy outside the scope of the state and the sole sovereign subject: the Spanish people as a whole.[16]

Participatory democracy makes it possible to circumvent the restrictions imposed by direct democracy, allowing all citizens to participate without the

---

autonomous regions (Valencia, Extremadura, Galicia, Cantabria, La Rioja, Madrid and the Balearic Islands) the threshold is increased to 5%. In the Canary Islands the percentage ranges from 4% in the single autonomous region constituency to 15% in the various island constituencies.

14 Constitutional Court Judgment 31, of 28 June 2010, clearly determined that the state's jurisdiction was not exclusively limited to the authorisation for a referendum to be held, but rather extends "to the referendum as an institution in its entirety", excluding any regional scope of action in the matter.

15 Constitutional Court Judgment 100, of 28 November 1984.

16 This has been noted in the abundant constitutional jurisprudence that has been generated as a result of the Catalan sovereignty process based on Constitutional Court Judgment number 42, of 25 March 2014, particularly in the Third Point of Law.

requirement of nationality being met.[17] However, precisely for this reason, the exercise of sovereignty is not affected.

3 Furthering the Scope of the Democratic Model in the Autonomous Regions

For many years, the autonomous regions did not depart from the state model. Their Statutes of Autonomy barely contained references to citizen participation, and those that did merely mimicked the constitutional structure. They replicated the mandate of Article 9.2 of the SC for the citizens of the autonomous regions with identical or similar wording. These Statutes allowed for the possibility of participating in a regional legislative procedure through the *citizens' legislative initiative*. In some cases, powers were held on matters related to citizens' consultations. Ultimately, provisions were introduced that enabled some autonomous regions to hold referendums to approve processes for reforming their Statutes (Catalonia, Galicia, the Basque Country and Andalusia) and referendum-type consultations for the unification or separation of territories (Aragón, Castilla y León and the Basque Country).

Citizen participation has not been a priority for the regional legislator either. For years there has been an indolent attitude towards furthering the scope of the democratic model. Leaving aside the social participation required to regulate different sectors (labour, environment, education, trade and provision of services, etc.), for a long time the autonomous region laws regulating *citizens' legislative initiatives* have reproduced the regulatory pattern of state regulations regarding the subjects, limits, and ultimately their extremely restricted operability as a form of participation.[18]

---

17 The expression 'participatory democracy' includes all those instruments that allow the intervention of citizens – individually or grouped in organizations that defend social interests – in some phase of the public decision-making process in order to influence the final decision adopted by the competent authority. This citizen participation is not considered political participation and, therefore, is excluded from the scope of protection of the fundamental right recognized in article 23 SC. Unlike the mechanisms of direct democracy (e.g. the referendum) – which are linked to the exercise of the right to political participation – in the procedures of participatory democracy (e.g. public hearings, citizen hearings in the procedure of discussion of a law) the legislator can contemplate the intervention of non-national citizens and minors. In addition, above all, their exercise is not surrounded by the electoral guarantees that do accompany the exercise of direct democracy.

18 Recent studies have revealed this limited effectiveness of the popular legislative initiative at the state level: Paloma Requejo, "El régimen jurídico de la iniciativa legislativa

3.1 *A Turning Point: The Crisis of Representation*

At the beginning of the 2000s there was a shift in the attitude of the autonomous regions towards the participatory phenomenon. This change was related to citizens' questioning of the institutional system and incumbent representatives, which reached its peak during the financial recession. While this was not the trigger for the institutional crisis, it did increase its severity. There was social unrest at various levels of society and a sense of weariness, disappointment and discontent among a large part of the population. At the core of public criticism was how representation operated. Citizens openly criticised the inability of public administrators to deal with the dismantling of the welfare state and the achievements it had made in times of economic prosperity. The failure of public representatives to make decisions that met the challenges resulting from the recession effectively was also widely reproved. Citizens felt excluded from the decision-making procedures that directly concerned them. It became bitterly apparent that there was a clear gap between citizens and their representatives. Fundamentally, this crisis of representation revealed the shortcomings of the institutional system and the exhaustion of a model whereby political leaders made decisions without involving the members of the public and the different sensitivities and interests of the people.[19]

In this context, the demand for more participation by citizens resulted from a desire to retake the reins of power conferred to them by their status as holders of sovereignty and to "empower" themselves with a dual purpose. First, to take part and be present in the decision-making processes so as not to be oblivious to what was decided on their behalf; and second, to take control and promote accountability.

The response to these shortcomings was provided by the autonomous regions. After many years of lethargy, they were receptive of the complaints in contrast to the passivity shown by the state. The autonomous regions played a decisive role in driving the renewal of democracy and giving citizens avenues to participate in decision-making processes beyond the boundaries of representative and direct democracy. In this way, the close link between the development of participatory institutions and political decentralisation became much more solid. This led to a regional model of participatory democracy in

popular: un presente insatisfactorio y un futuro incierto," *Teoría y Realidad Constitucional* 51 (2023): 259–281; Angel Fernández, "Teoría y práctica de la iniciativa legislativa popular en España," *Estudios de Deusto. Revista de Derecho Público* 71, no. 1 (2023): 199–227.

19 José Tudela et al., eds. *Libro blanco sobre la calidad democrática en España* (Madrid: Marcial Pons, 2018).

which citizens have more opportunities to take part in public decision-making processes than they have at state level.[20]

3.2 *The Response from the Legislator in the Autonomous Regions: A Clear Commitment to the Participatory Model*

The change mentioned above was apparent in the reforms of the autonomous regions' Statutes that took place from the mid-2000s. The new Statutes of Autonomy exponentially increased their participatory content, which was no longer merely anecdotal. They were intended to meet the demands for additional participation avenues in the reformed Statutes, as they had rigid provisions in this regard that were similar to those in the SC. In this way, the participatory phenomenon was somewhat "updated" within the regulatory framework. The reform placed participation at the core of the actions provided for by the autonomous regions' public powers. This therefore became one of the essential elements of both a political democracy and an advanced social (and economic) democracy.

3.2.1 The Proclamation of Participation Rights in the New Statutes of Autonomy

The new statutory cycle is promoted by some of the autonomous regions whose Statutes had not been changed since they were enacted (between 1979 and 1981). They initiated the reform procedures provided for in their regulations and used them to replace the old provisions with new ones. The process that began in Catalonia (2006) and Andalusia (2007) was later extended to other autonomous regions, namely, the Valencian Region, Aragon, the Balearic Islands, Extremadura, Navarre, the Canary Islands, Castilla y León, Castilla-La Mancha and the Murcia Region. Currently, these new provisions coexist with those in older Statutes of Autonomy that have not yet been subject to revision.

Under these new Statutes of Autonomy, participation is a right of the citizens of the region in question. To the extent that the Statutes specify and define the way citizens relate to their self-government institutions, they are part of the provisions prescribed in Article 147.2c SC and enable the exercise of regional powers to organise self-government institutions. In the words of the

20 María Reyes Pérez Alberdi, "El modelo autonómico de democracia participativa: la situación a partir de la aprobación de los nuevos estatutos de autonomía (Model of Participatory Democracy in Spain's Autonomous Communities: New Statutes of Autonomy)," *Oñati Socio-Legal Series* 7, no. 5 (2017): 1062. [https://opo.iisj.net/index.php/osls/article/view/832].

Constitutional Court, they constitute "central or nuclear aspects of the institutions they regulate".[21]

In this way, the new Statutes not only cover the right to active and passive suffrage for regional elections – using very similar or the same wording as that of Article 23 SC – and the right of petition (proclaimed in Article 29 SC). Most of them also confer the status of rights on *citizens' legislative initiatives* and participation in the law-making process, the right to file complaints (only in Catalonia) and the right to promote the holding of citizens' consultations (Andalusia, the Canary Islands, Castilla and León, Catalonia and the Balearic Islands).

Another new development that accompanied the proclamation of these participation rights was related to the rights-holders. The political participation set out in Article 23 SC only applies to national citizens.[22] This is expressly provided for in Article 13 of the SC, with a single exception referring to local elections. In local elections, non-nationals have the right to active and passive suffrage[23] as long as two conditions are met: It must be provided for in a treaty or law, and must take into account reciprocity criteria.

In this way, while political participation within the scope of representative and direct democracy is reserved for citizens who exist within the notion of a sovereign people (whose members are part of the electoral body), the paths of participatory democracy allow this sharp distinction between sovereign subject and citizen to be overcome. Insofar as the rights granted under the Autonomous Regions' Statutes are outside what is understood as *public affairs*, they should also be applied to all citizens of the autonomous region, whether or not they have Spanish nationality. For this reason, the citizen participation protected by the bills of rights contained in the Statutes is an instrument of democratic integration for all citizens and not only those who make

21 Judgments of the Constitutional Court numbers 247, of 12 December 2007 and 31, of 28 June 2010.

22 Organic Law 5/1985, of 19 June 1985, on the General Electoral Regime embraced a broad concept of "national" which includes both resident nationals and absent nationals who make up a single electoral roll despite being registered in different censuses.

23 Originally, Article 13 SC only referred to the right to active suffrage. In 1992, the reference to passive suffrage was incorporated into its provisions. This constitutional reform resulted from the signing of the Treaty of the European Union. It was intended to meet a requirement of the Constitutional Court which held "that the stipulation contained in the future Art. 8 B, paragraph 1, of the Treaty Establishing the European Economic Community, as it will be drafted in the Treaty of the European Union, is contrary to Art. 13.2 of the [Spanish] Constitution regarding the attribution of the right to passive suffrage in local elections to citizens of the European Union who are not Spanish nationals" (Declaration 1/1992, of 1 July 1992).

up their electoral body. Participatory democracy makes representation more inclusive.[24]

The clauses incorporated in the new Statutes of Autonomy followed the same path. Explicit mandates were formulated and were addressed to the self-government institutions, either to establish "appropriate avenues to facilitate and promote participation in decisions of general interest of resident foreign citizens" (Aragon), or to "extend to citizens of the European Union and resident foreigners" the rights of participation "under the Spanish Constitution, without prejudice to the rights of participation guaranteed by European Union law" (Andalusia). The formulation of these provisions is not in conflict with the constitutional framework in relation to the holding of the rights of political participation. However, on a more symbolic level, they succeeded in capturing the debate raised in some social and political sectors -supported by some scholars-[25] regarding the holding of rights of political participation applicable to non-nationals with stable residence in Spain.[26] These provisions paved the way for new prospects in terms of the holding of these rights which, until then, had only been applied to nationals, while also reinforcing the commitment to a more inclusive notion of citizenship underpinned by residence status.

Beyond the subjective aspect, the proclamation of these rights in the Statute of Autonomy contributed to qualifying their democratic operation in an attempt to bring decision-making processes closer to citizens. This reinforced the institutions of participatory democracy.

24 Enriqueta Expósito Gomez, *Deliberación y participación ciudadanas* (Madrid: Marcial Pons, 2021), 70–71.

25 Among others, Ignacio Villaverde, "La ciudadanía borrosa. Ciudadanías multinivel," *Fundamentos: Cuadernos monográficos de teoría del estado, derecho público e historia constitucional* 7 (2012): 285–308; Blanca Rodríguez, "Las dos caras de la ciudadanía moderna: entre la nacionalidad y el estatus participativo," *Revista Europea de Derechos Fundamentales* 27 (2016): 17–42; Ángel Rodríguez, "El voto de los ciudadanos de la unión europea en las elecciones autonómicas españolas: estado de la cuestión y propuestas de reforma," *Revista Europea de Derechos Fundamentales* 27 (2016): 203–227; Miguel A. Presno, "El sufragio de los extranjeros residentes en las elecciones generales como exigencia de una ciudadanía democrática," *Revista Europea de Derechos Fundamentales* 27 (2016): 257–283; Miguel Agudo, "Vías constitucionales para el reconocimiento del derecho de sufragio en las elecciones autonómicas españolas a los extranjeros residentes," *Revista Europea de Derechos Fundamentales* 27 (2016): 309–328.

26 This debate was also analysed in the Report on Proposals of Amendment of the General Electoral Regime, issued by the Council of State at the request of the government in February 2009.

3.2.2 The Regulatory Action of the Autonomous Regions

Only the autonomous regions that have approved new Statutes of Autonomy have proclaimed participation rights for their citizens. However, the response of regional legislators has had a wider scope. Currently, the vast majority of the autonomous regions have passed regulations that govern participation rights, regardless of whether their Statutes have been reformed or not.

Within the autonomous regions action affecting different areas of participation has been taken at two levels: legislative and executive. The same outcome has been achieved at both levels: citizen participation fosters an improvement in the democratic exercise of government, regenerating the link between power and the citizens who legitimise it. Nevertheless, the logic for participation at each of these levels is different. At the legislative level, citizen participation focuses on reinforcing deliberation and debate. At the executive level, participation is aimed more towards agreement: there is awareness of the interests involved and that a better solution can be provided for them accordingly. This last perspective incorporates the postulates of governance that demand collaboration between incumbent representatives and society for the common good.

3.2.2.1 *A More Receptive and Approachable Parliament*

Parliament is the body whose members are representatives of the people, understood as the electoral body (called upon to elect its representatives). As an institution, however, Parliament represents the whole of society, including those citizens who, due to age, nationality or any other circumstances, cannot participate in the election of its members. For this reason, in parliamentary terms, citizen participation is an instrument of inclusion and democratic integration of all groups that may consider themselves excluded or feel that their interests are not sufficiently represented by the majorities resulting from elections.

The instruments that enable citizen participation serve different functions in Parliament, especially concerning legislative and government control functions.

To perform the legislative function, participation has traditionally been channelled through the *citizens' legislative initiative*. As it originates in the people, it is a proactive form of power in the hands of citizens that is capable of changing the *status quo*.[27] In this way, there is a recognition of citizens' ability

27 David Altman, *Democràcia directa, democràcia representativa i apoderament ciutadà*. (Barcelona: Generalitat de Catalunya, 2010), 28–29 and 104.

to propose new regulations on issues that had not attracted the attention of the legislator or reforms to existing laws in order to adapt them to an increasingly changing and complex social reality.

The *citizens' legislative initiative* was first provided for in the SC (Article 87.3) and subsequently developed by Organic Law 3/1984, of 26 March 1984 (with reforms made in 2006 and 2015). It became a very limited instrument in the hands of nationals of legal age. After overcoming the relevant legal constraints, which involved obtaining a certain number of signatures and addressing some material and formal limitations, this form of participation became ineffective upon the mere submission of the bill in question before Parliament. This reduction of the participatory scope was also applicable to the autonomous regions. The regional legislators had originally adopted the same regulations as those implemented at state level with hardly any innovations.

The reforms carried out in the autonomous regions' laws and regulations have pointed in a single direction over the past two decades. Their purpose was to reinstate the essence of the *citizens' legislative initiative* as a true instrument of collaboration between citizens and constitutional bodies, moving away from its traditional consideration as a mechanism for interfering with and altering government programmes.[28]

Many new developments have been introduced, notably including the expansion of the categories of people who are eligible to submit *citizens' legislative initiatives*. In Catalonia, the reform of the law in 2006 meant that these initiatives may be submitted by any residents – nationality having no bearing – and by minors from the age of 16. The legislators of the Basque Country, the Balearic Islands and the Valencian Region adopted similar regulations in 2016. Nevertheless, their new provisions did not refer to age, as this was subject to electoral legislation. In the Valencian Region, this capacity is also provided to "associations, economic and social agents, NGOs and other non-profit entities with legal personality".

Some criteria for acceptance of initiatives that prioritised the Parliament option over the citizenship one were abrogated. In Catalonia and Aragon, a citizens' initiative cannot be rejected when there is another one in progress on the same matter, either as a draft bill or a bill. In these cases, the Parliament is required to offer the organisers the option of maintaining their proposal or withdrawing it. If they choose to maintain it, the Chamber's Bureau may

28 José M. Morales Arroyo, "El alcance y los límites de los instrumentos constitucionales de participación directa," *Revista General de Derecho Constitucional* 26 (2018): 9.

decide to accumulate all legislative initiatives dealing with the same issue and process them jointly.

The role of the organisers of citizens' initiatives has also been reinforced, as provisions have been introduced to involve them in the successive phases of parliamentary processing. This not only allows them to defend their initiative and its purpose; it also helps prevent potential misrepresentation. However, if their initiative is misrepresented, the organisers would be given the option to withdraw it and terminate the legislative procedure.

Finally, deadlines have been set for the debate on whether or not the citizens' initiative is accepted for processing in some autonomous regions (Andalusia, Catalonia, Aragon, Castilla y León, Galicia, the Valencian Region and the Balearic Islands), as well as at the state level. This prevents a citizens' initiative from remaining dormant from the time it is accepted until a decision is made to discuss it in a plenary session. This provision transformed the conception of this form of participation. As a result, it has become an instrument in the hands of citizens that forces representatives to adopt a public position by holding a debate in the plenary session of the Chamber. This change in perspective is highly significant. The legislative initiative has come to be a mechanism for *triggering* parliamentary debate, as it forces the Chambers to take a public stand on a specific question that incumbent representatives had not deemed a priority.[29]

This power of influencing the parliamentary agenda does not undermine the legislative function attributed to Parliaments. This participatory citizenship cannot aspire to engage in joint legislative powers or decision making. Parliament's discretion to circumvent citizens' initiatives is, however, limited; the fact that Parliament has the last word on what is legislated and what the content of the law should be does not mean that it should be a *blocking body*.[30] Exclusivity in the exercise of the legislative function does not endow Parliament with the power to steal the debate from citizens when it is in compliance with all criteria in the SC, Regional Statutes or other legal requirements. Parliamentary deliberation cannot be alien to or separate from the will of those represented.

29 Patricia García Majado "La configuración de la Iniciativa Legislativa Popular: resistencias y soluciones (The Configuration of the Popular Legislative Initiative: Resistances and Solutions)," *Oñati Socio-Legal Series* 7, no. 5 (2017): 1043. [https://opo.iisj.net/index.php/osls/article/view/836].

30 Morales Arroyo, "El alcance y los límites de los instrumentos constitucionales de participación directa," 23.

Citizens' amendments (*enmiendas populares*) operate along similar lines as *legislative initiatives*. At present they are only provided for in some parliamentary regulations of Autonomous Parliaments (Andalusia, Valencian Region, Aragon, Murcia Region, Madrid Region and the Balearic Islands). These amendments enable the citizens residing in these autonomous regions – or the organisations of which they are members – to submit proposals to modify, add or delete part of the content of a draft bill or a bill that is in progress. In the Valencian and Murcia regions, it is required that the reasons for said amendments be stated. In the Andalusian and Murcia regions, these amendments are not accepted when they refer to draft bills or bills that deal with matters excluded from the scope of citizens' legislative initiatives in these autonomous regions. Nor can they be submitted to the Madrid Region Parliament if they concern the processing of initiatives to reform the Statute of Autonomy or the bill for the General Budgets. Once formulated, their subsequent processing is subject to their being assumed by a parliamentary group.

The participatory channel that is most widespread in parliamentary regulations is *citizen appearances* (*comparecencias ciudadanas*). In Catalonia, Andalusia, Cantabria, Extremadura, the Valencian Region, Galicia, Aragon, and in the Murcia and Madrid regions, they are explicitly accepted as a stage of the legislative procedure. They ensure the presence of associations or groups representing public or private interests that are *affected* or *concerned* by the content of the draft bill or bill in the competent legislative Commission. This is even guaranteed for "the legal representatives of the most important recognised social groups and organisations" (Valencian Region). Attendance on an individual basis is exceptional and is only permitted when the individual in question is "considered an expert in the matter subject to regulation" (Andalusia, Extremadura and Murcia). The attendance of experts must be requested by members of Parliament.

Unlike what happens in legislative terms, the provision of citizens' instruments for participation in the *control function of the Government* is still in the minority. So far, only Andalusia, the Canary Islands, Galicia, the Murcia Region, Aragon and the Balearic Islands provide for this. Citizens of all of these autonomous regions may pose questions to any members of the Executive. In the Canary Islands, however, these questions cannot be addressed to the President of the autonomous region.

Despite their name, these citizen questions do not constitute a direct or immediate mechanism for participation. They must be submitted to the Autonomous Chamber and once they have been screened and approved, their subsequent processing will depend on whether they are taken on by a member of the Regional Parliament, who will pose the question to the Government, stating the author or origin.

Differences between autonomous regions and local governments aside, it is interesting to highlight how these forms of citizen participation that exercises control of the representative bodies is also making headway at the local level. The law for democratic participation of the Navarre Region (2019) is a pioneering development in this regard. It enables citizens to submit initiatives that express disapproval of members of local governments. This form of participation only covers the initial stage of the procedure. Disapproval cannot be expressed directly by citizens but is effected by submitting a letter with the names of all the citizens who subscribe to the initiative, indicating the reasons for disapproval. These reasons must be related to the performance of a given member of the local government. It must be endorsed by a certain number of signatures – which varies depending on the number of inhabitants of the municipality – of residents of legal age who have been registered in the corresponding municipality for more than a year. If it is accepted, its only impact is that the political groups in the local government are informed, so that they can raise a motion through the appropriate legal channels.

3.2.2.2 *Power Increased Transparency in Government*

While all the autonomous regions have taken actions on the functional scope of the Executive Power, not all of them have addressed it in the same way. In some cases, laws have been passed with the sole purpose of enabling citizen participation (Valencian Region, 2008 – now repealed – ; Canary Islands 2010; Galicia, 2015; Andalusia, 2017; Navarre and Castilla La Mancha, 2019). On other occasions, participation has been treated together with transparency and/or good governance or open government, as an essential part of the latter (Galicia, 2006; Balearic Islands, 2011; Extremadura, 2013; La Rioja and Murcia regions, 2014; Aragón and Castilla y León, 2015; Madrid Region, 2019 and Valencian Region, 2015 and 2022). And, other times, this regulatory arrangement has been accompanied by *citizens' consultations* (Catalonia, 2014 and the Balearic Islands, 2019). Despite this diversity, all these regulations have a shared purpose: to replace the image of opacity that surrounded the actions of the Executive and the administration. Greater openness and transparency are required of them. Citizen participation is one of the axes for bringing the exercise of power closer to the recipients of decisions. It encourages collaboration between governors and the governed, favouring the search for consensus among the various actors involved in public decision making.[31]

The premise for citizen participation requires that a specific interest be concerned. This requirement gives full meaning to the basic principle of the idea of governance contained in the provisions of many of these laws regulating regional participation. One of the most recent ones, the Law of the Basque Country 6/2022, of 30 June 2022, on the procedure for drawing up general provisions, literally refers to *collaborative governance* and alludes to the implementation of "active listening measures and collaboration from citizens to ensure their participation in the procedure for approving regulations".

In addition to reinforcing participation in the procedures for drawing up regulations, including the provision of citizens' initiatives to propose regulations – in many cases with the same material limitations as the *citizens' legislative initiative* in the autonomous regions – , the regional legislator has provided a range of participatory instruments. Their purpose is to involve citizens in policy making. Through *public hearings* (*audiencias públicas*), the citizens directly affected by a public policy, or an action taken by the public authorities can be heard before the decision is made. The *consultation or participation forums* (*foros de consulta o participación*), known as *expert exchange meetings* (*reuniones de contraste experto*) in Castilla-La Mancha, are spaces created by the public authorities to debate and analyse the effects of a given public policy. Using *citizen panels* (*panels ciudadanos*), the authorities respond to citizens' queries about any matter of public interest. Additionally, *citizen juries* (*jurados ciudadanos*) are aimed at examining the effects of a certain action, project or programme once it has been carried out. They may also use surveys and other demographic data collection methods to gather citizens' opinions, proposals, suggestions or complaints on any matter of interest that is within the remit of regional governments or related to public policies or administration. The common denominator of all these participatory channels is that they are operated and initiated by the public authorities.

Special mention should be made of *participatory budgets* (*presupuestos participativos*).[32] These have been a common practice in many municipalities

31 Enriqueta Expósito Gomez, "Las leyes de transparencia, participación, buen gobierno y gobierno abierto: ¿instrumentos útiles para hacer frente a la desafección ciudadana? La perspectiva legislativa autonómica," in *Problemas actuales de derecho constitucional en un contexto de crisis*, ed. Rosario Tur Alsina (Granada: Comares, 2015), 175–198 and Jorge Castellanos Claramunt, *Participación ciudadana y buen gobierno democrático* (Madrid: Marcial Pons, 2020), 189–195.

32 Through them, local and regional executives share with citizens the decisions on the use of the Community's financial resources. It offers the possibility for the citizens of the

for some time now. With participatory budgets being applied to autonomous regions, citizens have the opportunity to give their opinion and propose alternatives "in terms of the order of priorities in the different areas involved" (Extremadura, 2013) or affect "the distribution of part of the expenditure budgets of a public authority" by "submitting or assessing specific spending proposals, prioritising the allocation of public resources" (Balearic Islands, 2019). Normally, this places participation at the level of budget priorities or expenses. In Navarre, the regional legislature (2019) also extended it to "aspects related to revenue".

The instruments described above are common to the various autonomous regions. However, legislators in some regions have adopted different mechanisms. In the Madrid Region (2019), there is a provision for collaborative sectoral work groups, with meeting spaces between the competent Administration and specific affected sectors. In Castilla-La Mancha (2019) some deliberative and evaluative instruments have been provided that are implemented as a series of seminars on transversal public policies. And in Extremadura (2013) there is a *public debate* open to anyone interested in which the presidents of the parliamentary groups and/or any of their members are invited to participate, together with other representative political and social forces in that autonomous region.

Citizens' consultations (*consultas populares*) are remarkable forms of participation in this context. They make it possible to obtain the opinion of a certain sector or group of the population – rather than of all members of the public – on a specific matter or decision of public interest that affects them. These matters or decisions are always related to the powers held by the autonomous regions. The new Statutes of Autonomy refer to them either as a specific form of citizen participation (Canary Islands), or as a right to call citizens' consultations (Catalonia, Andalusia, Castilla y León and Balearic Islands). Moreover, all of them explicitly hold powers on this matter and exclude referendums from their scope of action,[33] despite their heterogeneous formulation. They have

Autonomous Community to propose spending alternatives or in the prioritization of the allocation of public resources. The law on democratic participation of the Community of Navarre, this participation is projected not only at the level of expenditure, but also in specifying aspects related to the revenues allocated by the autonomous executive. On this issue in Spain: Alfredo Ramírez Nárdiz, "Los presupuestos participativos como instrumento de democracia participativa," *Cuadernos Constitucionales de la Cátedra Fadrique Furió Ceriol* 66 (2009): 127–144 and Castellanos Claramunt, *Participación ciudadana*, 240–245.

33 In the Statute of Autonomy of Catalonia, unlike the rest of the Statutes that included powers in this matter, this exclusion was not explicit. Nevertheless, the Constitutional Court in Judgment no 31, of 28 June 2010, considered that it was implicit.

stronger provisions in four autonomous regions. In Andalusia and Navarre, they were incorporated as an important part of their respective participation laws. However, in Catalonia and the Balearic Islands, they are specifically regulated by the legislature together with other participatory processes.

By giving *citizens' consultations* their own status, separate from referendums, the regional legislator had a wide margin of discretion to regulate them more flexibly. This would facilitate calling citizens' consultations and circumventing the rigid provisions contained in State law. And yet, the reality has been rather different. Some autonomous regions, especially Catalonia, have taken the opportunity to turn them into pseudo referendums, substitutes for this form of direct democracy. In order to ensure that *citizens' consultations* could be called, the requirements contained in the regulations essentially reproduced the same conditions to which the referendum is subjected, transferring them to a sphere different from the electoral one. In this way, any intervention of the state bodies in the call was circumvented, leaving in the hands of the authorities of the autonomous region the power to decide on the object, the question, the times and, above all, whether to call a *citizens' consultation*.

None of the above participatory instruments is intended to replace the decision-making capacity of incumbent representatives. This is a peculiarity that is implicit in the very nature of democratic innovations, which is separate from political participation and, therefore, from the sphere of the decision-making power that the exercise of sovereignty entails. Only the regional legislature of Navarre (2019) assumed that all participatory processes "involve a democratic and political imperative for the institutions", without eliciting any subsequent effects. The same legislator also determined the binding effects of the consultation process when it is related to participatory budgets.

Citizen participation instruments connect representatives with citizens. They make it possible to know the interests and positions of society. This knowledge makes it possible for the decision to be taken by the public body to be appropriate to the interests involved, to respond to real problems and to satisfy current needs. For this reason, when the decision-making body departs from the positions expressed by citizens in a participatory process, it must provide explanations and make public the reasons that have led it not to take into account the allegations, citizen proposals or the results of the participatory process. From this perspective, citizen participation is a factor that increases the democratic quality of the decision-making process because it reinforces one of its essential elements: accountability.[34]

---

34 Expósito Gomez, *Deliberación y participación ciudadanas*, 171–173.

4 Final Remarks: The Link between Participatory Democracy and Decentralization

Participatory democracy has enabled autonomous regions to further the democratic quality of their self-government. Citizen participation has become a priority for regulatory action for regional legislators. It has made it possible for legislators to build their own model of democracy that is more participatory and inclusive of the citizens of the autonomous regions. The Spanish case fits into one of the potential ways in which deliberative democracy interacts with federalism, as pointed out in M. Trettel's chapter in this volume. It is a clear example of how the decentralised institutional structure evidently affects the development of participatory processes: it is the sub-national or local instance where most citizen participation is experienced, both from a normative perspective (it is the autonomous legislator who has regulated participatory processes) and in practice.

This model has been forged around participatory democracy, incorporating many of the elements that characterise federal logic. The objective of both approaches is the exercise of political power, although with different nuances. In the logic of (federal) decentralisation, the core of decision-making processes moves to the territorial units. In contrast, in participatory democracy, citizen intervention does not involve a shift in political power. Citizens participate in the decision-making process, but ultimately representatives make public decisions. In either case, the purpose is to bring power closer to the citizens, facilitating greater knowledge of their interests and needs. This also makes it possible to improve the effectiveness of decisions. A decision that responds appropriately to the conflicting interests known through the participatory processes favours its acceptance because it is not questioned and generates conviction among its addressees.

The territorial form of the state does not influence its qualification as a democratic state. There is no correlation between stronger democracy and federal structures compared to unitary or centralised states. This correspondence does not occur with the provision of direct participation mechanisms, apart from representation. A detailed regulation of these mechanisms does not determine the state's democratic status, although it does enable the measurement of its quality. Both federalism and participatory democracy foster representativeness, despite having more complex procedures due to the diversity of actors involved. As in the federal logic, participatory democracy seeks to integrate diversity in decision making. Citizens are not uniform. Different interests and realities among the members of the public can therefore be identified through this unique concept.

It is not accidental that a change of attitude on the part of the autonomous regions occurred at a specific point in recent Spanish history. The regions have managed to understand how to satisfy citizen aspirations, channelling them as a complement to representative democracy, which attempted to mitigate its shortfalls. After many years of lethargy, they have played a decisive role in promoting democratic renewal and in giving citizens avenues to participate in decision-making processes. In this way, participatory democracy preserves social diversity in a very similar way to how federalism protects diversity in territorial and/or cultural terms. Thus, the participatory democracy that develops at the autonomous or local levels of government responds to a model of governance that, like federalism, implies the same logic of diversity of decision-making centres.

Bibliography

Agudo, Miguel. "Vías constitucionales para el reconocimiento del derecho de sufragio en las elecciones autonómicas españolas a los extranjeros residentes." *Revista Europea de Derechos Fundamentales* 27 (2016): 309–328.

Altman, David. *Democràcia directa, democràcia representativa i apoderament ciutadà*. Barcelona: Generalitat de Catalunya, 2010.

Castellanos Claramunt, Jorge. *Participación ciudadana y buen gobierno democrático*. Madrid: Marcial Pons, 2020.

Expósito Gomez, Enriqueta. *Deliberación y participación ciudadanas*. Madrid: Marcial Pons, 2021.

Expósito Gomez, Enriqueta. "Las leyes de transparencia, participación, buen gobierno y gobierno abierto: ¿instrumentos útiles para hacer frente a la desafección ciudadana? La perspectiva legislativa autonómica." In *Problemas actuales de derecho constitucional en un contexto de crisis*, edited by Rosario Tur Alsina, 175–198. Granada: Comares, 2015.

Fernández, Angel. "Teoría y práctica de la iniciativa legislativa popular en España." *Estudios de Deusto. Revista de Derecho Público* 71, no. 1 (2023): 199–227.

García Majado, Patricia. "La configuración de la Iniciativa Legislativa Popular: resistencias y soluciones (The Configuration of the Popular Legislative Initiative: Resistances and Solutions)." *Oñati Socio-Legal Series* 7, no. 5 (2017): 1041–1057.

Morales Arroyo, José M. "El alcance y los límites de los instrumentos constitucionales de participación directa." *Revista General de Derecho Constitucional* 26 (2018): 1–24.

Pérez Alberdi, María Reyes. "El modelo autonómico de democracia participativa: la situación a partir de la aprobación de los nuevos estatutos de autonomía (Model of Participatory Democracy in Spain's Autonomous Communities: New Statutes of Autonomy)." *Oñati Socio-Legal Series* 7, no. 5 (2017): 1058–1081.

Presno, Miguel A. "El sufragio de los extranjeros residentes en las elecciones generales como exigencia de una ciudadanía democrática." *Revista Europea de Derechos Fundamentales* 27 (2016): 257–283.

Ramírez Nárdiz, Alfredo. "Los presupuestos participativos como instrumento de democracia participativa." *Cuadernos Constitucionales de la Cátedra Fadrique Furió Ceriol* 66 (2009): 127–144.

Requejo, Paloma. "El régimen jurídico de la iniciativa legislativa popular: un presente insatisfactorio y un futuro incierto." *Teoría y Realidad Constitucional* 51 (2023): 259–281.

Rodríguez, Ángel. "El voto de los ciudadanos de la unión europea en las elecciones autonómicas españolas: estado de la cuestión y propuestas de reforma." *Revista Europea de Derechos Fundamentales* 27 (2016): 203–227.

Rodríguez, Blanca. "Las dos caras de la ciudadanía moderna: entre la nacionalidad y el estatus participativo." *Revista Europea de Derechos Fundamentales* 27 (2016): 17–42.

Santamaría Pastor, Juan Alfonso. "Comentario al artículo 23.1 CE." In *Comentarios a la Constitución Española de 1978*, edited by Fernando Garrido Falla, XX. Madrid: Civitas, 1985.

Tudela, José et al., eds. *Libro blanco sobre la calidad democrática en España*. Madrid: Marcial Pons, 2018.

Villaverde, Ignacio. "La ciudadanía borrosa. Ciudadanías multinivel." *Fundamentos: Cuadernos monográficos de teoría del estado, derecho público e historia constitucional* 7 (2012): 285–308.

PART 3

Federalism and Legal Pluralism

CHAPTER 7

Federalism, Legal Pluralism and the Law of Diversity

Kyriaki Topidi

1 Introduction: The Diffusion of Normative Power in Plural Legal Orders

The emerging body of socio-legal research and literature on the *Law of diversity* seeks to observe and theorize empirical realities related to diversity governance. To do so, it attempts to reconcile legitimacy and efficacy in arrangements that are conducive to both top-down and bottom-up claims to equality.[1] The task entails an understanding of the Law of diversity as a normative framework that aims to fulfill the promise of empowering diversity while guaranteeing the unity of the legal system(s) it governs. This task may seem too ambitious, especially in contexts where multiple competing sources of normativity operate. It is also challenging as all normative legal orders to some extent include some while excluding others.[2] Focusing, however, on procedural and institutional design challenges connected to diversity accommodation calls for a broader vision (and definition) of law. This must mirror to some degree Lindahl's approach, which considers law to be "institutionalized and authoritatively mediated collected action."[3] Within such an understanding of law, jurisdictions and normative orderings serve as sites of contestation between multiple actors when attempting to articulate norms that are either products of consensus among various legal orders or of resistance to state sovereignty by a segment of such orders.[4]

1 Paul S. Berman, "Can Global Legal Pluralism Be Both "Global" and "Pluralist"?," *Duke Journal of Comparative and International Law* 29, no. 3 (2019): 383.

2 According to Hans Lindahl, *Authority and the Globalisation of Inclusion and Exclusion* (Cambridge: Cambridge University Press, 2018), 2: "No global legal order is universal or universalizable because unification and pluralisation are the two faces of the single, ongoing process of setting the boundaries of legal orders, global or otherwise".

3 Lindahl, *Authority*, 1.

4 Berman, "Can Global Legal Pluralism," 396.

DOI:10.1163/9789004707764_009

Federalism, as one important approach for managing a polycentric reality has been premised on its connection to territory and to the concept of the nation-state. There is indeed a wealth of definitions of federalism in this light. For the purposes of the present discussion, however, it will be understood on its more basic level as 'a system of government that divides power between a central administration and regional subunits, each with separate authority to directly regulate their mutual citizens.'[5] The aim of the present contribution, on the basis of this understanding of the term, is to explore federalism as both an analytical lens and a methodology to address diversity in connection to legal pluralism.

Broader understandings of legal pluralism include normative forces that derive authority from religious norms, indigenous law, corporate social responsibility and others.[6] More narrowly, accommodating legal pluralist claims from culturally diverse groups usually entails either forms of autonomy (e.g. in the form of personal status law) and/or processes of privatization of diversity (e.g. through religious arbitration regimes).[7] The two methodological approaches, federalism and legal pluralism, are brought together, aside from their normative contention to accommodate diverse groups, not only by the degree of autonomy that they provide to the different entities within each system but also by the opportunity structures provided to decision-makers to pursue varying solutions that are both more inclusive and locally related.[8]

Therefore, to study the overlaps and contrasts between the two approaches, the analysis will focus first on federalism in its pluralizing dimension as an approach to diversity governance, followed by a similar consideration of legal pluralism. The conceptual discussion will then be followed by an attempt to bring together federalism and legal pluralism, especially in relation to the issue of resolving conflicts within plural legal orders. The analysis will engage with 'deep' difference as a means to achieve sustainable governance and finally

---

5 Erin Ryan, *Federalism and the Tug of War* (Oxford: Oxford University Press, 2012), 7.

6 Erin Ryan, "Federalism as Legal Pluralism," in *The Oxford Handbook on Legal Pluralism*, ed. Paul S. Berman (Oxford University Press, 2020), 483. Legal pluralism is not without critiques of conflicts between liberal principles within Western societies and illiberal ones rooted in tribal and religious rules. See indicatively, Brian Z. Tamanaha, "Understanding Legal Pluralism: Past to Present, Local to Global," *Sydney Law Review* 30, no. 3 (2008): 375–411.

7 Jean-F. Gaudreault-DesBiens, "Religious Courts, Personal Federalism and Legal Transplants," in *Shariah in the West*, eds. Rex Adhar and Nicholas Aroney (Oxford, Oxford University Press, 2010), 159.

8 Paul S. Berman, "Federalism and International Law through the Lens of Legal Pluralism," *Missouri Law Review* 73, no. 4 (2008): 1149.

conclude with some thoughts on the challenges of polycentric governance as addressed by the approaches considered here.

2 The Pluralist Interpretations of Federalism

In empirical terms, cultural, legal and constitutional forms of pluralism operate synchronically within modern states. Federal systems are structured around the principles of superposed legal orders, degrees of autonomy of federated entities and (ideally) of participation of all entities in the process of governing.[9] Constitutional pluralism, in particular, as a constitutive element of federalism designed to respond to Law of diversity claims, includes the dialogue and negotiation that happens between institutions. Normative coexistence, in this frame, is neither dispute-free nor easily distinguished from legal pluralism and multiculturalism.

Among the benefits of having overlapping jurisdictional assertions, one can include the possibility for larger spaces for norm articulation and error correction.[10] In this context, flexibility becomes essential to ensure a minimum degree of unity of structure. However, managing diversity through flexible forms of federalism also has a cost, namely, coherence.[11] An indicative (though contested) example at hand could be European federalism in the frame of the European Union: largely asymmetric, the EU legal order has established the principle of unity without an automatic requirement towards uniformity through the CJEU (then ECJ).

Turning to the more cultural applications of the federal principle, these are empirically pluralistic and as such are more prone to post-national interpretations. As narratives on the national dimensions of identity they are constantly (re)-negotiated in light of more open and overlapping identities. Here lies the core challenge of federalism: developing understandings and practices of the concept that are attuned to multicultural societies. Thus, "[f]ederalism [becomes] a metaphor for imagining the manner in which citizens conceive

9 Laurence Potvin-Solis, ed., *Le Statut d'État membre de l'Union Européenne* (Brussels: Bruylant, 2018), especially the contribution by Godiveau.

10 Berman, "Federalism and International Law," 1152.

11 Joxerramon Bengoetxea, "Emancipatory Federalism and Juridical Pluralism: The Multinational European Context," *Les grandes conferences du Centre d'Analyse Politique Constitution Federalisme* (2020): 11, available at https://www.ehu.eus/documents/1687243/32914376/Emancipatory+Federalism+and+Juridical+Pluralism.pdf/5aac2c19-2171-1149-ceb4-f342e5718b13?t=1635239576942.

who they are and how they organize their relationships through which they pursue their purposes and ambitions in concert with others across the entire range of human interaction."[12] Two conceptualizations of federalism stand out as inherently linked to the aims of plurinormativity within consensus-building contexts, *personal* federalism and *negotiated* federalism, bringing federalism closer to legal pluralism.

2.1 *Personal Federalism*

Personal federalism can arguably be presented as a 'mediating' concept between federalism and legal pluralism: it describes a form of political organization that is designed around the principle of personality (as opposed to that of territoriality). It becomes relevant for groups that differentiate themselves on the basis of race, language and/or religion. In acknowledgement of these differences, it allows these groups to possess legal personhood in constitutional terms. This can imply self-governing powers and the application of a distinct body of norms in relation to certain matters.[13] The underlying goal in such cases is to promote inter-group equality while acknowledging asymmetries among groups in terms of access to power and resources.[14] Personal forms of federalism can also extend to the consideration of rules and principles governing conflicts between these different legal orders.

The applicability of personal federalism rationae personae can cover both 'old' minorities with unresolved claims (e.g. indigenous groups) but also 'new' minority groups connected to immigration but who resist assimilation (e.g. Muslim immigrants in Western Europe). Goudreault -DesBiens finds personal law-based regimes as 'largely rooted in non-Western societies', asking 'to what extent can such models be successfully transplanted in the West'.[15] The question of their 'suitability' for Western contexts does not erase, however, the fundamental undertone of any comparative law consideration, which is concerned with one of the oldest debates in minority rights: that of the collective aspects of the definition and protection of minority identity. Embracing state-endorsed forms of personal federalism signifies the at least de facto

12 Roderick A. Macdonald, "Kaleidoscopic Federalism," in *Le fédéralisme dans tous ses états: governance, identité et méthodologie – The States and Moods of Federalism: Governance, Identity and Methodology*, eds. Jean-F. Gaudreault-DesBiens and Fabien Gélinas (Cowansville-Bruxelles: Éditions Yvon Blais-Bruylant, 2005), 278–279.

13 Gaudreault-DesBiens, "Religious Courts," 160.

14 See the work of Antoine N. Messara on Lebanon in Antoine N. Messarra, *Theorie Generale du système politique libanais* (Paris: Cariscript, 1994).

15 Gaudreault-DesBiens, "Religious Courts," 167.

acceptance of collective minority rights through the recognition of equality and/or difference-based claims within specific sub-state communities. By extension, such a process can (and will) provoke shifts and adjustments to the nature of citizenship and sovereignty.[16] It also requires a certain degree of contextualization that will correspond to the needs of minority communities as these arise within a particular geographical and socio-legal context.

2.2 *Negotiated Federalism*

Given the inevitability of normative conflict in super-diverse societies, dialogic and relational consensus-building processes matter in order to bring the disagreeing groups into shared social spaces through procedural mechanisms, institutions and practices. Negotiated federalism is designed as a method used within multistakeholder governance that includes policymaking, participation and the opportunity to voice one's position and concerns. It aims not only at agreement among parties but constitutes at the same time a credible and realistic method to overcome disagreement, especially when all other governance mechanisms have failed.[17] It presupposes the commitment of all participating actors to both the process and outcome of negotiations and is connected to legal pluralism as a method of dialogic pluralist governance. It can be distinguished from traditional rulemaking whereby actors can react to proposed rules but are not involved in their making from the first moment. It can rely, according to Berman, on procedural tools based on subsidiarity schemes, hybrid participation agreements or purposeful jurisdictional redundancy.[18]

According to Ryan, this type of federalism has both advantages and disadvantages. It is likely to result in fewer errors and is more cost- and time-efficient. Additionally, it will likely generate a greater degree of compliance.[19] However, the limitations of negotiated federalism relate to issues of representation (who speaks for and understands best stakeholders), the inadequacy of certain subjects as a matter for negotiation (e.g. fundamental rights and illiberal practices of certain minorities) and the impossibility of achieving consensus.[20] It is also possible that at the end of the day the options available would

16 Gaudreault-DesBiens, "Religious Courts," 169.

17 Erin Ryan, "Negotiating Federalism," *Boston College Law Review* 52, no. 1 (2011): 1–136, especially 102–127.

18 Paul S. Berman, "Jurisgenerative Constitutionalism: Procedural Principles for Managing Global Pluralism," *Indiana Journal of Global Legal Studies* 22, no. 2 (2013): 680–694.

19 Ryan, "Federalism as Legal Pluralism," 505.

20 Ryan, "Federalism as Legal Pluralism," 506.

be either a deadlock due to lack of consensus despite inclusive processes or risk of non-implementation due a failure to consult all parties concerned.

3 Legal Pluralism

Legal pluralism operates on the premise that the state recognizes a plurality of normative frameworks that are legally accommodated.[21] This kind of accommodation is based on the delegation or sharing of power with non-state authorities (e.g. religious authorities on family law matters). It treats law as that which individuals and groups use as law, if one does not limit oneself to 'official' regulatory pronouncements.[22] It can also be applied to regulatory pronouncements between international organisations, states and/or transnational entities. If understood in the sense of diffusion of jurisdictional powers (as opposed to empirical multiplicity of normative orders), it can take three forms: that of a federal system, that of a con-sociational one or that of a personal status- based jurisdiction.[23] It is also commonly framed as a critique to *statism* and is relevant as a strategy for the management of difference as it 'demonopolizes' distinct areas of legal regulation.[24] It is tightly linked to the maintenance of group identity and its perpetuation along with respect for and promotion of cultural distinctiveness. This is because it carries the potential of facilitating exchange and of providing opportunities for non-state actors to contribute to governance and at the same time increases the efficiency of chosen measures, opening the process to more voices. It is, however, controversial when put forward as the 'normatively desirable' approach within diversity governance, especially because it disturbs the clear hierarchical line of authority within constitutional settings.[25]

21 See only indicatively Sally Engle Merry, "Legal Pluralism," *Law & Society Review* 22, no. 5 (1988): 869–896; Sally Falk Moore, "Law and Social Change: The Semi-Autonomous Social Field as an Appropriate Subject of Study," *Law & Society Review* 7, no. 4 (1973): 719; John Griffiths, "What is Legal Pluralism?," *The Journal of Legal Pluralism and Unofficial Law* 18, no. 24 (1986): 1.

22 Brian Z. Tamanaha, "A Non-Essentialist Version of Legal Pluralism," *Journal of Law & Society* 27, no. 2 (2000): 296.

23 Jean L. Cohen, "The Politics and Risks of the New Legal Pluralism in the Domain of Intimacy," *International Journal of Constitutional Law* 10, no. 2 (2012): 389. Consociational democracies focus on consensus building (e.g. by coalition building) through the autonomy of self-governing units while personal law systems cede control to private (usually religious or cultural) authorities over limited areas.

24 Cohen, "The Politics and Risks," 383–384.

25 Berman, "Can Global Legal Pluralism," 387.

Legal pluralism and federalism share a starting point: the idea that there can be multiple sources of sovereign authority and opportunities for dialectical legal interactions. This multiplicity, in the case of legal pluralism, is often justified by the multiple community affiliations that individuals hold, including to religious institutions, subnational ethnic groups, professional groups or even internet groups that are considered 'norm generating communities'[26] but that can often be outside the state-based system. Legal pluralism adds a focus on the intersecting factors shaping the general legal enterprise by making inquiries about the relationship between state and non-state sources of normative authority. The assumption is that the interaction between legal orders is bi-directional and the influence mutual.[27] Inclusive procedural mechanisms are hence at the core of both concepts although legal pluralism places greater emphasis on the provision of multiple ports of entry for normative communities to participate in society.[28]

Federalism and legal pluralism are drawn apart, however, regarding the fundamental assumption that the state should have the power to forge the identity of its legal subjects. For legal pluralism, this assumption is fundamentally flawed from the perspective of 'everyday' law.[29] This is because it operates on a decontextualized understanding of personal identities and towards a single/mono-dimensional source of national legal identity. Thus, for a legal pluralist, state ranking of identity-related claims is impossible because identity is related to assertions that individuals/groups make about themselves.[30] Any plural understanding of law therefore cannot function if law is pre-existing to identity. In the words of Macdonald, the challenge of legal pluralism is essentially the following: "The multiple, overlapping normative communities (whether territorial, affective, affiliative, economic or virtual) in which people live their everyday lives, as for example, children, parents, siblings spouses, neighbours, friends, co-religionists, workers, and in which they discover, negotiate, order, and reorder their particular identities are conceived of not as sites of law but simply as brute, and essentially mute, facts."[31] Can one still argue though that

26 Robert M. Cover, "Nomos and Narrative – Foreword," *Harvard Law Review* 97, no. 4 (1983): 43.

27 Peter Fitzpatrick, "Law and Societies," *Osgoode Hall Law Journal* 22, no. 1 (1984): 115.

28 Paul S. Berman, *Global Legal Pluralism: A Jurisprudence of Law Beyond Borders* (Cambridge, Cambridge University Press, 2012), 237.

29 Roderick A. Macdonald, "Legal Republicanism and Legal Pluralism: Two Takes on Identity and Diversity," in *Human Diversity and the Law: La diversité humaine et le droit*, eds. Mauro Bussani and Michele Graziadei (Brussels: Bruylant, 2005), 43–44.

30 Macdonald, "Legal Republicanism," 50.

31 Macdonald, "Legal Republicanism," 49.

federalism is in its essence a form of legal pluralism? The noteworthy parallels are evident: emphasis on systemic spaces of dialogue and contestation, negotiation between groups in cases of normative or jurisdictional conflicts, and procedural tools to create consensus when these conflicts persist.[32] Where legal pluralism distinguishes itself from more classic forms of federalism is in considering synergetic approaches to protecting difference between public and private entities. Classic federalist options emphasize public jurisdiction. The 'cost' that both approaches to diversity governance are confronted with is sometimes described as uncertainty and inefficiency.

For legal pluralism, however, there are additional inherent risks to consider: in some cases, the delegation of self-rule to non-state groups may lead to the freezing of a framed hierarchy within the group (e.g. along gendered lines) instead of accommodating difference. The demarcating function of non-state law, in these cases, operates both between the minority group and the rest of the society but also within the group itself, by preventing more egalitarian distributional decisions.[33] It also leads to questioning the meaningfulness of an 'exit' option of members, when the individual is presented with the well know dilemma of having to choose between one's rights versus one's culture. Other normative critiques against legal pluralism include the fragmentation of the polity, the privatization of the exercise of state power and the threat to shared citizenship as a result of overlapping commitments and of individuals.[34] A shared jurisdiction between the state and non-state authorities, following Shachar,[35] would still be considered in itself a 'federal' logic to the extent that communal decision-making is recognized but the state retains the ability to review if required. But to echo Cohen, can states really outlaw shunning and ostracism that minorities within minorities may suffer?[36]

32 Ryan, "Federalism as Legal Pluralism," 488.

33 Ayelet Shachar, *Multicultural Jurisdictions* (Cambridge: Cambridge University Press, 2001), 72 who proposed a model of shared jurisdiction between state and non-state authorities in the area of religion and family law (transformative accommodation).

34 Cohen, "The Politics and Risks," 390.

35 Shachar, *Multicultural Jurisdictions*.

36 Cohen, "The Politics and Risks," 388.

4 Bringing together Federalism and Legal Pluralism When Resolving Conflicts

The normative affinity between federalism and legal pluralism is based on their common logic of multi-tiered forms of governance, which combine shared rule with self-rule. The institutionalization of two or more orders, notably due to their cultural components, is necessary to grasp both institutional as well as non-institutional factors of how actors live and perform their difference. The two concepts can therefore be joined from a pragmatic perspective as their manifestations and operationalization matter in order to reflect on ways to manage and reconcile difference within plural societies. When answering the essential question of who should get to decide, both federalism and legal pluralism become relational, based on more complex power relation constellations among actors while questioning the limitations of the nation-state.[37] The remaining part of this section will briefly address first the implications of the relational features of both federalism and legal pluralism. It will then explore the space of opportunities arising from the combination of both frames for ethnoculturally diverse societies, with some examples to illustrate the points made.

The implications of this affinity between the two concepts are several and far-reaching: the first stems from the assumption of plural layers of government, which then leads to multiple (and sometimes conflicting) institutional expressions of autonomy. The second relies on the growth of the paradigm of public-private law relationships which remain marginalized in state-centric interpretations of law but which construct in practice functional forms of non-territorial autonomy. These forms of autonomy are premised on the existence and evolution of norm-producing authorities in the same political space. The third, more methodological, implication leads precisely to treat federalism and legal pluralism more as processes and less as fixed and static modes of diversity governance. For both concepts to function as evolving and context-based processes they presuppose one or more common objectives, values or beliefs among the groups concerned. Lastly, federalism and legal pluralism make a fundamental distinction between integration and differentiation as a result of their evolving and dynamic nature permitting to unveil the affinities between them. Communities can either be joined by a common 'project' or be

37 Jean-F. Gaudreault-DesBiens, "Towards a Deontic-Axiomatic Theory of Federal Adjudication," in *The Federal Idea*, ed. Amnon Lev (Oxford: Hart Publishing, 2017), 75–106.

separated and work in differentiated terms on decisions or policies that affect them in different ways.

The conceptual challenge in bringing together federalism and legal pluralism rests on how to extend the application of the federal analytical lens to more functionally defined jurisdictions.[38] The appeal of 'rapprochement' between the two is to give more prominence to the study of minority groups and their agency within, for example, cities, the education system or the public administration as 'sites of racial and political integration'.[39] Bringing the two together is also more likely to capture diverse forms of political contestation within plural societies and a wider range of normative forces in action.[40]

The core question, from a governance perspective, in managing diverse societies is how to pursue individual dignity within very diverse groups, allowing self-determination but at the same time maintaining a web of responsibilities among the groups in connection to their shared political and social space.[41] Federalism, as a 'strategy for good governance', in this sense allows for state-sponsored negotiation and potentially innovative solutions without eliminating conflict among the principles and/or values which can lead to different solutions for a given issue.

Federalism bargaining is one such technique of negotiation, consisting of 'negotiations between competing sovereign agents that range from conventional political haggling, as over the terms of proposed legislation; formalized methods of collaborative policymaking, as created by various federal statutes (…); and more remote signaling processes by which state and federal actors share responsibility for evolving decision-making over time (…).'[42] The example of a kind of dynamic federalism as applied in environmental law in the US context is illustrative: the conventional federal logic would dictate that the level of authority that retains competence is the one that roughly matches the geographic scope of the situation in need of regulation. According to a more dynamic approach and in light of the overlapping and shifting focus of environmental matters, however, competences may escape territorial concerns, for

38 Daniel Halberstam, "Federalism: Theory, Policy, Law." in *The Oxford Handbook of Comparative Constitutional Law*, eds. Michel Rosenfeld and András Sajó (Oxford, Oxford University Press, 2012), 605.

39 Heather K. Gerken, "Federalism All the Way Down," *Harvard Law Review* 124, no. 1 (2010): 9.

40 Ryan, "Federalism as Legal Pluralism," 484.

41 Ryan, "Federalism as Legal Pluralism," 492.

42 Ryan, "Federalism as Legal Pluralism," 503, discussing the application of the technique in the US context.

example in connection to issues related to climate change.[43] In these cases competences can be 'adjusted' organically at the most efficient level both from the local to the federal level and vice versa. The same or a similar approach can be relevant for policy areas that defy the strict boundaries of single state action such as the regulation of the internet, indigenous peoples claims or international trade matters.

Jurisdictional redundancy is another tool suitable for scenarios of overlapping authority used in federal contexts. The basic tenet of jurisdictional redundancy is that when two legal authorities claim competence or jurisdiction over a specific actor, one of them will refrain from asserting such jurisdiction in the understanding that the other will take action.[44] This technique has the advantage of avoiding hierarchy or influence. A well cited illustration of this practice concerns Article 17 of the International Criminal Court that stipulates that the ICC cannot prosecute someone unless the suspect country of nationality is unwilling or unable to do so.[45] As a solution to complementarity regimes, it has been nevertheless criticized as either an affront to state prerogatives or as a way to dilute the exercise of international justice.

From the perspective of federalism, clear values that can be used in instances of conflict can be accountability and transparency of decision-makers, autonomy through interjurisdictional innovation (and competition), the development of problem-solving synergies to resolve matters that cannot be resolved if actors acted alone and the maintenance of checks and balances among actors with power to protect individuals.[46] To use the American model, as a brief example, federal supremacy can be designed to privilege national authority by subjecting jurisdictional conflicts to a hierarchy (i.e. US Constitution's Supremacy Clause that gives priority to national power over municipal authority in cases of conflict).[47] This kind of clause, however, is not plural and ultimately limits relational and deliberative policy-making. More

43 See David E. Adelman and Kirsten H. Engel "Adaptive Federalism: The Case Against Reallocating Environmental Regulatory Authority," *Minnesota Law Review* 92, no. 6 (2008): 1796–1850.

44 Berman, "Federalism and International Law," 1164.

45 Rome Statute of the International Criminal Court, of 17 July 1998 2187 U.N.T.S. 90, Article 17.

46 Ryan, "Federalism as Legal Pluralism," 492.

47 Article IV of the US Constitution stipulates: "This Constitution, and the laws of the United States which shall be made in pursuance thererof; and all treaties made, or which shall be made; under the authority of the United States, shall be supreme law of the land; and the judges in every state shall be bound thereby, anything in the Constitution or laws of any state to the contrary notwithstanding."

dynamic forms of federalism, on the other hand, for both state-to-state but also state-to non-state communities, are more likely to increase participation, exchange and negotiation opportunities. In addition, by providing non-state lawmaking communities participation rights in substantive decisions, inclusion and tolerance are bolstered. As such, they bring federalism closer to legal pluralism by virtue of their consensus-based processes laying the foundations for more sustainable governance solutions.

Bringing together flexible forms of federalism with legal pluralism, Berman provides a road-map to identify and preempt conflicts while maintaining pluralism: he proposes, first, that decision-makers consider the kind of normative systems at play in any given context. He then invites decision-makers to question whether there is need to restrain one's voice as an actor in the process, especially if there are other decision-makers that are in a position to speak to the issue more appropriately. Following which, he proposes that decision-makers consider alternative, hybrid decisional frameworks that allow for more voices to be heard. Finally, he suggests the consideration of procedures and arrangements that constitutionally embed the abovementioned inquiries in the broader decision-making system.[48] To be clear, Berman's approach does not completely and exhaustively overcome the limitations and contestations that are born out of competing normative values and claims. It adopts, nevertheless, a pragmatic take on diversity governance that prioritizes avenues for dialogue and the procedural virtue of self-restraint as a modus operandi for co-existence.

The example of Canada provides an interesting illustration on how more co-operative forms of federalism can address the somehow problematic relationship between federalism and human rights. More concretely, Canada has resorted to the ratification and enforcement of international human rights treaties through processes of consultation, cooperation and negotiation between the federal government and its federated units (provinces).[49] The value of this approach is found in its use as a means to resolve differences between the federal government and the provinces and avoid deadlock in circumstances of divided jurisdiction under the Canadian constitution. In practice, upon ratification of human rights treaties by Canada, both the federal government and the provinces are in express agreement over their respective legal commitments to the text. This approach can be relevant when the federal

48 Berman, "Can Global Legal Pluralism," 402.

49 See indicatively Jamie Cameron, "Federalism, Treaties and International Human rights Under the Canadian Constitution," *The Wayne Law Review* 48, no. 1 (2002): 38–47.

nature of the system of governance poses challenges for the enforcement of human rights, with cultural and religious arguments used as a defense.[50]

In another Canadian example, the recent case of English-language school boards in Quebec illustrates very concretely how legal pluralities may be conceived as constitutionally autonomous forms of local government within a purely domestic context. The case essentially begs consideration of the extent to which a federal arrangement can be interpreted as containing a regime of personal federalism within education.[51] Personal federalism, according to Theo Jans, "implies that the recipients of state power would be population groups rather than territories."[52]

In *Hak,*[53] the Canadian court found that section 23 of the Canadian Charter of Rights and Freedoms grants constitutional protection to linguistic minorities in the management of their schools, particularly with respect to establishing policies for hiring, retention and promotion of the personnel of their choice. The Canadian Constitution, however, explicitly provides that provinces are responsible for determining the competences of local government within their jurisdiction.[54] In the meantime, the struggle to acknowledge (and protect) normatively different institutional actors and networks coexisting within specific territories in non-exclusivist terms persists.

Taking the question of linguistic autonomy a step further, the judge in *Hak* declared that "linguistic minorities must be able to control all aspects of their linguistic and cultural education and that the government cannot adversely affect the linguistic and cultural concerns of the minority" (at para.1003). By finding so, the outcome of the case confirmed that it would be impossible for the Quebec government to reform the English-language school board systems

50 See for example the prohibition of child marriage in Nigeria through a federal lens in Felix E. Eboibi, "The Impact of Federalism and Legal Pluralism on the Enforcement of International Human Rights Law against Child Marriage in Africa," *African Journal Human Rights* 1 (2017): 72–85.

51 Dave Guénette and Félix Mathieu, "Minority Language School Boards and Personal Federalism in Canada: Recent and Ongoing Developments in Quebec," *Constitutional Forum Constitutionnel* 31, no. 1 (2022): 19–28.

52 Maarten T. Jans, "Personal Federalism: A Solution to Ethno-National Conflicts? What is has meant in Brussels and what it could mean in Abkhazia," in *Federal Practice: Exploring Alternatives for Brussels and Abkhazia,* eds. Bruno Coppieters, David Darchiashvili, and Natella Akaba (Brussels: VUB Press, 2000), 219.

53 *Hak v Procureur Général du Québec,* 2021 QCCS 1446. The decision upheld the constitutionality of a legislative bill (Bill 21) which prohibits public service workers from wearing religious symbols with the exception of minority language school boards. The appeal of the case is scheduled to be heard in November 2022 before the Quebec Court of Appeal.

54 Constitutional Act 1867, section 91.

(i.e. by allowing the maintenance of school elections against the plans of the government).

5 'Deep' Difference within Sustainable Governance

Against challenges such as social inequalities, resource scarcity, globalization or demographic changes, states are called to generate legal and political decisions that among others reverse unequal participation opportunities for some groups. Sustainability as a constitutional duty and value within legal systems is an emerging concept in constitutional studies that aims to address these needs.[55] It signifies "a capacity to maintain some entity, outcome or process over time"[56] and has been generally connected in the existing literature to the notion of environmentally sustainable development.

Unlike terms such as *sovereignty, constitution* or the *rule of law*, it has known less systematic analysis in work related to the Law of diversity or within Federal Studies. It proposes an understanding of governance in terms of collective action towards the common good and towards responsibilities for present and future generations.[57] It can be related to federalism and legal pluralism in connection to the normative question of the value of accommodating diversity. As a justice inspired legal concept, sustainability is linked to the discussion of cultural diversity and survival of groups/entities based on the notions of dignity[58] and decent society.[59] At the same time, a sustainable approach to governance normatively connects well with the concept of 'deep diversity' as conceived by Charles Taylor, which concerns situations where one's belonging to a larger polity is conditional upon belonging to a smaller political community.[60]

In a similar spirit, both federalism and legal pluralism constitute attempts to celebrate and acknowledge local variations of norms, while also considering international orders. Both frames can be designed to preserve sites of

55 See for example Article 37 of the EU Charter of Fundamental Rights.

56 Justice Mensah, "Sustainable Development: Meaning, History, Principles, Pillars and Implications for Human Action: Literature Review," *Cogent Social Sciences* 5, no. 1 (2019): 1–21.

57 Ester Herlin-Karnell, "The Constitutional Concepts of Sustainability and Dignity," *Jus Cogens* (2023): 125–148, available at https://link.springer.com/article/10.1007/s42439-023-00078-9.

58 Herlin-Karnell, "The Constitutional Concepts".

59 Avishai Margalit, *The Decent Society* (Harvard, Harvard University Press, 1998).

60 Charles Taylor, "Shared and Divergent Values," in *Options for a New Canada*, eds. Ronald L. Watts and Douglas M. Brown (Toronto, University of Toronto Press, 1991), 155–186.

normative contestation on the basis of reciprocity, exchange and interdependence. This vision of governance of difference aims at guaranteeing the viability of community-based and bottom-up processes that complement the top-down authoritative decisions of state authorities.

A sustainable federalist and/or legal pluralist governance design protecting difference is not without obstacles: the uneasy coexistence between key constitutional principles and cultural differences is often expressed in the areas of equality, citizenship or the separation between the public and private spheres. It calls for the individualization of certain principles and/or norms and more controversially shows the impossibility of predicting normative outcomes, although based on sub-national governance schemes that move closer to the core issues surrounding the preservation of culturally diverse communities. Still, constitutional arrangements and frames that reject non-state normative influences, the foreign or international dimension of normative authority become untenable in an interconnected world.

Given however how consensus is neither guaranteed nor even attainable in some cases, systemic space for dialogue in procedural as well as substantial terms is a more realistic ambition if the aim remains to give voice to actors that are silenced in sustainable terms.[61] More concretely, some of the positive benefits of polycentric systems of governance, according to the related literature, are the recognition that local communities can govern themselves and the emphasis on the development of capacities for self-governance and participation; the more effective production and provision of public goods; the use of resources in accordance with local conditions and knowledge; the creation of more inclusive systems of law, rules and shared values among diverse communities and groups; the balancing between personal freedom and collective authority.[62]

To the extent that one subscribes to a definition of federalism in philosophical terms as "a normative judgment upon the ideal organization of human relations and content" it becomes tenable that it may function as a constitutional and political framework for the accommodation of diversity.[63] Indeed,

61 Berman, "Federalism in International Law", 1183.

62 See indicatively Paul Aligica and Vlad Tarko, "Polycentricity: From Polanyi to Ostrom and Beyond," *Governance* 25, no. 2 (2012): 237–262; Keith Carlisle and Rebecca Gruby, "Polycentric Systems of Governance: A Theoretical Ode for the Commons," *Policy Studies Journal* 47, no. 4 (2019): 927–951; Andrew Jordan et al., eds., *Governing Climate Change: Polycentricity in Action?* (Cambridge: Cambridge University Press, 2018).

63 Michael Burgess and Alain-G. Gagnon, eds., *Comparative Federalism and Federation: Competing Traditions and Future Directions* (Toronto, University of Toronto Press, 1993).

efforts towards cultural autonomy push minority groups to seek the expansion of self-government within existing state structures.[64] They do so, however, in largely asymmetrical terms, distinguishing themselves from 'classic' federations, where all constituent units enjoy equal powers. This plural kind of federalism offers prospects towards group identity preservation and development that can be seen as emancipatory, especially in contexts where there are dual or multiple national identities.[65]

An *emancipatory* kind of federalism, understood as 'one that respects pluralism, but also one that accommodates self-determination- the free will of its component entities to govern themselves on some matters and share sovereign powers on other (…)'[66] can be supportive of normative claims premised on multiple authorities navigating diverse normative claims in a sustainable way. The example of *state-enforced self-governance* introduced by Sarker is illustrative in this respect: based on natural resource case-studies in Japan, the study launched the idea that communities can require assistance from national and/or provincial government to achieve and sustain self-governance.[67] The legal foundation for such kinds of collaboration is found through the establishment of enabling conditions using legal, economic and democratic tools.[68]

Alongside the accommodation of such normative claims, it is important to highlight two additional connected dimensions in the functioning of plural legal orders: the first is to attempt to answer the question of who interprets and decides on the competencies/powers of actors in a federalist or legal pluralism frame and the second is focused on where the ultimate authority lies.[69] Based on the principle of accommodation, implied within federalism, which can afford legal recognition of minority claims, federalism as multi-level governance can defy territoriality while embracing inclusiveness, if aligned to legal pluralist frames, especially those that concern social regulation (e.g. family law or commercial law). This kind of inclusiveness has the potential to lead to self-determination processes and emancipation through cultural self-government, accommodation and participation.[70] And after all, no statement of law is

64 Jaime Lluch, "Autonomism and Federalism," *Publius: The Journal of Federalism* 42, no.1 (2011): 134–161.

65 Lluch, "Autonomism and Federalism," 21, discussing the US, Canada and Spain.

66 Bengoetxea, "Emancipatory Federalism", 5.

67 Ashutosh Sarker, "The Role of State-reinforced Self-governance in Averting the Tragedy of the Irrigation Commons in Japan," *Public Administration* 91, no. 3 (2013): 727–743.

68 See indicatively Daniel A. De Caro et al., "Legal and Institutional Foundations of Adaptive Environmental Governance," *Ecology and Society* 22, no. 1 (2017): 32–52.

69 Bengoetxea, "Emancipatory Federalism", 25.

70 Bengoetxea, "Emancipatory Federalism", 32.

final,[71] which is why diversity-prone decision-making in complex scenarios will remain a creative and jurisgenerative context-based process.

6 Concluding Remarks: Towards Polycentric Governance within a Federalist Context?

Renewed emphasis on constitutionally protected expressions of desire for identities through culture, language, social practices or history gives continuous weight to the question of whether federalism can be an answer for the governance of multicultural societies. Emancipatory federalism, as outlined above, constitutes one such framing encouraging cultural diversity. More broadly, however, polycentric governance systems may provide a relevant frame for diversity-inclined federalist frames to emerge, while offering a response to the perennial challenge of which level of power should exercise decision-making authority within plural legal orders.

Polycentric systems describe plural forms of governance where there are multiple centres of decision-making, each operating with some degree of autonomy.[72] They designate a form of political organization characterized by overlapping political units.[73] Autonomy is conceived in this case as decision-making without centralized coordination and is evaluated on the basis of rules-in-use, and not rules-in-form, where states can use incentives and indirect control mechanisms to limit degrees of autonomy (e.g. duties of excessive

71 The non-finality of normative outcomes is based on the assumption that increasingly diverse and interconnected societies are conducive to increasingly diverse and interconnected rules that map the co-evolution between law and society. The limitation in the law's representation of societal identity and authority is found in the law's understanding of society's culture as stable and singular. In that sense, and to the extent that "law (…) enforces an antecedent culture, or constitutes culture, or displaces culture" (Robert Post, "Law and Cultural Conflict," *Chicago-Kent Law Review* 78, no. 2 (2003): 489), it is challenged to either encourage or retard change when operating as an instrument for conflict resolution.

72 Carlisle and Gruby, "Polycentric Systems of Governance," 928. According to Vincent Ostrom, *The Meaning of American Federalism* (San Francisco: Institute for Contemporary Studies Press, 1991), 225, a polycentric political system would be composed of: (1) many autonomous units formally independent of one another, (2) choosing to act in ways that take account of others, (3) through processes of cooperation, competition, conflict, and conflict resolution.

73 Vincent Ostrom, Charles M. Tiebout and Robert Warren, "The Organization of Government in Metropolitan Areas: A Theoretical Inquiry," *American Political Science Review* 55, no. 4 (1961): 831–842.

reporting, use of financial incentives, compliance requirements). The ways that authorities/actors interact within such a framework are complex and in constant evolution. Despite seemingly uncoordinated practices, a system of social ordering can emerge that sustains individual liberty, group autonomy and self-governance.[74] These practices are focused on three elements of the relationship between state and non-state entities, which are exit, voice and self-organization.[75]

More specifically, the decision-making units (i.e. authorities/actors) can be organized according to overlapping jurisdictional levels and can have both competitive as well as cooperative relationships in addition to conflict resolution tasks.[76] More functional forms of polycentric governance offer a number of features such as higher degrees of adaptability to social change, more flexibility to address complex resource systems and lower risk of institutional failure due to redundant decision-making processes.[77] At the same time, they present risks and pitfalls linked to their inherent complexity and accountability mechanisms.

When applied to the study of constitutional arrangements that strive to promote and protect diversity, polycentric governance can respond to both formal and informal rules and strategies that form the basis of claims of minority groups. This is because as a model of governance, polycentricity acknowledges scale diversity, the diversity of human interests and values and multiple parallel goals of groups.[78] To achieve this aim, polycentric governance includes actors from the public, private and voluntary sectors, including community-based organizations, moving beyond state authorities, to perform state-related functions.[79] The determinant factor in identifying relevant actors is effective and efficient service as well as balance of interests and representation of all those concerned.[80]

74 Michael D. McGinnis, Elizabeth Baldwin and Andreas Thiel, "When is Polycentric Governance Sustainable? Using Institutional Theory to Identify Endogenous Drivers of Dysfunctional Dynamics," 2020, available at https://ostromworkshop.indiana.edu/pdf/seriespapers/2020fall-colloq/mcginnis.pdf. A well-known application of such type of governance is found within community-based management of natural resources.

75 See Andreas Thiel, William Blomquist and Dustin Garrick, eds., *Governing Complexity* (Cambridge: Cambridge University Press, 2019).

76 Ostrom et al., "The Organization of Government."

77 Carlisle and Gruby, "Polycentric Systems of Governance," 929.

78 Graham R. Marshall, "Polycentricity, Reciprocity and Farmer Adoption of Conservation Practices under Community-based Governance," *Ecological Economics* 68, no. 5 (2009):1507–1520.

79 Michael D. McGinnis and Elinor Ostrom, "Reflections on Vincent Ostrom, Public Administration and Polycentricity," *Public Administration Review* 72, no. 1 (2012): 15.

80 Carlisle and Gruby, "Polycentric Systems of Governance," 933.

The degree of autonomy introduced in these arrangements is nevertheless a matter of open debate, although de facto rather than formal forms of autonomy seem to matter most in polycentric governance studies.[81] The role and structure of actors within these constellations is also not neat and fixed but rather dense and evolving.[82] As crucially, the element of cooperation understood as voluntary and inclusive joint action among decision-making centres denotes the dialogical and synergetic dimension of the model that fits well within both federalist and legal pluralist conceptual frames. Cooperation possibilities do not preclude however competitive processes among actors in the provision of services to their communities or towards obtaining resources, highlighting the need for conflict resolution mechanisms to reconcile diverging interests. Conflicts and differences in power and values are indeed unavoidable in such constellations. The adaptation of rules and the creation of new institutional pathways when conflicts persist are possible avenues to avoid dysfunctionality of the arrangements in question, although the risk of ad hoc decision-making must be also considered. Governance literature further highlights that instead of hierarchical systems in the resolution of conflicts, systems that dispose of a diversity of fora and a variety of approaches (e.g. conciliation, mediation, arbitration) increase the degree of effective conflict resolution.[83] Cross-jurisdictional decision-making is also relevant (and a distinguishing feature of federalist solutions) insofar as it allows specialization in particular policy-matters.[84] The question of accountability is equally substantial: vulnerable groups will otherwise bear the risks and be disproportionately impacted by polycentric decision-making. Fairer distribution of resources (both material and non-material) can reduce conflict and reverse exclusion and marginalization of groups.

Far from an accurate predictor of successful plural and inclusive governance, an adaptation of polycentricity within federal systems of organization and distribution of power will bring closer federalist scenarios to legal pluralist ones. In fact, using polycentric governance as a background framework, and adapting it to the comparison of federalist and legal pluralist approaches to diversity governance, it could be argued that the two approaches share the following characteristics with polycentricity: the multiplicity of decision centres, the de jure independence or de facto autonomy of decision-making for

81 Carlisle and Gruby, "Polycentric Systems of Governance," 933.

82 Carlisle and Gruby, "Polycentric Systems of Governance," 933.

83 Elinor Ostrom, "The Challenge of Common Pool Resources," *Environment* 50, no. 4 (2008): 1–20.

84 McGinnis and Ostrom, "Reflections," 15.

each decision centre, overlapping jurisdictions, multiple processes of mutual adjustment among decision centres based on shared values and norms, as well as means of effective coordination.[85] They offer frameworks of possibility for individuals to hold multiple allegiances with room to change the order of prioritization of one's identity markers depending on the case at hand. Excessive delegation of public authority to non-state actors along with lack of coherence and alignment of governance constellations with society's goals are ultimately, however, the limitations of such arrangements.[86] Without neglecting the power relations between the coexisting legal orderings, both legal pluralism and federalism, as methodologies for governing cultural difference, ultimately depend on the degree to which they can indeed foster mutual 'relevance' between their normative components.[87]

Beyond these affinities, however, polycentric governance is in addition aligned to the implementation of Law of diversity insofar as it can increase our understanding of the quality and degree of autonomy arrangements necessary to guarantee diversity, along with the benefits of coordination mechanisms among the different layers of government across the public and private sectors and ultimately the adaptive efforts required to obtain social outcomes that enhance cultural diversity in our societies.

In sum, by placing hybridity and multiplicity at the service of collective identity development, "diversity (…) is not per se a problem to overcome but a situation to handle (…)" for states and minority groups.[88] As the example of states that become federal in order to ensure their survival demonstrates,[89] forms of power-sharing and participation have become increasingly relevant to assess sustainable contemporary federal arrangements, moving past sovereignty and statehood as heavily contested benchmarks of performance when sharing power while protecting difference.

---

85 Mark Stephan, Graham Marshall and Michael D. McGinnis, "An Introduction to Polycentricity and Governance," in *Governing Complexity*, eds. Andreas Thiel, William Blomquist and Dustin Garrick (Cambridge: Cambridge University Press, 2019), 41.

86 McGinnis, Baldwin and Thiel, "When is Polycentric Governance," 23.

87 See the concept of 'judicial relevance' of Santi Romano, *L'ordre juridique* (Paris: Dalloz, 1976), 106 that is based on the idea that not only should the co-existing legal orders recognize each other as relevant but must also create dialogical links between them.

88 Eva M. Belser, "Why the Affection of Federalism for Human Rights Is Unrequited and How the Relationship Could Be Improved," in *The Principle of Equality in Diverse States*, eds. Eva M. Belser et al. (Leiden-Boston: Brill, 2021), 93.

89 India is a good, though imperfect, illustration of this category of states. See Ambar K. Gosh, "The Paradox of Centralised Federalism: An Analysis to the Challenges of India's Federal Design," *ORF Occasional Paper* no. 272 (2020), available at https://www.orfonline.org/research/the-paradox-of-centralised-federalism/.

Bibliography

Adelman, David E. and Kirsten H. Engel. "Adaptive Federalism: The Case Against Reallocating Environmental Regulatory Authority." *Minnesota Law Review* 92, no. 6 (2008): 1796–1850.

Aligica, Paul and Vlad Tarko. "Polycentricity: From Polanyi to Ostrom and Beyond." *Governance* 25, no. 2 (2012): 237–262.

Belser, Eva M. "Why the Affection of Federalism for Human Rights Is Unrequited and How the Relationship Could Be Improved." In *The Principle of Equality in Diverse States*, edited by Eva M. Belser et al., 62–100. Leiden-Boston: Brill, 2021.

Bengoetxea, Joxerramon, "Emancipatory Federalism and Juridical Pluralism: The Multinational European Context." *Les grandes conferences du Centre d'Analyse Politique Constitution Federalisme* (2020): 1–34, available at https://www.ehu.eus/documents/1687243/32914376/Emancipatory+Federalism+and+Juridical+Pluralism.pdf/5aac2c19-2171-1149-ceb4-f342e5718b13?t=1635239576942.

Berman, Paul S. "Can Global Legal Pluralism Be Both "Global" and "Pluralist"?" *Duke Journal of Comparative and International Law* 29, no. 3 (2019): 381–403.

Berman, Paul S. "Federalism and International Law Through the Lens of Legal Pluralism." *Missouri Law Review* 73, no. 4 (2008): 1149.

Berman, Paul S. *Global Legal Pluralism: A Jurisprudence of Law Beyond Borders*. Cambridge, Cambridge University Press, 2012.

Berman, Paul S. "Jurisgenerative Constitutionalism: Procedural Principles for Managing Global Pluralism." *Indiana Journal of Global Legal Studies* 22, no. 2 (2013): 680–694.

Burgess, Michael and Alain-G. Gagnon, eds., *Comparative Federalism and Federation: Competing Traditions and Future Directions*. Toronto, University of Toronto Press, 1993.

Carlisle, Keith and Rebecca Gruby. "Polycentric Systems of Governance: A Theoretical Ode for the Commons." *Policy Studies Journal* 47, no. 4 (2019): 927–951.

Cohen, Jean L. "The Politics and Risks of the New Legal Pluralism in the Domain of Intimacy." *International Journal of Constitutional Law* 10, no. 2 (2012): 380–397.

Cover, Robert M. "Nomos and Narrative – Foreword." *Harvard Law Review* 97, no. 4 (1983): 4–68.

De Caro, Daniel A. et al., "Legal and Institutional Foundations of Adaptive Environmental Governance." *Ecology and Society* 22, no. 1 (2017): 32–52.

Eboibi, Felix E. "The Impact of Federalism and Legal Pluralism on the Enforcement of International Human Rights Law against Child Marriage in Africa." *African Journal Human Rights* 1 (2017): 72–85.

Fitzpatrick, Peter. "Law and Societies." *Osgoode Hall Law Journal* 22, no. 1 (1984): 115–138.

Gaudreault-DesBiens, Jean-F. "Religious Courts, Personal Federalism and Legal Transplants." In *Shariah in the West*, edited by Rex Adhar and Nicholas Aroney, 159–180. Oxford, Oxford University Press, 2010.

Gaudreault-DesBiens, Jean-F. "Towards a Deontic-Axiomatic Theory of Federal Adjudication." In *The Federal Idea*, edited by Amnon Lev, 75–106. Hart Publishing: Oxford, 2017.

Gerken, Heather K. "Federalism All the Way Down." *Harvard Law Rev*iew 124, no. 1 (2010): 4–74.

Gosh, Ambar K. "The Paradox of Centralised Federalism: An Analysis to the Challenges of India's Federal Design." *ORF Occasional Paper no. 272* (2020), available at https://www.orfonline.org/research/the-paradox-of-centralised-federalism/.

Griffiths, John. "What is Legal Pluralism?" *The Journal of Legal Pluralism and Unofficial Law* 18, no. 24 (1986): 1–55.

Guénette, Dave and Félix Mathieu. "Minority Language School Boards and Personal Federalism in Canada: Recent and Ongoing Developments in Quebec." *Constitutional Forum Constitutionnel* 31, no. 1 (2022): 19–28.

Halberstam, Daniel. "Federalism: Theory, Policy, Law." In *The Oxford Handbook of Comparative Constitutional Law*, edited by Michel Rosenfeld and András Sajó, 576–608. Oxford, Oxford University Press, 2012.

Herlin-Karnell, Ester. "The Constitutional Concepts of Sustainability and Dignity." *Jus Cogens* (2023): 125–148 available at https://link.springer.com/article/10.1007/s42439-023-00078-9.

Jans, Maarten T. "Personal Federalism: A Solution to Ethno-National Conflicts? What is has meant in Brussels and what it could mean in Abkhazia." In *Federal Practice: Exploring Alternatives for Brussels and Abkhazia,* edited by Bruno Coppieters, David Darchiashvili, and Natella Akaba, 215–229. Brussels: VUB Press, 2000.

Jordan, Andrew et al., eds., *Governing Climate Change: Polycentricity in Action?* Cambridge: Cambridge University Press, 2018.

Lindahl, Hans. *Authority and the Globalisation of Inclusion and Exclusion.* Cambridge: Cambridge University Press, 2018.

Lluch, Jaime. "Autonomism and Federalism." *Publius: The Journal of Federalism* 42, no. 1 (2011): 134–161.

Macdonald, Roderick A. "Kaleidoscopic Federalism." In *Le fédéralisme dans tous ses états: governance, identité et méthodologie – The States and Moods of Federalism: Governance, Identity and Methodology*, edited by Jean-F. Gaudreault-DesBiens and Fabien Gélinas, 261–283. Cowansville-Bruxelles: Éditions Yvon Blais-Bruylant, 2005.

Macdonald, Roderick A. "Legal Republicanism and Legal Pluralism: Two Takes on Identity and Diversity." In *Human Diversity and the Law: La diversité humaine et le droit*, edited by Mauro Bussani and Michele Graziadei, 43–70. Brussels: Bruylant, 2005.

Margalit, Avishai. *The Decent Society*. Harvard, Harvard University Press, 1998.

Marshall, Graham R. "Polycentricity, Reciprocity and Farmer Adoption of Conservation Practices under Community-based Governance." *Ecological Economics* 68, no. 5 (2009): 1507–1520.

McGinnis, Michael D., Elizabeth Baldwin and Andreas Thiel, "When is Polycentric Governance Sustainable? Using Institutional Theory to Identify Endogenous Drivers of Dysfunctional Dynamics." 2020, available at https://ostromworkshop.indiana.edu/pdf/seriespapers/2020fall-colloq/mcginnis.pdf.

Mensah, Justice. "Sustainable Development: Meaning, History, Principles, Pillars and Implications for Human Action: Literature Review." *Cogent Social Sciences* 5, no. 1 (2019): 1–21.

Merry, Sally Engle. "Legal Pluralism." *Law & Society Review* 22, no. 5 (1988): 869–896.

Messarra, Antoine N. *Theorie Generale du système politique libanais*. Paris: Cariscript, 1994.

Moore, Sally Falk. "Law and Social Change: The Semi-Autonomous Social Field as an Appropriate Subject of Study." *Law & Society Review* 7, no. 4 (1973): 719–746.

Ostrom, Vincent, Charles M. Tiebout and Robert Warren. "The Organization of Government in Metropolitan Areas: A Theoretical Inquiry." *American Political Science Review* 55, no. 4 (1961): 831–842.

Ostrom, Vincent. *The Meaning of American Federalism*. San Francisco: Institute for Contemporary Studies Press, 1991.

Post, Robert. "Law and Cultural Conflict." *Chicago-Kent Law Review* 78, no. 2 (2003): 485–508.

Potvin-Solis, Laurence, ed., *Le Statut d'État membre de l'Union Européenne* (Brussels: Bruylant, 2018).

Romano, Santi. *L'ordre juridique*. Paris: Dalloz, 1976.

Ryan, Erin. *Federalism and the Tug of War*. Oxford: Oxford University Press, 2012.

Ryan, Erin. "Federalism as Legal Pluralism." In *The Oxford Handbook on Legal Pluralism*, edited by Paul S. Berman, 482–518. Oxford University Press, 2020.

Ryan, Erin. "Negotiating Federalism." *Boston College Law Review* 52, no. 1 (2011): 1–136.

Sarker, Ashutosh. "The Role of State-reinforced Self-governance in Averting the Tragedy of the Irrigation Commons in Japan." *Public Administration* 91, no. 3 (2013): 727–743.

Shachar, Ayelet. *Multicultural Jurisdictions*. Cambridge: Cambridge University Press, 2001.

Stephan, Mark, Graham Marshall and Michael D. McGinnis. "An Introduction to Polycentricity and Governance." In *Governing Complexity*, edited by Andreas Thiel, William Blomquist and Dustin Garrick, 21–44. Cambridge: Cambridge University Press, 2019.

Tamanaha, Brian Z. "A Non-Essentialist Version of Legal Pluralism." *Journal of Law & Society* 27, no. 2 (2000): 296–321.

Tamanaha, Brian Z. "Understanding Legal Pluralism: Past to Present, Local to Global." *Sydney Law Review* 30, no. 3 (2008): 375–411.

Taylor, Charles. "Shared and Divergent Values." In *Options for a New Canada,* edited by Ronald L. Watts and Douglas M. Brown (Toronto, University of Toronto Press, 1991), 155–186.

Thiel, Andreas, William Blomquist and Dustin Garrick, eds., *Governing Complexity*. Cambridge: Cambridge University Press, 2019.

CHAPTER 8

Measurement and Change in Federalism and Legal Pluralism

Michael G. Breen

1 Introduction

Debates about the value and effects of federalism and legal pluralism have tended to occur in isolation, despite the apparent overlaps. This chapter, and this edited volume more generally, represent steps towards a more coherent or unifying research agenda that conceptualises and measures federalism, legal pluralism, and how they relate, specifically as steps towards the development of a "law of diversity". This chapter focuses on ethnic diversity and ethnic accommodation, building on an approach first detailed in Breen 2018.[1]

Federalism is a common yet often imprecisely used term. In some cases it is used interchangeably with respect to a specific system of government, a federation,[2] and at other times more loosely to capture a range of decentralised states and polities.[3] Traditionally, federalism was taken to refer to a system of government with at least two levels of territorially defined and constitutionally sovereign governments, each with their own powers derived from a constitution.[4] Wheare[5] reduced it to a system whereby each level of government has at least one matter on which they have the final say. These definitions were based largely on the US constitution, which was considered to be the paradigmatic case of federalism. But as different approaches to federalism proliferated, these definitions gave way to more nuanced perspectives.

1 Michael G. Breen, *The Road to Federalism in Nepal, Myanmar and Sri Lanka: Finding the Middle Ground, Politics in Asia* (London-New York: Routledge, 2018).

2 For example, Brian Galligan, *A Federal Republic: Australia's Constitutional System of Government* (Cambridge: Cambridge University Press, 1985).

3 See for example Daniel J. Elazar, *Exploring Federalism* (Tuscaloosa: University of Alabama Press, 1987).

4 For example, William H. Riker, *Federalism: Origin, Operation, Significance* (Boston: Little, Brown, 1964).

5 Kenneth Wheare, *Federal Government* (Oxford: Oxford University Press, 1947).

This paper adopts a definition of federalism following Ronald Watts.[6] Watts distinguishes between federalism as an ideology, or normative principle[7] and federal systems, or federal political systems, which refers to the particular institutional manifestation of that federal principle. The federal principle has been famously captured by Elazar[8] as "shared rule plus self-rule" and by Watts[9] as "unity in diversity" (and more recently unity through diversity). These principles in turn imply a federal logic that is centred on the accommodation of diversity, or pluralism, through the recognition, division and sharing of power between different groups defined on a territorial or identity basis (often both). It should be apparent at this point how legal pluralism can relate to federalism. But first, a discussion of federal systems themselves.

There are several different types of federal systems. The most well-known are the federations, such as the US, Australia and Switzerland. But Watts and others also conceive of constitutionally decentralised unions, where powers are divided according to a constitution, but the central government remains supreme, which are relatively commonplace in Asia. The European Union, according to Watts, represents a confederation. Iceland has a kind of federal system, whereby Greenland has autonomy but little role in the governance of Iceland as a whole, known as a federacy. Watts also established a kind of residual category of hybrid federal system. Using this approach, we can think of federalism as a set of normative principles and an organisational logic unrestricted by preconceptions based on existing federal systems, like the US federation.

In other words, federalism as a normative principle can underpin a framework for classifying the instruments and institutions for the accommodation of diversity. This acknowledges that not every institution of interest can be considered as a characteristic component of a federal system. For example, an electoral system is an institution that is often designed to maximise diversity accommodation, but an electoral system is not normally considered to be a federal feature. Nevertheless, we should consider such institutions alongside more specifically federal institutions because they interact and work towards the same or similar objectives. Thus, to understand how a federal system works in practice and the extent to which it achieves its (diversity accommodation)

6 Ronald L. Watts, *Comparing Federal Systems* (2nd ed., Montreal; London: Published for the School of Policy Studies, Queen's University by McGill-Queen's University Press, 1987).

7 See also Preston King, *Federalism and Federation*, (London: Croom Helm, 1982) and Elazar, *Exploring*.

8 Elazar, *Exploring*.

9 Watts, *Comparing*.

objectives, it needs to be analysed and understood in concert with the analysis of related interacting institutions. Hence in this paper, I refer to federalism as a broad overarching normative principle and framework, federal systems as the institutional configuration, and to additional institutions that are relevant to diversity accommodation.

Another way of categorising federalism is according to whether it is ethnic (multinational), territorial (regional) or some hybrid thereof. Minority ethnic groups and Indigenous Peoples tend to seek ethnic federalism, which is institutionalised through the design of provincial boundaries that reflect the distribution of different ethnic groups, or to recognise traditional homelands, and in doing so enable special rights for the given ethnic group(s).[10] This can be compared to territorial federalism, where the corresponding federal boundaries are based on non-ethnic factors, like geography, viability and infrastructure, and laws are based on principles of neutrality and are blind to ethnicity and cultural difference.[11]

Legal pluralism refers to different sets of laws or legal systems pertaining to different groups or territories within a single state or polity. Legal pluralism is present to at least some extent in all federal systems because federal systems have different legislative systems at the federal level as compared to the regional or provincial level, or some variation thereof. In those federal systems that are ethnic, or multinational, legal pluralism is much more prominent. This is because the state, at the time of federalisation, tends to recognise and (aims to) institutionalise ethnic diversity. This means that different subnational units will be empowered to create laws and legal systems that account for that unit's titular or dominant ethnic group's cultural and linguistic distinctiveness and, in many cases, their unique traditions and customary practices. Ethnic federal systems are also often asymmetrical. It is through this accommodation of diversity that we see the most fundamental overlap between the (recognition of) unity in diversity that is central to federalism and to legal pluralism. Indeed, conceived in this way, the two do not just overlap but are mutually reinforcing.

---

10 Will Kymlicka, *Multicultural citizenship: A Liberal Theory of Minority Rights* (Cambridge: Cambridge University Press, 1995); and, "Multi-nation Federalism," in *Federalism in Asia*, eds. Baogang He, Brian Galligan and Takashi Inoguchi (Cheltenham, UK: Edward Elgar, 2007), 33–56.

11 David Brown, "Regionalist Federalism: A Critique of Ethno-national Federalism," in *Federalism in Asia*, eds. Baogang He, Brian Galligan and Takashi Inoguchi (Cheltenham, UK: Edward Elgar 2007), 57–81; Yash Ghai and Jill Cottrell, *Federalism and State Restructuring in Nepal: The Challenge for the Constituent Assembly*, (Kathmandu: United Nations Development Programme, 2007).

Over recent decades, federal systems have been introduced predominately as a tool for the accommodation of ethnic diversity. These modern federal systems can be described as holding together,[12] formed in response to a secession risk, or some threat to the territorial integrity of the country.[13] Invariably, such risks have some kind of ethnic underpinning. One or more ethnic groups (whether based predominately on language, religion, caste or other) demand autonomy and often take up arms in order to pressure the government to accede to that demand. Whether overtly or not, a risk of the breakup or fracturing of the state becomes a goad to action, and when conditions are ripe, federalism results. The institutions of the federal system itself inevitably must address, at least to some extent, these demands, and so an ethnic federal system is developed. (Although we might call them ethnic federal systems, they are usually in fact a hybrid, incorporating some ethnic provinces, some territorially-based provinces and some mixture thereof).[14]

Thus, what defines an ethnic federal system in this context is the accommodation of ethnic diversity. This may be through the delineation of territories forming provinces, through political representation rights, through the recognition of different legal systems and customary laws, and through other special rights (e.g. language rights). Notably, these "ethnic" features are usually aimed towards minorities and the provision or recognition of minority rights. However, we are increasingly seeing a greater emphasis and incorporation of rights for all ethnic groups. For example, the recent Constitution of Nepal includes quotas for different ethnic groups, including the dominant Khas Arya, while the now defunct Constitution of Myanmar (2008), incorporated ethnic affairs ministries on a non-territorial basis where groups became small minorities in the territorial units (states and regions). The largest number of those ministries were allocated to the dominant group, the Bamar, who are also designated as one of the eight Indigenous "national races".

Hence, the accommodation of diversity is about more than just the institutions traditionally understood to characterise a federal system, as conceived by Watts.[15] The logic, the underpinning principles and the institutional approaches of federalism and legal pluralism overlap and in order to progress

12 Alfred C. Stepan, "Federalism and democracy: Beyond the US model," *Journal of Democracy* 10, no. 4 (1999): 19–34.

13 Michael G. Breen, "The Origins of Holding-Together Federalism: Nepal, Myanmar and Sri Lanka," *Publius: The Journal of Federalism* 48, no. 1 (2018): 26–50.

14 See Baogang He, Michael G. Breen and Laura Allison-Reumann, *Comparative Federalism in Asia: Democracy, Ethnicity and Religion*, (London-New York: Routledge, 2023).

15 Watts, *Comparing.*

a "law of diversity", they need to be considered together. In particular, federalism as an ideology should not be restricted to the logic of a division of powers between territorially-based tiers of government. Indeed, federalism is inherently pluralist and reflects a range of distinct and overlapping legal and normative systems without being 'ethnic' as such, as discussed by Alessi and Trettel in the introduction to this volume. Nevertheless, this chapter focuses on the ethnic dimension to the accommodation of diversity. Ethnicity here refers to culture, language, religion, caste and traditions.

This chapter puts forward an approach to the definition and measurement of the accommodation of diversity that is built around the institutions for federalism (broadly conceived). The measurement approach features a number of indicators that can be aggregated and disaggregated to focus on one or the other, and to understand how they relate. It is state-centric, but it does not need to be. It can be used, and has been used, to theorise how and why institutions change, and under what conditions, and to analyse the outcomes of different combinations of institutions.[16] From this we can make normative claims about (the desirability and design of) federalism and legal pluralism and the impact of various institutional configurations.

The paper is structured as follows. Following this introduction, Section 2 conceptualises federalism, legal pluralism and accommodation while Section 3 describes the measurement approach and the definition of key indicators. Section 4 applies the approach to three cases in Asia that have faced considerable challenges arising from their ethnic diversity, namely Myanmar, Nepal and Sri Lanka. Section 5 considers further the relationship with democracy, followed by a conclusion.

2 Conceptualising Federalism and Accommodation

Taking a principle-based approach to federalism and the accommodation of diversity means that federal systems should be considered along a continuum, between unitary on the one end, and federal on the other, and include a dimension of inclusion. Inclusion can be high or low, independent of the extent of federalisation. Federal systems can be more or less federal, depending on their institutional design and implementation. They can display, for example, the features of a federation, like the US, or a constitutionally decentralised union, like Sri Lanka, or even be a predominately unitary state with important federal

16 See Breen, "The Origins," and *The Road to Federalism*.

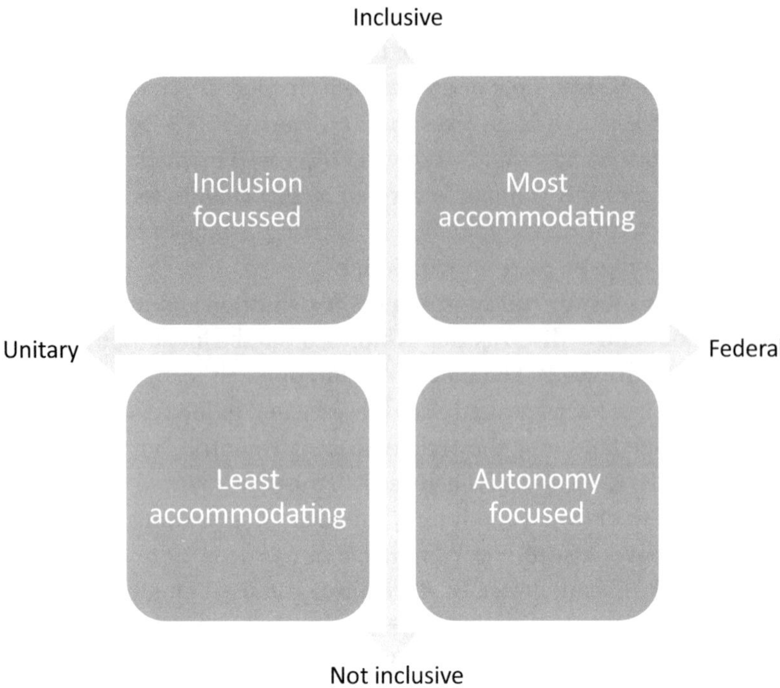

FIGURE 8.1 Matrix of federal and inclusion dimensions of the accommodation of diversity

features, like the Philippines. Each of these can be mapped along a continuum, as per Figure 8.1. Indeed, federalism is inherently a hybrid, starting in the US with the mapping of confederal features on a strong central government, through to the more recent innovations that we have seen in Nepal, for example, which institutionalises a strong local government and comparatively weak provinces. Hybridity can concern many elements – how ethnic and territorial elements are mixed, how federal and unitary characteristics combine, how religion and secularism are accommodated and how symmetry and asymmetry coexist.

At the same time, a federal system can be more or less accommodating of diversity. It is not necessarily true that a system that could be categorised on the far (federal) end of a federal continuum is also accommodating, as per Figure 8.1. For example, Australia's federal system emphasises legal neutrality and purports to be identity-blind. It has legal pluralism in its different orders of government, but it largely stops there. There is no part of its federalism that

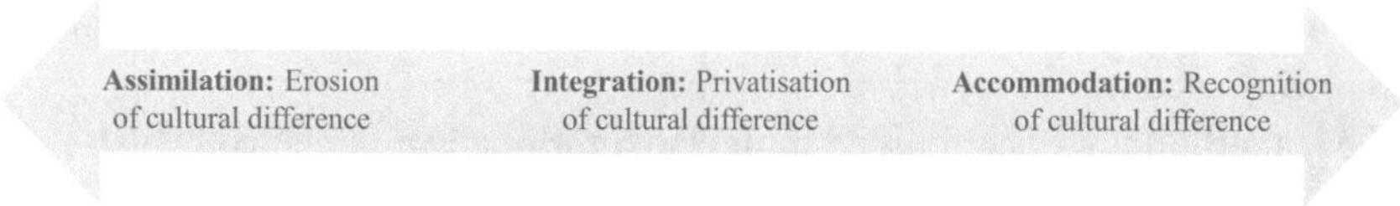

FIGURE 8.2 Continuum from assimilation to accommodation
ADAPTED FROM BREEN 2018B

can be said to be aimed towards the accommodation of ethnic or religious diversity (rather it enables regionally-based diversity).[17]

So, what do we mean when we talk about accommodation? I define accommodation as a mixture of inclusion (representation and voice in political institutions) and autonomy, which I elaborate on in the following section. Like federalism, accommodation can be measured along a continuum of assimilation to integration to accommodation, each defined according to their approach to cultural difference (see Figure 8.2).[18] Specifically, assimilation seeks to erode or eliminate cultural differences and to build a common identity. Integration respects cultural differences but treats them as private affairs within a framework that otherwise focuses on individual rights and state neutrality. Accommodation recognises cultural differences and institutionalises group rights.[19] Federal systems can be designed in a way that is accommodating, such as in an ethnic federal system; integrating; or assimilating. Several federal systems including the US and arguably Malaysia have been designed in a way that cross-cuts ethnicity, with a view towards assimilation.[20]

In the Asian region, federalism is invariably a kind of holding-together ethnic federalism.[21] The explicit treatment of ethnic groups in federal systems in Asia thus make it a fruitful ground for elaborating and testing an approach to

17 Galligan, *A Federal Republic.*

18 John McGarry, Brendan O'Leary, and Richard Simeon, "Integration or Accommodation? The Enduring Debate in Conflict Regulation," in *Constitutional Design for Divided Societies*, ed. Sujit Choudhry, (Oxford: Oxford University Press, 2008), 41–88.

19 McGarry, O'Leary and Simeon, "Integration or Accommodation."

20 Liam D. Anderson, *Federal Solutions to Ethnic Problems: Accommodating Diversity, Exeter studies in Ethno Politics* (London-New York: Routledge, 2013); and William Case, "Semi-democracy and Minimalist Federalism in Malaysia," in *Federalism in Asia*, eds. Baogang He, Brian Galligan and Takashi Inoguchi, (Cheltenham, UK: Edward Elgar, 2007), 124–133.

21 Breen, *The Road to Federalism*; and Michael G. Breen, "Federal and Political Party Reforms in Asia: Is there a New Model of Federal Democracy Emerging in Ethnically Diverse Countries," *Government and Opposition* 2, no. 7 (2022): 296–317.

the measurement of the accommodation of diversity, which I turn to in the following section.

My methodology is grounded in new institutionalism, specifically historical institutionalism, which pays attention to path dependencies and critical junctures as opportunities for substantive change. I define institutions following March and Olsen:[22] An institution is a relatively enduring collection of rules and organised practices, embedded in structures of meaning and resources that are relatively invariant in the face of turnover of individuals and relatively resilient to the idiosyncratic preferences and expectations of individuals and changing external circumstances.

My measurement approach distinguishes between formal and informal institutions, or institutions as formal rules and informal organised practices. This is consistent with approaches to legal pluralism that distinguish between formal and informal legal systems, with the former comprising those official and written laws and practices, and the latter encompassing traditional, customary and personal (family) laws, some of which may also become formal.

Taking a holistic approach to federalism requires us to consider its purposes when identifying features. I focus on Asia in my conceptualisation and apply the measurement approach to three countries. Asian federal systems, as holding together federal systems in ethnically divided contexts, focus on the accommodation (and sometimes integration or assimilation) of different ethnic groups. Therefore, institutions that seek to achieve or otherwise affect these ends should be incorporated into the concept and measured, especially when they interact with federal institutions and contribute to the aim of unity in diversity. This includes legal pluralism (outside of the conventional occurrence in federal systems), mechanisms for proportional representation and the recognition of cultural rights.

In doing so, I develop a new approach to understanding and evaluating federalism as a means of accommodating diversity. Together, these aspects work towards unity in diversity, "based on the presumed value and validity of combining unity and diversity and of accommodating, preserving and promoting distinct identities".[23] It does not have to be about minority ethnic groups alone, but it should be acknowledged that dominant groups are usually in effect already accommodated. It is well established that states, including

22 James March and Johan Olsen, "Elaborating the New Institutionalism," *The Oxford Handbook of Political Institutions*, eds. Sarah A. Binder, Roderock A. W. Rhodes and Bert A. Rockman, (Oxford: Oxford University Press, 2008), 3.

23 Watts, *Comparing*, 6.

liberal democratic states, are not neutral.[24] A purportedly neutral state will inevitably reflect to some degree the culture, language, preferences and biases of the dominant group. This bias combines with historical discrimination to prevent many minority groups from achieving equality.[25] In other words, my approach to accommodating diversity focuses on minority ethnic groups, as dominant groups are already accommodated in the overarching state structure and legal framework.

3 Measuring Federal Systems and Accommodation

My approaching to measuring the management of ethnic diversity maps formal and informal institutions along a continuum from assimilation to accommodation. The higher the score, the more accommodating it is. The indicators have been subcategorised to enable disaggregation and comparison of component parts, for example, consociational elements, those that address legal pluralism specifically, those that relate to traditional federal systems, and those that relate strictly to the ethnicity afforded in the federal design.

The formal federal system indicators and their operationalisation are:

- Autonomy: the extent of centralisation (e.g. intervention rights) offset against the extent of constitutional autonomy afforded to the units;
- Constitutionalism: the constitutional change, interpretation and dispute resolution processes;
- Bicameralism: how units are represented in the centre, such as whether there are two relatively equal houses of parliament, or whether units are formally represented in other central institutions.

But a federal system as mentioned is not necessarily accommodating, unless it is designed in such a way that ethnic groups have some kind of autonomy, such as through the provincial boundaries that are aligned with territorial clustering of ethnic groups or forms of special autonomy. Hence the incorporation of an ethnicity in federalism indicator, which is measured primarily according to the proportion of units which are based primarily in a single ethnicity, mixed or territorially based. Additional factors informing the measurement of this indicator are the extent of asymmetry, the strength of local government and presence of provisions for special autonomy.

---

24 Kymlicka, *Multicultural Citizenship*; and Ian O'Flynn, *Deliberative Democracy and Divided Societies*, (Edinburgh: Edinburgh University Press, 1995).

25 Kymlicka, *Multicultural Citizenship*; and Ian O'Flynn, *Deliberative Democracy*.

Other indicators included here that work towards unity in diversity, and their operationalisation, are:

- Representation: how ethnic groups are represented in key institutions, particularly the legislature, including electoral systems; and,
- Cultural rights: the extent to which diverse cultural rights, such as those relating to language and religion, are positively protected or undermined, such as through personal law systems and non-territorial autonomy.

Informal or behavioural components are recorded as actions that reinforce or undermine the formal institutions and their purposes, or as the implementation or not of those formal institutions. If a constitutional provision is not implemented within three years, its score is removed. Scores are also adjusted if either the legislature or executive of a unit is dissolved, or legislation is disallowed by a higher tier and according to the proportionality of electoral results and the basic composition of executives (such as whether minimum, oversized or consensus). Further details are provided in Table 8.1.

The scoring system is informed by the approach of Lijphart[26] but adapted. Lijphart famously used ten variables to identify and analyse the contrast between majoritarian and consensus democracies. I adapt his variables, although I do not measure central bank independence or the strength of civil society and I look at the specific mix of power allocation for autonomy and centralization measures. I use Gallagher's Index[27] to measure proportionality, and an adaptation thereof to look at ethnic inclusion. For comparing with and controlling for democracy and internal conflict, I use the Polity Project's timeseries data.[28]

I do not consider democracy as a prerequisite or essential element of federalism or accommodation. It is often argued that accommodation of minorities is less likely, and that federalism, or federal systems, cannot work in an authoritarian regime.[29] But this is to downplay or disregard the significance of hybrid arrangements and successful forms of accommodation in countries that are considered to be not fully democratic, such as those in Malaysia and

26 Arend Lijphart, *Patterns of Democracy: Government Forms and Performance in Thirty-six Countries*, (New Haven: Yale University Press, 1999).

27 Lijphart, *Patterns*, 145.

28 Monty G. Marshall, Ted Robert Gurr, and Keith Jaggers, *Political Regime Characteristics and Transitions, 1800–2015*, Polity IV Project, (Vienna: Centre for Systemic Peace, 2016).

29 For example, Stepan, *Federalism and Democracy*; Elazar, *Exploring*; Michael Burgess, *In Search of the Federal Spirit: New Comparative Empirical and Theoretical Perspectives*, (Oxford: Oxford University Press, 2012); Thomas O. Hueglin and Alan Fenna, *Comparative Federalism: A Systematic Inquiry* (2nd ed., Toronto: University of Toronto Press, 2015).

Myanmar.[30] Henders[31] and Bertrand & Laliberte[32] find little difference across regime types in whether and how minorities are accommodated, and in some cases, authoritarian regimes are more suited to protecting group rights and seeking consensus, given the lesser emphasis on individual rights and democratic competition.

Other controls and points of comparison that I have incorporated in order to understand the reasons for, and timing of, institutional change are the extent of internal conflict, when regime type changes occur, when there is either major marketisation or an economic crisis and when there is international intervention or other contingent event, like a natural disaster. Positive changes are scored as one, and negative changes as negative one, and are generally not cumulative.

I also measure infrastructural capacity. Infrastructural capacity, building on Ziblatt,[33] refers to the representational and institutional arrangements of minority ethnic groups. Infrastructural capacity in this sense can be taken to refer to an informal legal pluralism, and its presence incentivises the central state to recognise that legal pluralism through federal arrangements mitigates secession risk.[34] My measurement approach has been tried and tested in my 2018 book[35] and journal article[36] covering Nepal, Myanmar and Sri Lanka, and a subsequent article expanding its use to a further five countries in Asia.[37] The examples in Section 4 are drawn from these publications, which provide further detail on the methodology.

With respect to the accommodation of diversity, some institutions addressed here are clearly a representation of legal pluralism – autonomy being one, but also cultural rights. Some enable recognition of legal pluralism, or make it more likely, such as, for example, political inclusion. On the other hand, a constitutionally independent court designed to adjudicate disputes between

30 For examples see Will Kymlicka and Baogang He, *Multiculturalism in Asia*, (Oxon: Oxford University Press, 2005).

31 Susan J. Henders, *Territoriality, Asymmetry, and Autonomy: Catalonia, Corsica, Hong Kong, and Tibet*, (New York: Palgrave Macmillan, 2010).

32 Jacques Bertrand and Andre Laliberte, *Multination States in Asia*, (Cambridge: Cambridge University Press, 2010).

33 Daniel Ziblatt, "Rethinking the Origins of Federalism: Puzzle, Theory, and Evidence from Nineteenth-Century Europe," *World Politics* 57, no. 1 (2004): 70–98.

34 See Breen, "The Origins."

35 See Breen, *The Road to Federalism*.

36 See Breen, "The Origins."

37 See Breen, "Federal and Political Party," including supplementary online data.

TABLE 8.1 Federalism as the accommodation of diversity: indicators

Indicator	Operationalisation
Autonomy	Extent of autonomy, based on breadth indicated by the sharing of four key kinds of powers, and the scope of that autonomy (legislative, executive)
Constitutionalism	Constitutional change requirements (e.g. supermajority or minority veto), independence of judiciary and dispute resolution procedures
Interdependence	Bicameralism including type of representation and role of upper house, and legislative executive relations (parliamentary, presidential etc.)
Subnational units	Basis of provincial level units (ethnic) and presence and strength of local level and other special structures
Asymmetry	Differences in powers and representation of subnational units and constituent ethnic groups
Representation	Identity/ethnic elements of representation, such as reservations, proportional representation
Cultural rights	Recognition of languages, personal laws, traditional dispute resolution, customary laws, non-territorial autonomy
Federal behaviours	Increases or reductions in the powers of subnational units, changes in the number or boundaries of units, impositions of states of emergencies and other major acts of intervention, secession events, major changes to the independence of the courts
Behaviours associated with inclusion and cultural rights	Representation of ethnic groups in the executive, extent of proportionality (ethnic) in the legislature, empowerment of ethnic groups to manage own affairs (where not covered above such as in a constitution), exercise of minority veto, minus assimilating activities such as education or language reforms that prioritise the dominant group.
Infrastructural capacity	Strength of regional or identity-based administrative and representative structures, comprising existence and type of regional administration and its services, and the type(s) of political / negotiating organisation

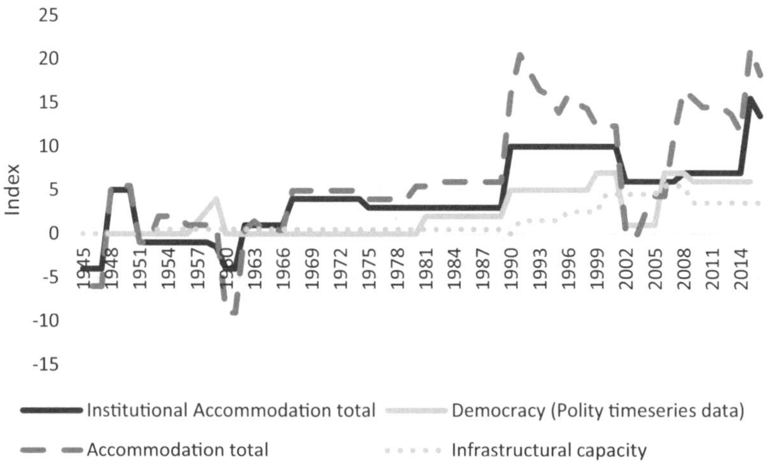

FIGURE 8.3 Accommodation, democratisation and infrastructural capacity in Nepal 1945–2016
ADAPTED FROM BREEN 2018B

subnational units, and between subnational units and the centre, cannot be said to be a form of legal pluralism.

4 Applying the Measures – Myanmar, Nepal and Sri Lanka

When applied to Myanmar, Nepal and Sri Lanka, these measures reveal several conditions and incentives for the accommodation of minorities,[38] and demonstrate the relationship between different kinds of institutions, for example federalism (that accommodates diversity) and democracy. Starting with Nepal, and its process towards federal democracy, Figure 8.3 maps the change in the level of accommodation (formal and combined) since the establishment of its modern state in 1948, along with the level of democracy (democratisation) and the peripheral infrastructural capacity.

Figure 8.3 shows that there have been three main approaches to the accommodation of diversity in Nepal. Firstly, Panchayats (people's assemblies), provided a bottom-up approach to decentralisation. They existed in both democratic and authoritarian regimes (see democracy line in Figure 8.4). The clustering of ethnic groups, and the deliberate delineation of Panchayats that aligned with this clustering meant that they entailed important approaches

38 For further detail, see Breen, *The Road to Federalism*, 83–119.

to the accommodation of diversity. But they were centrally controlled and restricted non-sanctioned forms of association (including political parties).[39] As indicated in Figure 8.3, the arrangements did not cross into the accommodation range of the continuum,[40] and were used primarily to progress an assimilation-based nation-building agenda. This arrangement was met with considerable resistance from minority groups and from the dominant group, which agitated for democratisation.

Secondly, a new democratic regime was put in place in 1990 in response to a popular uprising. But it was a highly centralised unitary system that reinforced the culture and identity of the dominant group. It did recognise multiethnicity and increase inclusion, but it kept in place identity-based nation-building tools, like a national religion and restrictive citizenship rules. There was some observance of customary laws, personal laws and traditional dispute resolution, though with little formal recognition. We can see a middle rating (integration) though in fact it was a mixture of accommodating and assimilating policies, with little space for formal legal pluralism.

Thirdly, the establishment of an interim and then federal constitution in 2008 and 2015 respectively, bought in a range of accommodating institutions and formal recognition of diversity and legal pluralism. For example, quotas and proportional representation in various sectors including politics, multilingualism, institutionalisation of personal laws and customary dispute resolution. The accommodation of diversity score is quite high. It is notable that this change followed internal conflict and a major contingent event (crisis), which provided an opportunity for significant change (i.e. a critical juncture that enabled a new path to be established).[41]

Figure 8.4 compares those elements marked as federal, those that encompass cultural rights, and those that are about inclusion (focused on representation). They are mutually reinforcing, but they are not the same. Sometimes they move independently of the other, at other times they are linked to a package of institutional reforms. Representation is a prime example, while cultural rights have also occurred at high levels in the absence of federal structures.

39 David N. Gellner, "Ethnic Rights and Politics in Nepal," *Himalayan Journal of Anthropology and Sociology* 2 (2005): 1–17; D.P. Kumar, *Nepal: Year of Decision*, (New Delhi: Vikas Publishing House, 1980); Thomas B. Smith, *The Ideology of Nepal's Panchayat Raj* (Master thesis, University of Arizona, 1967).

40 Although I do not specifically define ranges or definite lines between accommodation, integration and assimilation (being a continuum), scores above five may generally be regarded as accommodating, while assimilative approaches tend to score below zero.

41 See Breen, *The Road to Federalism*, 87–92.

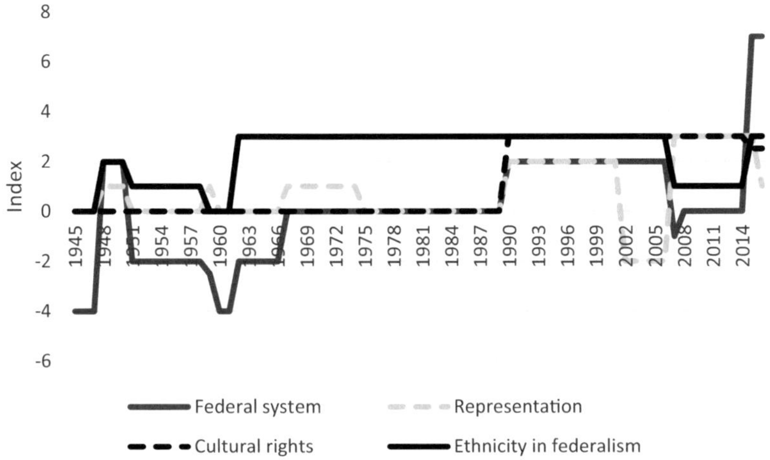

FIGURE 8.4 Institutions linked to the accommodation of diversity in Nepal, 1948–2016
ADAPTED FROM BREEN 2018B

In Myanmar, as displayed in Figure 8.5, the initial state structure was democratic, federal and accommodating in design, but with several underlying assimilation approaches, like the Burmese language being the only official language, and a special position for the Buddhist religion. This system was ended by the military coup in 1962 and a new kind of authoritarian federal system was established in 1974 (after 12 years of operating without a constitution). This was also accommodating in some respects and assimilating in others. Political association was highly restricted, a one-party system was enforced, and although the socialist blueprint that was applied purported to be ethnically neutral, it privileged the Bamar Buddhist culture, language and religion. At the same time, many areas of the country were practically autonomous, as ethnic armed groups held considerable tracts of land by force or under ceasefire with the military regime. This element (of legal pluralism) is represented in the infrastructural capacity indicator.

Following a series of crises, significant change began in 2008 with the establishment of a new semi-democratic constitution that was federal (a constitutionally decentralised union) with designated ethnic states, but still it privileged Bamar Buddhists and lacked recognition of customary and personal laws. The military also retained 25% of seats in all parliaments and executive offices, and conflict continued in significant parts of the country. This constitution and the federal system it established was effectively ended in 2021 by another military coup. Figure 8.6 below shows these substantial fluctuations

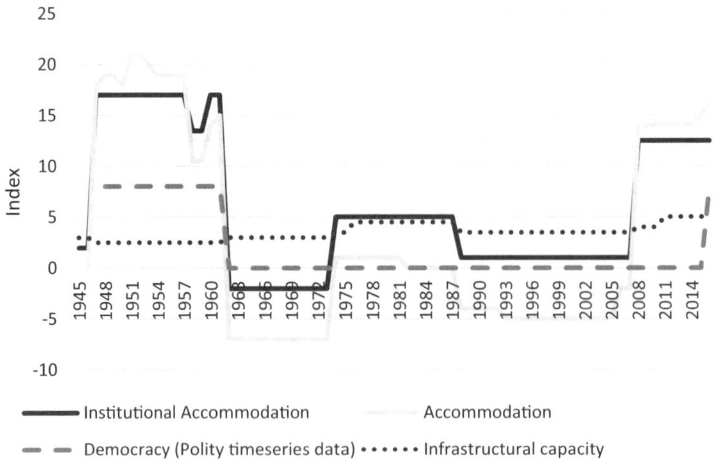

FIGURE 8.5 Accommodation, democratisation and infrastructural capacity in Myanmar 1945–2016
ADAPTED FROM BREEN 2018B

in accommodation, sometimes in concert with changes to the level of democracy, sometimes independently. The federal system indicator has, in this case, also tended to follow the development of infrastructural capacity. In other words, an informal legal pluralism precedes its recognition.

Figure 8.6 compares those elements marked as federal, those that encompass cultural rights, and those that focus on representation. In this case, there have been significant fluctuations in the federal system measures, but complete consistency with respect to (the lack of) representation and cultural rights.

In Sri Lanka, the state has been more or less a democracy since independence in 1948. However, it has consistently implemented an assimilating nation-building agenda, contributing to a gradual decline in the quality of its democracy (see democracy indicator in Figure 8.7). Similar to Myanmar and Nepal, it privileged one religion (Buddhism), had only one national language (Sinhala) and failed to respond to minority ethnic groups' demands for autonomy, leading eventually to a devastating twenty-five-year civil war. The major change that can be seen in Figure 8.7 in 1987 is the introduction of a kind of federal system (constitutionally decentralised union), involving two ethnic provinces (which were at one stage merged) and seven provinces for the dominant Sinhala group. However, many provisions of this constitutional change were not implemented, and it failed to halt the civil war.

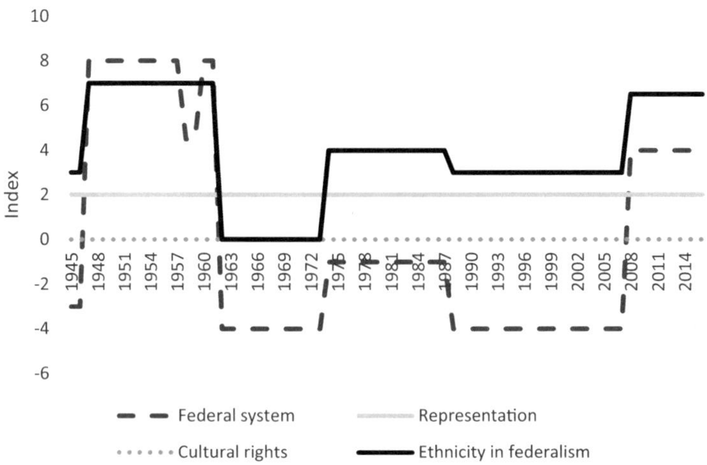

FIGURE 8.6 Institutions linked to the accommodation of diversity in Myanmar, 1945–2016
ADAPTED FROM BREEN 2018B

Importantly, Figure 8.7 demonstrates the significant differences between accommodation on paper and in practice, and major declines in accommodation in practice are visible, even while the accommodation on paper remained much the same. The trajectory of democracy is more closely related to this practical dimension than it is to the formal institutional arrangements. We can also see the link between the creation of infrastructural capacity and the subsequent establishment of a federal system. Again, informal legal pluralism precedes its recognition.

Recent efforts to reform the constitution and again establish an accommodating federal system were halted by the 2019 election of Gotabaya Rajapaksa, former defence minister and brother of former president Mahinda Rajapaksa, as president. They campaigned on an agenda of ethnic and religious nationalism and did little to appease aggrieved minorities. At the time of writing, there is a major economic crisis, and we can anticipate that this will precipitate further institutional reform.

Figure 8.8 compares those elements marked as federal, those that encompass cultural rights, and those that are about inclusion (focused on representation). There is no change in the level of cultural rights, representation or ethnicity in federalism. It maintained much the same provincial structure and continued to preference Sinhala language. Although Sri Lanka introduced proportional representation in its electoral system, the threshold was so high

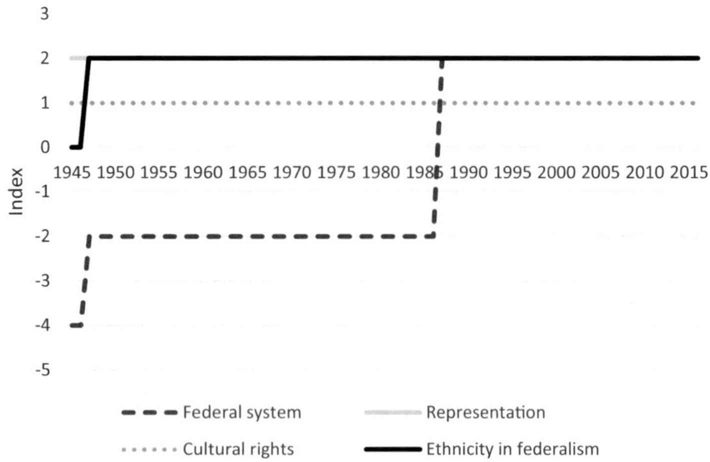

FIGURE 8.7 Accommodation, democratisation and infrastructural capacity in Sri Lanka 1945–2016
ADAPTED FROM BREEN 2018B

that it failed to accommodate minority ethnic groups or make any substantive difference to the level of inclusion.

From the analysis of these changes, we can conclude that the accommodation of diversity is more likely to occur, and to be more robust, in a democratic

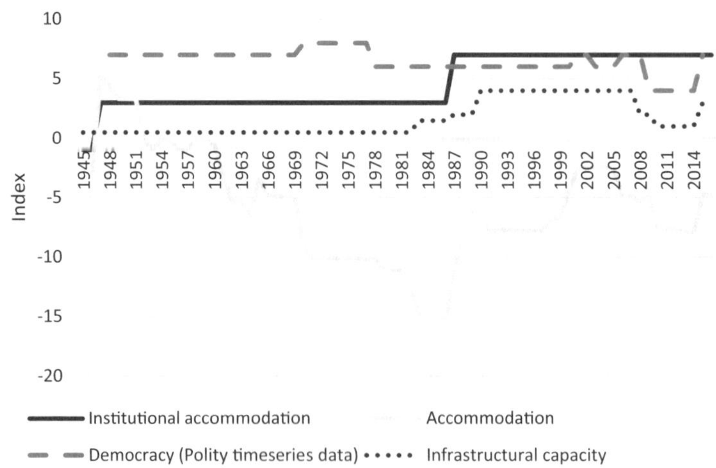

FIGURE 8.8 Institutions linked to the accommodation of diversity in Sri Lanka, 1945–2016
ADAPTED FROM BREEN 2018B

regime, in particular at the time of initial democratisation; and that the mixing of accommodating and assimilating institutions is unlikely to sustain itself long-term. In addition, we can see the importance of infrastructural capacity, which represents a form of legal pluralism, as a necessary condition for the federalisation and the formal recognition of that legal pluralism.

5 Applying the Measures – Federalism and Democracy in Asia

In a separate study, I applied the same federal system measure, without the cultural rights and representation (inclusion) features, but with a measure of ethnicity in provincial design, to a study of eight countries in Asia that have a federal system.[42] This used the four key institutions: autonomy (powers) of provinces, intervention powers or dominance of the centre, bicameralism and constitutionalism (including an independent court), as described in Table 8.2, as well as the measure of the extent of ethnicity in federalism based on the proportion of provinces based on ethnicity. From this I compared at an aggregate and individual level federalism with democracy, proportionality, the effective number of political parties and executive (in)stability. I report here on the relationship with democracy.

Figure 8.9 shows the positive relationship between federal systems and democracy, which should be no surprise. But even controlling for overlap of institutions, the relationship is still strongly positive. Several institutions are mutually reinforcing, like an independent court. Federalism makes democratic participation easier by bringing government closer to the people, and it is more accommodating of diversity. Indeed, between 2010 and 2020, democracy in each of the eight federal countries was maintained at the same level or increased, whereas many unitary countries in Asia have seen their democracies go backwards (such as Bangladesh, Cambodia, Thailand).[43]

Notably, Figure 8.9 shows three distinct periods in the history of federalism in Asia. The first period (from about 1948 to the early 1960s) shows an initially high level of democracy and a low level of federal institutionalisation. A series of democratic failures followed, as these initial institutions failed to adequately accommodate diversity. The second period shows experimentations with undemocratic federal systems, like Nepal's partyless Panchayats (assemblies) and Myanmar's single party federal structures. These too failed. Finally,

42 See Breen, "Federal and Political Party," including supplementary online data.

43 Breen, "Federal and Political Party," 314.

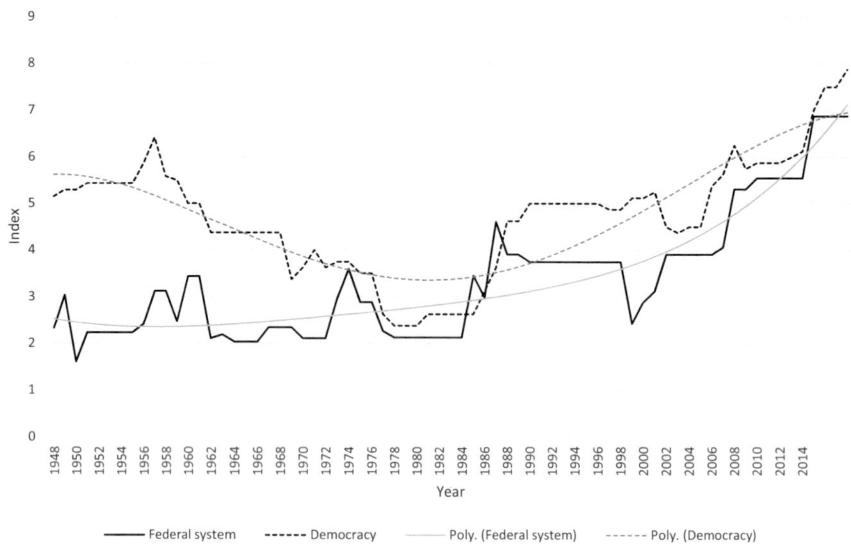

FIGURE 8.9 Federalism and democracy averages for eight countries in Asia: 1948–2017
ADAPTED FROM BREEN 2022

the third period (from the late 1980s up to now) shows that democracy and federalism are being combined – and apparently sustainably so. On this basis, we may propose that one aspect of a Law of diversity is that accommodation is likely to be higher in democratic regimes than in authoritarian regimes. We can also posit that democracy in ethnically divided societies is more likely to sustain when it is federal than when it is unitary.

6 Conclusion

Federalism is an ideological and normative principle encompassed in the phrases "unity in diversity" and "self-rule plus shared rule". In this sense, federalism is fundamentally about the accommodation of diversity. Federalism in its institutional manifestation can be described as a federal system, but even this is too narrow. Federalism as a principle and a federal system as an institutional configuration should be able to provide us with a framework for understanding, organising and assessing the accommodation of diversity through a range of mechanisms, including legal pluralism, non-territorial autonomy, participatory and deliberative processes and political inclusion. Ethnic federalism is a logic of federalism that prioritises the accommodation of ethnic diversity.

This paper argues that federalism, legal pluralism and the accommodation of diversity can be simultaneously measured. The measures can be aggregated or disaggregated in a variety of ways, including to focus purely on those institutions that indicate a form of legal pluralism. In doing so, we can compare the effects and the evolution over time of different combinations of institutional approaches to accommodation and identify conditions, causal mechanisms, and even laws for the accommodation of diversity.

In the preceding discussion, I have demonstrated that accommodation of diversity is more likely to occur, and to be higher, in a democratic regime, and that the mixing of accommodating and assimilating institutions is likely to contribute to instability and conflict, and is unlikely to be sustainable. Further, substantive change in the extent of accommodation is more likely to occur at times of crisis, particularly when economic crises converge with other crises (e.g. natural disasters).[44] Elsewhere,[45] I have shown that federalism (as accommodation of diversity) reduces conflict, secession and regime instability. But only under arrangements that incentivise deliberation and inter-ethnic engagements, at the same time as enabling autonomy, through ethnoterritorial provinces, mixed party systems and mixed yet majoritarian executives.

We can use the above conclusions towards the construction of a Law of diversity. We can see the different (potential components) and how they relate. We can make the claim that accommodation should be democratic because it is likely to be of a greater extent and more sustainable. The experience of Asia also indicates the importance of local participatory institutions, which can accommodate a broader range of (smaller and scattered) minorities. And we can also argue that federalism is a major and potentially necessary underpinning principle of a system that accommodates diversity and recognises and institutionalises legal pluralism.

This approach to the measurement of accommodation is one that can contribute to the development of a Law of diversity, its assessment, and its further refinement. But it is only one step. It is fundamentally an institutional analysis (even if it includes informal institutions and behavioural elements) and can inform theory development but not take the place of it. As such a theory develops, we can build on the framework and refine measures, add new measures, and make it adaptable to the idea that federalism can provide a framework for analysis but not provide a prescription or model for accommodation. Models

44 Breen, *The Road to Federalism.*

45 Breen, "Federalism and Political Party."

can be identified empirically and idealised, but they are fundamentally contextual and dynamic.

One potential avenue for further development is to address more explicitly the deliberative and participatory institutions. In Breen (2018)[46] I drew out the deliberative incentives that are incorporated within the above analysis and proposed that the incorporation of deliberative incentives in federal design can help to overcome tensions between competing theories of consociationalism and centripetalism for ethnic conflict management. In Breen and He,[47] I demonstrated that deliberative methodologies are effective means of moderating ethnic division and overcoming polarisation. I believe this, together with the further development of measures of participation, provides fruitful ground for further empirical analysis of the effects and benefits of different approaches to the accommodation of diversity and the associated theoretical development.

Bibliography

Anderson, Liam D. *Federal Solutions to Ethnic Problems: Accommodating Diversity, Exeter studies in Ethno Politics*. London-New York: Routledge, 2013.

Bertrand, Jacques and Andre Laliberte. *Multination States in Asia*. Cambridge: Cambridge University Press, 2010.

Breen, Michael G. "Federal and Political Party Reforms in Asia: Is there a New Model of Federal Democracy Emerging in Ethnically Diverse Countries." *Government and Opposition* 2, no. 7 (2022): 296–317.

Breen, Michael G. "The Origins of Holding-Together Federalism: Nepal, Myanmar and Sri Lanka." *Publius: The Journal of Federalism* 48, no. 1 (2018): 26–50.

Breen, Michael G. *The Road to Federalism in Nepal, Myanmar and Sri Lanka: Finding the Middle Ground, Politics in Asia*. Abingdon, London-New York: Routledge, 2018.

Brown, David. "Regionalist Federalism: A Critique of Ethno-national Federalism." In *Federalism in Asia*, edited by Baogang He, Brian Galligan and Takashi Inoguchi, 57–81 (Cheltenham, UK: Edward Elgar 2007).

Burgess, Michael. *In Search of the Federal Spirit: New Comparative Empirical and Theoretical Perspectives*. Oxford: Oxford University Press, 2012.

46 Breen, *The Road to Federalism*, 172–175.

47 Michael G. Breen and Baogang He, "Moderating Polarised Positions on Questions of National Identity and Sovereignty: Deliberative Surveys on Federalism in Myanmar," *International Area Studies Review* 23, no. 1 (2020): 93–113.

Case, William. "Semi-democracy and Minimalist Federalism in Malaysia." In *Federalism in Asia*, edited by Baogang He, Brian Galligan and Takashi Inoguchi, 124–133. Cheltenham, UK: Edward Elgar, 2007.

Elazar, Daniel J. *Exploring Federalism*. Tuscaloosa: University of Alabama Press, 1987.

Galligan, Brian. *A Federal Republic: Australia's Constitutional System of Government*. Cambridge: Cambridge University Press, 1985.

Gellner, David N. "Ethnic Rights and Politics in Nepal." *Himalayan Journal of Anthropology and Sociology* 2 (2005): 1–17.

Ghai, Yash and Jill Cottrell. *Federalism and State Restructuring in Nepal: The Challenge for the Constituent Assembly*. Kathmandu: United Nations Development Programme, 2007.

He, Baogang, Michael G. Breen and Laura Allison-Reumann. *Comparative Federalism in Asia: Democracy, Ethnicity and Religion*. London-New York: Routledge, 2023.

Henders, Susan J. *Territoriality, Asymmetry, and Autonomy: Catalonia, Corsica, Hong Kong, and Tibet*. New York: Palgrave Macmillan, 2010.

Hueglin, Thomas O. and Alan Fenna. *Comparative Federalism: A Systematic Inquiry*. 2nd ed., Toronto: University of Toronto Press, 2015.

King, Preston. *Federalism and Federation*. London: Croom Helm, 1982.

Kumar, D.P. *Nepal: Year of Decision*. New Delhi: Vikas Publishing House, 1980.

Smith, Thomas B. *The Ideology of Nepal's Panchayat Raj*. Master thesis, University of Arizona, 1967.

Kymlicka, Will and Baogang He. *Multiculturalism in Asia*. Oxon: Oxford University Press, 2005.

Kymlicka, Will. *Multicultural citizenship: A Liberal Theory of Minority Rights*. Cambridge: Cambridge University Press, 1995.

Kymlicka, Will. "Multi-nation Federalism." In *Federalism in Asia*, edited by Baogang He, Brian Galligan and Takashi Inoguchi, 33–56. Cheltenham, UK: Edward Elgar, 2007.

Lijphart, Arend. *Patterns of Democracy: Government Forms and Performance in Thirty-six Countries*. New Haven: Yale University Press, 1999.

March, James and Johan Olsen. "Elaborating the New Institutionalism." *The Oxford Handbook of Political Institutions*, edited by Sarah A. Binder, Roderock A. W. Rhodes and Bert A. Rockman, 3–20. Oxford: Oxford University Press, 2008.

McGarry, John, Brendan O'Leary, and Richard Simeon. "Integration or Accommodation? The Enduring Debate in Conflict Regulation." In *Constitutional Design for Divided Societies*, edited by Sujit Choudhry, 41–88. Oxford: Oxford University Press, 2008.

Marshall, Monty G., Ted Robert Gurr, and Keith Jaggers. *Political Regime Characteristics and Transitions, 1800–2015*, Polity IV Project. Vienna: Centre for Systemic Peace, 2016.

O'Flynn, Ian. *Deliberative Democracy and Divided Societies*. Edinburgh: Edinburgh University Press, 1995.

Riker, William H. *Federalism: Origin, Operation, Significance*. Boston: Little, Brown, 1964.

Stepan, Alfred C. "Federalism and democracy: Beyond the US model." *Journal of Democracy* 10, no. 4 (1999): 19–34.

Watts, Ronald L. *Comparing Federal Systems.* 2nd ed., Montreal; London: Published for the School of Policy Studies, Queen's University by McGill-Queen's University Press, 1987.

Wheare, Kenneth. *Federal Government.* Oxford: Oxford University Press, 1947.

Ziblatt, Daniel. "Rethinking the Origins of Federalism: Puzzle, Theory, and Evidence from Nineteenth-Century Europe." *World Politics* 57, no. 1 (2004): 70–98.

CHAPTER 9

Some Ideas on Diversities, Federalisms, and Pluralisms

Roberto Toniatti

1 Introduction

In contemporary societies, issues such as recognition of identities (of minorities and of the majority as well), protection of diversities as an inherent substantive content of equality, and the search for institutional tools meant to achieve mutual accommodation of differences and homogeneity – both of them relative and at least to some extent reciprocally compatible – represent a major and permanent area of concern for social cohesion and political leadership. A noticeable increase in human mobility, an unprecedented development of information and communication technologies and widespread processes of globalisation in all fields provide the factual background of such challenging concerns and contribute to setting the basic coordinates of the problems to be addressed.

Multidisciplinary scientific research is attempting to explain the causes of such phenomena and to suggest rational solutions. Apart from their intrinsic soundness, these solutions must receive social support and political consensus. This presents a challenge in a scenario in which conflicts are frequent and emotional, just as current manifestations of nationalistic, populist, antisemitic, islamophobic and, at large, racist, xenophobic and authoritarian attitudes are. These positions show how structurally uninterested their supporters are in looking for solutions of balanced accommodation.

Research in comparative constitutional law in particular is committed to exploring the legal context that frames the foundation of established normative models in the field and to critically examining their respective rationale. This is accomplished by borrowing concepts and analysis from other scientific areas, such as legal anthropology, sociology, and political science. The purpose of such endeavours is to distinguish and classify historical arrangements and to acknowledge that such models are not easily interchangeable and applicable in all scenarios, thus encouraging the quest for development of further arrangements and models.

The main object of this paper is to evaluate whether federalism is (or might be) an adequate pluralist framework for a reasonable accommodation of diversities, in particular those endowed with their own legal system.

To do so, we will recall some basic notions and combine them in an appropriate framework. The main assumption is that all such basic notions are to be considered under a plural perspective, so that we will have to deal with several sorts of diversit*ies*, rather than with diversity of one kind only, with distinct forms of federalism*s*, rather than with federalism *per se*, and with a multifaceted set of pluralism*s*, rather than with pluralism as a unitary category.

A second relevant assumption is that most classifications and categories in comparative constitutional law as well as its technical legal language and idioms owe much of their present use to the Western legal tradition and, while they are undoubtedly appropriate when applied to the North of the world, do not often appear as appropriate when dealing with the Global South and its participation in the global phenomena that are relevant in this context.[1] Furthermore, the English language itself is not always the most effective means of communication for expressing concepts that do not belong to the world of the common law.[2]

Thirdly, it should be stressed that the present attempt at dealing with the main research hypothesis indicated above does not intend to be in any way final. Quite to the contrary, it is meant to provide some constructive ideas, fragments of knowledge and intuition that might ultimately contribute to further reasoning and ideas.

2 On Federalisms and the Homogeneity Clause

The well-established theoretical definition of federalism is "a combination of self-rule and shared rule".[3]

1 On the need to acknowledge (and respect) the plurality of conceptions of the constitution in the global context and to (try to) employ scientific classifications consistent with the specific conception one is dealing with, see Roberto Toniatti, "Comparing Constitutions in the Global Era: Opportunities, Purposes, Challenges, 2019 Casad Comparative Law Lecture," *Kansas Law Review* 67, no. 4 (2019): 693–711.

2 For example – as is well known -, the formula "rule of law" or "law of the land" cannot be literally translated into other languages and reliance on formulas that are their functional equivalent is therefore necessary.

3 See Daniel J. Elazar, *Exploring Federalism* (Tuscaloosa: University of Alabama Press, 1991), 5; a further contribution to the definition of federalism based on a comparative research indicates that "in essence, a federal arrangement is one of partnership, established and regulated by a covenant, whose internal relationships reflect the special kind of sharing that must

The definition seems well positioned to accommodate diversities within a unitary frame: the first segment of the definition ("self-rule") is understood to indicate the exercise of government of and by a specific part of the population over a portion of the territory of a larger polity. This arrangement enables that segment of the population to support a set of qualified perspectives, based upon distinct historical foundations and an identity of their own, and aimed at achieving a common good that belongs to that community and represents a local and particular public interest. On the contrary, "shared rule" is meant to refer to setting general common values, goals, and to pursuing broader priorities that make up the governmental public interest of the larger polity. "Sharing" entails participation by smaller units in central governmental institutions – both as concerns their composition and the exercise of their functions – thus ultimately contributing to balanced decision-making.

The concept of "combination" is the third segment of the definition. It acts as a structural link between the other two. It is sufficiently vague and flexible as to allow constant and progressive adjustments and yet stable enough to rely on as the foundation of the relationship between self and shared rule. Consequently, the concept is also consistent with the construction of federalism as an ongoing process.[4] The principle of loyal cooperation (or federal trust, *Bundestreue*) – borrowed from a context of intergovernmental relations regulated by international law – complements the distribution of powers and adds an originally non-legal factor to the static architecture of federalism.

The concept of "combination" is a crucial element in any comparative survey of federal systems: the notion of combination, in fact, includes a variety of arrangements of power distribution. It is compatible with marginal participation in the procedure for amending the constitution and with a lack of some essential state functions, such as the judicial one. It is consistent with a plurality of historical experiences bearing several denominations – beyond "federal" – such as "supranational" or "regional" ones.[5] Consequently, this paper

---

prevail among the partners, based on a mutual recognition of the integrity of each partner and the attempt to foster a special unity among them"; see Elazar, *Exploring*, 5.

4 Carl J. Friedrich, *Trends of Federalism in Theory and Practice* (London: Pall Mall, 1968); Giovanni Bognetti, "Federalismo," in *Digesto* (4th ed., Turin: UTET, 1992), 276; Roberto Toniatti, "Federalismo e separazione dei poteri," in *Bognetti comparatista*, ed. Giuseppe F. Ferrari (Milano: Gruppo 24 Ore, 2014), 139.

5 See Francesco Palermo and Karl Kössler, *Comparative Federalism: Constitutional Arrangements and Case Law* (Oxford: Hart Publishing, 2017), 3: "There is no universal agreement on what federalism means, nor is the agreement on how to classify federal countries. Non can there be one". For a critical survey of the main "manifestations" of the manifold concept of federalism, see pages 34–66.

will make reference to a wide range of "federalisms", not holding to a single theoretical abstract model but considering a very wide set of systems based on different combinations of self-rule and shared rule.

The short description provided so far offers a fair representation of the theoretical suitability of federalism to hosting diversities within a unitary frame. Nevertheless, some further observations on the nature and types of diversities compatible with a unitary federal legal order need to be developed.[6]

Federal constitutions themselves, in fact, set some systemic conditions that are to be respected by the constitutive units. Such conditions are part of the "combination" issue, as they affect the federal context as much as the federated units.[7]

Such conditions refer to the so called "homogeneity clause", meaning the basic ordering principles that place a systemic *Weltanschauung* at the foundation of the constitutional order. The constitutional homogeneity clause reflects a balanced degree of stability, continuity, individuals' equality, social and economic cohesion and cultural compatibility. This balance is required to ensure the achievement of the *raison d'être* of the original motivation for combining self-rule and shared rule among those same partners.[8]

The homogeneity clause also includes the federal power of intervention for protecting the constitutional order of the subnational units of government, as mutual constitutional consistency in all institutional spheres is a shared public interest.[9]

---

6 See Rosalind Dixon, Ron Levy and Mark Tushnet, "Theories and Practices of Federalism in Deeply Divided Societies," *Federal Law Review* 46, no. 4 (2017): 481.

7 In fact, such conditions also affect future members of the original federal compact, as indicated by the "conditionality" policy of the European Union based on the Copenhagen criteria and on art. 49 of the treaty establishing the European Union.

8 Nevertheless, it is to be noticed that "homogeneity does not always promote unity [...] various forms of unity and disunity are to be considered, as well as more varieties of diversity. There is a difference between consolidated unity (for example, France) and federal unity (for example, Switzerland). Diversity is manifested through nationality or ethnic, religious, ideological, social, and interest factors that may or may not gain political expression. Consolidated unity attempts either to depoliticize or carefully limit the political effects of diversity, relegating manifestations of diversity to other spheres. Federal unity, on the other hand, not only is comfortable with the political expression of diversity but is from its roots a means to accommodate diversity as a legitimate element in the polity. Thus, consolidated polities can be diverse but, for them, diversity is not considered desirable per se, even if reality requires its reconciliation within the body polity. The question remains open as to what kinds or combinations of diversity are compatible with federal unity and which ones are not", in Elazar, *Exploring*, 67.

9 Supremacy clauses as well as homogeneity clauses are dealt with as limits on constitutional autonomy of subnational units "that exist, in one form or another, explicitly or

Clear examples of federal homogeneity clauses are expressed in the Constitutions of the United States,[10] Austria,[11] Germany[12] and Switzerland.[13]

Consequently, as much as federalism may be virtually regarded as an appropriate context for hosting diversities, it is obvious that in reality, hosting is selective and not all diversities are entitled to claim the status of a federated subnational unit of government of a federal polity.

3 On Diversities and Equal Citizenship

Differences and cleavages of all sorts are very common in any society and, historically, constitutional democracies are expected to manage the conflicts inevitably raised in divided societies more efficiently.[14]

---

implicitly, in all constitutions of compound states", Palermo and Kössler, *Comparative Federalism*, 130. See also Giacomo Delledonne, *L'omogeneità costituzionale negli ordinamenti composti* (Naples: Editoriale Scientifica, 2017); Davide Strazzari, "La clausola di omogeneità dell'UE: connotazione costituzionale o internazionale? Riflessioni da un'analisi comparata," *Federalismi.it*, no. 24 (2014): 1–55.

10 See art. 4, sec. 4 "The United States shall guarantee to every State in this Union a Republican Form of Government".

11 See art. 99: "The *Land* Constitution to be enacted by a Land constitutional law can, inasmuch as the Federal Constitution is not affected thereby, be amended by *Land* constitutional law".

12 See art. 28.1: "The constitutional order in the *Länder* must conform to the principles of a republican, democratic and social state governed by the rule of law, within the meaning of this Basic Law", and art. 28.3: "The Federation shall guarantee that the constitutional order of the *Länder* conforms to the basic rights and to the provisions of paragraphs (1) and (2) of this Article". It is noteworthy to recall that "since the 18th century, the purpose of homogeneity clauses can be described as connecting federalism and constitutionalism and allowing the normative claims of constitutionalism to permeate federal orders. This is particularly true of Germany both in the 19th century and after 1949, with the fight for constitutionalisation and later democratisation inevitably questioning the basic structures of the constitutional orders in the Länder"; on this, see Giacomo Delledonne, "Federalism: Tragic Compromise and Conflicts," *Estudios de Deusto* 67, no. 1 (2019): 89.

13 See Sec. 4 "Federal Guarantees", Art. 51 "Cantonal constitutions": "1. Each Canton shall adopt a democratic constitution. This requires the approval of the People and must be capable of being revised if the majority of those eligible to vote so request. 2 Each cantonal constitution shall require the guarantee of the Confederation. The Confederation shall guarantee a constitution provided it is not contrary to federal law".

14 See Claus Offe, "Homogeneity and Constitutional Democracy: Coping with Identity Conflicts through Group Rights," *The Journal of Political Philosophy* 6, no. 2 (1998): 113–119 and his description of differences, all of which can potentially undermine the coherence and integration of the political community: "In fact, there are three different kinds of differences: interest-based, ideology-based and identity-based (the three "i"s) [...] The

The expectation is even higher in a federal order, as federalism may be – and in several cases actually is – a proper method meant to manage such conflicts and still preserve a sufficient degree of unity. Subnational governments enjoy variable margins of autonomy in policy making and legislative autonomy as a core content of self-rule, in conformity with the homogeneity clause, while at the same time not endangering the well-being of the federation as a whole.

Diversities may concern the economic interests of one part of the territory that are very different and even incompatible with those of other parts. They can also concern the national origin of different segments of the population, as happens to be the case in countries such as the United States (or Australia and Canada), where immigration from all areas of the world has contributed to shaping – according to the "melting pot" theory – a people with a fairly high degree of unitary awareness and yet which keep a high sense of their own original identity (from a community of W.A.S.PS. to the so called "hyphenated Americans").[15]

One source of diversity is related to the distinct languages spoken in the territories of a federation. However, experience tells us that this not unmanageable. This is the case with Switzerland, the European Union, Belgium and Canada, although in the latter two cases a careful and strict normative regulation has been implemented after reiterated formal attempts or political challenges of secession. In Switzerland, a civil war took place (the *Sonderbund* war, 1847), thus providing the grounds for the adoption of a new federal Constitution in 1848. In the United States, the political movement favourable to establishing English as the official language has never passed the stage of a (legislative or even constitutional amendment) proposal. In the European Union, the regulation "determining the languages to be used by the European Economic Community" bears the symbolic number 1.[16]

"valued things" that are contested in these conflicts can be categorized, respectively, in terms of three "r"s: resources, rights and recognition (or respect)".

15 For the argument that it is the federal Constitution that provides the main (if not exclusive) ground for the establishment of the "nation-state" in the United States, see Roberto Toniatti, "La "nazione costituzionale": genesi e consolidamento dell'identità repubblicana dell'ordinamento federale statunitense quale Stato-nazione," *Diritto Pubblico Comparato ed Europeo* (2011): 1150–1169.

16 All the languages of the member states are official languages of the Union. The regulation was published in the Official Gazette in 1958 and has been repeatedly modified at any "linguistic" enlargement of the Union. There are two noteworthy flexibility clauses: "the institutions of the Community may stipulate in their rules of procedure which of the languages are to be used in specific cases" (art. 6); and " if a Member State has more than one official language, the language to be used shall, at the request of such State, be governed by the general rules of its law" (art. 8). Furthermore, "the languages to be used in

Coexistence of a national language with minority languages is a common phenomenon in several European continental countries (Finland, Italy, Spain, and all states in Central, Eastern and South-Eastern Europe), where the latter have the *status* of official language only in the territory where they are largely spoken, alongside the common national language.[17]

The 1995 European Framework Convention for the protection of national minorities – "considering that a pluralist and genuinely democratic society should not only respect the ethnic, cultural, linguistic and religious identity of each person belonging to a national minority, but also create appropriate conditions enabling them to express, preserve and develop this identity; considering that the creation of a climate of tolerance and dialogue is necessary to enable cultural diversity to be a source and a factor, not of division, but of enrichment for each society"[18] – declares that "the Parties undertake to recognise that every person belonging to a national minority has the right to use freely and without interference his or her minority language, in private and in public, orally and in writing" (art. 10.1). Also, the Charter of fundamental rights of the European Union (2007) affirms that "the Union shall respect cultural, religious and linguistic diversity".[19]

In other words, historical evidence and normative sources show that law can facilitate the coexistence of more than one language within the same federal polity when political will of all parties concerned acknowledges that the reasons for preserving the unity of the whole – under the homogeneity clause – ought to prevail, while at the same time acknowledging and respecting linguistic diversities.

Of course, what appears simple in the abstract world of ideas is not always easy in reality. Language, religion, nationality and economic interests are all but single elements of culture and eventually of identity, which is a complex concept that recently has become the object of regulation and legal analysis. Conflicts based on diversity of identity have been defined as "the most intractable of all".[20]

Beyond diversities and before conflicts, a crucial role in ensuring homogeneity – which is not synonymous with uniformity – is played by the notion of

---

the proceedings of the Court of Justice shall be laid down in its rules of procedure" (art. 7). Specific litigation in front of the Court of Justice has been relatively low.

17 See Giovanni Poggeschi, *I diritti linguistici: un'analisi comparata* (Carocci: Roma, 2010).

18 Preamble.

19 See art 22, headed "cultural, religious and linguistic diversity" in Title III centred on equality.

20 See Offe, "Homogeneity and Constitutional Democracy," 123.

citizenship and the principle of equality. The status of all individuals under the law is defined by their permanent relationship with the state, regardless of diversities.[21] Equal citizenship has proved to be a strong factor of national and federal aggregation, also – and perhaps with even more visibility – when substantive equality requires that diversities be protected through exceptions to general rules and accommodated with special laws.

Equal citizenship, thus implemented, combines diversities and homogeneity and is instrumental to both.

A new substantive understanding of citizenship – without prejudice for its undifferentiated formal condition of citizenship *tout court* – leads to a descriptive notion of "cultural citizenship", namely the ground for holding rights based on one's own differentiated identity. In fact, such rights are equivalent to those belonging to the rest of the population and are not, therefore, intrinsically special and do not constitute a privilege.[22] And yet, they do differ in their nature, as they are bestowed upon individuals not as such – that is, as isolated individuals – but inasmuch as those individuals are members of a group or community. These group or communitarian rights, as a sort of hybrid arrangement, are meant to be consistent with the roots of the Western legal tradition and the homogeneity clause as well as conform to the requirements of inclusion of diversities.[23]

---

21 In the current post-apartheid Constitution of South Africa, for obvious historical reasons, the provision on citizenship (art. 3) strongly establishes that "there is a common South African citizenship. (2) All citizens are – (a) equally entitled to the rights, privileges and benefits of citizenship; and (b) equally subject to the duties and responsibilities of citizenship. (3) National legislation must provide for the acquisition, loss and restoration of citizenship".

22 On cultural citizenship see Roberto Toniatti, "Pluralismo e autodeterminazione delle identità negli ordinamenti culturalmente composti: osservazioni in tema di cittadinanza culturale," in *Tutela delle identità culturali, diritti linguistici e istruzione: dal Trentino-Alto Adige/Südtirol alla prospettiva comparata*, eds. Eleonora Ceccherini and Matteo Cosulich (Padova: Cedam, 2012), 5.

23 The situation is described as follows: "The antidote that constitutional democracies have available in order to cope with this type of conflict is group rights. These come, as far as political life is concerned, in three varieties: rights to self-government, polyethnic rights and special representation rights [...] The logic behind the granting of such group rights to religious, linguistic, racial, ethnic, gender, regional and other categories of people is clear enough: Members of these groups are to be assured, through tangible guarantees and concessions, of their full inclusion into the citizenship; and feelings of alienation, resentment and hostility are thus to be overcome or prevented from emerging in the first place" in Offe, "Homogeneity and Constitutional Democracy," 123. See Shlomo Avineri and Avner de-Shalit, eds., *Communitarism and Individualism* (Oxford: Oxford University Press, 1992).

At this stage, however, the focus is no longer on federalisms as a form of territorial arrangement coupled with the management of identity diversities: recognition of group rights is not the equivalent of the establishment of a sort of "cultural federalism". Although a guarantee of cultural identity through group rights is substantively related to territorial self-government, the covenantal federal relation is not between "cultures". It is between state and subnational institutions and, consequently, it refers formally only to the shaping of the respective governmental establishments. The motivation for this may be different from the one inspiring the status of units of self-government where no diversities need to be recognised and protected, but the legal machinery is largely the same. The group is not entitled to rights (and duties) of its own in a corporate capacity, nor are territorial governmental institutions entitled to act on behalf of a respective culture or encroach on their cultural sphere.

Mainstream Western constitutionalism and international law are opposing a scenario of ethnic states – that maybe the outcome of tragic policies of ethnic cleansing – and the concepts of "nation" and "nation state" (founded on a *demos*) standing out and beyond the one of *ethnos*. Even the *principe des nationalités* – based on the coincidence between nation and state – has evolved more toward indicating the principle of self-determination of peoples out of colonial rule.[24]

---

24 A fairly rare provision was introduced as one of the fundamental constitutional principles in the *interim* Constitution of South Africa (1993) in order to accommodate the claims by the descendants of the Dutch-speaking Afrikaners or *Afrikaans* people (formerly supporters of *apartheid*) to live in a federated state of their own (*Volksstaat*). See the text (Schedule 4, Constitutional Principles XXXIV): "1. This Schedule and the recognition therein of the right of the South African people as a whole to self-determination, shall not be construed as precluding, within the framework of the said right, constitutional provision for a notion of the right to self-determination by any community sharing a common cultural and language heritage, whether in a territorial entity within the Republic or in any other recognised way. 2. The Constitution may give expression to any particular form of self- determination provided there is substantial proven support within the community concerned for such a form of self-determination. 3. If a territorial entity referred to in paragraph 1 is established in terms of this Constitution before the new constitutional text is adopted, the new Constitution shall entrench the continuation of such territorial entity, including its structures, powers and functions". The provision did not receive any further implementation. Quite to the contrary, the Constitution of Namibia (1990) gives the National Assembly the function – among others – "to remain vigilant and *vigorous for the purposes of ensuring that the scourges of apartheid, tribalism and colonialism* do not again manifest themselves in any form in a free and independent Namibia" (art. 63); and (art. 108) declares that "the delineation of the boundaries of the regions and local authorities [...] shall be geographical only, without any reference to the race, colour or ethnic origin of the inhabitants of such areas".

There is one more argument to support the separation of territorial institutional federalism from any form of cultural and group rights-based federalism: under the homogeneity clause, the state has the exclusive role of lawmaker, rendering all other non-state sources of law invalid and illegitimate in the larger legal order. The state alone can endow law-making power to subnational governmental authorities, provided that such subnational legislation is part of and consistent with the same legal family (or tradition).

In other words, federalism is founded upon premises of normative pluralism, not of legal pluralism.[25]

4 On Diversities and Legal Pluralism

The law is a complex cultural phenomenon, as is a legal order. Both may have more than one definition, theoretically as well as historically, in conformity with processes of evolution (and involution) over time and in different geopolitical contexts.

Diversities have a deep impact on the law and different state legal systems react differently to them.[26] Consequently, the notions of law and legal system are easily associated with a plural scenario, deeply influenced by the respective cultural frame. Hence the efforts by scholarship to identify the main features that contribute to characterising the varying concepts of law and legal system and to elaborating their grouping and classification according to a set of criteria.[27]

25 *Contra*, Topidi's chapter in this volume, which illustrate that federalism and legal pluralism can be brought together through the concepts of "personal federalism" and "negotiated federalism".

26 See Marie-C. Foblets, Jean-F. Gaudreault-DesBiens and Alison Dundes Rentels, eds., *Cultural Diversity and the Law: State Responses from Around the World* (Cowansville-Bruxelles: Éditions Yvon Blais-Bruylant, 2010).

27 Traditional scholarship on systemology include Gilles Cuniberti, *Grands systèmes de droit contemporaines* (2nd ed, Paris: LGDJ, 2011); René David and Camille Jauffret-Spinosi, *Les grands systèmes de droit contemporaines* (11th ed., Paris: Dalloz, 2002); Antonio Gambaro and Rodolfo Sacco, *Sistemi giuridici comparati*, (Turin: UTET, 2018); Raymond Legeais, *Grands systèmes de droit contemporaines. Approche comparative* (2nd ed., Paris: Litec, 2005); Mario G. Losano, *I grandi sistemi giuridici. Introduzione ai diritti europei ed extraeuropei* (Bari: Laterza, 2000); Konrad Zweigert and Hein Kötz, *An Introduction to Comparative Law* (3rd ed., Oxford: Oxford University Press, 1999).

A valuable parameter of classification of legal systems is the method of law-making.[28] In synthesis, the law may be the outcome (i) of a political process, as the result of a determination by an elected and representative assembly in liberal and democratic settings or by the uncontrolled will of an individual autocrat or of an unelected military or bureaucratic *élite*; or (ii) of judicial decision-making to settle controversies in conformity with precedent case-law; or (iii) of conventional methods, as is mostly the case with international sources of law as well as, domestically, with a plurality of forms of agreements and compacts mutually binding governmental institutions;[29] or (iv) of a divine will, expressed through a revelation and enshrined in religious texts that are devotedly guarded by clergy and venerated by the faithful; or (v) of customs having their origins in time immemorial and being continuously shared and implemented by the community. More particularly, this is the case with customs – enriched by a spiritual force – as experienced by indigenous populations (chthonic law).[30]

A setting of legal pluralism is characterised by the official, actual and effective coexistence of more than one legal family in the same jurisdiction.[31] The opposite setting is one of legal monism, when only one legal family is regarded

28 The parameter has been indicated and elaborated upon by Alessandro Pizzorusso, *Sistemi giuridici comparati* (2nd ed., Milano: Giuffrè, 1995).

29 The most interesting case is likely to concern the conventions of the constitution, that are mostly regarded as only politically binding and non-justiciable. Although derived by scholarship from the system of sources of constitutional law of the United Kingdom, conventions of the constitution are detectable in many (if not all) jurisdictions (also in civil law countries in spite of their detailed written constitutions); they perform the function of regulating those margins of discretion of governmental institutions not regulated by positive law, thus filling the gaps of normative regulations and ensuring predictability and consistency in their respective behaviour without having to employ formal normative instruments.

30 On the rich and complex worldview related to chthonic law see H. Patrick Glenn, *Legal Traditions of the World* (5th ed., Oxford: Oxford University Press, 2014), 61, quoting Edward Goldsmith, *The Way: An Ecological World View* (London: Rider, 1992), 62: "the chtonic worldview [...] when people really knew how to live in harmony with the natural world" and the following explanatory statement: "to describe a legal tradition as chtonic is thus to attempt to describe a tradition by criteria internal to itself, as opposed to imposed criteria. It is an attempt to see the tradition from within, in spite of all problems of language and perception, and to see it from a time prior to the emergence of colonial language".

31 See Brian Z. Tamanaha, *Legal Pluralism Explained: History, Theory, Consequences* (Oxford, Oxford University Press, 2021); William Twining, "Normative and Legal Pluralism: A Global Perspective," *Duke Journal of Comparative & International Law* 20, no. 3 (2010): 473.

as valid law and consequently implemented by citizens and enforced by the authorities.[32]

Legal pluralism is clearly to be distinguished from normative pluralism, when there is indeed a variety of sources of law (national, subnational, international, supranational) but all such sources are the result of the same political method of law-making, be it formalised in sources of law at state, sub-state, inter-state or supra-state levels.

In the Western legal tradition, since the Enlightenment and with the consolidation of the constitutional ideology inspired by the English, American and French revolutions, the rule is legal monism controlled by state law. The state has the exclusive power of law-making, both through the political process and the judiciary subject to and bound by the law.[33]

In other parts of the world – most notably in Asia, in the South Mediterranean countries (including Israel),[34] in Africa[35] and, more recently, in Latin America[36]

---

32 The classification is somehow abstract, as it should be acknowledged that, apart from those experiences that are admittedly of a hybrid or mixed nature – typically, the case of Québec in Canada –, all legal orders present a combination of one main legal system with elements of the others. On mixed jurisdictions, combining mostly civil law and common law, see Vernon V. Palmer, *Mixed Jurisdictions Worldwide: The Third Legal Family* (Cambridge, Cambridge University Press, 2001).

33 In opposition to legal pluralism, there is the "ideology of legal centralism" as defined in John Griffiths, "What is Legal Pluralism?," *Journal of Legal Pluralism and Unofficial Law* 18, no. 24 (1986): 5 ("law is and should be the law of the state, uniform for all persons, exclusive of all other law, and administered by a single set of state institutions"); furthermore, "legal pluralism is the fact. Legal centralism is a myth, an ideal, a claim, an illusion. Nevertheless, the ideology of legal centralism has had such a powerful hold on the imagination of lawyers that its picture of the legal world has been able successfully to masquerade as fact and has formed the foundation stone of social and legal theory".

34 See Will Kymlicka and Eva Pföstl, eds., *Multiculturalism and Minority Rights in the Arab World* (Oxford: Oxford University Press, 2014).

35 Roberto Toniatti, "La razionalizzazione del «pluralismo giuridico debole»: le prospettive di un nuovo modello giuridico e costituzionale nell'esperienza africana," in *Le trasformazioni costituzionali del secondo millennio. Scenari e prospettive dall'Europa all'Africa*, ed. Marina Calamo Specchia (Sant'Arcangelo di Romagna: Maggioli, 2016), 449.

36 See Roberto Toniatti, "Il paradigma costituzionale dell'inclusione della diversità culturale in Europa e in America latina: premesse per una ricerca comparata sui rispettivi modelli," in *La ciencia del derecho constitucional comparado: Estudios en homenaje a Lucio Pegoraro*, eds. Silvia Bagni, Giovanni A. Figueroa Mejía and Giorgia Pavani (Ciudad de México: tirant lo Blanch, 2017), 1445; Roberto Toniatti, "El paradigma constitucional de la inclusion de la diversidad cultural. Notas para una comparación entre los modelos de protección de las minorías nacionales en Europa y de los pueblos indígenas en Latinoamérica," *Inter-American and European Human Rights Journal/Revista Interamericana y Europea de derechos humanos* 9, no. 1 (2016): 118.

legal pluralism, in the form of recognition of the legitimate validity of religious, customary or chthonic law, is the rule with regard to matters that are regarded as "personal" and concern mostly family law, broadly defined. However, the political will – if and when manifested – may still prevail in all circumstances.[37]

Non-state law, however, has an intrinsic normative force that significant segments of society – according to the various contexts – are willing to respect, for reasons that include conscientious objection to state law or religion affiliation, irrespective of the systematic claim of primacy and exclusivity of state law. Governmental institutions, therefore, may find it politically more convenient to mitigate the rigidity of its own monopolistic claim and acknowledge a limited role for non-state law through explicit exceptions to the general rule.

A historic model and a widely circulated source of inspiration of legal pluralism related to religious law is the "millet system", established by the former Ottoman Empire and still practiced in the Mediterranean countries that developed from its collapse in the early 20th century. Within a systemic political scenario of Islam, the millet arrangement allowed the other "peoples of the Book" – namely Jews and Christians – and other ethnic and religious communities to regulate the sphere of private relationships according to their respective sources of law.[38] This system consisted mainly of collective personal

---

37 India offers a very interesting study case on the matter: religious "personal laws" for the different communities are the source of regulation of family life, covering marriage, divorce, inheritance, adoption and alimony. The 1949 Constitution includes a provision (art. 44) saying that "the State shall endeavour to secure for the citizens a uniform civil code throughout the territory of India". In spite of some attempts to implement it fully, only a Special Marriage Act has been enacted in 1954, regulating marriage between persons irrespective of their religious affiliation and inter-religious marriages. The Supreme Court, deciding the Shah Bano case (*Mohd. Ahmad Khan v. Shah Bano Begum*) in 1985, tried to settle the right of the Muslim wife to receive maintenance for life by the former husband but the Islamic community considered it to be a violation of their faith – as of all other communities – empowered by the Constitution "to manage its own affairs in matters of religion" (art. 26). The controversy raised by the judicial decision prompted Congress to enact legislation meant to reform its effects, but further judicial cases managed to re-establish the right. On these matters see Domenico Francavilla, *Il diritto nell'India contemporanea: sistemi tradizionali, modelli occidentali e globalizzazione* (Turin: Giappichelli, 2010).

38 See Abdulaziz Sachedina, *The Islamic Roots of Democratic Pluralism* (Oxford: Oxford University Press, 2001), 96: "The millet system in the Muslim world provided the premodern paradigm of a religiously pluralistic society by granting each religious community an official status and a substantial measure of self-government"; Christoph Herzog and Malek Sharif, eds., *The First Ottoman Experiment in Democracy* (Istanbul: Orient Institute, 2016); Latif Tas, "The Myth of the Ottoman *Millet* System: Its Treatment of Kurds and a Discussion of Territorial and Non-Territorial Autonomy," *International Journal on Minority and Group Rights* 21, no. 4 (2014): 497; Ergun Cahal, "Pluralism, Tolerance and

autonomy, although it was founded on the basis of political loyalty to the centre of power.

Based on this framework, a new phenomenon has arisen that permits differentiation between legal pluralism in a strong sense – whose effectiveness defies all inconsistencies with state law and constitutes, as it were, the "authentic" legal pluralism[39] – and legal pluralism in a weak sense, whose applicability depends on an act of recognition by state law, thus contradicting any claim of an original status of non-state law.[40]

While legal pluralism in a strong sense is undoubtedly present in Europe, mostly at a societal level because it is in breach of civil and criminal law, the focus of our reasoning must be centred on the several fields of "weak" legal pluralism that have found their way into some European countries.

One such area – and a crucial one – is represented by religious law, which expresses a permanent tension between individual freedom of religion and from religion, on the one hand, and the principles of state secularism, on the other, with the factor of group rights standing as a relevant third complement.

Historically, because of its direct involvement in temporal powers, the relationship between the emerging nation-state and the Roman Catholic Church was dealt with through bilateral agreements, named concordats. The same pattern has continued throughout the 20th century and into the 21st. A reformed version of it has been adopted with other religious denominations.[41] Some states in Europe (namely, Italy, Poland, and Spain) constitutionally require that parliamentary statutes regulating the relationship between state and religious

Control: On the *Millet* System and the Question of Minorities," *International Journal on Minority and Group Rights* 27, no. 1 (2020): 34.

39 An example is offered by the traditional practice of female genital mutilation on young girls from migrating families (mostly from African countries), even when born in Europe.

40 In fact, a radical criticism is that "it would be a complete confusion to think of "legal pluralism" in the weak sense as fundamentally inconsistent with the ideology of legal centralism. It is merely a particular arrangement in a system whose basic ideology is centralist. The very notion of "recognition" and all the doctrinal paraphernalia which it brings with it are typical reflections of the idea that "law" must ultimately depend from a single validating source. "Legal pluralism" is thus but one of the forms in which the ideology of legal centralism can manifest itself. It is, to be sure, by the terms of that ideology an inferior form of law, a necessary accommodation to a social situation perceived as problematic", Griffiths, *What is*, 8.

41 See the various chapters in Cinzia Piciocchi, Davide Strazzari and Roberto Toniatti, eds., *State and Religion: Agreements, Conventions and Statutes* (Naples: Edizioni Scientifiche Italiane, 2021) available in open access (https://iris.unitn.it/retrieve/handle/11572/328977/520716/P.S.T.%20per%20IRIS.pdf) (accessed 25 May 2023).

organisations reflect a previously negotiated agreement; some others follow this conventional practice because of its political expediency.[42]

The agreements cover matters such as spiritual assistance in prisons, hospitals, and with armed services; rights and duties of the clergy; protection of religious sites; the teaching of religion in private and/or public schools and the recognition of civil effects of marriage. The outcome is the creation of an experience of a (direct or indirect) form of "consensual legal pluralism" that allows the coexistence, side by side, of distinct sets of rules on the same substantive issue within the same state jurisdiction.

It is important to underline how the negotiable margins of such negotiations are limited by the "public policy" or "*ordre public*" clause – the functional equivalent of the "homogeneity" clause of federal settings – inasmuch as it establishes the priority of fundamental principles and values of state law over religious legal sources.[43]

The same clause is applied to determine the process of recognition of effects of foreign judicial decisions adopted in a distinct jurisdiction.[44]

An interesting innovation has been attempted in England, by the introduction of *shari'ah councils* organised as private arbitration jurisdictions, whose decisions do not have legally recognised effects in state law.[45] Making use of Alternative Dispute Resolutions (ADR) mechanisms is partially consistent with

42 Roberto Toniatti, "Consensual Legal Pluralism: Assessing the Method and the Merits in Agreements between State and Church(es) in Italy and Spain," in Cinzia Piciocchi, Davide Strazzari and Roberto Toniatti, eds., *State and Religion: Agreements, Conventions and Statutes* (Naples: Edizioni Scientifiche Italiane, 2021), 55.

43 Roberto Toniatti and Davide Strazzari, eds., *Legal Pluralism and the* Ordre Public *Clause Exception: Normative and Judicial Perspectives* (Trento: The Pluralist Papers Ebooks 2016), available at http://www.jupls.eu/images/JPs_eBook_OrdrePublic.pdf (accessed 25 May 2023).

44 A clear and frequent example is provided by the denial of recognition as a divorce of the unilateral repudiation of the wife by the husband (*talaq*) known and practiced in Islamic law and accepted by a foreign (state or religious) court because that procedure is found to be in violation of the principle of a fair trial, as decided by the Italian *Corte di Cassazione* (decision n.16804, *Cassazione civile* sez. I, 07/08/2020). In the case *Soha Sahyouni v. Raja Mamisch* (2017) the Court of Justice of the European Union has declared that EU law concerns "only situations in which divorce is pronounced by a national court or by, or under the supervision of, another public authority" and does not recognise "other types of divorce, such as those which, as in the present case, are based on a "private unilateral declaration of intent" pronounced before a religious court".

45 See more in Paola Parolari, *Diritto policentrico e interlegalità nei paesi europei di immigrazione: il caso degli shari'ah councils in Inghilterra* (Turin: Giappichelli, 2020); Angelo Rinella, *La shari'a in Occidente: Giurisdizioni e diritto islamico: Regno Unito, Canada e Stati Uniti d'America* (Bologna: Il Mulino, 2020).

the tenets of legal pluralism in a weak form insofar as it is reserved to members of a religious community and is framed on the foundation of personal law and freedom of choice.[46]

Issues regulated by provisions introduced mainly in European legal orders according to legal pluralism in a weak form are as varied as the exception to the general rule of wearing a helmet while riding a motorcycle or allowing the practice of wearing a sacred knife (*kirpan*), both reserved to *Sikhs*; or Islamic and Jewish ritual slaughtering of animals for human consumption according to the respective religious law;[47] or the freedom to choose (or not) a given therapy on cultural and religious ground.[48]

All of them are concerned mostly with religious law, customary and traditional law occupying a very small area.

Recognition of customary law is, in fact, another area suitable for a limited manifestation of legal pluralism, although with almost the same substantive results.

This may be the case of the Sami population in the northern part of Scandinavia – whose claims are quite limited[49] – as well as of the Roma population in Europe, who may be perceived as quite reluctant to have their

---

46 In April 2024 a Sikh court was inaugurated in the United Kingdom: see Liz Harris and Jonathan Ames, "First Sikh court open in London," in *The Times*, April 25th, 2024 where the basic explanations given are that "The court will operate as an alternative dispute resolution forum for British Sikhs caught in family and civil disputes"; and that "British lawyers have launched a world-first Sikh court amid claims that secular judges lack expertise to deal with the religion's sensitivities". A further interesting comment that denies it is a "religious court" is that "Unlike Islam and Judaism, Sikhism does not have its own legal code" and, therefore, the purpose of such court will be "to assist Sikh families in their time of need when dealing with conflict and disputes in line with Sikh principles". See also Liz Harris, "The world's first Sikh court opens in London," in *Religion Media Center*, April 25th, 2024 with experts' further critical comments.

47 See Roberto Toniatti, "Sul bilanciamento costituzionale fra libertà religiosa e protezione degli animali," in *Il divieto di macellazione rituale* (*Shechità Kosher e Halal*) *e la libertà religiosa delle minoranze*, eds. Pablo Lerner and Alfredo M. Rabello (Trento: Università degli Studi di Trento, 2010).

48 See Cinzia Piciocchi, *La libertà terapeutica come diritto culturale: Uno studio sul pluralismo nel diritto costituzionale comparato* (Padova: Cedam, 2006); and *Id.*, *Courts, Pluralism and Law in the Everyday: Food, Clothing and Days of Rest* (London-New York: Routledge, 2024).

49 See Christina Allard, "Judicial Pluralism and the Sami: an Indigenous People," in *Europe, Indigenous Peoples' Sovereignty and the Limits of Judicial and Legal Pluralism: American Tribes, Canadian First Nations and Scandinavian Sami Compared*, eds. Roberto Toniatti and Jens Woelk (Trento: The Pluralist Papers Ebook, 2014) 49, available at http://www.jupls.eu/images/ebook%20JPs%20-%202014.pdf (accessed on 3 June 2023).

customs recognised and protected as long as the general environment surrounding them is mainly hostile.[50]

A fairly systematic approach has been implemented in France with regard to the recognition of traditional indigenous law – the "*coutume Kanak*" – in New Caledonia. Following several stages of negotiation and failed voting on independence, the powerful formula "shared sovereignty" ("*souveraineté partagée*") was established: the validity of Kanak customary law – with limits that

---

50 The European Court of Human Rights, in deciding the case *Muñoz Diaz v. Spain* (Appl. no. 49151/07) in 2011 (the Spanish state had refused to recognise the effects of a Roma marriage only after the husband's death and consequently denied the payment of the retirement pension to the surviving widow), declared that "The importance of the beliefs that the applicant derives from belonging to the Roma community – a community which has its own values that are well established and deeply rooted in Spanish society. The Court observes, in the present case, that when the applicant got married in 1971 according to Roma rites and traditions, it was not possible in Spain, except by making a prior declaration of apostasy, to be married otherwise than in accordance with the canon-law rites of the Catholic Church. The Court takes the view that the applicant could not have been required, without infringing her right to religious freedom, to marry legally, that is to say under canon law, in 1971, when she expressed her consent to marry according to Roma rites. […] The Court takes the view that the force of the collective beliefs of a community that is well-defined culturally cannot be ignored" (57–60). Nevertheless, the Court decided in favour of Mrs. Muñoz on the ground that "the applicant's good faith as to the validity of her marriage, being confirmed by the authorities' official recognition of her situation, gave her a legitimate expectation of being regarded as the spouse of M.D. and of forming a recognised married couple with him" (63). Furthermore, the Court found that "civil marriage in Spain, as in force since 1981, is open to everyone, and takes the view that its regulation does not entail any discrimination on religious or other grounds. The same form of marriage, before a mayor, a magistrate or another designated public servant, applies to everyone without distinction. There is no requirement to declare one's religion or beliefs or to belong to a cultural, linguistic, ethnic or other group. It is true that certain religious forms of expression of consent are accepted under Spanish law, but those religious forms (Catholic, Protestant, Muslim and Jewish) are recognised by virtue of agreements with the State and thus produce the same effects as civil marriage, whereas other forms (religious or traditional) are not recognised. The Court observes, however, that this is a distinction derived from religious affiliation, which is not pertinent in the case of the Roma community. But that distinction does not impede or prohibit civil marriage, which is open to the Roma under the same conditions of equality as to persons not belonging to their community, and is a response to considerations that have to be taken into account by the legislature within its margin of appreciation, as the Government have argued. Accordingly, the Court finds that the fact that Roma marriage has no civil effects as desired by the applicant does not constitute discrimination prohibited by Article 14" (79–81).

are both personal and territorial – extends to family law, property and some areas of criminal law.[51]

The scenario we have referred to so far tends to distinguish between the Western (and mostly European) legal tradition and the rest of the world, namely state jurisdictions in Africa, Asia and Latin America. Each one of these geopolitical areas needs to be dealt with while emphasising their distinct features, although it is important to note that all of them, generally, practice legal pluralism much more than the West.

The innovative phenomena taking place in this field in Latin America are of particular interest because of the European civil law framework behind their modern origins, as well as because of the quite radical reforms recently attempted. Such reforms are basically meant to give a more visible and appropriate role not only – at last – to the autochthonous population but, in particular, to their peculiar cultural paradigm, including their legal and judicial systems. The reforms therefore appear more as a new way of setting the legal order in general than as a marginal recognition of a restricted space for minorities.

In fact, what is currently known as the "new Latin American constitutionalism" is introducing not only "Western" rights and empowerment to participation in public affairs by indigenous populations but also a robust injection of legal pluralism (yet, in the weak sense) related to chthonic law of tribes scattered in the territory.[52]

Such trends aim at distancing themselves from the cultural roots of the original European blueprint of the nation-state and at achieving a new qualification of the form of state, described as "plurinational" and "intercultural", and

---

51 See Angelica Ignisci, *Prospettive della* "souveraineté partagée"*: spazi di pluralismo giuridico nell'esperienza di autonomia della Nuova Caledonia* (Trento: The Pluralist Papers Ebook, 2020), available in open access at http://www.jupls.eu/images/Ignisci_e_book_.pdf (accessed on 31 May 2023).

52 See Roberto Gargarella, *Latin American Constitutionalism, 1810–2010: The Engine Room of the Constitution* (Oxford: Oxford University Press, 2010). One relevant trend in some countries in the region shows that "reforms have resulted in a truly new and transformative form of constitutionalism", as noticed in Rodrigo Uprimny, "The Recent Transformation of Constitutional Law in Latin America: Trends and Challenges," *Texas Law Review* 89, no. 7 (2011): 1587. See also Silvia Bagni, "Il ruolo delle Corti costituzionali tra pluralismo giuridico, plurinazionalità e interculturalità," 2020, available in open access in https://www.robertotoniatti.eu/contributi/il-ruolo-delle-corti-costituzionali-tra-pluralismo-giuridico-plurinazionalita-e-interculturalita (accessed on 5 June 2023); Silvia Bagni, "Le forme di Stato in America Latina," in *Latinoamérica: viaggio nel costituzionalismo comparato dalla Patagonia al Río Grande*, eds. Silvia Bagni and Serena Baldin (Turin: Giappichelli, 2021), 35.

in syntony with the ecological inspiration provided by the consideration of the rights of the "*Pacha Mama*" (Mother Earth).[53]

The experience of reforms in Latin America – still too young for a reliable scientific assessment, considering the considerable opposition as well as objective obstacles to be overcome – indicates the structural difficulties that Western constitutionalism must face when trying to go beyond its conceptual roots, such as the central ideological role of the nation-state and its legal monism.

Another geopolitical area in the world which is going through a stage of constitutional recognition of legal pluralism in a weak form, providing for reference to chthonic, traditional and indigenous law, is Africa.

What is remarkable – and most likely suitable for a proper justification by historians and political scientists – is that, while in Latin America the inspiring force of the reforms is going well beyond the boundaries of mainstream constitutionalism of European origin, in Africa the trend is quite the opposite. The process of rationalisation of the margins of applicability of chthonic law started by some African countries, in fact, is trying to reduce the scope of legal pluralism in a strong sense and make traditional indigenous law more compatible with the fundamental values of their constitutions. Such values – it should be added – are currently interpreted as their own (and not necessarily imported from the former European colonizers).[54]

Furthermore, among current constitutional values, a great attention is given to the protection of women, also in view of a sort of ideal compensation for the hardships they have suffered in the (very recent) past.[55]

---

53 See art. 71 of the Constitution of Ecuador: "Nature, or Pacha Mama, where life is reproduced and occurs, has the right to integral respect for its existence and for the maintenance and regeneration of its life cycles, structure, functions and evolutionary processes".

54 Some clear examples are provided by the Constitution of Kenya (art.2), that very clearly establishes that it is "the supreme law of the Republic [...] and that "any law, including customary law, that is inconsistent with this Constitution is void to the extent of the inconsistency, and any act or omission in contravention of this Constitution is invalid"; and by the Constitution of Namibia (art. 66, Customary and Common Law): "(1) Both the customary law and the common law of Namibia in force on the date of Independence shall remain valid to the extent to which such customary or common law does not conflict with this Constitution or any other statutory law".

55 Some constitutional texts are framed to emphasise very strongly the radical innovations to be introduced in social practices: see again art. 23 of the Constitution of Namibia (1) "In the enactment of legislation and the application of any policies and practices contemplated by Sub-Article (2) hereof, it shall be permissible to have regard to the fact that women in Namibia have traditionally suffered special discrimination and that they need to be encouraged and enabled to play a full, equal and effective role in the political, social, economic and cultural life of the nation"; art. 35 of the Constitution of

It is obvious that normative texts do not necessarily correspond to reality and that they do not have the power to reform centuries-old and deeply held beliefs and practices. Nevertheless, such constitutional statements are indeed sufficient to indicate a political will that could realistically take notice of the reality and attempt to affect it in conformity with the words – and "spirit" – of the constitution.

One further paradigmatic piece of evidence is offered by a decision by the Constitutional Court of South Africa, in the case *Shilubana and Others v. Sidwell Nwamitwa* (2007). The case concerned the power of the royal dynasty of a tribe to change the traditional rules in order to allow a woman to become the head of the community, a power challenged in court by a son of the deceased who would have inherited the title as Chief of the *Valoyi* without the said reform.

The Court elaborated the notion of a "living" customary law, consequent to the fact that "customary law is by its nature a constantly evolving system". Besides that, "customary law, like any other law, must accord with the Constitution".[56] Furthermore, there is a distinction between a situation in which development of customary law is determined by a customary community and one when such development is the result of actions of a court, as

Ethiopia: "(1) Women shall, in the enjoyment of rights and protections provided for by this Constitution, have equal right with men. (2) Women have equal rights with men in marriage as prescribed by this Constitution. (3) The historical legacy of inequality and discrimination suffered by women in Ethiopia taken into account, women, in order to remedy this legacy, are entitled to affirmative measures. The purpose of such measures shall be to provide special attention to women so as to enable them to compete and participate on the basis of equality with men in political, social and economic life as well as in public and private institutions. (4) The State shall enforce the right of women to eliminate the influences of harmful customs. Laws, customs and practices that oppress or cause bodily or mental harm to women are prohibited"; art. 80.3 of the Constitution of Zimbabwe: "All laws, customs, traditions and cultural practices that infringe the rights of women conferred by this Constitution are void to the extent of the infringement".

56 The Constitutional Court started its reasoning by saying that "customary law must be recognised as 'an integral part of our law' and is 'an independent source of norms within the legal system' […] It is a body of law by which millions of South Africans regulate their lives and must be treated accordingly". Furthermore, "it is important to respect the right of communities that observe systems of customary law to develop their law […] The right of communities under section 211(2) includes the right of traditional authorities to amend and repeal their own customs. As has been repeatedly emphasised by this and other courts, customary law is by its nature a constantly evolving system. Under pre-democratic colonial and apartheid regimes, this development was frustrated and customary law stagnated. This stagnation should not continue, and the free development by communities of their own laws to meet the needs of a rapidly changing society must be respected and facilitated" (43–45).

"a court engaged in the adjudication of a customary law matter must remain mindful of its obligations under section 39(2) of the Constitution to promote the *spirit, purport and objects* of the Bill of Rights".[57]

The status and the very nature of customary law is further explained: "customary law must be permitted to develop, and the enquiry must be rooted in the contemporary practice of the community in question". The Court further states that "the legal status of customary law norms cannot depend simply on their having been consistently applied in the past, because that is a test which any new development must necessarily fail".

The Court elaborates an original understanding of "customary law": "Development implies some departure from past practice. A rule that requires absolute consistency with past practice before a court will recognise the existence of a customary norm that would therefore prevent the recognition of new developments as customary law. This would result in the courts applying laws which communities themselves no longer follow, and would stifle the recognition of the new rules adopted by the communities in response to the changing face of South African society. This result would be contrary to the Constitution and cannot be accepted".

In other words, the development of customary law can be superseded by political will – by the traditional leadership – as long as such (extra-customary) political will allows customary law to develop in conformity with the changes introduced from above by the Constitution.[58] The arguments elaborated by the Constitutional Court are an authoritative comment on the systematic meaning of the process of rationalisation of customary law in the African context.

57 Italics in the original, at 48.

58 See the text: "Accordingly, if it is true that the authorities presently have no power to bring the law and practice of customary leadership into line with the Constitution, their power must be expanded. It must be held that they have the authority to act on constitutional considerations in fulfilling their role in matters of traditional leadership. Their actions, reflected in the appointment of Ms Shilubana, accordingly represent a development of customary law", at 75. And: "It follows that if the traditional authority has only those powers accorded it by the narrow view, it would be contrary to the Constitution and frustrate the achievement of the values in the Bill of Rights. Section 39(2) of the Constitution obliges this Court to develop the customary law in accordance with the spirit, purport and aims of the Bill of Rights. This power should be exercised judiciously and sensitively, in an incremental fashion. As the Supreme Court of Canada has held in relation to the common law, "[t]he judiciary should confine itself to those incremental changes which are necessary to keep the common law in step with the dynamic and evolving fabric of our society." The same remarks apply to customary law. It is appropriate for the Court to exercise its section 39(2) powers in a manner that will empower the community itself to continue the development" (at 75).

A radically different orientation, quite far from both the Latin American and the African trends, is needed when qualifying the prevailing status of legal pluralism in many countries in Asia (leaving China out, obviously). In fact, in this geopolitical area, a legal system not inclusive of legal pluralism as an integral component would be inconceivable.

In Asia, generally, the system based on different personal laws is reflective of the strength of the distinct religious communities and it corresponds to a deeply and sincerely felt religious sensitivity of most of the population, although quite inconsistent with an abstract secular conception of the state and its construction of equal citizenship, without any further cultural qualification (presumably imported from Europeans).[59]

5 Final Remarks

Diversities reflect the variety, richness and creativity of the human condition. Respecting and preserving them is crucial for a basic acknowledgement of the dignity of the human being. Individual and collective diversities are an authentic resource, as they are expressions of living identities and contribute to the development of cultures. Inevitably, different cultures tend to socialise into distinct groups and communities on the ground of a shared worldview, leaving some others out.

And yet, cultures may also choose to co-exist with each other, while keeping their own identity and, at the same time, respecting the identity of others (and, obviously, have their identity respected as well). In fact, diversities may discover that they are, at some stage, mutually compatible and that, provided that an adequate frame and suitable mechanisms for the governance of such compatibility are adopted, coexistence is eventually feasible.

59 It is interesting to point out that the principle of secularism has been introduced in the 1949 Constitution of India through an amendment to its preamble only in 1976, indicating that India is a secular country without any established state religion and recognising religious pluralism. The same pluralist perspective may explain the textual contradiction in the 1972 Constitution of Bangladesh, which is declared being adopted "*In the name of Allah, the Beneficient, the Merciful, In the name of the Creator, the Merciful*", and whose preamble proclaims secularism as one of the fundamental features of the state; art. 12 further declares that "The principle of secularism shall be realised by the elimination of (a) communalism in all its forms; (b) the granting by the State of political status in favour of any religion; (c) the abuse of religion for political purposes; (d) any discrimination against, or persecution of, persons practicing a particular religion".

However, not all diversities and cultural identities are prepared to make such a choice. There is, indeed, a problem related to the "quality of diversity" and, consequently, to the "potential for togetherness and inclusion of diversities". Such a problem requires designing the composition of the social fabric of a community. The operation is obviously complex and costly in terms of general cohesion. It takes mutual efforts to soften divergences and establish a constructive dialogue and it is not guaranteed to achieve a final positive result. Any positive result achieved may be only provisional. The operation, furthermore, requires and at the same time produces rules that constitute "the law of diversity".

These varying social dynamics prepare the basic pre-legal scenario of "the law of diversity", on which we have elaborated some ideas, referring to the interaction between diversities, federalism and legal pluralism and questioning whether federalism and legal pluralism might be the overarching frame for hosting diversities under the same roof.

The answer is negative: federalisms – although broadly defined –, historically and theoretically require a homogeneity clause and are meant to be regulated by a setting of normative pluralism, based on sharing the political method of law-making. This does not go farther than confirming the mutual compatibility between the common law and the civil law legal traditions (while rejecting the socialist legal tradition). At least historically, federalisms have not (yet) expressed any significant experience in the adoption of a setting inspired by legal pluralism.[60]

Federalism is normally identified with a territorially compound system, although – at least with regard to autochthonous language and national minorities – it should be seen as a compound system also from the cultural point of view. However, what is relevant is the "quality of diversity" and, although federalism has failed – thus far – to accommodate legal pluralism, one might consider the hypothesis of an abstract construction of the features of a "multicultural (or intercultural) federalism".[61]

Furthermore, it must be stressed that legal pluralism also assumes some systemic limits of homogeneity. This is not true, obviously, when it comes to legal pluralism in a strong sense, which is mainly unnoticed and unknown – save for the precious investigations of anthropologists – either for fear of criminalisation in industrialised societies or for lack of communication in marginalised

60 On the potential of federalism as a set of tools to solve conflicts in pluralist settings, see Topidi and Alessi in this volume.

61 A concept that is reminiscent of the models of personal and negotiated federalism developed by Topidi in this volume.

territorial contexts. This situation, in other words, refers to a kind of legal pluralism that is thoroughly out of any control and may be the self-referential expression of its own principles and values.

The opposite perspective that has been the focus of our present reasoning is known as legal pluralism in a weak sense: the basic assumption of it is that state law is physiologically expected to control practices that are part of a distinct cultural and legal setting and are regarded as being intolerable, radically contrary to and not compatible with the characterising features of state law.

Therefore, neither unlimited normative pluralism nor any known federal arrangement is the proper instrument for unselectively, uncritically and, ultimately, blindly regulating diversities.

This is the approach cherished by Western mainstream constitutionalism – with larger or narrower margins of tolerance (and, indeed, it would be most interesting to elaborate a taxonomy of the margins of tolerance adopted by individual states with regard to legal pluralism) – and progressively transferred also into sources of international law. This is not to say that the implementation of the approach is intrinsically to be praised in all circumstances and regarded as the best and only one. But the approach should be noted and recorded as the one that is prevailing in this field.

This approach is, after all, perfectly in line with the universalist perspective systematically manifested by Western culture: whether this be the outcome of Christian eschatology or of enlightened and rational secularism, the fact is that the self-imposed "mission" of selecting values for the rest of the world is a historically characteristic attitude of all the main policies of the West. Paradoxically, the universalist approach in the field of recognition of human rights turns out to be – as is well known – a sort of boomerang that hits back supporting criticism of "eurocentrism" or of "cultural imperialism". And human rights – or, the Western view of human rights – are the structural limits of admissibility of legal pluralism, even in its weak form.

The focus of further research ought to be, therefore, on comparing conflictual relationships between human rights and legal pluralism, including the judicial implementation of the "public policy (or *ordre public*) exception", in the recognition of the effects of judicial decisions between private parties originating in a different (religious) legal tradition.

The outcome of this research might be to critically establish the preconditions for enlarging to some extent the margins of tolerance with regard to the enforcement of rules of other legal traditions. Hypothetically, a more tolerant attitude might be seen, indirectly, as an enlargement of individual self-determination, of religious freedom (although not necessarily of freedom from religion), and of the right to one's own culture (yet to be defined).

A more tolerant attitude, however, would not take place in a historical vacuum, as it would necessarily overlap with policies of inclusion of immigrants, not only as individuals but also and mostly as families, language groups, ethnic and national settlements, and religious communities. What integration of such cultural diversities really implies is not as clear as it might appear: is assimilation feasible and, if feasible, is it desirable? Is cultural assimilation a more efficient integration of diversities than an authentic and respectful dialogue with them? Is the prohibition of "policies or practices aimed at assimilation of persons belonging to [communities of migrants] against their will" – provided for by the Framework Convention for the Protection of National Minorities (art. 5.2) – applicable also to migrants?

In other words, the hypothesis of an alternative option – to be built as an inspiring vision – should not be between human rights, on the one hand, and legal pluralism, on the other. Both hopefully and realistically, it ought to be encouraging more human rights within a wider setting of legal pluralism, thus improving both.[62]

Bibliography

Allard, Christina. "Judicial Pluralism and the Sami: an Indigenous People." In *Europe, Indigenous Peoples' Sovereignty and the Limits of Judicial and Legal Pluralism: American Tribes, Canadian First Nations and Scandinavian Sami Compared*, edited by Roberto Toniatti and Jens Woelk, 49–60. Trento: The Pluralist Papers Ebook, 2014.

Avineri, Shlomo and Avner de-Shalit, eds., *Communitarism and Individualism*. Oxford: Oxford University Press, 1992.

Bagni, Silvia. "Il ruolo delle Corti costituzionali tra pluralismo giuridico, plurinazionalità e interculturalità," 2020, available at the following link https://www.robertotoniatti.eu/contributi/il-ruolo-delle-corti-costituzionali-tra-pluralismo-giuridico-plurinazionalita-e-interculturalita.

Bagni, Silvia. "Le forme di Stato in America Latina," in *Latinoamérica: viaggio nel costituzionalismo comparato dalla Patagonia al Río Grande*, edited by Silvia Bagni and Serena Baldin, 35–59. Turin: Giappichelli, 2021.

Bognetti, Giovanni. "Federalismo." in *Digesto*, 273–302. 4th ed., Turin: UTET, 1992.

62 Reference is to be made to the 'Research Agendas' suggested in Giselle Corradi, Eva Brems and Mark Goodale, eds., *Human Rights Encounter Legal Pluralism: Normative and Empirical Approaches* (London: Bloomsbury, 2017).

Cahal, Ergun. "Pluralism, Tolerance and Control: On the *Millet* System and the Question of Minorities." *International Journal on Minority and Group Rights* 27, no. 1 (2020): 34–65.

Corradi, Giselle, Eva Brems and Mark Goodale, eds., *Human Rights Encounter Legal Pluralism: Normative and Empirical Approaches*. London: Bloomsbury, 2017.

Cuniberti, Gilles. *Grands systèmes de droit contemporaines*. 2nd ed, Paris: LGDJ, 2011.

David, René and Camille Jauffret-Spinosi. *Les grands systèmes de droit contemporaines.* 11th ed., Paris: Dalloz, 2002.

Delledonne, Giacomo. "Federalism: Tragic Compromise and Conflicts." *Estudios de Deusto* 67, no. 1 (2019): 83–96.

Delledonne, Giacomo. *L'omogeneità costituzionale negli ordinamenti composti.* Naples: Editoriale Scientifica, 2017.

Dixon, Rosalind, Ron Levy and Mark Tushnet. "Theories and Practices of Federalism in Deeply Divided Societies." *Federal Law Review* 46, no. 4 (2017): 481–490.

Elazar, Daniel J. *Exploring Federalism*. Tuscaloosa: University of Alabama Press, 1991.

Francavilla, Domenico. *Il diritto nell'India contemporanea: sistemi tradizionali, modelli occidentali e globalizzazione*. Turin: Giappichelli, 2010.

Friedrich, Carl J. *Trends of Federalism in Theory and Practice.* London: Pall Mall, 1968.

Foblets, Marie-C., Jean-F. Gaudreault-DesBiens and Alison Dundes Rentels, eds., *Cultural Diversity and the Law: State Responses from Around the World.* Cowansville-Bruxelles: Éditions Yvon Blais-Bruylant, 2010.

Gambaro, Antonio and Rodolfo Sacco. *Sistemi giuridici comparati.* Turin: UTET, 2018.

Gargarella, Roberto. *Latin American Constitutionalism, 1810–2010: The Engine Room of the Constitution.* Oxford: Oxford University Press, 2010.

Glenn, H. Patrick. *Legal Traditions of the World.* 5th ed., Oxford: Oxford University Press, 2014.

Goldsmith, Edward. *The Way: An Ecological World View*. London: Rider, 1992.

Griffiths, John. "What is Legal Pluralism?" *Journal of Legal Pluralism and Unofficial Law* 18, no. 24 (1986): 1–55.

Herzog, Christoph and Malek Sharif, eds., *The First Ottoman Experiment in Democracy.* Istanbul: Orient Institute, 2016.

Ignisci, Angelica. *Prospettive della* "souveraineté partagée"*: spazi di pluralismo giuridico nell'esperienza di autonomia della Nuova Caledonia*. Trento: The Pluralist Papers Ebook, 2020.

Kymlicka, Will and Eva Pföstl, eds., *Multiculturalism and Minority Rights in the Arab World.* Oxford: Oxford University Press, 2014.

Legeais, Raymond. *Grands systèmes de droit contemporaines. Approche comparative.* 2nd ed., Paris: Litec, 2005.

Losano, Mario G. *I grandi sistemi giuridici. Introduzione ai diritti europei ed extraeuropei.* Bari: Laterza 2000.

Offe, Claus. "Homogeneity and Constitutional Democracy: Coping with Identity Conflicts through Group Rights." *The Journal of Political Philosophy* 6, no. 2 (1998): 113–141.

Palermo, Francesco and Karl Kössler. *Comparative Federalism: Constitutional Arrangements and Case Law*. Oxford: Hart Publishing, 2017.

Palmer, Vernon V. *Mixed Jurisdictions Worldwide: The Third Legal Family*. Cambridge, Cambridge University Press, 2001.

Parolari, Paola. *Diritto policentrico e interlegalità nei paesi europei di immigrazione*: *il caso degli shari'ah councils in Inghilterra*. Turin: Giappichelli, 2020.

Piciocchi, Cinzia. *Courts, Pluralism and Law in the Everyday: Food, Clothing and Days of Rest*. London-New York: Routledge, 2024.

Piciocchi, Cinzia, Davide Strazzari and Roberto Toniatti, eds., *State and Religion: Agreements, Conventions and Statutes.* Naples: Edizioni Scientifiche Italiane, 2021.

Piciocchi, Cinzia. *La libertà terapeutica come diritto culturale: Uno studio sul pluralismo nel diritto costituzionale comparato*. Padova: Cedam, 2006.

Pizzorusso, Alessandro. *Sistemi giuridici comparati.* 2nd ed., Milano: Giuffrè, 1995.

Poggeschi, Giovanni. *I diritti linguistici: un'analisi comparata*. Carocci: Roma, 2010.

Rinella, Angelo. *La shari'a in Occidente: Giurisdizioni e diritto islamico: Regno Unito, Canada e Stati Uniti d'America*. Bologna: Il Mulino, 2020.

Sachedina, Abdulaziz. *The Islamic Roots of Democratic Pluralism*. Oxford: Oxford University Press, 2001.

Strazzari, Davide. "La clausola di omogeneità dell'UE: connotazione costituzionale o internazionale? Riflessioni da un'analisi comparata." *Federalismi.it*, no. 24 (2014): 1–55.

Tamanaha, Brian Z. *Legal Pluralism Explained: History, Theory, Consequences*. Oxford, Oxford University Press, 2021.

Tas, Latif. "The Myth of the Ottoman *Millet* System: Its Treatment of Kurds and a Discussion of Territorial and Non-Territorial Autonomy." *International Journal on Minority and Group Rights* 21, no. 4 (2014): 497–526.

Toniatti, Roberto and Davide Strazzari, eds., *Legal Pluralism and the* Ordre Public *Clause Exception: Normative and Judicial Perspectives*. Trento: The Pluralist Papers Ebooks 2016.

Toniatti, Roberto. "Comparing Constitutions in the Global Era: Opportunities, Purposes, Challenges, 2019 Casad Comparative Law Lecture." *Kansas Law Review* 67, no. 4 (2019): 693–711.

Toniatti, Roberto. "Consensual Legal Pluralism: Assessing the Method and the Merits in Agreements between State and Church(es) in Italy and Spain." in *State and Religion: Agreements, Conventions and Statutes*, edited by Piciocchi, Cinzia, Davide Strazzari and Roberto Toniatti, 55–124. Naples: Edizioni Scientifiche Italiane, 2021.

Toniatti, Roberto. "El paradigma constitucional de la inclusion de la diversidad cultural. Notas para una comparación entre los modelos de protección de las minorías nacionales en Europa y de los pueblos indígenas en Latinoamérica." *Inter-American and European Human Rights Journal/Revista Interamericana y Europea de derechos humanos* 9, no. 1 (2016): 118–137.

Toniatti, Roberto. "Federalismo e separazione dei poteri." In *Bognetti comparatista*, edited by Giuseppe F. Ferrari, 139–163. Milano: Gruppo 24 Ore, 2014.

Toniatti, Roberto. "Il paradigma costituzionale dell'inclusione della diversità culturale in Europa e in America latina: premesse per una ricerca comparata sui rispettivi modelli." In *La ciencia del derecho constitucional comparado: Estudios en homenaje a Lucio Pegoraro*, edited by Silvia Bagni, Giovanni A. Figueroa Mejía and Giorgia Pavani, 1445–1478. Ciudad de México: tirant lo Blanch, 2017.

Toniatti, Roberto. "La "nazione costituzionale": genesi e consolidamento dell'identità repubblicana dell'ordinamento federale statunitense quale Stato-nazione." *Diritto Pubblico Comparato ed Europeo* (2011): 1150–1169.

Toniatti, Roberto. "La razionalizzazione del «pluralismo giuridico debole»: le prospettive di un nuovo modello giuridico e costituzionale nell'esperienza africana." In *Le trasformazioni costituzionali del secondo millennio. Scenari e prospettive dall'Europa all'Africa*, edited by Marina Calamo Specchia, 449–484. Sant'Arcangelo di Romagna: Maggioli, 2016.

Toniatti, Roberto. "Pluralismo e autodeterminazione delle identità negli ordinamenti culturalmente composti: osservazioni in tema di cittadinanza culturale." In *Tutela delle identità culturali, diritti linguistici e istruzione: dal Trentino-Alto Adige/Südtirol alla prospettiva comparata*, edited by Eleonora Ceccherini and Matteo Cosulich, 5–29. Padova: Cedam, 2012.

Toniatti, Roberto, "Sul bilanciamento costituzionale fra libertà religiosa e protezione degli animali." In *Il divieto di macellazione rituale (Shechità Kosher e Halal) e la libertà religiosa delle minoranze*, edited by Pablo Lerner and Alfredo M. Rabello. Trento: Università degli Studi di Trento, 2010.

Twining, William. "Normative and Legal Pluralism: A Global Perspective." *Duke Journal of Comparative & International Law* 20, no. 3 (2010): 473–518.

Uprimny, Rodrigo. "The Recent Transformation of Constitutional Law in Latin America: Trends and Challenges." *Texas Law Review* 89, no. 7 (2011): 1587–1609.

Zweigert, Konrad and Hein Kötz. *An Introduction to Comparative Law*. 3rd ed., Oxford: Oxford University Press, 1999.

Index

Printed in the United States
by Baker & Taylor Publisher Services